Jon E. Lewis lives in Wandsworth and Herefordshire. He is the author of numerous books including *England: The Autobiography*, *The British Soldier: The Autobiography*, *Eye-Witness D-Day*, *Eye-Witness The 20th Century* and *The New Rights of Man*.

Praise for his previous books

England: The Autobiography:

'A triumph.'
Saul David, author of *Victoria's Army*

The British Solider: The Autobiography:

'This thoughtful compilation . . . almost unbearably moving.'
Guardian

'[A] compelling tommy's eye view of war.'
Daily Telegraph

'What a book. Five Stars.'
Daily Express

London

THE AUTOBIOGRAPHY

*2000 Years of the Capital's History
by Those who Saw it Happen*

EDITED BY

Jon E. Lewis

ROBINSON

RUNNING PRESS
PHILADELPHIA · LONDON

Constable & Robinson Ltd
3 The Lanchesters
162 Fulham Palace Road
London W6 9ER
www.constablerobinson.com

First published in the UK by Robinson,
an imprint of Constable & Robinson Ltd.

A copy of the British Library Cataloguing in
Publication data is available from the British Library

UK ISBN: 978-1-84529-942-2

1 3 5 7 9 10 8 6 4 2

First published in the United States in 2009 by Running Press Book Publishers

9 8 7 6 5 4 3 2 1
Digit on the right indicates the number of this printing

US Library of Congress Control Number: 2009920964
US ISBN: 978-0-7624-3734-4

Running Press Book Publishers
2300 Chestnut Street
Philadelphia, PA 19103-4371

www.runningpress.com

Printed and bound in the EU

For Penny, a London girl

Contents

~~~

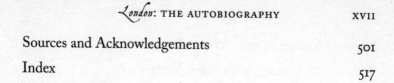

Illustrations

※ ※ ※

1 Map of Roman London with its grid of straight roads. *Mary Evans Picture Library* (10052954)

2 London Bridge and the Tower, from *Mediaeval London*, William Benham & Charles Welch, 1901

3 Wat Tyler, leader of the 1381 Peasants' Revolt, is slain at Smithfield. *Mary Evans Picture Library* (10047290)

4 Sir Richard 'Dick' Whittington, Mayor of London, pictured with his legendary cat. *Topfoto* (0829217)

5 *Londinium Feracissimi Angliae Regni Metropolis* (Map of London published in George Baum & Fransiscus Hogenburg, *Civites Orbis Terrarum*, 1572).

6 The execution of King Charles I with portraits of his adherents, from *The Story of Old Whitehall*, Austin Brereton, 1912

7 The Great Fire of London, 1666, from an engraving by Hollar, from *Mediaeval London*, William Benham & Charles Welch, 1911

8 A Frost Fair on the Thames, 1683. *Ann Ronan Picture Library* (hip0012229)

21 The Dome of St Paul's Cathedral, London, photographed on the night of 7 June 1941, after surviving a night of Luftwaffe bombing © *Topham / Topfoto* (0113204)

22 A London bus is guided by its fog lamps along the Embankment, 6 December 1952 © *Topham Picturepoint / Topfoto* (0521874)

23 The Kray brothers © 2002 *Topham Picturepoint / Topfoto* (0250069)

24 An East End street party celebrating the Queen's Jubilee, 1977 © *Nobby Clark / Getty Images* (71782278)

25 The bombed bus in Tavistock Square on 7 July 2005 © *Jeff Moore / Topfoto* (0915705)

Foreword

No, Sir, when a man is tired of London, he is tired of life . . .

YOU DON'T HAVE to be a Londoner to love London so. Or even to be Dr Johnson to appreciate the truth of his bon mot. After all London has been, variously, the world's biggest city, the crucible of ideology (capitalism *and* communism), the front line against Hitler's Luftwaffe, the home of parliamentary democracy, the clearing house of the world, the port of the world, and the hippest, 'swingingest' Sixties city in the world. With all due apologies to the also-rans – New York, Moscow, Paris, Rome, Tokyo – London is the most interesting city in global history. And, dare I say it, the most important.

There was little about London's birth that suggested such future grandeur. Founded by the Romans sometime in the first century AD, Londinium was intended solely as a humdrum supply camp. The capital status was unplanned; but then little or nothing in London's history – unlike, say, straight-roaded Paris – would ever be planned. London early took on a life of its own. This book is the story of that life by London's citizens and its visitors. In other words, it is London in its own words.

Something of London's destiny was given by its birthplace, the furthest upstream bridgeable point of the Thames (the present Tower Bridge is only yards from the Romans' own bridging site). London was the strategic crossing point between southern and mid England. He who controlled London controlled England. London was also a natural port and thus a natural market. The smart-spieling London barrow-boy is one of England's oldest social stereotypes.

If the Romans only belatedly understood that London was the natural site for Britannia's capital city, the succeeding Saxons were even more tardy in coming to this realization. Wessex, the dominant Saxon kingdom, preferred bucolic Winchester for its capital, and when Edward the Confessor finally deigned to accord London its due status he confused the issue by building the royal palace outside the city at Westminster. In other words, the Crown and the historic city were separate entities. One result was that the monarch was only able to exercise relative, not absolute, control over the city.

The Crown was not the only Dark Age institution to find its grip on London to be a decidedly weak one. The Church, despairing of Londoners' bloody-minded paganism, concluded that Canterbury was much the better base for its spiritual endeavours.

So, London became a place of self-government (and freedom) to a degree unusual, even unique, for a city. With its capacity for money making, it also became a formidable, discrete power in the land. The Mayor of London was the only commoner to sign Magna Carta in 1215. People flocked to this cocky city of profit and pleasure by the thousand. London's gargantuan growth from the late medieval period onwards (the city's population in 1497 was approximately 70,000; in 1837 it was 1.5 million) had little to do with the local birth rate and much more to do with the ceaseless migration there of people on the make or on the run. Historically, most of these refugees came from the British countryside, though there were large influxes of foreigners too. So large were these influxes, indeed, that by the late twentieth century London had ceased to be an English city and had become instead a 'Cosmopolis', a city of indeterminate ethnicity in a Babel of languages.

But then London never was a truly English city. London was always London. The Midlands out-of-towner whose visit to the capital is recorded in the fifteenth-century poem 'London Lickpenny' found it to be an alien place beyond his experience. Utterly so. His eyewitness description is just one of the more than 150 accounts that appear in the following pages. These records by 'those who were there' vary from official reports to private diary jottings, from newspaper journalism to personal letters. They may not have the plumb-the-depths, turn-every-stone analysis of the historian's work but they are simply more vivid. They are also unassailably authentic.

Here, then, London speaks for itself. As editor I have merely threaded the eyewitness accounts together in an attempt to make a readable, coherent story, adding context and explanation where needed. I did, though, have a guiding spirit in helping London to find its voice: Dr Johnson. In 1763 Johnson told the young James Boswell, newly arrived in the city, that 'If you wish to have a just notion of the magnitude of this city, you must not be satisfied with seeing its great streets and squares, but must survey the innumerable little lanes and courts.'

Dr Johnson's advice can be transferred to London's history. If one wishes to understand the magnitude of London's past one must remember the little backyards of social history as much as the great boulevards of political, religious and cultural history. The result is to let London reveal itself, truthfully and completely.

There are touching revelations to be found in these obscure corners of London's life, such as – a personal favourite – the obvious hurt to the civic pride of the Mayor over the state of Farringdon ward in 1422, particularly the public loo in Ludgate. (It is perhaps a surprise in itself that the medieval city even had public latrines). John Evelyn's amazement at a whale in the Thames is infectious even three centuries down the historical line, while the sheer joie de vivre of jivers at the Paramount Ballroom in 1947 dances off the page.

Equally, there are some unpleasant surprises in the shaded crannies of London's past life. Mayhew's depiction of Victorian 'toshers' (those who subsisted by trawling the city's sewers for saleable refuse) makes for squeamish reading, while the long-standing xenophobia of London is deeply disquieting, stretching back as it does to the massacre of the Jews in 1189. Indeed, violence of all sorts seems imprinted in London's DNA. The Brixton riots of 1981 were just one part of a chain of Mob outbursts against the Establishment, beginning with the Tallage riots of 1194. The Krays, meanwhile, would have recognized the professional violence of the Edwardian gangster Arthur Harding, who in turn would have appreciated the menacing technique of the highwaymen who robbed the Duke of Ormond in 1674. Similarly, there should be no astonishment in the twenty-first century over anti-social teenagers, because they have been in London's make-up for centuries: in 1326 the Calendar of the Coroners' Rolls recorded the death of Roger Styward, an eel-seller, who was kicked to death by Simon de Peckham, an apprentice; in 1712 Lady Stafford was one of many terrorized by the street gang known as the 'Mohocks'. Violence in London is not accident or happenstance. It is nature, and the most pertinent reminder that the city is a living entity with definite character traits.

The life of London is vast. It is made vaster still by its role as the governmental capital of the British nation. No one book can encompass every event in the life of London the city, let alone London the city and London the national capital. I should make clear that this is the story of London the city, and national events that occurred in London are only included when they have a particular London resonance. Obviously, it would be madness to treat national happenings as part of London's story just because they happened to take place there.

Even with this codicil, events and people teem and fight for space on the following pages: King Olaf pulling down London Bridge, John Evelyn at the Great Fire, the Blitz, the Sex Pistols at St Martin's College, the execution of Charles I, the cholera epidemic of 1832, Jack the Ripper, Engels walking around the slums of St Giles, the Gordon Riots, the Great Exhibition, the Iranian Embassy siege, smogs, the battle of Cable Street, Wren rebuilding St Pauls, George Orwell in a doss-house . . .

A man who is tired of London is tired of life. Johnson might have added: So is the man or woman who is tired of reading the life of London. After all, what could beat it for drama and variety?

This book is an inside account by those who truly have the knowledge, who are the black cab drivers of the city's past: Londoners themselves, together with some of their guests.

It is London's autobiography.

Boudicca Sacks Londinium, *AD* 60
Tacitus

The uprising against Roman rule led by Boudicca, Queen of the Iceni, introduced London into history. A supply camp beside a ford on the Thames, Londinium had been granted a name by the Romans but little else. There was no fortification, no bath, no grand civic buildings. No Roman thought the place worthy of record – until Boudicca decided to march on the Thameside settlement with her 100,000 followers, following the sack of Camulodunum.

Tacitus, though not a direct eye-witness to Boudicca's revolt, was the most informed of Roman historians on Britain: his father-in-law, Agricola, was tribune in the isles at the time of the rising. Tacitus begins with the march of the Roman governor, Suetonius, to reach London before the Iceni:

SUETONIUS, UNDISMAYED, MARCHED through disaffected territory to Londinium. This town did not rank as a Roman settlement, but was an important centre for business-men and merchandise. At first, he hesitated whether to stand and fight there. Eventually, his numerical inferiority – and the price only too clearly paid by the divisional commander's rashness – decided him to sacrifice the single city of Londinium to save the province as a whole. Unmoved by lamentations and appeals, Suetonius gave the signal for departure. The inhabitants were allowed to accompany him. But those who stayed because they were women, or old, or attached to the place, were slaughtered by the enemy. Verulamium suffered the same fate.

The natives enjoyed plundering and thought of nothing else. Bypassing forts and garrisons, they made for where loot was richest and protection weakest. Roman and provincial deaths at the places mentioned are estimated at 70,000. For the British did not take or sell prisoners, or practise other wartime exchanges. They could not wait to cut throats, hang, burn, and crucify – as though avenging, in advance, the retribution that was on its way.

Boudicca's slaughterous attack on London is testified to by the archaeologist's trowel, which has uncovered significant evidence of burning along King Street, Milk Street in the old city and across the river in Southwark. It is touching that the first Londoners were so attached to their city that they would not leave before Boudicca's arsonists arrived. Londoners refused to leave London in 1940 too, the last time the city burned.

After his tactical withdrawal from London, Suetonius turned and bested Boudicca in battle. If folklore is to be believed, the site of Boudicca's last stand was near present-day King's Cross, with the queen herself allegedly buried under Platform 10. More probably, the battleground was further out, in Hertfordshire.

From the ashes rose a more substantial Roman London. A basilica was built on the site that would later become Leadenhall Market, together with a fort at Cripplegate and an amphitheatre at Guildhall. Streets were wide and paved and laid out in grid fashion. By AD 90 the first permanent London Bridge was built, a wooden construction to the east of the present bridge, ending on the north bank at Fish Street Hill. A century later the Romans built a city wall around Londinium, two miles long and 18 feet high.

୬ ୬ ୬

The Romans in London: Graffiti
Various

Within the walled area, which extended to 326 acres, the
population reached as high as 90,000, making Londinium
by far the largest settlement in Britain. Londinium was
never Rome-on-the-Thames but, as befitted its status as the
colony's administrative centre, it achieved a fair facsimile
of Latin civilization. The spread of literacy allowed the city's
inhabitants, Romans and Romano-British alike, to inscribe
their advertisements and thoughts:

AUSTALIS HAS BEEN GOING OFF ON HIS OWN EVERY DAY
THIS FORTNIGHT.
  (scratched on a tile)

ENOUGH!
  (scratched on a tile)

LONDON; NEXT DOOR TO THE TEMPLE OF ISIS
  (scratched on a jug)

TO THE SPIRITS OF THE DEPARTED: FLAVIUS AGRICOLA,
SOLDIER OF THE SIXTH LEGION, LIVED 42 YEARS, 10 DAYS;
ALBIA FAUSTINA HAD THIS MADE FOR HER PEERLESS
HUSBAND
  (tombstone, found in the Minories in 1787)

AULUS AUFIDIUS OLUSSA OF THE POMPTINE VOTING TRIBE,
AGED 70, BORN AT ATHENS, LIES HERE. IN ACCORDANCE
WITH HIS WILL HIS HEIR SET THIS UP
(tombstone, found on Tower Hill in 1852)

GAIUS VALERIUS AMANDUS' DROPS FOR DIM SIGHT
(stamp for proprietary eye tonics)

FOR SHAME!
(scratched underneath an illegible scrawl on a wall)

In the fourth century, London was renamed Augusta. The Romans' bright new nomenclature for their Thameside city did not disguise its depressing fall in fortune. The Roman Empire was in decline; Londinium/Augusta simply waned with it. In 410 the empire withdrew its last two legions in Britain in a desperate attempt to prevent the barbarians from entering the eternal city itself.

In Britain, the barbarians were already through the gates and making themselves at home. In one of English history's biggest blunders the Romano-British invited the Saxons to the isles as mercenaries against the Picts; the Saxons came across the North Sea in their 'wave horses', liked what they saw, and decided to conquer. In 457 London received the British survivors of a battle fought in Kent (possibly at Crayford) against the Saxon chieftain Hengist. Although the Romano-British under King Arthur trounced the Saxons at Mount Badon in *c.* 516, Saxon control spread like a stain from the south-east coast into the Thames Valley. By 550 London was engulfed in the Saxon advance.

London disappeared into the Dark Ages. The Saxons were congenitally averse to urban living; more, they considered the stone buildings of the Romano-British cities to be the work of Giants – and so best avoided. London fell into ruin. An Anglo-Saxon poet, wandering around the remains of an unknown abandoned British city, versed his impressions of such a place:

WELL WROUGHT THIS wall: Wierds [fates] broke it.
The stronghold burst . . .
Snapped rooftrees, towers fallen,

the work of the Giants, the stonesmiths,
mouldereth.
Rime scoureth gatetowers
rime on mortar.
Shattered the showershields, roofs ruined,
age under-ate them.

And the wielders and wrights?
Earthgrip holds them – gone, long gone,
fast in gravesgrasp while fifty fathers
and sons have passed.

Wall stood,
grey lichen, red stone, kings fell often,
stood under storms, high arch crashed –
stands yet the wall stone, hacked by weapons,
by files grim-ground . . .
    . . . shown the old skilled work
    . . . sank to loam-crust . . .

The first Saxons did not entirely ignore the London of the Giants; large areas within the walls were given over to pasture land and some public buildings were seemingly put to use – even if it was not the use they were intended for. (The amphitheatre under the present-day Guildhall is a contender for the site of the Saxon folkmoot – a meeting place for the people). But generally the Saxons had little use and less liking for the stones of London, and so built outside the wall another London, of wood and mud and thatch, 200 acres of it stretching along the

Thames to the west: Lundenwic. 'Wic' was the Anglo-Saxon for market; Old Saxon 'market-boy' London lives on in the name of 'Aldwych'.

By the seventh century London, courtesy of its thriving *wic*, had regained some of its old prestige. Enough prestige, indeed, for the fledgling Christian mission to England to grant the city its own bishop. But London proved stony ground for Mellitus, the Roman monk charged with saving its soul.

Londoners Reject Christianity, 616
The Venerable Bede

The Venerable Bede, a monk at Jarrow, was the author of the *Historica Ecclesiastica Gentis Anglorum* (Ecclesiastical History of the English People), completed in 731:

*I*N THE YEAR of our Lord 604, Augustine, Archbishop of Britain, ordained ... [bishop] Mellitus to preach to the province of the East Saxons, who are divided from Kent by the river Thames, and border on the Eastern sea. Their metropolis is the city of London, which is situated on the bank of the aforesaid river, and is the mart of many nations resorting to it by sea and land. At that time, Sabert, nephew to Ethelbert through his sister Ricula, reigned over the nation, though he was under subjection to Ethelbert, who, as has been said above, had command over all the nations of the

English as far as the river Humber. But when this province also received the word of truth, by the preaching of Mellitus, King Ethelbert built the church of St. Paul the Apostle, in the city of London, where he and his successors should have their episcopal see ...

IN THE YEAR of our Lord 616 ... the death of Sabert, king of the East Saxons ... left three sons, still pagans, to inherit his temporal crown. They immediately began openly to give themselves up to idolatry, which, during their father's lifetime, they had seemed somewhat to abandon, and they granted free licence to their subjects to serve idols. And when they saw the bishop [Mellitus], whilst celebrating Mass in the church, give the Eucharist to the people, filled, as they were, with folly and ignorance, they said to him, as is commonly reported, 'Why do you not give us also that white bread, which you used to give to our father Saba (for so they were wont to call him), and which you still continue to give to the people in the church?' To whom he answered, 'If you will be washed in that font of salvation, in which your father was washed, you may also partake of the holy Bread of which he partook; but if you despise the lover of life, you can in no wise receive the Bread of life.' They replied, 'We will not enter into that font, because we know that we do not stand in need of it, and yet we will be refreshed by that bread.' And being often earnestly admonished by him, that this could by no means be done, nor would any one be admitted to partake of the sacred Oblation without the holy cleansing, at last, they said, filled with rage, 'If you will not comply with us in so small a matter as that which we require, you shall not stay in our province.' And they drove him out and bade him and his company depart from their kingdom.

Mellitus was forced to flee to Gaul; at the insistence of the Archbishop of Canterbury, Laurentius, Mellitus returned to London. Bede recorded:

... BUT THE people of London would not receive Bishop Mellitus, choosing rather to be under their idolatrous high priests; for King Eadbald [the Saxon overlord of southern and mid England] had not so much authority in the kingdom as his father, and was not able to restore the bishop to his church against the will and consent of the pagans.

Such independence of mind would become a distinguishing characteristic of Londoners. Not until 675 did London irretrievably enter the Christian fold. The Church, meanwhile, despairing of the paganism of the Londoner, established the seat of the Primate of England not in Londinium, as intended, but in Canterbury. And there it has remained.

Viking Raids, 842–1009
The Anglo-Saxon Chronicle

The Venerable Bede's 'mart of many nations' attracted more than traders. The vocational plunderers who were the Vikings were drawn to London by its vulnerable riches and its strategic position astride the Thames.

*8*42. IN THIS year there was a great slaughter in London and Quentavic [near Etaples, France] and Rochester.

851. IN THIS year Ealdorman Ceorl with the contingent of the men of Devon fought against a heathen army at Wicganbeorg, and the English made a great slaughter there and had the victory. And for the first time, heathen men stayed through the winter on Thanet. And the same year 350 ships came into the mouth of the Thames and stormed Canterbury and London and put to flight Brihtwulf, king of the Mercians, with his army, and went south across the Thames into Surrey.

Once again London lay in ruins. Sixteen years later, the Danes came back. This time, however, they did not destroy – they occupied. Halfdere the Norse leader minted coins and used London as the garrison town for the Thames basin.

If the English were to prevail in their long war against the Vikings, London had to be retaken. He who controlled London controlled the use of the Thames as a waterway for war galleys; he also controlled the crossing point between the south-east and the Midlands. So it was that King Alfred, England's last great hope against the invader, besieged Viking London in 883.

Three years later the city was his and the Vikings sued for peace. They were allotted settlements east of the river Lea. Asser, a member of Alfred's court, recorded:

IN THE SAME year [886], Alfred, King of the Anglo-Saxons, after the burning of the cities and the slaying of the people, honourably rebuilt the city of London, and made it again habitable. He gave it into the custody of his son-in-law, Ethelred, earl of Mercia, to which king all the Angles and Saxons, who before had been dispersed everywhere, or were in captivity with the pagans, voluntarily turned and submitted themselves to his dominion.

Inside the relieved London, Alfred stimulated commerce by building a road between Ludgate and Aldgate, refurbishing the Thameside quays and granting strips of land inside the walls at Eastcheap and Westcheap markets to magnates with money to spend. (These land grants originated the city's patchwork of wards and parishes.) To protect his ninth-century experiment in town planning, Alfred restored the city's walls and organized its citizens into a militia under his son-in-law, Ethelred, the governor.

A century later, London's *burgwara* army had the chance to prove its worth: England was enveloped by another tide of Norsemen:

994. IN THIS year Olaf and Swein [Sweyn Forkbeard, king of the Danes] came to London on the Nativity of St Mary with 94 ships, and they proceeded to attack the city stoutly and wished also to set it on fire; but there they suffered more harm and injury than they ever thought any citizens would do to

them. But the holy Mother of God showed her mercy to the citizens on that day and saved them from their enemies.

1009. THEN AFTER Martinmas they [the Vikings] went back again to Kent, and took up winter quarters on the Thames, and lived off Essex and off the shires which were nearest, on both sides of the Thames, and often they attacked the borough of London. But, praise be to God, it still stands untouched, and they always suffered loss there.

Even London could not resist the Danes forever. After a lengthy blockade the city surrendered to Sweyn in 1013; in turn Sweyn was besieged by the English king Ethelred, who was accompanied by an improbable ally: the Viking Olaf of Norway. Olaf's trustworthiness might have been questionable; his military genius was not.

London Bridge is Pulled Down by King Olaf, c. 1014

Snorri Sturluson

Sturluson's account of Olaf's fêted attack on London Bridge, written in *c.*1225, was based on the sung sagas of the Norse warriors. The incident is likely the inspiration for the children's nursery rhyme, 'London Bridge is Falling Down'.

ETHELRED ... SENT an invitation to all the men who would enter into his pay, to join him in recovering the country. Then many people flocked to him; and among others, came King Olaf with a great troop of Northmen to his aid. They steered first to London, and sailed into the Thames with their fleet; but the Danes had a castle within. On the other side of the river is a great trading place, which is called Sudvirke [Southwark]. There the Danes had raised a great work, dug large ditches, and within had built a bulwark of stone, timber, and turf, where they had stationed a strong army. King Ethelred ordered a great assault; but the Danes defended themselves bravely, and King Ethelred could make nothing of it. Between the castle and Sudvirke there was a bridge, so broad that two wagons could pass each other upon it. On the bridge were raised barricades, both towers and wooden parapets, in the direction of the river, which were nearly breast high; and under the bridge were piles driven into the bottom of the river. Now when the attack was made the troops stood on the bridge everywhere, and defended themselves. King Ethelred was very anxious to get possession of the bridge, and he called together all the chiefs to consult how they should get the bridge broken down. Then said King Olaf he would attempt to lay his fleet alongside of it, if the other ships would do the same. It was then determined in this council that they should lay their war forces under the bridge; and each made himself ready with ships and men.

King Olaf ordered great platforms of floating wood to be tied together with hazel bands, and for this he took down old houses; and with these, as a roof, he covered over his ships so widely, that it reached over the ships' sides. Under this screen he set pillars so high and stout, that there both was room for swinging their swords, and the roofs were strong enough to withstand the stones cast down upon them. Now when the fleet and men were ready, they rowed up along the river; but when they came near the bridge, there were cast down upon them so many stones and missile weapons, such as arrows and spears, that neither helmet nor shield could hold out against it; and the ships themselves were so greatly damaged, that many retreated out of it. But King Olaf, and the Northmen's fleet with him, rowed quite up under the bridge, laid their cables around the piles which supported it, and then rowed off with all the ships as hard as they could down the stream. The piles were thus shaken in the bottom, and were loosened under the bridge. Now as the armed troops stood thick of men upon the bridge, and there were likewise many heaps of stones and other weapons upon it, and the piles under it being loosened and broken, the bridge gave way; and a great part of the men upon it fell into the river, and all the others fled, some into the castle, some into Sudvirke. Thereafter Sudvirke was stormed and taken. Now when the people in the castle saw that the river Thames was mastered, and that they could not hinder the passage of ships up into the country, they became afraid, surrendered the tower, and took Ethelred to be their king.

So says [the scald] Ottar Svarte: 'London Bridge is broken

down. Gold is won, and bright renown. Shields resounding, War-horns sounding, Hild is shouting in the din! Arrows singing, Mail-coats ringing – Odin makes our Olaf win!'

Olaf was later beatified. At least six churches in London were named after him. The church of St Olave in Hart Street still stands.

With the final surrender of England to the Danish king Cnut in 1016, London had little choice but to follow suit. The *Chronicle* recorded: '. . . the Londoners came to terms with the [Danish] army and bought peace for themselves, and the army brought their ships into London and took up winter quarters there.'

Cnut took fiscal revenge on the unenthusiastic Londoners; he made them render one-eighth of the entire tribute of England. He also ensured that they could not rise against him, stationing pockets of loyal Danes across the city. Cnut's sailors camped at St Clement Danes on the Westminster road, close to their ships.

Londoners did have something to thank Cnut for – he made the city the unambiguous capital of England. The land's previous monarchs, from the house of Wessex, had ruled from Winchester. London's pre-eminence was only confirmed when the Danish line died out with the death of Harthacnut from 'excess of drinking' at Lambeth in 1042 (the occasion was the wedding of the daughter of Osgod Clapa, the settler who gave Clapham its name) and the throne reverted to the house of Wessex in the pale saintly form of Edward the Confessor; he too ruled from London. He did, however, move the royal palace from St Paul's a mile and a half upstream to the island of Thornea, where his new minster was already under construction.

Edward the Confessor Builds Westminster Abbey,
1060–5

A Monk of St Bertin's Abbey

O UTSIDE THE WALLS of London, upon the River Thames, stood a monastery dedicated to St. Peter, but insignificant in buildings and numbers, for under the abbot only a small community of monks served Christ. Moreover, the endowments from the faithful were slender, and provided no more than their daily bread. The king, therefore, being devoted to God, gave his attention to that place, for it both lay hard by the famous and rich town and also was a delightful spot, surrounded with fertile lands and green fields and near the main channel of the river, which bore abundant merchandise of wares of every kind for sale from the whole world to the town on its banks. And, especially because of his love of the Prince of the Apostles, whom he worshipped with uncommon and special love, he decided to have his burial place there. Accordingly he ordered that out of the tithes of all his revenues should be started the building of a noble edifice, worthy of the Prince of the Apostles; so that, after the transient journey of this life, God would look kindly upon him, both for the sake of his goodness and because of the gift of lands and ornaments with which he intended to ennoble the place. And so the building, nobly begun at the king's command, was successfully made ready; and there was no weighing of the costs, past or future, so long as it proved worthy of, and acceptable to, God and St. Peter. The princely house of the altar, noble with its most lofty vaulting, is surrounded by dressed stone evenly jointed. Also the passage round that temple is enclosed on both sides by a double arching of stone with the joints of the structure strongly consolidated on this side and that. Furthermore, the crossing of the church, which is to hold in its midst the choir of God's choristers, and to uphold with like support from either side the high apex of the central tower, rises simply at first with a low and sturdy vault, swells with many a stair spiralling up in artistic profusion, but then with a plain wall climbs to the wooden roof which is carefully covered with lead. Above and below are built out chapels methodically arranged, which are to be consecrated through their altars to the memory of apostles, martyrs, confessors, and virgins. Moreover, the whole complex of this enormous building was started so far to the East of the old church that the brethren dwelling there should not have to cease from Christ's service and also that a sufficiently spacious vestibule might be placed between them.

This 'Westminster', built in sumptuous Caen stone, was consecrated at Christmas 1065, only weeks before the death of its pious founder. The move to Westminster had profound implications – the basing of the monarchy outside the capital allowed the city to develop in relative autonomy. Six hundred years of rivalry between the Crown and the city were birthed by Edward's decision to move palaces.

Harold Godwinson, meanwhile, the next king of England, considered Westminster Abbey to be the ideal venue for his coronation – as did the Norman upstart who beat him in battle.

The Coronation of William the Conqueror, Westminster, Christmas Day 1066

Orderic Vitalis

After defeating Harold at Hastings on 14 October 1066, William of Normandy marched on London, where the English resistance had gathered behind the wall. Few Londoners doubted that William the Bastard could be kept out – the motto of the time was that, courtesy of its Alfredian defences, London 'neither fears enemies nor dreads being taken by storm'. Traitors were another matter. A group of Saxon nobles secretly treated with William and opened the Ludgate to him. Even so, the citizens rallied and attacked William's soldiers near Cheapside. According to the chronicler William of Jumièges, the ensuing street fighting caused 'no little mourning to the city because of the very many deaths of her own sons and citizens'. Only now did London submit; only now could William have the crown placed on his head. For Vitalis the new year started on Christmas Day, hence his date of 1067 for the coronation.

So AT LAST on Christmas Day in the year of Our Lord 1067, the fifth Indiction, the English assembled at London for the king's coronation, and a strong guard of Norman men-at-arms and knights was posted round the minster to prevent any treachery or disorder. And, in the presence of the bishops, abbots, and nobles of the whole realm of Albion, Archbishop Ealdred consecrated William duke of Normandy as king of the English and placed the royal crown on his head. This was done in the abbey church of St Peter the chief of the apostles, called Westminster, where the body of King Edward lies honourably buried.

But at the prompting of the devil, who hates everything good, a sudden disaster and portent of future catastrophes occurred. For when Archbishop Ealdred asked the English, and Geoffrey bishop of Coutances asked the Normans, if they would accept William as their king, all of them gladly shouted out with one voice if not in one language that they would. The armed guard outside, hearing the tumult of the joyful crowd in the church and the harsh accents of a foreign tongue, imagined that some treachery was afoot, and rashly set fire to some of the buildings. The fire spread rapidly from house to house; the crowd who had been rejoicing in the church took fright and throngs of men and women of every rank and condition rushed out of the church in frantic haste. Only the bishops and a few clergy and monks remained, terrified, in the sanctuary, and with difficulty completed the consecration of the king who was trembling from head to foot. Almost all the rest made for the scene of conflagration, some to fight the flames and many others hoping to find loot for themselves in the general confusion. The English, after hearing of the perpetration of such misdeeds, never again trusted the Normans who seemed to have betrayed them, but nursed their anger and bided their time to take revenge.

The distrustful William promptly left London for Barking, while 'certain strongholds were made in the town [of London] against the fickleness of the vast and fierce populace.' These perimeter stockades were Montfichet Tower, Baynard's Castle and lastly the White Tower, where the old Roman wall ran down to the river in the east. The forbidding 90-feet-high White Tower is now the central feature of the Tower of London.

Oddly enough, under the watchful eye of the Norman military occupation, London life went on much as before. The local system of civic administration, based on wards electing aldermen, grew unchecked, as did the vogue for building parish churches (which would eventually see some 120 erected within the city confines). William, doubtless to his chagrin, was obliged to acknowledge the unique privileges of the Londoner, with the consequence that the city escaped the land seizures by which William rewarded his followers.

The special position of London was confirmed in 1133 by Henry I.

✃ ✃ ✃

The Charter of Henry I in Favour of the Citizens of London, Michaelmas 1130–August 1133

Henry I

*H*ENRY, BY THE grace of God, king of the English, to the archbishop of Canterbury, and to the bishops and abbots, and earls and barons and justices and sheriffs, and to all his liegemen, both French and English, of the whole of England, greeting. Know that I have granted to my citizens of London that they shall hold Middlesex at 'farm' for 300 pounds 'by tale' for themselves and their heirs from me and my heirs, so that the citizens shall appoint as sheriff from themselves whomsoever they may choose, and shall appoint from among themselves as justice whomsoever they choose to look after the pleas of my crown and the pleadings which arise in connection with them. No other shall be justice over the men of London. And the citizens shall not plead outside the walls of the city in respect of any plea; and they shall be quit of scot and of Danegeld and the murder-fine. Nor shall any of them be compelled to offer trial by battle. And if any one of the citizens shall be impleaded in respect of the pleas of the crown, let him prove himself to be a man of London by an oath which shall be judged in the city. Let no one be billeted within the walls of the city, either of my household, or by the force of anyone else. And let all the men of London and their property be quit and free from toll and passage and lestage and from all other customs throughout all England and at the seaports. And let the churches and barons and citizens hold and have well and in peace their sokes, with all their customs, so that those who dwell in these sokes shall pay no customs except to him who possesses the soke, or to the steward whom he has placed there. And a man of London shall not be fined at mercy except according to his 'were', that is to say, up to 100 shillings: this applies to an offence which can be punished by a fine. And there shall no longer be 'miskenning' in the hustings court, nor in the folk-moot, nor in other pleas within the city. And the hustings court shall sit once a week, to wit, on Monday. I will cause my citizens to have their lands and pledges and debts within the city and outside it. And in respect of the lands about which they make claim to me, I will do them right according to the law of the city. And if anyone has taken toll or custom from the citizens of London, then the citizens of London may take from the borough or village where toll or custom has been levied as much as the man of London gave for toll, and more also may be taken for a penalty. And let all debtors to the citizens of London discharge their debts, or prove in London that they do not owe them; and if they refuse either to pay or to come and make such proof, then the citizens to whom the debts are due may take pledges within the city either from the borough or from the village or from the county in which the debtor lives. And the citizens shall have their hunting chases, as well and fully as had their predecessors, namely, in Chiltern and Middlesex and Surrey. Witness: the bishop of Winchester; Robert, son of Richer; Hugh Bigot; Alfred of Totnes; William of Aubigny; Hubert the king's chamberlain; William of Montfiquet; Hagulf 'de Tani'; John Belet; Robert, son of Siward. Given at Westminster.

The right of London to appoint its own sheriff was a very notable concession since the official role of the 'shire reeve' was to act as the king's agent on the spot.

A Description of the City of London, c. 1173

William Fitz Stephen

Fitz Stephen's portrait of London in the age of Henry II was penned as the prologue to his *Life of Becket*. Thomas à Becket, the martyred Archbishop of Canterbury, was the first Englishman to rise to high office following the Norman takeover. As Fitz Stephen understood, Becket would not have achieved so much so young without the confidence that came from being a London-born boy – a proto-cockney. Hence the fulsome description of the capital and its 40,000 citizens with which Fitz Stephen begins the biography:

MONG THE NOBLE and celebrated cities of the world that of London, the capital of the kingdom of the English, is one which extends its glory farther than all the others and sends its wealth and merchandise more widely into distant lands. Higher than all the rest does it lift its head. It is happy in the healthiness of its air; in its observance of Christian practice; in the strength of its fortifications; in its natural situation; in the honour of its citizens; and in the modesty of its matrons. It is cheerful in its sports, and the fruitful mother of noble men. Let us look into these things in turn.

If the mildness of the climate of this place softens the character of its inhabitants, it does not make them corrupt in following Venus, but rather prevents them from being fierce and bestial, making them liberal and kind.

In the church of St Paul there is the episcopal seat. Once it was metropolitan, and some think it will again become so, if the citizens return to the island, unless perhaps the archiepiscopal title of the blessed martyr, Thomas, and the presence of his body preserves that dignity for ever at Canterbury where it is at present. But as St Thomas has made both cities illustrious, London by his rising and Canterbury by his setting, each can claim advantage of the other with justice in respect of that saint. As regards the practice of Christian worship there are in London and its suburbs thirteen greater conventual churches and, besides these, one hundred and twenty-six lesser parish churches.

It has on the east the Palatine castle,* very great and strong: the keep and walls rise from very deep foundations and are fixed with a mortar tempered by the blood of animals. On the west there are two castles very strongly fortified, and from these there runs a high and massive wall with seven double gates and with towers along the north at regular intervals. London was once also walled and turreted on the south, but the mighty Thames, so full of fish, has with the sea's ebb and flow washed against, loosened, and thrown down those walls in the course of time. Upstream to the west there is the royal palace† which is conspicuous above the river, a building incomparable in its ramparts and bulwarks. It is about two miles from the city and joined thereto by a populous suburb.

Everywhere outside the houses of those living in the suburbs, and adjacent to them, are the spacious and beautiful gardens of the citizens, and these are planted with trees. Also there are on the north side pastures and pleasant meadow lands through which flow streams wherein the turning of mill-wheels makes a cheerful sound. Very near lies a great forest with woodland pastures in which there are the lairs of wild animals: stags, fallow deer, wild boars and bulls. The tilled lands of the city are not of barren gravel, but fat Asian

---

* The Tower of London
† Westminster

plains that yield luxuriant crops and fill the tillers' barns with the sheaves of Ceres.

There are also outside London on the north side excellent suburban wells with sweet, wholesome and clear water that flows rippling over the bright stones. Among these are Holywell, Clerkenwell and St Clement's Well, which are all famous. These are frequented by great numbers and much visited by the students from the schools and by the young men of the city, when they go out for fresh air on summer evenings. Good indeed is this city when it has a good lord!

The city is honoured by her men, glorious in its arms, and so populous that during the terrible wars of King Stephen's reign the men going forth from it to battle were reckoned as twenty thousand armed horsemen and sixty thousand foot-soldiers, all equipped for war. The citizens of London are regarded as conspicuous above all others for their polished manners, for their dress and for the good tables which they keep. The inhabitants of other towns are called citizens, but those of London are called barons. And with them a solemn pledge is sufficient to end every dispute.

The matrons of this city are very Sabines.

In London the three principal churches (that is to say, the episcopal church of St Paul, the church of the Holy Trinity, and the church of St Martin) have famous schools by special privilege and by virtue of their ancient dignity. But through the favour of some magnate, or through the presence of teachers who are notable or famous in philosophy, there are also other schools. On feast-days the masters hold meetings for their pupils in the church whose festival it is. The scholars dispute, some with oratory and some with argument; some recite enthymemes;* others excel in using perfect syllogisms. Some dispute for ostentation like wrestlers with opponents;

---

* A form of philosophical disputation

others argue in order to establish the truth in its perfection. Sophists who speak paradoxes are praised for their torrent of words, while others seek to overthrow their opponents by using fallacious arguments. Now and then orators use rhetoric for persuasion, being careful to omit nothing essential to their art. Boys of different schools strive against each other in verses, or contend about the principles of grammar and the rules governing past and future tenses. Others use epigrams, rhythm and metre in the old trivial banter; they pull their comrades to pieces with 'Fescennine Licence': mentioning no names, they dart abuse and gibes, and mock the faults of their comrades and sometimes even those of their elders, using Socratic wit and biting harder even than the tooth of Theon in daring dithyrambics. Their hearers, ready to enjoy the joke, wrinkle up their noses as they guffaw in applause.

Of the Ordering of the City

Those engaged in business of various kinds, sellers of merchandise, hirers of labour, are distributed every morning into their several localities according to their trade. Besides, there is in London on the river bank among the wines for sale in ships and in the cellars of the vintners a public cook-shop. There daily you may find food according to the season, dishes of meat, roast, fried and boiled, large and small fish, coarser meats for the poor and more delicate for the rich, such as venison and big and small birds. If any of the citizens should unexpectedly receive visitors, weary from their journey, who would fain not wait until fresh food is bought and cooked, or until the servants have brought bread or water for washing, they hasten to the river bank and there find all they need. However great the multitude of soldiers and travellers entering the city, or preparing to go out of it, at any hour of the day or night – that these may not fast too long, and those may not go out supperless – they turn aside thither, if they please, where every man can refresh himself in his own way. Those who would cater for themselves fastidiously need not search to find sturgeon or the bird of Africa or the Ionian godwit. For this is a public kitchen, very convenient to the city, and part of its amenities. Hence the dictum in the Gorgias of Plato that the art of cookery is an imitation of medicine and flatters a quarter of civic life.

Immediately outside one of the gates there is a field which is smooth* both in fact and in name. On every sixth day of the week, unless it be a major feast-day, there takes place there a famous exhibition of fine horses for sale. Earls, barons and knights, who are in the town, and many citizens come out to see or to buy. It is pleasant to see the high-stepping palfreys with their gleaming coats, as they go through their paces, putting down their feet alternately on one side together. Next, one can see the horses suitable for esquires, moving faster though less smoothly, lifting and setting down, as it were, the opposite fore and hind feet: here are colts of fine breed, but not yet accustomed to the bit, stepping high with jaunty tread; there are the sumpter-horses, powerful and spirited; and after them there are the war-horses, costly, elegant of form, noble of stature, with ears quickly tremulous, necks raised and large haunches. As these show their paces, the buyers first try those of gentler gait, then those of quicker pace whereby the fore and hind feet move in pairs together. When a race is about to begin among such chargers that are so powerful to carry and so swift to run, a shout is raised, and orders are given that the inferior animals should be led apart. Three jockeys who mount these flying steeds (or at times two, as may be agreed) prepare themselves for the contest; skilled in managing them,

---

* Smithfield

they curb their untamed mouths with bitted bridles. To get a good start in the race is their chief concern. Their mounts also enter into the spirit of the contest as they are able; their limbs tremble, and so impatient are they of delay that they cannot keep still. When the signal is given, they stretch their limbs to the uttermost, and dash down the course with courageous speed. The riders, covetous of applause and ardent for victory, plunge their spurs into the loose-reined horses, and urge them forward with their shouts and their whips. You would agree with Heraclitus that all things are in motion! You would know Zeno to be completely wrong when he said that there was no motion and no goal to be reached!

By themselves in another part of the field stand the goods of the countryfolk: implements of husbandry, swine with long flanks, cows with full udders, oxen of immense size, and woolly sheep. There also stand the mares fit for plough, some big with foal, and others with brisk young colts closely following them.

To this city from every nation under heaven merchants delight to bring their trade by sea. The Arabian sends gold; the Sabaean spice and incense. The Scythian brings arms, and from the rich, fat lands of Babylon comes oil of palms. The Nile sends precious stones; the men of Norway and Russia, furs and sables; nor is China absent with purple silk. The Gauls come with their wines.

London, as historians have shown, is a much older city than Rome, for though it derives from the same Trojan ancestors, it was founded by Brutus before Rome was founded by Romulus and Remus. Wherefore they still have the same laws from their common origin. This city is like Rome divided into wards; it has annual sheriffs instead of consuls; it has its senatorial order and lower magistrates; it has drains and aqueducts in its streets; it has its appointed places for the hearing of cases deliberative, demonstrative and judicial; it has its several courts, and its separate assemblies on appointed days.

I do not think there is a city with a better record for church-going, doing honour to God's ordinances, keeping feast-days, giving alms and hospitality to strangers, confirming betrothals, contracting marriages, celebrating weddings, providing feasts, entertaining guests, and also, it may be added, in care for funerals and for the burial of the dead. The only plagues of London are the immoderate drinking of fools and the frequency of fires.

To this it may be added that almost all the bishops, abbots and magnates of England are in a sense citizens and freemen of London, having their own splendid town-houses. In them they live, and spend largely, when they are summoned to great councils by the king or by their metropolitan, or drawn thither by their private affairs.

Of the Sports of London

We now come to speak of the sports of the city, for it is not fitting that a city should be merely useful and serious-minded, unless it be also pleasant and cheerful. For this cause on the seals of the supreme pontiff, down to the time of the last Pope Leo, on one side of the lead was engraved the figure of Peter the fisherman and above him a key, as it were, held out to him from heaven by the hand of God, and around it was inscribed the verse, 'For me didst thou leave the ship, receive now the key.' And on the other side was engraved a city with the inscription 'Golden Rome'. Moreover, it was said in honour of Augustus Caesar and Rome, 'It rains all night, games usher in the day; Caesar, thou dost divide dominion with Jove.' Instead of shows in the theatre and stage-plays, London provides plays of a more sacred character, wherein are presented the miracles worked by saintly confessors or the sufferings which made illustrious the constancy of martyrs. Furthermore, every year on the day called Carnival – to begin with the sports of boys (for we were all boys once) – scholars from the different schools bring fighting-cocks to their masters, and the whole morning is set apart to watch their cocks do battle in the schools, for the boys are given a holiday that day. After dinner all the young men of the town go out into the fields in the suburbs to play ball. The scholars of the various schools have their own ball, and almost all the followers of each occupation have theirs also. The seniors and the fathers and the wealthy magnates of the city come on horseback to watch the contests of the younger generation, and in their turn recover their lost youth: the motions of their natural heat seem to be stirred in them at the mere sight of such strenuous activity and by their participation in the joys of unbridled youth.

Every Sunday in Lent after dinner a fresh swarm of young men go out into the fields on war-horses, steeds foremost in the contest, each of which is skilled and schooled to run in circles. From the gates there sallies forth a host of laymen, sons of the citizens, equipped with lances and shields, the younger ones with spears forked at the top, but with the steel point removed. They make a pretence at war, carry out field-exercises and indulge in mimic combats. Thither too come many courtiers, when the king is in town, and from the households of bishops, earls and barons come youths and adolescents, not yet girt with the belt of knighthood, for the pleasure of engaging in combat with each other. Each is inflamed with the hope of victory. The fiery steeds neigh with tremulous limbs and champ their bits; impatient of delay they cannot stand still. When at last their trampling hooves ring on the ground in rapid flight, their boy riders divide their ranks; some pursue those immediately in front of them, but fail to catch up with them; others overtake their fellows, force them to dismount and fly past them.

At the Easter festival they play at a kind of naval warfare. A shield is firmly bound to a tree in mid-stream, and a small boat, swiftly impelled by many an oar and the current of the river, carries on the stern a youth armed with a lance with which to strike the shield. If he breaks the lance by striking the shield, and yet keeps his footing, he has achieved his aim and gratified his wish, but if he strikes the shield firmly and the lance remains unbroken, he is thrown overboard into the flowing river, and the boat, impelled by its own motion, rushes past him. There are, however, two other boats moored, one on each side of the target, with several youths on board to seize hold of the striker who has been engulfed by the stream, as soon as he comes into view or when he rises on the crest of the wave for the second time. On the bridge and the terraces fronting the river stand the spectators, ready to laugh their fill.

On feast-days throughout the summer the young men indulge in the sports of archery, running, jumping, wrestling, slinging the stone, hurling the javelin beyond a mark and fighting with sword and buckler. Cytherea leads the dance of maidens, and until the moon rises, the earth is shaken with flying feet.

In winter on almost every feast-day before dinner either foaming boars, armed with lightning tusks, fight for their lives 'to save their bacon', or stout bulls with butting horns, or huge bears do battle with the hounds let loose upon them. When the great marsh that washes the north wall of the city is frozen over, swarms of young men issue forth to play games on the ice. Some, gaining speed in their run, with feet set well apart, slide sideways over a vast expanse of ice. Others make seats out of a large lump of ice, and while one sits thereon, others with linked hands run before and drag him along behind them. So swift is their sliding motion that sometimes their feet slip, and they all fall on their faces. Others, more skilled at winter sports, put on their feet the shin-bones of animals, binding them firmly round their ankles, and, holding poles shod with iron in their hands, which they strike from time to time against the ice, they are propelled swift as a bird in flight or a bolt shot from an engine of war. Sometimes, by mutual consent, two of them run against each other in this way from a great distance, and, lifting their poles, each tilts against the other. Either one or both fall, not without some bodily injury, for, as they fall, they are carried along a great way beyond each other by the impetus of their run, and wherever the ice comes in contact with their heads, it scrapes off the skin utterly. Often a leg or an arm is broken, if the victim falls with it underneath him; but theirs is an age greedy of glory, youth yearns for victory, and exercises itself in mock combats in order to carry itself more bravely in real battles.

Many of the citizens take pleasure in sporting with birds of the air, with hawks, falcons and such-like, and with hounds that hunt their prey in the woods. The citizens have the rights of the chase in Middlesex, Hertfordshire, all the Chiltern country, and in Kent as far as the river Cray. The Londoners, who were then known as Trinobantes, drove back Julius Caesar, whose delight it was to wade through paths steeped in blood.

Fitz Stephen omitted to mention the immigrants huddled in enclaves around the city – principally Germans, French, Dutch and Flemings engaged in crafts and import-export. The Jews, who inhabited Jewry Street and Old Jewry, were, unlike Christians, allowed to loan money; for this trade of 'usury' they were widely despised, even by their biggest customers, the kings of England. The eye-witness compiler of the *Itinerary of Richard I* commented on that king's coronation:

ON THE 3RD day of September, in the year of our Lord 1189, Richard [I] was appointed king, on a Sunday, with the dominical letter A., viz., in the year after leap year. Many were the conjectures made, because the day above that was marked unlucky in the calendar; and in truth it was unlucky, and very much so to the Jews in London, who were destroyed that day, and likewise the Jews settled in other parts of England endured many hardships.

Thirty Jews died in the attacks of 1189, their bodies interred in the Jewish graveyard outside Cripplegate, the only Jewish cemetery in England. More anti-Semitic pogroms followed in the capital in 1215, 1264 and 1272. Finally, in 1290 Edward I expelled all the Jews from England and confiscated their property. He also relieved Christians of any obligations to repay debts to them. As bankers to the Crown and city the Jews were replaced by the Italian merchants who settled in Lombard Street.

Building Regulations, 1189
The London Assizes

W HEN TWO NEIGHBOURS shall have agreed to build between themselves a wall of stone, each shall give a foot and a half of land, and so they shall construct, at their joint cost, a stone wall three feet thick and sixteen feet in height. And, if they agree, they shall make a gutter between them, to carry off the water from their houses, as they may deem most convenient. But if they should not agree, either of them may make a gutter to carry the water dripping from his own house on to his own land, except he can convey it into the high street ...

And if any one shall build his own stone wall, upon his own land, of the height of sixteen feet, his neighbour ought to make a gutter under the eaves of the house which is placed on that wall, and receive in it the water falling from that house, and lead it on to his own land, unless he can lead it into the high street.

Also, no one of two parties having a common wall built between them, can, or ought, to pull down any portion of his part of the said wall, or lessen its thickness, or make arches in it, without the assent and will of the other.

And if any one shall have windows looking towards the land of a neighbour, and although he and his predecessors have long been possessed of the view of the aforesaid windows, nevertheless, his neighbour may lawfully obstruct the view of those windows, by building opposite to them on his own ground, as he shall consider most expedient; except he who hath the windows can show any writing whereby his neighbour may not obstruct the view of those windows ...

A decree made by the counsel of the citizens, for the setting into order of the city and to provide, by God's help, against fire.

First, they advise that all ale-houses be forbidden, except those which shall be licensed by the common council of the city at Guildhall, excepting those belonging to persons willing to build of stone, that the city may be secure. And that no baker bake, or ale-wife brew, by night, either with reeds or straw or stubble, but with wood only.

They advise also that all the cook-shops on the Thames be whitewashed and plastered within and without, and that all inner chambers and hostelries be wholly removed, so that there remain only the house [hall] and bed-room.

Whosoever wishes to build, let him take care, as he loveth himself and his goods, that he roof not with reeds, nor rush, nor with any manner of litter, but with tile only, or shingle, or boards, or, if it may be, with lead, within the city and Portsoken. Also all houses which till now are covered with reed or rush, which can be plastered, let them be plastered within eight days, and let those which shall not be so plastered within the term be demolished by the aldermen and lawful men of the venue.

All wooden houses which are nearest to the stone houses in Cheap, whereby the stone houses in Cheap may be in peril, shall be securely amended by view of the mayor and sheriffs, and good men of the city, or, without any exception, to whomsoever they may belong, pulled down.

The watches, and they who watch by night for the custody of the city shall go out by day and return by day, or they by whom they may have been sent forth shall be fined forty shillings by the city. And let old houses in which brewing or baking is done be whitewashed and plastered within and without, that they may be safe against fire . . .

They say also that it is only proper that before every house should be a tub full of water, either of wood or stone.

The fire ordinances were prompted by London's ingrained habit of setting itself alight. Fire in 1087 had reduced St Paul's to ashes for the third time, and in 1135 flames consumed the city between the Fleet river and London Bridge. Doubtless to the relief of the locals the peculiarly flame-friendly timber span over the Thames was replaced in 1209 by a stone version, which lasted until 1830.

As the London Assizes recognized, expensive stone buildings were found throughout the city – rich Londoner lived cheek-by-jowl with poor Londoner. Proximity, though, did not always lessen class tensions:

～～～

Tax Riot, 1194
Roger of Wendover

An early entrance into history for the notorious London 'Mob' (*mobile vulgus*):

ABOUT THIS TIME there arose a dispute in the city of London between the poor and the rich on account of the talllage, which was exacted by the king's agents for the benefit of the exchequer: for the principal men of the city, whom we call mayors and aldermen, having held a deliberation at their hustings, wished to preserve themselves free from the burden, and to oppress the poorer classes. Wherefore William Fitz-Robert, surnamed 'with the beard,' because his ancestors in anger against the Normans never shaved, made opposition to the same, and called the mayors of the city traitors to our lord the king for the cause above-named; and the disturbances were so great in the city that recourse was had to arms. William stirred up a large number of the middle and lower classes against the mayors and aldermen, but by their pusillanimity and cowardice the plans of William's confederates in resisting the injury done them were dissipated and defeated: the middle and lower classes were repressed, and the king, his ministers, and the chief men of the city charged the whole crime on William. As the king's party were about to arrest him, he, being a distinguished character in the city, tall of stature and of great personal strength, escaped, notwithstanding their exertions, defending himself with nothing but a knife, and flying into the church of St. Mary of the Arches, demanded the protection of our Lord, St. Mary, and her church, saying that he had resisted an unjust decree for no other purpose than that all might bear an equal share of the public burden, and contribute according to their means. His expostulations, however, were not listened to, the majority prevailed, and the archbishop, to the surprise of many, ordered that he should be dragged from the church to take his trial, because he had created a sedition and made such a disturbance among the people of the city. When this was told to William, he took refuge in the tower of the church, for he knew that the mayors, whom he had contradicted, sought to take away his life. In their obstinacy they applied fire, and sacrilegiously burnt down a great part of the church. Thus William was forced to leave the tower, almost suffocated with the heat and smoke. He was then seized, dragged out of the church, stripped, and, with his hands tied behind his back, conveyed away to the Tower of London. Soon after, at the instigation of the archbishop, the principal citizens, and the king's ministers, he was taken from the Tower, and dragged, tied to a horse's tail, through the middle of London to Ulmet, a pitiable sight to the citizens arid to his own respectable relations in the city: after which he was hung in chains on a gallows. Thus William of the Beard was shamefully put to death by his fellow citizens for asserting the truth and defending the cause of the poor: and if the justice of one's cause constitutes a martyr, we may surely set him down as one. With him also were hanged nine of his neighbours or of his family, who espoused his cause.

Although the tallage riot was easily quelled it could be dangerous, even fatal, for the Crown to provoke London. So affronted was London by the high-and-mighty attitude of Empress Matilda that the city rose against her and caused her to flee in 1141. Half a century later, during the Barons' War with King John, the populace of London threw in their lot with the uppity aristocrats and enforced Magna Carta in 1215. The Mayor of London was the only commoner to sign the agreement. A weak king always presented a chance for London – thus John was also obliged to grant the city a new charter in 1215, which introduced the principle of an annually elected mayor.

The Thames Floods, *1241*
Matthew Paris

Paris was a monk at St Albans.

O N THE FEAST of St Edmund in the same year, distinct thunder attended by lightning, a sad presage of the approach of a lengthened tempest, alarmed the hearts and ears of mortals; nor was the warning false, for it was followed by continued unseasonable weather, and by an unpleasant and disturbed state of the air, which continued for several days. Such deluges of rain fell, that the river Thames, overflowing its usual bounds and its ancient banks, spread itself over the country towards Lambeth, for six miles, and took possession, far and wide, of the houses and fields in that part. Owing to the inundation of the water, people rode into the great hall at Westminster on horseback ... Thus this year passed away, having afforded an abundance of fruits and vegetables, notwithstanding it was arid and hot, and towards the end, generating epidemics and quartan agues.

Misadventures in Childhood, 1301–37
Calendar of the Coroners' Rolls

A Game on the Way to School, 1301

O N TUESDAY (19 July), Richard, son of John le Mazon, who was eight years old, was walking immediately after dinner across London Bridge to school. For fun, he tried to hang by his hands from a beam on the side of the bridge, but his hands giving way, he fell into the water and was drowned. Being asked who were present, the jurors say a great multitude of passers-by, whose names they know not, but they suspect no one of the death except mischance.

Playing on the Timber Pile, 1322

ON THE SUNDAY before the Feast of St Dunstan, Robert, son of John de St Botulph, a boy seven years old, Richard, son of John de Chesthunt, and two other boys whose names are unknown were playing on certain pieces of timber in the lane called 'Kyroune-lane' in the ward of Vintry, and one piece fell on Robert and broke his right leg. In course of time Johanna his mother arrived and rolled the timber off him and carried him to the shop, where he lingered until the Friday before the Feast of St Margaret, when he died at the hour of prime, of the broken leg and of no other felony; nor do the jurors suspect anyone of the death, but only the accident and the fracture.

A Lost Ball, 1337

ON TUESDAY IN Pentecost week John, son of William atte Noke, chandler, got out of a window in the rent of John de Wynton, plumber, to recover a ball lost in a gutter at play. He slipped and fell, and so injured himself that he died on the Saturday following, of the fall.

Misadventure was only one of the many deaths to befall children in the dangerous playground that was fourteenth-century London. It was 'full of pits and sloughs' overflowing with human and animal faeces in which dread diseases bred. Typhus, smallpox and tuberculosis were common killers. Infant mortality throughout the fourteenth century was typically 35 per cent.

Street Life, 1301–80

Various

'Then Kicked Him as He Lay': A Fatal Fight, 1326, Calendar of the Coroners' Rolls

ON FRIDAY [AUGUST 15] at the hour of prime, Roger Styward was walking in Cordwainer Street carrying eels in a bucket for sale. He threw down on the street some skins of eels opposite the shops of Simon de Peckham and John de Keslyngbury; whereupon Simon and Richard de

Keslyngbury, apprentice of John, remonstrated with him. A quarrel arising, the apprentice left the shop and struck Roger with the palm of his hand under the left jaw and returned to the shop. Simon followed Roger as far as the churchyard of St. Mary-le-Bow and there struck him with his fist on the head under the left ear, so that he fell to the ground, and then kicked him as he lay. Roger rose with difficulty and went towards Cheapside, when he again fell and immediately died. Simon and Richard, on hearing of his death, took refuge in the church of St. Mary-le-Bow. Richard, after the inquest was held, surrendered and was taken to Newgate, but Simon refused to surrender.

A Home Owner Attacks Drunken Roisterers, 1322, Calendar of the Coroners' Rolls

AT MIDNIGHT ON a certain Tuesday in January [1321/22], Reginald de Freestone 'settere,' John Bocche, Walter le Skynnere, and eleven others whose names were unknown were passing the shop of William de Grymesby in the ward of Broad Street. [They were] singing and shouting, as they often did at night, when William de Grymesby, who was in his shop, begged them to allow him and the neighbors to sleep and rest in peace.

Whereupon Reginald de Freestone, John Bocche, Walter le Skynnere, and their companions invited William de Grymesby to come out of his shop if he dared.

At last he seized a staff called a 'balstaf' and did run after them. He struck Reginald with the staff on the left side of the head and smashed the whole of it. Reginald fell to the ground at the entrance of the tenement of Jordan de Langelegh and there lingered without speaking until break of day on Tuesday, when he died of the blow.

Alice de Breynford first discovered Reginald lying dead, and she raised the cry so that the country came.

The goods of William de Grymesby were appraised and found to be: two small pigs, at 3*s*.; one 'shippingbord,' at 3*d*.; one broken chest and a table, at 6*d*.; one pair of worn linen sheets, at 4*d*.; a blanket, a worn linen cloth, and other small things, at 2*s*. 9 ½*d*. Total, 6*s*. 11½*d*., for which Richard de Hakeneye, the sheriff, was to answer.

A Hit and Run Cart Driver, 1337, Calendar of the Coroners' Rolls

ON THURSDAY [FEBRUARY 13], about the hour of vespers, two carters taking two empty carts out of the city were urging their horses apace, when the wheels of one of the carts collapsed opposite the rent of the hospital of St. Mary, Bishopsgate, so that the cart fell on Agnes de Cicestre, who immediately died. The carter thereupon left his cart and three horses and took flight in fear, although he was not suspected of malicious intent. The cart and its trappings were appraised by jurors of the ward of Bishopsgate at 6*s*. 8*d*.; the first horse, of a dun color, at 10*s*., the second, a gray, and blind of both eyes, at 4*s*., and the third, a black, at 6*s*.; also five old sacks and five pounds of candles of 'coton' which were in the cart at the time of the accident at 16½*d*. Total 28*s*. ½*d*., for which John de North-halle, one of the sheriffs, will answer.

The city, incidentally, later implemented a speed limit for carts, viz: 'No carter with liberties shall drive his cart more quickly when it is unloaded than when it is loaded.'

Traders Riot, 1378, City of London Letter-Book

ON SUNDAY [. . .] before the hour of noon a conflict arose in Westcheap between certain persons of the trade of goldsmiths and others of the trade of pepperers, from a certain rancor that had existed between them; by reason of which conflict no small affray arose throughout the whole city, and that, too, while the bishop of Carlisle was preaching in St. Paul's churchyard. In which place, because of such conflict, and the wounded fleeing thither with great outcry, no little tumult and alarm ensued. Upon which Nicholas Brembre, the then mayor, being informed thereof, together with other aldermen, immediately went to Westcheap to restore peace there and to maintain it.

False Beggars, 1380, City of London Letter-Book

ON THE 24TH day of October, in the 4th year of Richard II, John Warde, of the County of York, and Richard Lynham, of The County of Somerset, two impostors, were brought to the Hall of the Guildhall of London, before John Hadlee, Mayor, the Aldermen, and the Sheriffs, and questioned for that, whereas they were stout enough to work for their food and raiment, and had their tongues to talk with, they, the same John Warde and Richard Lynham, did there pretend that they were mutes, and had been deprived of their tongues; and went about in divers places of the city aforesaid, carrying in their hands two ell measures, an iron hook and pincers, and a piece of leather, in shape like part of a tongue, edged with silver, and with writing around it, to this effect – THIS IS THE TONGUE OF JOHN WARDE – with which instruments, and by means of divers signs, they gave many persons to understand that they were traders, in token whereof they carried the said ell measures; and that they had been plundered by robbers of their goods; and that their tongues had also been drawn out with the said hook, and then cut off with the pincers; they making a horrible noise, like unto a roaring, and opening their mouths; where it seemed to all who examined the same, that their tongues had been cut off: to the defrauding of other poor and infirm persons, and in manifest deceit of the whole of the people.

Wherefore, they were asked how they would acquit themselves thereof; upon which, they acknowledged that they had done all the things above imputed to them. And as it appeared to the Court that of their evil intent and falsity they had done the things aforesaid, and in deceit of all the people; and to the end that other persons might beware of such and the like evil intent, falsity, and deceit, it was awarded that they should be put upon the pillory on three different days, each time for one hour in the day; namely, on the Wednesday, Friday, and Saturday, before the Feast of St Simon and St Jude; the said instruments being hung about their necks each day . . . which punishment being completed, they were instructed to have them taken back to the Gaol of Newgate, there to remain until orders should be given for their release.

Trick of the Trade: A Fraudulent Baker, 1327
The City of London Letter Book

A CONGREGATION OF ... aldermen, and Roger Chauntecler, one of the sheriffs of London, holden at the Guildhall, on Thursday in the week of Pentecost, that is, on the 4th day of June AD 1327 ...

John Brid, baker, was attached to make answer as to certain falsehood, malice, and deceit, by him committed, to the nuisance of the common people; as to which, the mayor, aldermen and sheriffs of the City were given to understand that the same John, for falsely and maliciously obtaining his own private advantage, did skilfully and artfully cause a certain hole to be made upon a table of his, called a '*moldingborde*,' pertaining to his bakehouse, after the manner of a mouse-trap, in which mice are caught; there being a certain wicket warily provided for closing and opening such hole.

And when his neighbours and others, who were wont to bake their bread at his oven, came with their dough or material for making bread, the said John used to put such dough or other material upon the said table, called a '*moldingborde*' as aforesaid, and over the hole before-mentioned for the purpose of making loaves therefrom, for baking; and such dough or material being so placed upon the table aforesaid, the same John had one of his household, ready provided for the same, sitting in secret beneath such table; which servant of his, so seated beneath the hole, and carefully opening it, piecemeal and bit by bit craftily withdrew some of the dough aforesaid, frequently collecting great quantities from such dough, falsely, wickedly, and maliciously; to the great loss of all his neighbours and persons living near, and of others, who had come to him with such dough to bake, and to the scandal and disgrace of the whole City, and, in especial, of the mayor and bailiffs for the safe-keeping of the assizes of the City assigned. Which hole, so found in his table aforesaid, was made of aforethought; and in like manner, a great quantity of such dough that had been drawn through the said hole, was found beneath the hole, and was . . . brought here into Court.

And the same John, here present in court, being asked how he will acquit himself of the fraud, malice, and deceit aforesaid, personally in court says that of such fraud, malice, and deceit, he is in no way guilty; and puts himself upon the country thereon, etc. Therefore, let inquisition as to the truth of the matter be made by the country, etc . . .

And after counsel and treaty had been held among the mayor and aldermen, as to passing judgment upon the falsehood, malice, and deceit aforesaid; seeing that, although there is no one who prosecutes them, or any one of them, the said deed is, as it were a certain species of theft, and that it is neither consonant with right nor pleasing to God that such falsehood, deceit, and malice shall go unpunished; the more especially as all those who have come to the said bakers, to bake their bread, have been falsely, wickedly, and maliciously deceived, they themselves being wholly ignorant thereof, and have suffered no little loss thereby; it was agreed and ordained, that all those of the bakers aforesaid, beneath whose tables with holes dough had been found, should be put upon the pillory, with a certain quantity of such dough hung from their necks; and that those bakers in whose houses dough was not found beneath the tables aforesaid, should be put upon the pillory, but without dough hung from their necks; and that they should so remain upon the pillory until vespers at St. Paul's in London should be ended.

Among the keenest in London to bring such a fraudster to justice would have been the guild of bakers. By the late 1320s there were nearly 30 merchant and craft associations in London, all of which existed – their charitable works notwithstanding – to protect themselves by policing their craft, its reputation and the admittance to the craft's 'mysteries'. To this end the guilds drew up stringent rules, of which the Spurriers' Ordinances is a prime example.

૪ ૪ ૪

The Ordinances of the Spurriers, 1346
Anonymous

Spurriers were makers of spurs.

B E IT REMEMBERED that on Tuesday, the morrow of St. Peter's Chains, in the nineteenth year of the reign of King Edward III, the articles underwritten were read before John Hammond, mayor, Roger de Depham, recorder, and the other aldermen; and seeing that the same were deemed befitting, they were accepted and enrolled in these words.

In the first place, that no one of the trade of spurriers shall work longer than from the beginning of the day until curfew rung out at the church of St. Sepulcher ... by reason that no man can work so neatly by night as by day. And many persons of the said trade, who compass how to practice deception in their work, desire to work by night rather than by day; and then they introduce false iron, and iron that has been cracked; for tin, and also they put gilt on false copper, and cracked. And further, many of the said trade are wandering about all day, without working at all at their trade; and then, when they have become drunk and frantic, they take to their work, to the annoyance of the sick, and all their neighborhood, by reason of the broils that arise between them and the strange folks who are dwelling among them.

And then they proceed to blow up their fires so vigorously that their forges begin all at once to blaze, to the great peril of themselves and of all the neighborhood around. And then, too, all the neighbors are much in dread of the sparks, which so vigorously issue forth in all directions from the mouths of the chimneys in their forges. By reason thereof it seems best that working by night should be put an end to, in order to avoid such false work and such perils; and therefore the mayor and the aldermen do will, by the assent of the good folks of the said trade, and for the common profit, that from henceforth such time for working, and such false work made in the trade, shall be forbidden. And if any person shall be found in the said trade to do the contrary hereof, let him be amerced, the first time in 40d., one-half thereof to go to the use of the Chamber of the Guildhall of London, and the other half to the use of the said trade; the second time, in half a mark, and the third time in 10s., to the use of the same Chamber and trade; and the fourth time, let him forswear the trade forever.

Also, that no one of the said trade shall hang his spurs out on Sundays, or any other days that are double feasts; but only a sign indicating his business; and such spurs as they shall so sell they are to show and sell within their shops, without exposing them without, or opening the doors or windows of their shops, on the pain aforesaid.

Also, that no one of the said trade shall keep a house or shop to carry on his business unless he is free of the city; and that no one shall cause to be sold, or exposed for sale, any manner of old spurs for new ones, or shall garnish them or change them for new ones.

Also, that no one of the said trade shall take an apprentice for a less term than seven years, and such apprentice shall be enrolled according to the usages of the said city.

Also, that if any one of the said trade, who is not a freeman, shall take an apprentice for a term of years, he shall be amerced as aforesaid.

Also, that no one of the said trade shall receive the apprentice, serving man, or journeyman of another in the same trade, during the term agreed upon between his master and him, on the pain aforesaid.

Also, that no alien of another country, or foreigner of this country, shall follow or use the said trade, unless he is enfranchised before the mayor, aldermen, and chamberlain; and that, by witness and surety of the good folks of the said trade, who will undertake for him, as to his loyalty and his good behavior.

Also, that no one of the said trade shall work on Saturdays, after noon has been rung out in the city; and not from that hour until Monday morning following.

The guilds continued to proliferate, with the most prestigious of them – the Mercers, Haberdashers, Fishmongers and Grocers – building imposing mansions or halls in the City. The guilds wielded enormous power over the medieval city, and guild membership was a pre-requisite of citizenship.

Perhaps 25 per cent of London's population were guild members and citizens; below them on the social ladder were the 'foreigns' – serfs who had fled the land, unskilled workers, aliens, criminals and beggars.

But, guild member or 'foreigner', the bacillus that came to London in 1348 did not discriminate.

City of the Dead: The Black Death, 1348
Robert of Avesbury

The Black Death was a form of bubonic plague. It was widely believed that the Black Death was caused by exhalations from the Earth, or carried on the wind. Those Londoners who could not flee the arrival of the Black Death sealed up their houses with waxed cloth and burnt aromatic woods to purify the air. To little or no avail.

THE PESTILENCE WHICH had first broken out in the land occupied by the Saracens became so much stronger that, sparing no dominion, it visited with the scourge of sudden death the various parts of all the kingdoms, extending from that land to the northward, including even Scotland, destroying the greater part of the people. For it began in England in Dorsetshire . . . in the year of the Lord 1348, and immediately advancing from place to place it attacked men without warning and for the most part those who were healthy. Very many of those who were attacked in the morning it carried out of human affairs before noon. And no one whom it willed to die did it permit to live longer than three or four days. There was moreover no choice of persons, with the exception, at least, of a few rich people. In the same day twenty, forty or sixty corpses, and indeed many times as many more bodies of those who had died, were delivered to church burial in the same pit at the same time. And about the feast of All Saints, reaching London, it deprived many of their life daily, and increased to so great an extent that from the feast of the Purification till after Easter there were more than two hundred bodies of those who had died buried daily in the cemetery which had been then recently made near Smithfield, besides the bodies which were in other graveyards of the same city. The grace of the Holy Spirit finally intervening, that is to say about the feast of Whitsunday, it ceased at London, proceeding continuously northward. In these parts also it ceased about the feast of St. Michael, in the year of the Lord 1349.

Around half of London's population of 80,000 had fallen victim to the buboes. Not until the later sixteenth century would the city's population regain its pre-1381 heights.

Flagellants, Michaelmas 1349
Robert of Avesbury

Flagellants, usually members of the Dominican or Franciscan monastic orders, underwent public voluntary whipping in atonement for society's sins. The numbers of flagellants increased dramatically in the wake of the Black Death, widely believed by the godly to be a Heaven-sent punishment.

ABOUT MICHAELMAS 1349 over six hundred men came to London from Flanders, mostly of Zeeland and Holland origin. Sometimes at St Paul's and sometimes at other points in the city they made two daily public appearances wearing cloths from the thighs to the ankles, but otherwise stripped bare. Each wore a cap marked with a red cross in front and behind. Each had in his right hand a scourge with three tails. Each tail had a knot and through the middle of it there were sometimes sharp nails fixed. They marched naked in a file one behind the other and whipped themselves with these scourges on their naked and bleeding bodies. Four of them would cant in their native tongue and, another four would chant in response like a litany. Thrice they would all cast themselves on the ground in this sort of procession, stretching out their hands like the arms of a cross. The singing would go on and, the one who was in the rear of those thus prostrate acting first, each of them in turn would step over the others and give one stroke with his scourge to the man lying under him. This went on from the first to the last until each of them had observed the ritual to the full tale of those on the ground. Then each put on his customary garments and always wearing their caps and carrying their whips in their hands they retired to their lodgings. It is said that every night they performed the same penance.

Friars were concerned with more than the citizens' souls. They performed material good works amongst the poor and were involved in setting up the first hospitals, including St Bartholomew's and St Thomas'.

Expulsion of a Leper, 1372
The City of London Letter-Book

Lepers were formally excluded from the city in 1346 to prevent them contaminating others 'by the contagion of their polluted breath . . . by carnal intercourse with women in stews and other secret places'. If lucky, the exiled lepers might find a place in one of the nearby suburban leper hospitals. These 'Lazarus Houses' were invariably situated by crossroads, providing the lepers with a steady procession of people from whom they might beg alms. Despite official strictures, lepers frequently sought to re-enter the city.

ON MONDAY NEXT before the Feast of St Barnabas the Apostle [7 June], in the 46th year etc., John Mayn, baker, who had oftentimes before been commanded by the mayor and aldermen to depart from the City, and provide for himself some dwelling outside it, and avoid the common conversation of mankind – seeing that he, John, was smitten with the blemish of leprosy – and not to go wandering about the City to communicate with other sound persons, by reason of the infection of that disease, on the peril that awaits the same etc.; was sworn before the mayor and aldermen, at the Husting holden on the said Monday, that he would depart forthwith from the City, and would make no longer stay within it; but would take up his abode elsewhere without the City, and not return thereto, on pain of undergoing the punishment of the pillory, if he should contravene the same etc.

An Inventory of the Goods in a Fishmonger's City House, *1373*
Calendar of Plea and Memoranda Rolls

Thomas Mocking, 'late citizen and fishmonger', had an eight-room house furnished thus:

In the chamber:	Value
A new bed and a tapestry	42*s*
Another bed with a tapestry	6*s*. 8*d*.
3 quilts and 1 mattress	8*s*.
3 rugs (*chalones*)	
1 framework (*supellex*)	
1 tester	18*s*.
1 blanket	
2 pillows (*cervical*)	
4 pairs of sheets	8*s*.
5 feather beds	17*s*.
5 pillows (*wongers*)	2*s*.
panels around the bed (*tabule circa lectum*)	3*s*.
2 curtains (*rydelli*)	3*s*.
2 chests and 2 counters (*computoria*)	10*s*.
1 silver girdle	20*s*.
2 pairs of amber paternosters	6*s*.

In the hall:	
3 dorsers	
3 bankers	£4 15*s*. 8*d*.
6 cushions	
3 old bankers and 5 cushions	3*s*. 4*d*.

1 board (*tabula*) ⎫
2 trestles ⎬   8s.
5 stools ⎭
3 checker boards (*scacar'*)   2s.
1 fireplace of iron and 1 pair of tongs   31s. 3d.
5 basins, whereof one is round
7 wash bowls (*lavatoria*), whereof one is a hanging bowl
4 candelabra weighing ½ cwt., 15 lb.
       at 2d. a pound   16s. 3d. [sic]

In the storehouse (dispensa):

7 cloths (*nappe*) ⎫
6 hand towels (*manutergia*) ⎬   24s.
4 napkins (*manapia*) ⎭
1 cupboard or locker (*aumbry*) ⎫
                      ⎬   4s.
4 vats (*fates*) ⎭
5 barrels   2s.
1 gallon jug ⎫ all of pewter, weighing
5 pottle jugs ⎬ 35 lbs. at 2d. a lb.   7s. 3d.
2 quart jugs ⎭
3 chargers ⎫ all of pewter weighing
12 small platters (*platerell*) ⎬ ½ cwt., 17 lbs,   13s.11d. [sic]
12 plates ⎭ at 2½d. a pound
12 salt cellars
1 broken silver cup called
    a biker   ⎫ weighing by goldsmith's
1 silver gilt cup with a silver foot ⎬ weight £8 5s. at 25s.
4 silver cups without feet   ⎭ a goldsmith £,
24 silver spoons   £10   6s. 3d.
3 nuts (*nuces*) with silver feet   40s.
4 broken cups of mazer
1 broken cup of warre (*werr*)   46s. 8d.

In the parlor (interlocutorium):
   1 dorser and 1 banker   10*s.*
   1 board (*tabula*) and 1 counter   5*s.*
   1 board (*tabula*) for cups, called a cupboard   4*s.*

In the chamber next the parlor:
   1 cupboard or locker (*aumbry*)
   3 chairs   4*s.*

In the workmen's room:
   1 chest
   1 board   2*s.*

In the solar above the same, called the apprentices' chamber:
   2 boards   12*d.*
   4 forms   3*s.*

In the kitchen:
   2 mortars   2*s.*
   2 vats (*fates*)   7*s.*
   1 water tankard   2*s.*
   5 tubs   12*d.*
   1 sieve called a hairsieve (*hersive*)   4*d.*
   1 board for a form   8*d.*
   2 large spits
   3 small spits
   2 tripods
   2 gridirons (*creticula*)   weighing
   1 frying pan (*patella frixoria*)   in all
   1 hook (*grom*)   220 lbs. at 27*s.* 6*d.*
   1 firepan (*ferpanne*)   1½*d.* a lb.
   4 iron rods for curtains

5 pitchers (*urcieli*)	weighing 2 cwt.,
7 pots (*olle*)	3 quarters, 10 lbs., 47s. 6d. [sic]
7 pans	at 2d. a lb.
2 caldrons	

Total value of furnishing: £238 16s. 3d.

The Peasants' Revolt Comes to London, 1381

Sir John Froissart

The sparks which ignited the Peasants' Revolt were the Poll Tax of 1379 and the wage-limiting Statute of Labourers of 1381. Initially, as its name suggests, the revolt was largely confined to the countryside but then the peasants, like protestors before and after, decided to bring their case to London.

*I*N ORDER THAT this disastrous rebellion may serve as an example to mankind, I will speak of all that was done from the information I had at the time. It is customary in England, as well as in several other countries, for the nobility to have great privileges over the commonality; that is to say, the lower orders are bound by law to plough the lands of the gentry, to harvest their grain, to carry it home to the barn, to thrash and winnow it; they are also bound to harvest and carry home the hay. All these services the prelates and gentlemen exact of their inferiors; and in the counties of Kent, Essex, Sussex, and Bedford, these services are more oppressive than in other parts of the kingdom. In consequence of this the evil disposed in these districts began to murmur, saying, that in the beginning of the world there were no slaves, and that no one ought to be treated as such, unless he had committed treason against his lord, as Lucifer had done against God; but they had done no such thing, for they were neither angels nor spirits, but men formed after the same likeness as these lords who treated them as beasts. This they would bear no longer; they were determined to be free, and if they laboured or did any work, they would be paid for it. A crazy priest in the county of Kent, called John Ball, who for his absurd preaching had thrice been confined in prison by the Archbishop of Canterbury, was greatly instrumental in exciting these rebellious ideas. Every Sunday after mass, as the people were coming out of church, this John Ball was accustomed to assemble a crowd around him in the marketplace and preach to them. On such occasions he would say, 'My good friends, matters cannot go on well in England until all things shall be in common; when there shall be neither vassals nor lords; when the lords shall be no more masters than ourselves. How ill they behave to us! for what reason do they thus hold us in bondage? Are we not all descended from the same parents, Adam and Eve? And what can they show, or what reason can they give, why they should be more masters than ourselves? They are clothed in velvet and rich stuffs, ornamented with ermine and other furs, while we are forced to wear poor clothing. They have wines, spices, and fine bread, while we have only rye and the refuse of the straw; and when we drink, it must be water. They have handsome seats and manors, while we must brave the wind and rain in our labours in the field; and it is by our labour they have wherewith to support their pomp. We are called slaves, and if we do not perform our service we are beaten, and we have no sovereign to whom we can complain or who would be willing to hear us. Let us go to the King and remonstrate with him; he is young, and from him we may obtain a favourable answer, and if not we must ourselves seek to amend our condition.' With such language as this did John Ball harangue the people of his village every Sunday after mass. The Archbishop, on being informed of it, had him arrested and imprisoned for two or three months by way of punishment; but the moment he was out of prison, he returned to his former course. Many in the city of London envious of the rich and noble, having heard of John Ball's preaching, said among themselves that the country was badly governed, and that the nobility had seized upon all the gold and silver. These wicked Londoners, therefore, began to assemble in parties, and to show signs of rebellion; they also invited all those who held like opinions in the adjoining counties to come to London; telling them that they would find the town open to them and the commonalty of the same way of thinking as themselves, and that they would so press the King, that there should no longer be a slave in England.

By this means the men of Kent, Essex, Sussex; Bedford, and the adjoining counties, in number about 60,000, were brought to London, under command of Wat Tyler, Jack Straw, and John Ball. This Wat Tyler, who was chief of the three, had been a tiler of houses – a bad man and a great enemy to the nobility. When these wicked people first began their disturbances, all London, with the exception of those who favoured them, was much alarmed. The Mayor and rich citizens assembled in council and debated whether they should shut the gate and refuse to admit them; however, upon mature reflection they determined not to do so, as they might run the risk of having the suburbs burned. The gates of the city were therefore thrown open, and the rabble entered and lodged as they pleased. True it is that full two-thirds of these people knew neither what they wanted, nor for what purpose they had come together; they followed one another like sheep. In this manner did many of these poor fellows walk to London from distances of one hundred, or sixty leagues, but the greater part came from the counties I have mentioned, and all on their arrival demanded to see the King. The country gentlemen, the knights and squires, began to be much alarmed when they saw the people thus assembling, and indeed they had sufficient reason to be so, for far less causes have excited fear. As the Kentish rebels were on their road towards London, the Princess of Wales, the king's mother, was returning from a pilgrimage to Canterbury; and when they saw her the scoundrels attacked her car and caused the good lady much alarm; but God preserved her from violence, and she came the whole journey from Canterbury to London without venturing to make any stoppage. On her arrival in London, King Richard was at the Tower; thither then the Princess went immediately, and found the King, attended by the Earl of Salisbury, the Archbishop of Canterbury, Sir Robert de Namur, and several others, who had kept near his person from suspicion of the rebels. King Richard well knew that this rebellion was in agitation long before it broke out, and it was a matter of astonishment to every one that he attempted to apply no remedy.

In order that gentlemen and others may take example and learn to correct such wicked rebels, I will most amply detail how the whole business was conducted. On the Monday preceding the feast of the Holy Sacrament in the year 1381, these people sallied forth from their homes to come to London, intending, as they said, to remonstrate with the King, and to demand their freedom. At Canterbury, they met John Ball, Wat Tyler, and Jack Straw. On entering this city they were well feasted by the inhabitants, who were all of the same way of thinking as themselves; and having held a council there, resolved to proceed on their march to London. They also sent emissaries across the Thames into Essex, Suffolk, and Bedford, to press the people of these parts to do the same, in order that the city might be quite surrounded. It was the intention of the leaders of this rabble, that all the different parties should be collected on the feast of the Holy Sacrament on the day following. At Canterbury the rebels entered the church of St Thomas, where they did much damage; they also pillaged the apartments of the Archbishop, saying as they were carrying off the different articles, 'The Chancellor of England has had this piece of furniture very cheap; he must now give us an account of his revenues, and of the large sums which he has levied since the coronation of the King.' After this they plundered the abbey of St Vincent, and then leaving Canterbury took the road towards Rochester. As they passed they collected people from the villages right and left, and on they went like a tempest, destroying all the houses belonging to attorneys, king's proctors, and the Archbishop, which came in their way. At Rochester they met with the same welcome as at Canterbury, for all the people were anxious to join them. Here they went at once to the castle, and seizing a knight by name Sir John de Newtoun, who was constable of the castle and captain of the town, told him that he must accompany them as their commander-in-chief and do whatever they wished. The knight endeavoured to excuse himself; but they met his excuses by saying, 'Sir John, if you refuse you are a dead man.' Upon which, finding that the outrageous mob were ready to kill him, he was constrained to comply with their request.

In other counties of England the rebels acted in a similar manner, and several great lords and knights, such as the Lord Manley, Sir Stephen Hales, and Sir Thomas Cossington, were compelled to march with them ... When the rebels had done all they wanted at Rochester, they left that city and came to Dartford, continuing to destroy all the houses of lawyers and proctors on the right and left of the road; from Dartford they came to Blackheath, where they took up their quarters, saying, that they were armed for the King and commons of England. When the principal citizens of London found that the rebels were quartered so near them, they caused the gates of London Bridge to be closed, and placed guards there, by order of Sir William Walworth, Mayor of London; notwithstanding there were in the city more than 30,000 who favoured the insurgents. Information that the gates of London Bridge had been closed against them soon reached Blackheath, whereupon the rebels sent a knight to speak with the King and to tell him that what they were doing was for his service; for the kingdom had now for many years been wretchedly governed, to the great dishonour of the realm and to the oppression of the lower orders of the people, by his uncles, by the clergy, and more especially by the Archbishop of Canterbury, his chancellor, from whom they were determined to have an account of his ministry. The knight who was appointed to this service would willingly have excused himself, but he did not dare to do it; so advancing to the Thames opposite the Tower, he took a boat and crossed over. The King and those who were with him in the Tower were in the greatest possible suspense and most anxious to receive some intelligence when the knight's arrival was announced, who was immediately conducted into the royal presence. With the King at this time were the Princess his mother, his two natural brothers, the Earl of Kent and Sir John Holland, the Earls of Salisbury, Warwick, and Suffolk, the Archbishop of Canterbury, the great Prior of the Templars, Sir Robert de Namur, the Mayor of London, and several of the principal citizens. Immediately upon entering the apartment the knight cast himself on his knees before the King, saying, 'My much redoubted lord, do not be displeased with me for the message which I am about to deliver to you; for, my dear lord, I have been compelled to come hither.' 'By no means, sir knight,' said the King. 'Tell us what you are charged with, we hold you excused.' 'My most redoubted lord, the commons of this realm have sent me to entreat you to come to Blackheath and speak with them. They wish to have no one but yourself: and you need not fear for your person, as they will not do you the least harm; they always have respected you as their king, and will continue to do so; but they desire to tell you many things which they say it is necessary you should hear: with these, however, they have not empowered me to make you acquainted. Have the goodness, dear lord, to give me such an answer as may satisfy them, and that they may be convinced that I have really been in your presence; for they have my children as hostages for my return, and if I go not back they will assuredly put them to death.' To this the King merely replied, 'You shall have my answer speedily'; and when the knight had withdrawn, he desired his council to consider what was to be done; after some consultation, the King was advised to send word to the insurgents, that if on Thursday they would come down to the river Thames, he would without fail speak with them. The knight on receiving this answer was well satisfied, and taking leave of the King and his barons, returned to Blackheath, where upwards of 60,000 men were assembled. He told them from the King, that if they would send their leaders the next morning to the Thames, the King would come and hear what they had to say. The answer was deemed satisfactory; and the rebels passed the night as well as they could, but you must know that one-fourth of them were without provisions.

On Corpus Christi day King Richard heard mass in the Tower of London, after which he entered his barge, attended by the Earls of Salisbury, Warwick, and Suffolk, and some other knights, and rowed down the Thames towards Rotherhithe, a royal manor, where upwards of 10,000 of the insurgents had assembled. As soon as the mob perceived the royal barge approaching, they began shouting and crying as if all the spirits of the nether world had been in the company. With them, also, was the knight whom they had sent to the Tower to the King; for if the King had not come, they determined to have him cut to pieces, as they had threatened him.

When the King and his lords saw this crowd of people, and the wildness of their manner, the boldest of the party felt alarm, and the King was advised not to land, but to have his barge rowed up and down the river. 'What do you wish for?' he demanded of the multitude; 'I am come hither to hear what you have to say.' Those near him cried out, 'We wish you to land, and then we will tell you what our wants are.' Upon this the Earl of Salisbury cried out, 'Gendemen, you are not properly dressed, nor are you in a fit condition for a King to talk with.' Nothing more was said on either side, for the King was prevailed upon at once to return to the Tower. The people seeing this were in a great passion, and returned to Blackheath to inform their companions how the King had served them; upon hearing which, they all cried out, 'Let us instantly march to London.' Accordingly they set out at once, and on the road thither destroyed all the houses of lawyers and courtiers, and all the monasteries they met with. In the suburbs of London, which are very handsome and extensive, they pulled down many fine houses: they demolished also the King's prison, called the Marshalsea, and set at liberty all who were confined in it; moreover, they threatened the Londoners at the entrance of the bridge for having shut the gates of it, declaring that they would take the city by storm, and afterwards burn and destroy it.

With regard to the common people of London, numbers entertained these rebellious opinions, and on assembling at the bridge asked of the guards, 'Why will you refuse admittance to these honest men? They are our friends, and what they are doing is for our good.' So urgent were they, that it was found necessary to open the gates, when crowds rushed in and took possession of those shops which seemed best stocked with provisions; indeed, wherever they went, meat and drink were placed before them, and nothing was refused in the hope of appeasing them. Their leaders, John Ball, Jack Straw, and Wat Tyler, then marched through London, attended by more than 20,000 men, to the palace of the Savoy, which is a handsome building belonging to the Duke of Lancaster, situated on the banks of the Thames on the road to Westminster: here they immediately killed the porters, pushed into the house, and set it on fire. Not content with this outrage, they went to the house of the Knight-hospitalers of Rhodes, dedicated to St John of Mount Carmel, which they burned, together with their church and hospital.

After this they paraded the streets, and killed every Fleming they could find, whether in house, church, or hospital; they broke open several houses of the Lombards, taking whatever money they could lay their hands upon. They murdered a rich citizen, by name Richard Lyon, to whom Wat Tyler had formerly been servant in France, but having once beaten him, the varlet had never forgotten it; and when he had carried his men to his house, he ordered his head to be cut off, placed upon a pike, and carried through the streets of London. Thus did these wicked people act, and on this Thursday they did much damage to the city of London. Towards evening they fixed their quarters in a square, called St Catherine's, before the Tower, declaring that they would not depart until they had obtained from the King everything they wanted – until the Chancellor of England had accounted to them, and shown how the great sums which were raised had been expended. Considering the mischief which the mob had already done, you may easily imagine how miserable, at this time, was the situation of the King and those who were with him. In the evening, he and his barons, together with Sir William Walworth, and some of the principal citizens, held a council in the Tower, when it was proposed to arm themselves and fall by night upon these wretches while they were drunk and asleep, for they might have been killed like so many fleas, as not one of them in twenty had arms: and the citizens were very capable of doing this, for they had secretly received into their house their friends and servants properly prepared for action. Sir Robert Knolles remained in his house guarding it, with more than six score companions completely armed, who could have sallied forth at a minute's notice. Sir Perducas d'Albret was also in London at this period, and would of course have been of great service, so that altogether they could have mustered upwards of 8000 men well armed. However, nothing was done; they were really too much afraid of the commonality; and the King's advisers, the Earl of Salisbury and others, said to him, 'Sir, if you can appease them by fair words, it will be so much the better; for, should we begin what we cannot go through, it will be all over with us and our heirs, and England will be a desert.' This council was followed, and the Mayor ordered to make no stir; who obeyed, as in reason he ought. On Friday morning the rebels, who lodged in the square of St Catherine's, before the Tower, began to make themselves ready. They shouted much and said, that if the King would not come out to them, they would attack the Tower, storm it, and slay all who were within. The King, alarmed at these menaces, resolved to speak with the rabble; he therefore sent orders for them to retire to a handsome meadow at Mile End, where, in the summertime, people go to amuse themselves, at the same time signifying that he would meet them there and grant their demands. Proclamation to this effect was made in the King's name, and thither, accordingly, the commonalty of the different villages began to march; many, however, did not care to go, but stayed behind in London, being more desirous of the riches of the nobles and the plunder of the city. Indeed, covetousness and the desire of plunder was the principal cause of these disturbances, as the rebels showed very plainly. When the gates of the Tower were thrown open, and the King, attended by his two brothers and other nobles, had passed through, Wat Tyler, Jack Straw, and John Ball, with upwards of 400 others, rushed in by force, and running from chamber to chamber, found the Archbishop of Canterbury, by name Simon, a valiant and wise man, whom the rascals seized and beheaded. The Prior of St John's suffered the same fate, and likewise a Franciscan friar, a doctor of physic, who was attached to the Duke of Lancaster, also a sergeant-at-arms whose name was John Laige.

The heads of these four persons the rebels fixed on long spikes and had them carried before them through the streets of London; and when they had made sufficient mockery of them, they caused them to be placed on London Bridge, as if they had been traitors to their king and country. The scoundrels then entered the apartment of the Princess and cut her bed to pieces, which so terrified her that she fainted, and in this condition was carried by her servants and ladies to the riverside, when she was put into a covered boat and conveyed to a house called the Wardrobe, where she continued for a day and night in a very precarious state. While the King was on his way to Mile End, his two brothers, the Earl of Kent and Sir John Holland, stole away from his company, not daring to show themselves to the populace. The King himself, however, showed great courage, and on his arrival at the appointed spot instantly advanced into the midst of the assembled multitude, saying in a most pleasing manner, 'My good people, I am your king and your lord, what is it you want? What do you wish to say to me?' Those who heard him made answer, 'We wish you to make us free for ever. We wish to be no longer called slaves, nor held in bondage.' The King replied, 'I grant your wish; now therefore return to your homes, and let two or three from each village be left behind, to whom I will order letters to be given with my seal, fully granting every demand you have made: and in order that you may be the more satisfied, I will direct that my banners be sent to every stewardship, castlewick, and corporation.'

These words greatly appeased the more moderate of the multitude, who said, 'It is well: we wish for nothing more.' The King, however, added yet further, 'You, my good people of Kent, shall have one of my banners; and you also of Essex, Sussex, Bedford, Suffolk, Cambridge, Stafford, and Lincoln, shall each have one; I pardon you all for what you have hitherto done, but you must follow my banners and now return home on the terms I have mentioned,' which they unanimously consented to do. Thus did this great assembly break up. The King instantly employed upwards of thirty secretaries, who drew up the letters as fast as they could, and when they were sealed and delivered to them, the people departed to their own counties. The principal mischief, however, remained behind: I mean Wat Tyler, Jack Straw, and John Ball, who declared, that though the people were satisfied, they were by no means so, and with them were about 30,000, also of the same mind. These all continued in the city without any wish to receive the letters or the King's seal, but did all they could to throw the town into such confusion, that the lords and rich citizens might be murdered and their houses pillaged and destroyed. The Londoners suspected this, and kept themselves at home, well armed and prepared to defend their property.

After he had appeased the people at Mile End Green, King Richard went to the Wardrobe, in order that he might console the Princess, who was in the greatest possible alarm. But I must not omit to relate an adventure which happened to these clowns before Norwich and to their leader, William Lister, who was from the county of Stafford. At the same time that a party of these wicked people in London burned the palace of the Savoy, the church and house of St John's, and the hospital of the Templars, there were collected numerous bodies of men from Lincolnshire, Norfolk, and Suffolk, who, according to the orders they had received, were marching towards London. On their road they stopped near Norwich, and forced everyone whom they met to join them.

The reason of their stopping near Norwich was, that the governor of the town was a knight, by name Sir Robert Salle, who was not by birth a gentleman; but who, because of his ability and courage, had been created a knight by King Edward: he was, moreover, one of the handsomest and strongest men in England. Lister and his companions took it into their heads that they would make this man their commander. They, therefore, sent orders to him to come out into the fields to speak with them, declaring, in case he refused, that they would attack and burn the city. The knight, considering it was much better for him to go to them than that they should commit such outrages, mounted his horse and went out of the town alone to hear what they had to say. On his approach they showed every mark of respect, and courteously entreated him to dismount and talk with them. He did dismount, and in so doing committed a great folly, for immediately the mob surrounded him, and at first conversed in a friendly way, saying, 'Robert, you are a knight and a man of great weight in this country, renowned for your valour; yet, notwithstanding all this, we know who you are; you are not a gentleman, but the son of a poor mason, such as ourselves. Come with us therefore, as our commander, and we will make you so great a man that one-quarter of England shall be under your control.'

The knight, on hearing them speak thus, was exceedingly

enraged, and, eyeing them with angry looks, said, 'Begone, scoundrels and false traitors, would you have me desert my natural lord for such a company of knaves as you are? Would you have me dishonour myself? I would rather have you all hanged, for that must be your end.' On saying this, he attempted to mount his horse; but his foot slipping from the stirrup, the animal took fright, and the mob upon this cried out, 'Put him to death.' Upon hearing which, Sir Robert let go his horse, and drawing a handsome Bordeaux sword, began to skirmish, and soon cleared the crowd from about him in an admirable manner. Many attempted to close with him; but each stroke he gave cut off heads, arms, feet, or legs so that the boldest became afraid to approach him. The wretches were 40,000 in number, and he killed twelve of them and wounded many before they overpowered him, which at last they did with their missiles; and as soon as he was down, they cut off his arms and legs and rent his body piecemeal. Such was the pitiable end of Sir Robert Salle.

On Saturday morning the King left the Wardrobe and went to Westminster, when he and his lords heard mass in the abbey. In this church there is a statue of Our Lady, in which the kings of England have much faith. To this on the present occasion King Richard and his nobles paid their devotions and made their offerings; they then rode in company along the causeway to London; but when they had proceeded a short distance, King Richard, with a few attendants, turned up a road on the left to go away from the city.

This day all the rabble again assembled under Wat Tyler, Jack Straw, and John Ball, at a place called Smithfield, where every Friday the horsemarket is kept. There were present about 20,000, and many more were in the city, breakfasting, and drinking Rhenish wine and Malmsey Madeira in the taverns and in the houses of the Lombards, without paying for anything; and happy was he who could give them good cheer to satisfy them. Those who collected in Smithfield had with them the King's banner, which had been given to them the preceding evening; and the wretches, notwithstanding this, wanted to pillage the city, their leaders saying, that hitherto they had done nothing. 'The pardon which the King has granted will be of no use to us; but if we be of the same mind, we shall pillage this rich and powerful town of London before those from Essex, Suffolk, Cambridge, Bedford, Warwick, Reading, Lancashire, Arundel, Guildford, Coventry, Lynne, Lincoln, York and Durham shall arrive; for they are on their road, and we know for certain that Vaquier and Lister will conduct them hither. Let us, then, be beforehand in plundering the wealth of the city; for if we wait for their arrival, they will wrest it from us.' To this opinion all had agreed, when the King, attended by sixty horses, appeared in sight; he was at the time not thinking of the rabble, but had intended to continue his ride, without coming into London; however, when he arrived before the Abbey of St Bartholomew, which is in Smithfield, and saw the crowd of people, he stopped, saying that he would ascertain what they wanted, and endeavour to appease them. Wat Tyler, seeing the King and his party, said to his men, 'Here is the King, I will go and speak with him; do you not stir until I give you a signal.' He then made a motion with his hand, and added, 'When you shall see me make this signal, then step forward, and kill everyone except the King; but hurt him not, for he is young, and we can do what we please with him; carrying him with us through England, we shall be lords of the whole country, without any opposition.' On saying which he spurred his horse and galloped up to the King, whom he approached so near that his horse's head touched the crupper of the King's horse.

His first words were these: 'King, dost thou see all these men here?' 'Yes,' replied the King; 'Why dost thou ask?' 'Because they are all under my command, and have sworn by their faith and loyalty to do whatsoever I shall order.' 'Very well,' said the King; 'I have no objection to it.' Tyler, who was only desirous of a riot, made answer: 'And thou thinkest, King, that these people, and as many more in the city, also under my command, ought to depart without having thy letters? No, indeed, we will carry them with us.' 'Why,' replied the King, 'it has been so ordered, and the letters will be delivered out one after another; but, friend, return to thy companions, and tell them to depart from London; be peaceable and careful of yourselves; for it is our determination that you shall all have the letters by towns and villages according to our agreement.' As the King finished speaking, Wat Tyler, casting his eyes round, spied a squire attached to the King's person bearing a sword. This squire Tyler mortally hated, and on seeing him cried out, 'What has thou there? Give me thy dagger.' 'I will not,' said the squire; 'why should I give it thee?' The King upon this said, 'Give it to him; give it to him'; which the squire did, though much against his will. When Tyler took the dagger, he began to play with it in his hand, and again addressing the squire, said, 'Give me that sword.' 'I will not,' replied the squire, 'for it is the King's sword, and thou being but a mechanic art not worthy to bear it; and if only thou and I were together, thou wouldst not have dared to say what thou hast, for a heap of gold as large as this church.' 'By my troth,' answered Tyler, 'I will not eat this day before I have thy head.' At these words the Mayor of London, with about twelve men, rode forward, armed under their robes, and seeing Tyler's manner of behaving, said 'Scoundrel, how dare you to behave thus in the King's presence?' The King, also enraged at the fellow's impudence, said to the Mayor, 'Lay hands on him.' Whilst King Richard was giving this order, Tyler still kept up the conversation, saying to the Mayor, 'What have you to do with it; does what I have said concern you?' 'It does,' replied the Mayor, who found himself supported by the King, and then

added, 'I will not live a day unless you pay for your insolence.'
Upon saying which he drew a kind of scimitar, and struck
Tyler such a blow on the head as felled him to his horse's
feet. As soon as the rebel was down, he was surrounded on all
sides, in order that his own men might not see him; and one
of the King's squires, by name John Standwich, immediately
leaped from his horse, and drawing his sword, thrust it into
his belly, so that he died.

When the rebels found that their leader was dead, they
drew up in a sort of battle array, each man having his bow
bent before him. The King at this time certainly hazarded
much, though it turned out most fortunately for him; for
as soon as Tyler was on the ground, he left his attendants,
giving orders that no one should follow him, and riding up
to the rebels, who were advancing to revenge their leader's
death, said, 'Gentlemen, what are you about? You shall have
me for your captain: I am your King, remain peaceable.' The
greater part, on hearing these words, were quite ashamed, and
those among them who were inclined for peace began to slip
away; the riotous ones, however, kept their ground. The King
returned to his lords, and consulted with them what next
should be done. Their advice was to make for the fields; but
the Mayor said that to retreat would be of no avail. 'It is quite
proper to act as we have done; and I reckon we shall very soon
receive assistance from our good friends in London.'

While things were in this state, several persons ran to
London, crying out, 'They are killing the King and our Mayor';
upon which alarm, all those of the King's party sallied out
towards Smithfield, in number about seven or eight thousand.
Among the first came Sir Robert Knolles and Sir Perducas
d'Albret, well attended; then several aldermen, with upwards
of 600 men-at-arms, and a powerful man of the city, by name
Nicholas Bramber, the king's draper, bringing with him a
large force on foot. These all drew up opposite to the rebels,

who had with them the King's banner, and showed as if they intended to maintain their ground by offering combat.

The King created at this time three knights: Sir William Walworth, Sir John Standwich, and Sir Nicholas Bramber. As soon as Sir Robert Knolles arrived at Smithfield, his advice was immediately to fall upon the insurgents, and slay them; but King Richard would not consent to this. 'You shall first go to them,' he said, 'and demand my banner; we shall then see how they will behave; for I am determined to have this by fair means or foul.' The new knights were accordingly sent forward, and on approaching the rebels made signs to them not to shoot, as they wished to speak with them; and when within hearing said, 'Now attend; the King orders you to send back his banners; and if you do so, we trust he will have mercy upon you.' The banners, upon this, were given up directly, and brought to the King. It was then ordered, under pain of death, that all those who had obtained the King's letters should deliver them up. Some did so, but not all; and the King on receiving them had them torn in pieces in their presence. You must know that from the time the King's banners were surrendered, these fellows kept no order; but the greater part, throwing their bows upon the ground, took to their heels and returned to London. Sir Robert Knolles was very angry that the rebels were not attacked at once and all slain; however, the King would not consent to it, saying, that he would have ample revenge without doing so.

When the rabble had dispersed, the King and his lords, to their great joy, returned in good array to London, whence the King immediately took the road to the Wardrobe, to visit the Princess his mother, who had remained there two days and two nights under the greatest apprehension. On seeing her son, the good lady was much rejoiced, and said, 'Ah, ah, fair son, what pain and anguish have I not suffered for you this day!' 'Madam,' replied the King, 'I am well assured of that; but now rejoice, and thank God, for it behoves us to praise him, as I have this day regained my inheritance – the kingdom of England, which I had lost.'

This whole day the King passed with his mother, and a proclamation was made through all the streets, that every person who was not an inhabitant of London, and who had not resided there for a whole year, should instantly depart; for if any of a contrary description were found in the city on Sunday morning at sunrise, they would be arrested as traitors to the King, and have their heads cut off. This proclamation no one dared to infringe, but all instantly departed to their homes quite discomfited.

John Ball and Jack Straw were found hidden in an old ruin, where they had secreted themselves, thinking to steal away when things were quiet; but this they were prevented doing, for their own men betrayed them. With this capture the King and his barons were much pleased, and had their heads cut off, as was that of Tyler's, and fixed on London Bridge, in the room of those whom these wretches themselves had placed there.

News of this total defeat of the rebels in London was sent throughout the neighbouring counties, in order that all those who were on their way to London might hear of it; and as soon as they did so, they instantly returned to their homes, without daring to advance farther.

Facing down the Peasants' Revolt was Richard II's one and only fine hour. His taste for autocracy and Frenchified habits eventually alienated the city.

❧ ❧ ❧

Richard II Quarrels with the City of London, 1392

The Monk of Westminster

AT THIS TIME the lord king, by the advice of his chancellor and treasurer, removed all his courts from London to York; these officials thought that by this move they would injure not a little the city of London, but they inflicted rather much greater injuries on the king and the men of the kingdom than on the said noble city. For poor men lost their pleas on account of this removal of the courts, not only because they did not have the money to go to such a remote place, but because such a sudden removal left them without the means of counsel ... These officials incited our lord king against the Londoners on account of certain seditions done recently amongst them and certain of his household. The Duke of Lancaster and the Earl of Huntingdon supported these officials. Behaving therefore as sons of iniquity, these officials, with others joined to them, wished to show all the malice they could think of against the Londoners, and devised a royal writ against them so terrible and horrible that it thundered in the ears of those who heard it.

The king's letter, addressed to mayor, sheriffs and aldermen of London, ordered them peremptorily, on account of certain causes specially moving the king, to appear with twenty-one of their fellow citizens at Nottingham on the morrow of St John Baptist next coming, with full power on behalf of the city to reply to charges to be made and to do what should be ordained by the king and his council, on pain of loss of their lives, members and all their possessions if they did not appear. The mayor, aldermen and sheriffs expressed their readiness to answer this summons and chose twenty-one fellow citizens to accompany them to Nottingham as directed.

The reason why the king was so angry with the Londoners was, according to some people, as follows. The king had been short of money and had therefore sent to certain citizens of London asking them on the security of a certain jewel of great price to lend him 5,000 marks or pounds. This jewel was worth more than the aforesaid sum. Nevertheless they excused themselves, saying that they could lend but little after the loss of their freedom, since the foreigners in the city enjoyed as much liberty as they did, and in view of such lost opportunities they could not raise such a large sum. The king was rather surprised by this answer and therefore consulted a certain Lombard, who at once promised to satisfy the king in his desires, and on the morrow came to the king with the needed sum. The king asked him how he had been able to raise such a large sum so quickly, to which he replied: 'I borrowed from various merchants of London.' When the king heard this, he was most indignant against the Londoners, who were evidently willing to lend more readily to a foreigner than to him.

On 19 June the Londoners came to Nottingham, where the chancellor explained the charges against them, and accused them of many derelictions of duty in the government of the city. The mayor was committed to Windsor Castle, the sheriffs were imprisoned in other castles, one at Odiham, the other at Wallingford, and the rest of the citizens were told to go home. A royal warden was appointed to govern London, along with two sheriffs chosen by the king, and all the liberties of London were revoked. In July the former mayor and former sheriffs made their humble submission to the king at Windsor and were released from prison, but the liberties of London were not restored. Various friends of theirs pleaded for them and several times the queen went down on her knees before the king to plead their cause. At last the king relented and yielded to the prayers of the queen and of various nobles, and condescended to agree to come to London on 21 August. The king was received with all the splendour of a coronation entry. Coming from Sheen he was met at Wandsworth by the warden, who presented him with the keys and sword of the city. The warden was followed by the craft gilds in their proper liveries 'to the number of 20,000 horsemen, with an infinite number of men on foot'. At London Bridge the king was presented with two coursers, one white, one red, with silver gilt saddles, and the queen received a palfrey with a golden saddle. The streets of London were adorned with bunting, etc. In the Cheap two boys dressed like angels offered two golden crowns, of great value, to the king and queen, and at Temple Bar they were presented with a gold table valued at a hundred marks. The royal party went on to Westminster, where they were received by the prior and convent in full vestments and entered the abbey for a solemn thanksgiving. This included a procession to the shrine of the Confessor, where the antiphon 'Hail, holy St Edward!' was sung. On the morrow the warden of London invited the king to a feast at which the Londoners offered the lord king a silver gilt table nine feet in length worth five hundred marks. Not many days afterwards the king seated on his royal throne in the great hall at Westminster restored the liberties of London with three exceptions. The following October the Londoners elected a mayor as usual; and at the following Epiphany the Londoners came to the king at Eltham and presented him with a dromedary with a boy sitting on it, and they gave to the queen a great and wonderful bird with a very wide throat.

But London never did forgive Richard II for his high-handed treatment and it took a drastic revenge upon him: The City supported the 1399 coup d'état of Henry Bolingbroke, who crowned himself Henry IV of England.

London Lickpenny, c. 1410
Anonymous

A lickpenny is someone or something that soaks up money. In this satirical poem the narrator, an out-of-towner (probably from the Midlands), comes to London to seek restoration for fraud but finds that without money it is impossible to get justice in London. And any money he might have he is relieved of. He even suffers the indignity of having his hood stolen in Westminster and then finding it for sale on a stall at Eastcheap. He finally quits London vowing never to return.

TO LONDON ONCE my steps I bent,
    Where truth in no wise should be faint;
To Westminster-ward I forthwith went
    To a man of law to make complaint.
    I said: 'For Mary's love, that holy saint,
        Pity the poor that would proceed!'
        But for lack of money I could not speed.

And as I thrust the press among,
    By froward chance my hood was gone;   *evil*

Yet for all that I stayed not long
   Till at the King's Bench I was come.
  Before the judge I kneeled anon
    And prayed him for God's sake to take heed;
    But for lack of money I might not speed . . .

Unto the Common Place I yode tho   *went then*
   Where sat one with a silken hood;
I did him reverence – for I ought to do so –
   And told my case as well as I could,
   How my goods were defrauded me by falsehood.
    I gat not a mum of his mouth for my meed,   *word*
    And for lack of money I might not speed . . .

In Westminster Hall I found out one
   Which went in a long gown of ray;
I crouched and kneeled before him anon,
   For Mary's love of help I him pray.
   'I wot not what thou meanst', gan he say;
    To get me thence he did me beed: *bid*
    For lack of money I could not speed.

Within this hall neither rich nor yet poor
   Would do for me aught, although I should die;
Which seeing, I gat me out of the door,
   Where Flemings began on me for to cry:
   'Master, what will you copen or buy?   *purchase*
    Fine felt hats, or spectacles to read?
    Lay down your silver, and here you may speed.' . . .

Then unto London I did me hie –
   Of all the land it beareth the prise!
'Hot peascods!' one began to cry,

'Strawberry ripe!' and 'cherries in the rise!'   *on the branch*
One bad me come near and buy some spice;
    Pepper and saffron, they gan me beede;   *proffer*
    But for lack of money I might not speed.

Then to the Cheap I gan me drawn,
    Where much people I saw for to stand:
One offered me velvet, silk, and lawn;
    Another he taketh me by the hand,
    'Here is Paris thread, the finest in the land'.
      I never was used to such things in deed,
      And, wanting money, I might not speed.

Then went I forth by London Stone,
    Throughout all Canwike Street: *Cannon Street*
Drapers much cloth me offered anon;
    Then comes me one, cried 'Hot sheep's feet!'
    One cried 'Mackerel!'; 'Rishes green!' another   *rushes*
                      gan greet,
    One bad me buy a hood to cover my head;
    But for want of money I might not speed.

Then I hied me into East Cheap.
    One cries 'Ribs of beef and many a pie!'
Pewter pots they clattered on a heap;
    There was harp, pipe, and minstrelsie.
    'Yea, by cock!' 'Nay, by cock!' some began cry.
      Some sung of Jenken and Julian for their meed.
      But for lack of money I might not speed.

Then into Cornhill anon I yode,
    Where was much stolen gear among;
I saw where hong mine own hode

That I had lost among the throng.
To buy my own hood I thought it wrong –
   I knew it well as I did my Creed:
   But for lack of money I could not speed.

The taverner took me by the sleeve:
   'Sir', saith he, 'will you our wine assay?'
I answered: 'That can not much me grieve;
   A penny can do no more than it may.'
   I drank a pint and for it did pay;
      Yet sore a-hungered from thence I yede,
      And, wanting money, I could not speed.

Then hied I me to Billingsgate,
   And one cried: 'Hoo! go we hence!'
I prayed a barge-man for God's sake
   That he would spare me my expense.
   'Thou 'scapst not here', quod he, 'under two pence;
      I list not yet bestow my alms-deed.'
      Thus, lacking money, I could not speed.

Then I conveyed me into Kent,
   For of the law would I meddle no more;
Because no man to me took entent
   I dight me to do as I did before.   *prepared*
   Now Jesus that in Bethlem was bore,
      Save London, and send true lawyers their meed!
      For whoso wants money with them shall not speed.

Of course, it wasn't just hicks visiting from the sticks who lacked money. The masses of medieval London tottered on at subsistence level.

Inside this poor London there was a distinct wave of sympathy for the Lollards, the ascetic proto-Protestant religious sect who followed the teachings of John Wyclif. Lollardy seemed so significant in the capital that in 1414 the Lollards launched a putsch from St Giles Fields. The rebellion was easily put down – Londoners liked Lollardy, but not as much as they liked their skins. Of the uprising's leader, Sir John Oldcastle, *The Brut* recorded:

'CONVYCTE BE [BY] the clergy of Lollardye, and dampned before the Iustice unto deth for treson he was hadde into the Tour [Tower] agen, and there he was laide on a hurdil, and drawn through the cite to Saint Gyles Felde, and there was made a new paire of galows, and a strong chayne, and a coler of yron for hym, and there he was hanged and brent on the gallous.'

Henry V's Victory March After Agincourt, 23 November 1415

Anonymous

Few monarchs seduced London as much as Henry V; before embarking for France, during the Hundred Years War, he personally explained his mission's aims to the Mayor and aldermen. London was flattered and opened its financial chests and its emotional heart. The city's regard for Henry V was only increased when he won, against all the odds, the battle of Agincourt on 25 October 1415. On the monarch's return home, the capital greeted him with full pageantry:

HE TOOK HIS journey by way of the sacred thresholds of the churches of Canterbury and St Augustine's Canterbury to his manor of Eltham, proposing to honour the city of London on the following Saturday with his presence. The citizens, hearing with the greatest joy the news of his approach, prepared themselves and the city in the meanwhile . . . And when the desired day of Saturday dawned, the citizens went out to meet the king at the brow of Blackheath, I.e. the mayor and 24 aldermen in scarlet, and the rest of the lesser citizens in red cloaks with red-and-white party-coloured hoods, to the number of about 20,000 horsemen . . . And when the king came through the midst of them about ten o'clock, and the citizens had given glory and honour to God, and congratulations to the king . . . the citizens rode before him towards the city, and the king followed . . .

When they arrived at the tower at the entrance to the bridge . . . there placed on top of the tower was an enormous figure, with ... a great axe in his right hand and the keys of the city hanging from a staff in his left hand, like a doorkeeper. On his right side stood an effigy not much smaller, of a woman dressed in a scarlet cloak and feminine ornaments, as if they were man and wife who in their best clothes were looking for the desired face of their lord and were receiving him with full honour. The tower was adorned with spears bearing the royal arms, projecting from the battlements, and trumpets and horns sounded in manifold melody; spread across the front of the tower was this elegant and convenient inscription, 'The City of the King of Justice'. And when they reached the little bridge, they found on both sides before them a lofty pillar in the manner of a tower ... made of wood, covered with linen cloth painted the colour of white marble and green jasper, to imitate the blocks and stones of mason's work. On top of the column on the right hand side was the effigy of an antelope ... with a splendid shield blazoned with the royal arms hanging from its neck, and bearing the royal sceptre in the right foot. On the top of the other column stood the image of a lion, which held aloft in its right claws ... the banner of the king displayed; across ... the road rose a turret ... in the middle of which under a splendid canopy stood a most impressive image of St George, armed, except for his head, which was adorned with a laurel wreath sown with gems sparkling like precious stones, having behind him a scarlet tapestry gleaming with his arms in a number of shields. On his right hung a triumphal helmet, and on his left a great shield of his arms; ... in his right hand he held the hilt of the sword with which he was girt and in his left he held a scroll extended across the battlements with the words: 'Honour and glory be to God alone'. And aloft on the tower in front was displayed this prophesy of congratulation: 'The streams of the river make glad the city of God' ... And in a house near the tower was a great crowd of boys representing the angelic host clad in white robes, with faces gleaming with gilt paint, with shining wings and the hair of girls crowned with laurel crowns, who sang on the king's approach with sweet voices to the accompaniment of an organ a song according to the programme in English.

And when they reached the tower of the aqueduct in Cornhill they found the tower hidden under a scarlet cloth stretched in the form of a tent, on spears hidden under the cloth. Surrounding the middle of the tower in four prominent positions were the arms of St George, St Edward, St Edmund, and of England, interspersed with small shields of royal arms and inset with this pious legend:

'Since the king hopes in the Lord and in the mercy of the Highest, he shall not be moved.' ... Under a covering was a band of venerable white-haired prophets in tunics and golden cloaks, with their heads hidden in turbans of gold and red who released, when the king came by, sparrows and other small birds in a great cloud as a sacrifice of thanksgiving to God for the victory He had given, some of the birds resting on the king's breast, some of them alighting on his shoulder, and some flying round his head, while the prophets sang in a sweet voice, according to the programme, this psalm of recognition: 'Sing to the Lord a new song, Hallelujah. For he hath done marvellous things, Hallelujah.'

Then they went on to the tower of the conduit at the entrance to Cheapside which was decked with an awning of green ... woven with little shields of the city's arms set in florid profusion, supported on posts covered in the same colour and erected to resemble a building. The tower was decorated above with shafts of spears of arms placed on the battlements ... and below the awning were venerable old men, twelve in number, clothed like the apostles and having the names of the twelve apostles written on their brows. With them were twelve kings, martyrs and confessors of the succession of England, with golden girdles round their loins, sceptres in their hands, and crowns on their heads ... who sang in unison on the king's approach a sweet song ... And they wafted to him round foils of silver intermingled with thin round wafers, and wine from the channels and cocks of the conduit, so that they might receive him with bread and wine as Melchisedech received Abraham when he returned from the fall of the four kings.

And when they came to the cross in Cheapside ... it was hidden by a beautiful castle of wood, very ingeniously and prettily constructed, and adorned with three beautiful columns, ... which had ... arches on either side projecting over the street, and stretching to the buildings on each side of the road ... And across the front of the arches was written, 'Glorious things of thee are spoken, O city of God'. This castle was covered with linen painted the colour of white marble, and green and red jasper, as if the whole work had been the result of the mason's art, fashioned from blocks of masonry and perfect precious stones. The top of the castle ... was adorned with the arms of St George, flanked on one side by the arms of the king and on the other by those of the emperor; ... on the lower turrets were the arms of the king's ancestors and of the greater magnates of the realm. From the middle of the castle ... projected a beautiful gateway, no less cunningly contrived, from which stretched a wooden bridge almost fifteen paces in length, of good width and about the height of a man's waist ... adorned with tapestries. When the king approached there came out on to the bridge a chorus of beautiful girls dressed in virgin white ... and playing on tambourines as a mark of rejoicing, as if to a David rejoicing at the fall of Goliath, who ... represented the pride of the French, and singing: 'Welcome, Henry the Fifth, King of England and of France'. From the top of the castle downwards, on the turrets, battlements, arches, and columns, were innumerable boys, dressed in white garments as angels and archangels, with shining wings and hair strewn with gems ... who threw down on the ... king as he passed underneath gold coins and laurel leaves, to the honour of Almighty God and as a sign of victory; and all sang together this angelic hymn as previously arranged: 'We praise thee O God, we acknowledge thee to be the Lord'.

And when they came to the tower of the conduit at the exit of Cheapside towards St Paul's, the tower had been surrounded with many ... niches, and in each niche was a beautiful young girl, in the posture of a statue; and in their hands were golden cups from which they very lightly puffed gold leaf upon the king's head as he rode by. Above the tower was stretched a canopy sky-blue in colour decorated with clouds and many other contrivances; and the top of the canopy was adorned by an archangel in shining gold, and the four posts which held up the canopy were supported by four angels equally cunning in workmanship. Below the canopy ... was a figure of majesty represented by a sun darting out flashing rays. Round the top of the canopy fluttered archangels singing sweetly all kinds of music ... And so that this tower might conform in its legend to the preceding praises to the honour and glory of God, not of men, it presented to the gaze of the passers-by this conclusion of praise: 'Thanks be to God'.

... Such was the dense throng of people in Cheapside from one end to the other that horsemen had scarcely ... room to ride through the crowds, and the upper storeys and windows on either side were filled with the more noble ladies and women of the realm and with honest and honourable men, who flocked to such a delectable sight, adorned in garments of gold and satin and scarlet, and other types of dress; so that a bigger or more impressive crowd had never gathered before in London.

But the king himself went along, amidst these shouts of praise and celebrations of the citizens, dressed in a purple robe, not with a haughty look and a pompous train ... but with a serious countenance and a reverend pace accompanied by only a few of his most faithful servants; following him, guarded by knights, were the captive dukes, counts and the marshal. From his silent face and ... sober pace it could be inferred that the king, silendy contemplating, was giving thanks and glory to God alone and not to man. And when he had visited the sanctuary of SS Peter and Paul, he rode away to his palace of Westminster, escorted by the citizens.

Doubtless among those watching Henry's triumphal return was Sir Richard 'Dick' Whittington, city merchant and one of Henry's principal bankrollers.

Richard Whittington is Elected Mayor for the Third Time, 13 October 1419

The City of London Letter Book

As befitted a city which was self-governing but under royal rule, the role of London's Mayor combined two elements: he was the king's representative in the city and simultaneously the city's ambassador to the king.

The office of mayor emerged around 1200. 'Dick' Whittington was first elected Mayor of London in 1398.

O N FRIDAY, THE Feast of St. Edward the King and Confessor [13 October] ... after the Mass of the Holy Spirit devoudy and becomingly celebrated with solemn music in the Chapel of the Guildhall of the City of London, according to the Ordinance made thereon in the time of John Wodecok ... in presence of William Sevenok, Mayor [with the Recorder, Aldermen and Sheriffs] and an immense number of the Commonalty of the citizens of the said city, summoned to the Guildhall of London for the election of a Mayor for the ensuing year, by their common assent, consent, and desire, Richard Whitingtone was chosen Mayor for the ensuing year; and on the morrow of the said Feast was presented before the Barons of the Exchequer of our Lord the King, at Westminster, admitted, and accepted as such.

Sixteen days later, Whittington led the annual Mayor's show. The City's *White Book* (Liber Albus) recorded:

ON THE MORROW of the Feast of the Apostles Simon and Jude it was the custom for both the new and the past mayor and the aldermen as well, in a like suit of robes, attended by the sheriffs and as many as were of the mayor's livery and of the several mysteries arrayed in their respective suits, to meet on horseback upon the place without the Guildhall about nine of the clock, the sword being borne upright before the person nominated as mayor. Departing thence, they rode together along Cheap through the gate of Newgate and then turning into Fleet Street passed on to Westminster. [The ceremony of oath-taking then took place.] Which done, they returned, the commons preceding on horseback in companies arrayed in the suits of their respective mysteries. Those, however, who were members of the mystery to which the mayor belonged, as also those who were of his livery, proceeded next before the mayor. No person, however, moved so close to the mayor but that there was a marked space between; while the sergeants-at-arms, the mace-bearers, and his sword-bearer went before him, with one sheriff on his right hand and the other on his left, bearing white wands in their hands The recorder and the other aldermen followed next in order and accompanied him through the middle of the market of Westcheap to his house; after which they returned home, as many, that is, as had not been invited to the feast.

Whittington, the legend aside, was not a noted lover of felines. Cats in the fourteenth century were thought to be bringers of good luck. Every Tom and Harry, as well as Dick Whittington, had a cat as a prop in their portrait. Neither was Whittington born poor – the younger son of a minor Gloucestershire knight, Whittington was apprenticed as a boy to the Mercers Company. He made a fortune and on his death in 1423 left £5,000 to found a college, establish the Guildhall and Greyfriars Libraries and to rebuild Newgate Prison.

Among Mayor Whittington's duties was keeping the crowded, medieval city sanitary. The Sanitation Orders made by Whittington and his fellow mayoral incumbents were legion. Abridged they include:

THAT NO ONE shall throw dung into the King's Highway, or before the house of his neighbour . . .

That each person shall make clean of filth the front of his house, under penalty of half a mark . . .

Item that the Pavements shall be mended, and all refuse removed . . .

If swine shall be found in the Streets or in the Fosses [moats], or in the Suburbs, they shall be killed, and he who kills them shall have them . . .

That the Scavengers shall have the power to survey the Pavements, and that all filth in the Streets shall be removed . . .

Such orders were honoured more in the breach than the observance:

Public Nuisances, 1422

The General Court of the Mayor of the City of London

GENERAL COURT OF Robert Chichele, Mayor of the City of London, held in the Guildhall of the said city, on Monday next after the feast of the Epiphany, 9 Henry V.

These are nuisances and defects found in the ward of Faringdon Without, taken in the wardmoot, before Rankyn Barton', Alderman of the same ward, the year of the king abovesaid.

First, that the master of Ludgate often puts out dung in the street gutter and stops the water from flowing, to the great nuisance of all the folk passing there. Also that a mud wall in the bailey by the High Street, between the house of Shelhard, haberdasher, and Hay, spurrier, falls down piecemeal into the High Street, and makes the way foul, to the annoyance of folk passing and dwelling there. Also William Emery, horsedealer, often lays much dung in the high street and allows it to lie yet, to the great nuisance and annoyance of all folk passing and dwelling thereabout. Also the pavements before the chamber house in the bailey, and before the door of Harry Gras, barber, and of Walsh's door, are defective and need to be mended. Also the common privy of Ludgate is very defective and perilous and the filth thereof decays the stone walls, so that it is likely to be very costly and dangerous to those walls in time to come, unless it be put right as soon as possible. Also that the barriers at Shoe-Lane end are all broken with water carts, and the pavements defective in divers places of the same parish. Also that John Taverner at Bell is not a freeman of the city. Also John Whitlok at Bell at Carter Lane end and his wife are common bauds, and therefore have lately been put out of other wards. Also John Swayn and his wife are forestallers, regrators, and extortioners often, and especially lately they hired a page of the Queen's household to arrest a boatful of rushes, and brought it from Queenhithe to Fleet Bridge, and there took up from it 30 loads of rushes, and laid them in Sir Walter Beauchamp's place, and then paid to the Boatman only 26*d* for 30 loads, whereas he should have been paid for every burden 3*d* and because of this the boatman made much noise and open slander. Also the taverners of St Bride's parish set their empty tuns and pipes in the high street, to the annoyance of all folk passing there.

With the premature death of Henry V in 1422 the throne passed to his son, Henry VI, whose rule was both a blessing and curse for London. His distinctly un-warrior-like personality meant that, instead of traipsing around foreign battlefields, he stayed in Westminster, which encouraged a fantastic growth in the machinery of government. Courtiers, flunkeys, civil servants, ecclesiasts and lawyers flocked to Westminster, as did tradespeople and prostitutes to service them. Naturally, they all needed somewhere to live. Some settled in Westminster itself (the population of which reached about 3,000 by the mid-fifteenth century), but many settled in the leafy villages and lanes between the city and Westminster, with the Strand lane being a favourite location for the mansions of magnates.

The selfsame magnates were Henry VI's undoing. Henry VI was a schizophrenic simpleton – consequently royal government lurched between incompetence and oppression. One result was a popular uprising in Kent in 1450, which (shades of the Peasants' Revolt) marched to Blackheath, this time under the leadership of Jack Cade. The rebellion fizzled out after some looting and a royal pardon. Another result, which was of more historical damage to London, was the incipient faction-fighting for the throne between Henry VI's Lancastrian dynasty and its rival house of York. John Stodely presents a good description of the aristocratic gang-fighting and power-playing in London which opened the so-called 'Wars of the Roses'.

Wars of the Roses:
The Beginning of Strife, 1454
John Stodely

As TOUCHING TIDINGS, please it you to know that at the Prince's coming to Windsor, the Duke of Buckingham took him in his arms and presented him to the King in goodly wise, beseeching the King to bless him, and the King gave no manner answer. Nevertheless the Duke abode still with the Prince by the King; and when he could no manner answer have, the Queen came in, and took the Prince in her arms and presented him in like form as the Duke had done, desiring that he should bless it; but all their labour was in vain, for they departed thence without any answer or countenance, saving only that once he looked on the Prince, and cast down his eyes again, without any more.

Item, the Cardinal hath charged and commanded all his servants to be ready with bowe and arrows, sword and buckler, crossbows and all other habiliments of war, such as they can meddle with, to wait upon the safeguard of his person.

Item, the Earl of Wiltshire and the Lord Bonvile have caused to be cried at Taunton in Somerset shire, that every man that is likely and will go with them and serve them, shall have 6d. every day as long as he abideth with them ...

Item, Thorpe of the exchequer articuleth fast against the Duke of York, but what his articles be it is yet unknown.

Item, Tresham, Joseph, Daniel, and Trevilian have made a bill to the Lords, desiring to have a garrison kept at Windsor for the safeguard of the King and of the Prince ...

Item, the Duke of Somerset's herberger hath taken up all the lodging that may be gotten near the Tower, in Thames street, Mart lane, Saint Katherine's, Tower hill and there about.

Item, the Queen hath made a bill of five articles, desiring these articles to be granted; whereof the first is that she desireth to have the whole rule of this land; the second is that she may make the Chancellor, the Treasurer, the Privy Seal, and all other officers of this land, with sheriffs and all other officers that the King should make; the third is that she may give all the bishoprics of this land, and all other benefices belonging to the King's gift; the fourth is that she may have sufficient livelode assigned her for the King and the Prince and herself. But as for the fifth article, I cannot yet know what it is.

Item, the Duke of York will be at London justly on Friday next coming at night, as his own men tell for certain, and he will come with his household meynee, cleanly beseen and likely men. And the earl of March cometh with him, but he will have another fellowship of good men that shall be at London before him ... The Earl of Salisbury will be at London on Monday or Tuesday next coming with seven score knights and squires, beside other meynee. The Earls of Warwick, Richmond and Pembroke come with the Duke of York, as it is said, every each of them with a goodly fellowship. And nevertheless the Earl of Warwick will have 1000 men awaiting on him beside the fellowship that cometh with him, as far as I can know. And as Geoffry Poole saith, the King's brothers be likely to be arrested at their coming to London, if they come. Wherefore it is thought by my Lord's servants and well wishers here that my Lord, at his coming hither shall come with a good and cleanly fellowship, such as is likely and according to his estate to have about him; and their harness to come in carts, as my Lord of York's men's harness did the last term, and shall at this time also. And over that, that my Lord shall have another good fellowship to wait on him and be here afore him, or else soon after him, in like wise as other Lords of his blood will have . . .

The Duke of Somerset hath spies going in every Lord's house of this land; some gone as friars, some as shipmen taken on the sea, and some in other wise; which report unto him all that they can see or hear touching the said Duke. And therefore make good watch, and beware of such spies . . .

The mayor and merchants of London, and the mayor and merchants of the staple of Calais, were with the Chancellor on Monday last passed at Lamhithe and complained on the Lord Bonvile for taking of the ships and goods of the Flemings and other of the Duke of Burgoynes Lordships, and the Chancellor gave them none answer to their pleading; wherefore the substance of them with one voice cried aloud, 'Justice, justice, justice!' whereof the Chancellor was so dismayed that he could nor might no more say to them for fear.

Eventually London plumped for the Yorkist cause in the Wars of the Roses, chiefly because the Yorkist Edward IV (who ruled from 1461 to 1483) promised the sort of efficiency and stability that allowed the capital's burghers to make money.

❧ ❧ ❧

The Dignity of the Mayor of London, 1464
Anonymous

THIS YEAR [1464], about midsummer, at the royal feast of the serjeants of the coif, the mayor of London was desired to be at that feast. And at dinner time, he came to that feast with his officers, in accordance and agreement with his degree; for within London he is next to the king in all manner of things. And at the time of washing the Earl of Worcester was led forward before the mayor and set down in the middle of the high table. And the mayor, seeing that his place was occupied, held himself content, and went home again without meat or drink or any thanks. He rewarded himself as the dignity of the city required and he took with him the majority of his brethren, the aldermen, to his place. And they were set and served as soon as any man could devise, both of cygnet and of other delicacies enough, so that all the house marvelled how well all things were done in so short a time and prayed all men to be merry and glad, for it should be amended another time. Then the officers of the feast, thoroughly ashamed, informed the masters of the feast of this mishap that had befallen. And they, considering the great dignity and costs and charge that belonged to the city, at once sent to the mayor a present of meat, bread, wine, and many divers confections in sugar. But when they who had come with the presents saw all the gifts and the service that was at the board, the one who had to give the message was sorely ashamed, for the present was not better than the service of meats that was being made before the mayor, and throughout the high table. But his behaviour was such that he had love and thanks for his message, and a great reward withal. And so the worship of the city was kept and not lost for him; and I trust that it never shall be, by the grace of God.

The Joust Between Lord Scales and the Bastard of Burgoyne, *1467*
Edward Hall

Cheapside, the broadest street in the city, was the usual venue for jousts, though London Bridge, Westminster Abbey Green and Smithfield were all used as well. For the knightly class jousting was both sport and score-settler.

THE BASTARD OF Burgoyne, a man of a haute corage, chalenged Anthony lord Scales, brother to the Quene, a man both egall in harte, and valyantnes with the bastard to fight with hym bothe on fote & on horsbacke, the lord Scales gladly receyved hys demaunde and promised hym on the othe of a gentleman, to aunswere hym in the felde, at the day appoynted: lyke chalenges were made by other Burgonyons, to the gentelmen of Englande, which you may surely beleve were not refused. The Kyng entendyng to see thys marciall sport and valiant chalenge performed, caused lystes royall for the champions, and costely galleries for Ladies to loke on, to be newly erected and edefied in West Smythfelde in London. And at the day by the Kyng assigned, the. 11. Lordes entered within the listes, well mounted, richely trapped and curiouslye armed. On whiche daye they ran together, certayne courses wyth sharpe speres, and so departed with egall honor. The next daye, they entered the felde, the bastarde sitting on a bay courser, beinge somewhat dymme of sight, and the lord Scales had a gray courser, on whose schaffron was a long and a sharpe pyke of stele. When these. 11. valeant persones coped together at the tornay, the lord Scales horse by chance or by custome, thrust hys pyke into the nostrelles of the horse of the bastarde, so that for very payne he mounted so hygh, that he fell on the one syde with hys master, & the lord Scales rode round about him with his sworde shakyeng in hys hand, tyll the Kyng commaunded the Marshall to helpe up the bastarde, whiche openly sayed, I can not holde by the cloudes, for though my horse fayled me, surely I will not fayle my conter-conpaignions. And when he was remounted, he made a countenaunce to assayle his adversarie, but the Kyng either favoryng his brothers honor then gotten, or mistrustyng the shame, whiche mighte come to the bastarde, if he were agayne foyled, caused the Heraldes to cry, *a lostel*, and every man to departe. The morrow after, the two noble men came in to the felde on fote, with two Poleaxes, and there fought valiantly lyke two coragious champions, but at the laste, the point of the axe of the lord Scales happened to enter into the sight of the healme of the bastard, & by fyne force might have plucked hym on his knees, the Kynge sodaynely caste doune his warder, and then the Marshalls them severed.

For some of the land's nobles there was real fighting to be done. For another two decades the Wars of the Roses ran their tiresome course until, in 1485, the Lancastrian contender, Henry Tudor, triumphed at Bosworth Field. Always keen to back a winner, London greeted him at Shoreditch with loyal verses. The miserly Henry VII, however, was probably more interested in the emollient 1,000 marks proffered him.

London had another visitor in 1485, one which money could not buy off.

ᘓ ᘓ ᘓ

The Sweating Sickness, 1485
Edward Hall

Modern epidemiology suggests that the 'sweating sickness' was a version of hantavirus pulmonary syndrome.

*I*N THE SAME yere a newe kynde of sicknes came sodenly through the whole region even after the first entryng of the Kyng into this Isle, which was so sore, so peynfull, & sharp that the lyke was never harde of, to any manes remembrance that tyme: For sodenly a dedly & burnyng sweate invaded their bodyes & vexed their bloud with a most ardent heat, infested the stomack & the head grevously: by the tormentyng and vexacion of which sicknes, men were so sore handled and so painfully pangued that if they were layed in their bed, beyng not hable to suffre the importunate heat, they cast away the shetes & all the clothes liyng on the bed. If they were in their apparell and vestures, they would put of all their garmentes even to their shirtes. Other were so drye that they dranke the colde water to quenche their importunate heate and insaciable thirst. Other that could or at the least woulde abyde the heate & styntche (for in dede the sweate had a great and a strong savoure) caused clothes to be layed upon theim as much as they coulde beare, to dryve oute the sweate if it might be. All in maner as sone as the sweate toke them, or within a short space after, yelded up their ghost. So that of all them that sickened ther was not one emongest an hundreth that escaped: in so muche, that beside the great nombre which deceased within the cytie of London, two Mayres successively dyed of the same disease within, viij daies and VI. Aldermen.

Mayors and aldermen were typical victims of the sweating sickness, which, unlike most of the pestilences to descend on London, preferred the bodies of the rich. The disease rarely attacked foreigners, and seldom broke past the borders of England, hence its alternative name – 'English sweate' (*sudor anglicus*).

Tudor London: A Portrait, 1497
Andreas Franciscus

At the turn of the Tudor century, the population of London was around 70,000 – to the pride of the locals and the awe of foreigners:

THE TOWN ITSELF stretches from East to West, and is three miles in circumference. However, its suburbs are so large that they greatly increase its circuit ... Throughout the town are to be seen many work-shops of craftsmen in all sorts of mechanical arts, to such an extent that there is hardly a street which is not graced by some shop or the like ... This makes the town look exceedingly prosperous and well-stocked, as well as having the immediate effect of adding to its splendour. The working in wrought sil-ver, tin, or white lead is very expert here, and perhaps the fin-est I have ever seen. There are many mansions, which do not, however, seem very large from the outside, but inside they contain a great number of rooms and garrets and are quite considerable ...

All the streets are so badly paved that they get wet at the slightest quantity of water, and this happens very frequently owing to the large numbers of cattle carrying water, as well as on account of the rain ... A vast amount of evil-smelling mud is formed, which does not disappear quickly but lasts a long time, in fact nearly the whole year round. The citizens, therefore, in order to remove mud and filth from their boots, are accustomed to spread fresh rushes on the floors of all houses ...

Merchants from not only Venice but also Florence and

Lucca, and many from Genoa and Pisa, from Spain, Germany, the Rhine valley and other countries meet here to handle business with the utmost keenness, having come from different parts of the world . . .

Londoners have such fierce tempers and wicked dispositions that they not only despise the way we Italians live, but actually pursue them with uncontrollable hatred, and whereas at Bruges foreigners are hospitably received and complimented . . . by everybody, here the Englishmen use them with the utmost contempt and arrogance, and make them the object of insults . . . They eat very frequently, at times more than is suitable.

Almost every foreign visitor to London complained of the locals' xenophobia, which sometimes went beyond insults to violence:

Evil May Day, 1 May 1517
The Chronicle of the Grey Friars

Incited by a priest in Spitalfields, over 1,000 young men rampaged around the city in the worst anti-alien riot of the Tudor years:

THYS YERE WAS yell [evil] May day, that yong men and prentes [apprentices] of London rose in the nyght, and wolde have had James Mottas ane owte-landych mane [man] and wolde have slayne hym, but he hyde hym in hys gotters in hys howse; and from thense they wente un to sent [Saint] Martyns, and there spoyled the shomakers shoppes of shone; and thane rose the mayer and shreffes [sheriffs] and wolde have cessyd them, but they cowde not. And then rose the erle of Surre, and he wolde have spoyled them. And iiij. or v. dayes after the corte kepte the citte in harnes with divers lordes, and at the last there ware dyvers of them hongyd within the citte on gallos, as at sent Martyns gatte at Ludgate, at Algate, Bysshoppes gate, Doggate, sent Manguns, Ledynhall, in the Powltre, and at the stondert in Cheppe; and there was hongyd and qwarterd one Lyncon; and another gallows at Newgate. And within shorte space the kynge satte in Westmyster halle, and there was commandyd the citte to come in their clothynge, and the rest of them that was pardent to come with halters abowte their neckes and to aske pardone, and soo a generall pardone was gevyne unto theme alle that came that tyme.

In total Henry VIII executed 15 Evil May Day participants. No more serious anti-alien riots occurred in London until the Georgian era, though xenophobia remained a swirling undercurrent of local life.

Henry's eagerness to send the rioters to the hangman was occasioned by more than a desire to promote good race relations in England's capital. He used the occasion to cut London down to size: the rioters had been tried for treason, not riot.

But nothing could stop London becoming the hub of history. London was *prime parus* populous. London was the main port for the exportation of the golden fleeces that were the Tudor age's main money-spinner. London was the permanent (more or less) headquarters for court and Parliament.

Under the Tudors, national events were increasingly acted out on the local stage of London.

The Beheading of Sir Thomas More, 1535
William Roper

More was born in London in 1478 and rose to become Lord Chancellor. Despite a desire for a more rational theology he opposed Henry VIII's Protestant Reformation and was accordingly found guilty of high treason. Still refusing to recant his Roman Catholicism, the author of *Utopia* was beheaded.

William Roper was More's son-in-law.

NOW AFTER THIS arraignement departed hee from the barre to the Towre againe, ledd by Sir William Kingston, a tall, stronge, and cornlye Knight, Constable of the Towre, his very deare frend, whoe when he had brought him from Westminster to the ould Swanne towardes the Towre, there with a heavie hart, the teares runninge downe his cheekes, bad him farewell. Sir Thomas Moore seinge him soe sor-rowfull, comforted him with as good wordes as he could, saying, 'Good Mr. Kingston, trouble not your selfe, but be of good cheare. For I will pray for you, and my good Ladie your wif, that we may meete in heaven togeather, where we shall be merrie for ever and ever.' Soone after Sir William Kingston talkinge with mee of Sir Tho. Moore, sayd, 'In faith Mr. Roper, I was ashamed of my selfe, that at my departure from your father, I found my harte soe feeble, and his soe stronge, that he was fayne to comforte me which should rather have comforted him.' When Sir Tho. Moore came from Westminster to the Towreward againe, his daughter my wife, desireous to see her father, whome shee thought shee should never see in this world after, and alsoe to have his finall blessinge, gave attendaunce aboutes the Towre wharfe, where shee knewe he should passe by, e're he could enter into the Towre. There tarriinge for his cominge home, assoone as shee sawe him, after his blessinges on her knees reverentlie receaved, shee, hastinge towards, without consideration of care of her-selfe, pressinge in amongest the midst of the thronge and the Companie of the Guard, that with Hollbards and Billes weare round about him, hastily ranne to him, and there openlye in the sight of all them embraced and tooke him about the necke and kissed him, whoe well likeinge her most daughterlye love and affection towardes him, gave her his fatherlie blessinge, and many godlie wordes of comfort besides, from whome after shee was departed, shee not satisfied with the former sight of her deare father, havinge respect neither to her self, nor to the presse of the people and multitude that were about him, suddenlye turned back againe, and rann to him as before, tooke him about the necke, and divers tymes togeather most lovingely kissed him, and at last with a full heavie harte was fayne to departe from him; the behouldinge whereof was to manye of them that weare present thereat soe lamentable, that it made them for very sorrow to mourne and weepe. Soe remayned Sir Thomas Moore in the Towre more then a seaven night after his Judgment. From whence the daye before he suffered he sent his shirt of hare, not willinge to have it seene, to my wyfe, his dearely beloved daughter, and a letter, written with a Cole, contayned in the foresaid booke of his workes, plainely expressinge the fervent desire he had to suffer on the morrowe in these wordes: 'I comber you, good Margarett, much, but I would bee sorrie if it should be any longer then to morrowe. For to morrow is St. Thomas even, and the Utas of St. Peeter, and therefore to morrow longe I to goe to God, that weare a daye very meet and convenient for mee. And I never liked your manners better, then when you kissed mee last. For I like when daughterlie Love, and deare Charitie hath noe leasure to looke to worldlie Curtesie.' And soe uppon the next morninge, beinge tuesday, St Thomas even, and the Utas of St Peeter in the yeare of our Lord God 1535, accordinge as he in his letter the day before had wished, earlie in the morninge came to him Sir Thomas Pope, his singular frend, on messadge from the Kinge and his Councell, that hee should before nyne of the clocke in the same morninge suffer death, and that therefore fourthwith he should prepare himselfe thereto. 'Mr. Pope,' sayth hee, 'for your good tydinges I most hartily thanke you. I have beene allwayes bounden much to the Kinge's Highnes for the benefitts and honors which he hath still from tyme to tyme most bountifully heaped upon mee, and yete more bounden I ame to his Grace for puttinge me into this place, where I have had convenient tyme and space to have remembraunce of my end, and soe helpe me God most of all, Mr. Pope, am I bound to his Highnes, that it pleased him soe shortlie to ridd me of the miseries of this wretched world. And therefore will I not fayle most earnestlye to praye for his Grace both here, and alsoe in an other world. The Kinge's pleasure is further,' quoth Mr. Pope, 'that at your Execution you shall not use many words.' 'Mr. Pope,' (quoth hee) 'you do well that you give mee warninge of his Grace's pleasure. For otherwise had I purposed at that tyme somewhat to have spoken, but of noe matter wherewith his Grace, or any other should have had cause to be offended. Neverthelesse what soever I intend I am readie obediently to conforme my self to his Grace's Commaundment. And I beseech you, good Mr Pope, to be a meane unto his Highnes, that my daughter Margerette may be present at my buriall.' 'The King is well contented allreadie' (quoth Mr Pope) 'that your Wife, Children, and other frendes shall have free libertie to be present thereat.' 'O how much behoulden,' then said Sir Thomas Moore, 'am I to his Grace, that unto my poore buriall vouchsafeth to have so gratious Consideration.' Wherewithall Mr Pope takeinge his leave of him could not refrayne from weepinge, which Sir Tho. Moore perceavinge, comforted him in this wise, 'Quiete your selfe, good Mr Pope, and be not discomforted. For I trust that we shall once in heaven see each other full merily, where we shall bee sure to live and love togeather in joyfull blisse eternally.' Upon whose departure Sir Tho. Moore, as one that had beene invited to a solempne feast, chaunged himselfe into his best apparell; which Mr Lieuetenaunt espyinge, advised him to put it off, sayinge, That he that should have it was but a Javill. 'What Mr Lieuetenaunt' (quoth he) 'shall I accompte him a Javill, that will doe mee this daye so singular a benefitt? Naye, I assure you, weare it cloath of gould I would accompte it well bestowed on him, as St Cyprian did, who gave his executioner xxx peeces of gold.' And albeit at length, through Mr Lievetenaunte's perswasions, he altered his apparell, yete, after the example of that holy Martyr St Ciprian, did hee of that litle money that was left him, send one Angell of gold to his Executioner. And soe was he brought by Mr Lieuetenaunt out of the Towre, and from thence ledd towardes the place of execution, where goeinge upp the Scaffold, which was soe weake that it was readie to fall, he sayde to Mr Lievetenaunt, 'I pray you, I pray you, Mr Lievetenaunt, see mee safe upp, and for my cominge downe lett mee shift for my selfe.' Then desired hee all the people thereaboutes to pray for him, and to beare witnesse with him, that he should then suffer death in and for the faith of the holie Catholique Church, which done hee kneeled downe, and after his prayers sayed, hee turned to the executioner, and with a cheerefull Countenance spake unto him, 'Plucke upp thie spirittes, man, and be not affrayed to do thine office, my necke is verye short. Take heede therefore thou scute not awrie for savinge thine honestie.' Soe passed Sir Thomas Moore out of this world to God uppon the verie same daye in which himselfe had most desired. Soone after whose death came intelligence thereof to the Emperor

Charles, whereuppon he sent for Sir Thomas Eliott, our English Embassodor, and sayd unto him, 'My Lord Embassodor, wee understand that the Kinge your Master hath putt his faithfull servaunt and grave wise Councellor Sir Thomas Moore to death.' Where unto Sir Thomas Eliott answeared, that hee understood nothinge thereof. 'Well,' sayd the Emperor, 'it is verye true, and this will we saye, that if wee had bine Mr. of such a servaunt, of whose doinges our selves have had these many yeares noe small experience, wee would rather have lost the best Cittie of our Dominiones, then have lost such a worthie Councellor.' Which matter was bye Sir Thomas Eliott to my selfe, to my wife, to Mr. Clement and his wife, to Mr. John Haywood and his wife, and divers others of his frends acordingely reported.

Thomas More turned out to be an atypical Londoner. The city's inhabitants inclined towards the reformed faith, especially the merchant class, since it was linked through trade and personal relations to the Rhineland and Low Countries, the well-springs of Protestantism.

So sympathetic, indeed, was London to the Reformation that it barely voiced a qualm over the suppression of the monasteries. As early as 1531 Henry suppressed the Convent of St Clare, Aldgate, and St James' Hospital for Lepers (which provided the site for St James' Palace). Five years later the king acquired most of Westminster Abbey's estates in London, including Hyde Park, Covent Garden and Pimlico.

The mature Henry VIII's leaning in religion was towards Catholicism without the Pope. His son was made of sterner Protestant stuff.

⚜ ⚜ ⚜

Protestant Revolution: Edward VI Suppresses Popery in London, 1547
The Chronicle of the Grey Friars

On Edward VI's premature death, a faction at court, headed by the Duke of Northumberland, declared Lady Jane Grey queen in a bid to ensure a Protestant succession. Grey had no legitimate claim, and Edward's half-sister, the Catholic-to-the-bone Mary, made a play for the crown.

ITEM THE 5TH day after in September began the king's visitation at Paul's and all images pulled down: and the 9th day of the same month the said visitation was at St. Bride's, and after that in divers other parish churches; and so all images pulled down through all England at that time, and all churches new white-limed with the commandments written on the walls. And at that time was the bishop of London put into the Fleet, and was there more than eight days; and after him was the bishop of Winchester put there also.

Item at this same time was pulled up all the tomes, great stones, all the altars, with the stalls and walls of the quire and altars in the church that was some time the Gray friars and sold, and the quire made smaller . . .

Item the 17th day of the same month at night was pulled down the Rode in Paul's with Mary and John, with all the images in the church, and two of the men that laboured at it was slain and divers others sore hurt. Item also at that time was pulled down through all the king's dominion in every church all Roddes with all images, and every preacher preached in their sermons against all images. Also the new

years day after preached *doctor* Latemer that some time was
bishop of Worcester preached at Paul's cross, and two Sundays
following, etc. Also this same time was much speaking again
the sacrament of the altar, that some called it Jack of the
box, with divers other shameful names: and then was made
a proclamation against such sayers, and it both the preachers
and others spake against it, and so continued; and at Easter
following there began the communion, and confession but of
those that would, as the book doth specify. And at this time
was much preaching against the mass. And the sacrament
of the altar pulled down in divers places through the realm.
Item after Easter began the service in English (at Paul's
at the commandment of the dean at the time, William
May,) and also in divers other parish churches. Item also at
Whitsuntide began the sermons at St. Mary spital. Item also
this year was Barking chapel at the Tower hill pulled down,
and Saint Martin's at the chambulles end, Saint Nicolas in
the chambulles, and Saint Ewyns, and within the Gatte of
Newgate these were put into the church that some time was
the Gray Friars: and also Strand church was pulled down to
make the protector duke of Somerset's place larger.

Item this year was all the chantries put down . . .

Item also the bishop of Winchester at that time Stephyn
Gardner preached before the king at saint James in the field
on Saint Peter's day at afternoon the which was then Friday,
and in the morrow after was committed into the tower of
London in ward . . .

Item all those preachers that preached at Paul's cross at that
time spake much against the bishop of Winchester; and also
Cardmaker, that talked in Paul's 3 times a week had more or
less of him.

Item this same time was put down all going abroad of
processions, and the sensyng at Paul's at Whitsuntide, and the
Skinners' procession on Corpus Christi day, with all others,

and had none other but the English procession in their churches.

Item at this time was much preaching through all England against the sacrament of the altar, save only M. Laygton, and he preached in every place that he preached against them all: and so was much controversy and much besynes in Paul's every Sunday and sitting in the church and of none that were honest persons, but boys and persons of little reputation: and would have made more if there had not a way a bene tane. And at the last the 28. of December following there was a proclamation that none of both parties should preach unto such time as the council had determined such things as they were in hand with all . . .

Queen Mary Seizes the Crown, 1553
Henry Machyn

Machyn was a London grocer.

THE IX DAY of July was sworne unto the qwen Jane alle the hed offesers and the gard as qwen of England ... doythur of the duke of Suffolke, and servyd as qwen of ...

The x day of July was reseyvyd in to the Towre [the Queen Jane] with a grett compeny of lords and nobulls of ... after the qwen, and the duches of Suffoke her mother, bering her trayn, with mony lades, and ther was a shot of gunnes and chamburs has nott be sene oft be-tweyn iiii and v [of the clock]; by vi of the cloke be-gane the proclamasyon the same [after-] non [of] qwen Jane with ii harold[s] and a trompet blohyng, [declaring] that my lade Mare was unlafully be-gotten, and so [went through] chepe to Fletstrett, proclamyng qwen Jane; and ther was a yong man taken that tym for spykyng of serten wordes of qwen Mare, that she had the ryght tytle ...

The xix day of July was qwene Mare proclamyd qwene of England, France and Yrland, and alle domyn[ni]ons, [as the] syster of the late kyng Edward the vi and doythur unto the nobull kyng Henry the viii be-twyn v and vi of the cloke at nyght and ther wher at proclamasyon iiii trumpeters and ii harold[s] of armes, and the erle of Arundell, the erle of Shrossbery, th'erle Penbroke, my lord Tressorer, my lord Preveselle, my lord Cobham, my lord Warden, master Masun, and my lord Mare, and dyvers odur nobull men; and thys was done at the crosse in Chepe, and from that plasse thay whent unto Powlls and ther was Te Deum Laudamus, wyth song, and the organes playhyng, and all the belles ryngyng thrugh London, and bone-fyres, and tabuls in evere strett, and wyne and bere and alle, and evre strett full of bon-fyres, and ther was money cast a-way.

It was the acclamation of the London crowd which ensured that Mary took the throne. Londoners' dislike of usurpation was greater than their liking for Protestantism. This was to change.

❧ ❧ ❧

Mary Persecutes the Protestants: The Burning of Bradford and Leaf at Smithfield, 1555
John Foxe

Whatever goodwill London harboured for Queen Mary soon evaporated. She wished to marry a foreigner – Philip II of Spain – which prompted the xenophobic citizens of the capital to acquiesce in Sir Thomas Wyatt's uprising against her, and only the locking of the Ludgate by the corporation at the last minute prevented Wyatt from marching into the city. Mary's stock sank lower still when she tried to return the country to Catholicism by burning its Protestants. Over 300 'heretics' were set afire by Mary I, their executions meticulously recorded by John Foxe in his bestselling *Book of Martyrs*, published in 1563.

ND WHEN BRADFORD and Leaf came to the Stake in *Smithfield* to be burned, Mr. *Bradford* lying prostrate on the one side of the Stake, and the young man *John Leaf* on the other side, they lay flat on their faces, praying to themselves the space of a minute of an hour. Then one of the Sheriffs said to Mr. *Bradford*, Arise and make an end; for the press of the People is great.

At that word they both stood upon their feet, and then Mr. *Bradford* took a Fagot in his hand, and kissed it, and so likewise the Stake. And when he had so done, he desired of the Sheriffs, that his Servant might have his Raiment. For (said he) I have nothing else to give him: and besides that, he is a poor man. And the Sheriff said he should have it. And so forthwith Mr. *Bradford* did put off his Raiment, and went to the Stake: and holding up his hands, and casting his countenance to Heaven, he said thus, O England, England, *repent thee of thy sins, repent thee of thy sins. Beware of Idolatory, beware of false Antichrists, take heed they do not deceive you.* And as he was speaking these words, the Sheriff bid tye his hands, if he would not be quiet. O master Sheriff (said Mr. *Bradford*) I am quiet: God forgive you this, Master Sheriff. And one of the Officers which made the fire, hearing Mr. *Bradford* speaking to the Sheriff, said If you have no better learning than that, you are but a fool, and were best hold your peace. To the which words Mr. *Bradford* gave no answer; but asked all the world forgiveness, and forgave all the world, and prayed the people to pray for him, and turned his head unto the young man that suffered with him, and said, Be of good comfort Brother; for we shall have a merry Supper with the Lord this night: And so spake no more words that any man did hear, but imbracing the Reeds, said thus; *Strait is the way, and narrow is the gate that leadeth to eternal salvation, and few there be that find it.*

And thus they both ended their mortal lives, most like

two Lambs, without any alteration of their countenance, being void of all fear, hoping to obtain the price of the Game they had long run at; to the which I beseech Almighty God happily to conduct us, through the merits of Jesus Christ our Lord and Saviour. Amen.

'Bloody Mary's' cruelty, the memory of which was long kept alive by Foxe's book, proved the best recruiting agent for Protestantism and its Puritanical variant.

Mary died of 'dropsy' (modern-day oedema – organ swelling due to fluid increase) in 1558. The throne passed to her 25-year-old Protestant half-sister Elizabeth, daughter of Henry VIII and Anne Boleyn.

The new queen's capital was entering a period of unparalleled growth; on her accession the population stood at 120,000. On her death in 1603 the population of London was 200,000, 140,000 of which lived in the ancient 26 wards (leading to extreme overcrowding in places), the remainder in the burgeoning suburbs which surrounded the city. Almost the entire population rise was caused by migration. London became a vast building site, with many of the new homes erected on the site of former monasteries.

In this time of flux Elizabeth gave London what it needed: stability. She promoted a middle-of-the-road Anglicanism, to which few people, except Catholic die-hards, could object. She also avoided the sort of foreign adventures that leached the city's money and conspicuously respected city institutions. After all, her maternal line included a former mayor.

Elizabethan London: City Life,
1564–99
Various

Theft from the Queen, 1564, John Stow

John Stow (1525–1605) was the author of *A Survey of London*.

ON THE XXVj day of Septembar, in anno 1564, beynge Tweseday, ware arraynyd at ye Gyldhalle of London iiij personas and there caste, for ye stelynge and receyvynge of ye queens lypott,* combe, and lokynge glasse, with a bodkyn of gold to brayd hir heare, and suche othar small ware out of hir chambar in her progresse. And on Thursday next afftar, beynge Myhilmas even, and ye xxviij day of September, ij of them whiche had bene servantis in Chepesyd, one of them with Master Bakehowse, dwellyng agaynst ye Standard, beyng a sylke man, were bothe hangyd before ye Cowrte gatte, upon ye gallows that stode on Haye Hyll, whiche was for that tyme removyd for that purpose to Saynt James, before ye wall, beynge at that tyme ye queens cowrte.

A Legacy for the Relief of the Poor, 1568, John Stow

SIR THOMAS ROE, Marchant Taylor, Mayor (of London), 1568, gave to the Marchant Taylors lands or Tenements, out of them to bee given to ten poore men Clothworkers, Carpentars, Tilars, Plasterers, and Armorers, 40 pounds yearely, viz. 4 pounds to each, also 200 pounds to bee lent to 8 poore men.

---

* Chamber pot

A School for Pick-pockets, 1581, William Fleetwood,
The Recorder of London

Fleetwood reported to William Cecil, Elizabeth's chief secretary of state. Petty crime was a preoccupation of Elizabethan Londoners, who were overrun, as they saw it, by beggars and relocated young men on the make.

RIGHT HONOURABLE AND my very good Lord ... upon Friday last we sat at the Justice Hall at Newgate from seven in the morning until seven at night, where were condemned certain horsestealers, cut-purses, and such like, to the number of ten, whereof nine were executed and the tenth stayed by a means from the court. These were executed upon Saturday in the morning. There was a shoemaker also condemned for wilful murder committed in the Blackfriars, who was executed upon Monday in the morning. The same day, my Lord Mayor being absent about the goods of the Spaniards, and also my Lords the Justices of the Benches being also away, we few that were there did spend the same day about the searching out of sundry that were receptors of felons, where we found a great many as well in London, Westminster, Southwark, as in all other places about the same. Amongst our travels, this one matter tumbled out by the way, that one Wotton, a gentleman born and sometime a merchant man of good credit, who falling by time into decay kept an alehouse at Smart's Key near Billingsgate, and after, for some misdemeanour being put down, he reared up a new trade of life, and in the same house he procured all the cut-purses about this City to repair to this said house. There was a schoolhouse set up to learn young boys to cut purses. There were hung up two devices, the one was a pocket, the other was a purse. The pocket had in it certain counters and was hung about with hawk's bells, and over the top did hang a little sacring-bell; and he that could take out a counter without any noise was allowed to be a *public foister*. And he that could take a piece of silver out of the purse without any noise of any of the bells, he was adjudged a *judicial nipper*. Nota that a foister is a pickpocket and a nipper is termed a pickpurse or a cutpurse. And as concerning this matter, I will set down no more in this place, but refer your Lordship to the paper herein enclosed.

Sentenced for Libel, 1581, John Stow

THE 13. OF October were arraigned at Westminster hall, John Stubs, Hugh Singleton, and William Page, these were all three condemned to lose their right hands, for writing, printing, and dispersing a libell, which they entituled, the Gaping Gulph, against Monsieur Francis, Duke of Anjow, the French Kings brother. And on the 3. day of November, they were all led to Westminster, where John Stubs, and William Page lost their hands by chopping off, but Hugh Singleton had his pardon.

A Scaffold Collapses at a Sports Match, c.1582, John Stow

C. 1582:– AND whereas, upon a *Lord's* Day, a great Number of People being met for Sport at *Paris* Garden, all the Scaffolds fell down at once to the Slaying and Wounding of a great many People; this Mayor piously looked upon it as a Judgment of God for Breach of the *Lord's Day*, and wrote to the Lord Treasurer to this Tenor: 'That it gave great Occasion to acknowledge the Hand of God for such Abuse of his *Sabbath-Day*; and moved him in Conscience to beseech his Lordship to give Order for Redress of such Contempt of God's Service. And that he had for that End treated with some Justices of Peace of that County, who shewed themselves to have very good Zeal, but alledged Want of Commission; which they humbly referred to his honourable Wisdom.'

Swans and Freaks, 1584, Lupold von Wedel

I AGAIN STEPPED into my boat, sailing down the river thirty miles towards London, where I arrived at twelve o'clock. All the time the river was full of tame swans, who have nests and breed on small islands formed by the river. They are exclusively used for the Queen's table, and it is on pain of death forbidden to meddle with them ... On 6 March I saw here in London a woman only twenty-eight breadths of a thumb high. She had very short legs, about a span in length; her steps were not longer than a cock's ... On the 13th I saw a young fellow with red and black spots on his head, resembling a pig.

Chauvinism and Clothes, 1592, Frederick, Duke of Württemberg

IT IS A very populous city, so that one can scarely pass along the streets, on account of the throng.

The inhabitants are magnificently appararelled, and are extremely proud and overbearing: and because the greater part, especially the trades people, seldom go into other countries, but always remain in their houses in the city attending to their business, they care little for foreigners, but scoff and laugh at them; and moreover one dare not oppose them, else the street-boys and apprentices collect together in immense crowds and strike to the right and left unmercifully without regard to person; and because they are the strongest, one is obliged to put up with the insult as well as the injury.

The women have much more liberty than perhaps in any

other place; they also know well how to make use of it, for they go dressed out in exceedingly fine clothes, and give all their attention to their ruffs and stuffs ... whilst at home perhaps they have not a piece of dry bread.

The Brothels of Southwark, 1598, John Stow

Southwark, outside the city limits, had been London's main red-light district since medieval times.

NEXT ON THIS banke was sometime the Bordello or stewes, a place so called, of certaine stew houses priuiledged there, for the repaire of incontinent men to the like women, of the which priuiledge I haue read thus.

In a Parliament holden at Westminster the 8. of *Henry* the second, it was ordayned by the commons and confirmed by the king and Lords, that diuers constitutions for euer should bee kept within that Lordship or franchise, according to the olde customes that had been there vsed time out of mind. Amongest the which these following were some, *vz.*

That no stewholder or his wife should let or staye any single Woman to goe and come freely at all times when they listed.

No stewholder to keepe any woman to borde, but she to borde abroad at her pleasure.

To take no more for the womans chamber in the weeke then foureteene pence.

Not to keepe open his dores vpon the holydayes.

Not to keepe any single woman in his house on the holy dayes, but the Bayliffe to see them voyded out of the Lordship.

No single woman to be kept against her will that would leaue her sinne.

No stewholder to receiue any Woman of religion, or any mans wife.

No single woman to take money to lie with any man, but shee lie with him all night till the morrow.

No man to be drawn or inticed into any stewhouse.

The Constables, Balife, and others euery weeke to search euery stewhouse.

No stewholder to keepe any woman that hath the perilous infirmitie of burning, nor to sell bread, ale, flesh, fish, wood, coale, or any victuals, &c.

These and many more orders were to be obserued vpon great payne and punishment: I haue also seene diuers Patentes of confirmation, namely one dated 1345. the nineteenth of *Edwarde* the third. Also I find that in the fourth of *Richarde* the second, these stew houses, belonging to *William Walworth* then Mayor of London, were farmed by Froes of Flaunders, and spoyled by *Walter Tighler*, and other rebelles of Kent: notwithstanding I finde that ordinances for the same place and houses were againe confirmed in the raigne of *Henry* the sixt, to be continued as before. Also *Robert Fabian* writeth that in the yeare 1506. the 21. of *Henry* the seuenth, the saide stewe houses in Southwarke were for a season inhibited, and the dores closed vp, but it was not long saith he, ere the houses there were set open againe, so many as were permitted, for (as it was said) whereas before were eighteene houses, from thenceforth were appointed to bee vsed but twelue onely. These allowed stewhouses had signes on their frontes, towardes the Thames, not hanged out, but painted on the walles, as a Boares heade, the Crosse keyes, the Gunne, the Castle, the Crane, the Cardinals Hat, the Bel, the Swanne, &c. I haue heard ancient men of good credite report, that these single women were forbidden the rightes of the Church, so long as they continued that sinnefull life, and were excluded from christian buriall, if they were not reconciled before their death. And therefore there was a plot of ground, called the single womans churchyeard, appoynted for them, far from the parish church.

In the yeare of Christ, 1546. the 37. of *Henry* the eight, this row of stewes in Southwarke was put downe by the kings commandement, which was proclaymed by sounde of Trumpet, no more to be priuiledged, and vsed as a common Brothel, but the inhabitants of the same to keepe good and honest rule as in other places of this realme, &c.

The next is the Clinke, a Gayle or prison for the trespassers in those parts, Namely in olde time for such as should brabble, frey, or breake the Peace on the saide banke, or in the Brothell houses, they were by the inhabitantes there about apprehended, and committed to this Gayle, where they were straightly imprisoned.

As Stow remarks, brothels were required to display a prominent design: the most famous was the 'Cardinal's Hat' in honour of the Bishop of Winchester, who owned the land on which many of the 'stews' were built. Thus London slang for prostitutes was 'Winchester geese'.

Bear-Baiting, 1599, *Thomas Platter*

Platter was a Swiss visitor to London.

EVERY SUNDAY AND Wednesday in London there are bear-baitings ... The theatre is circular, with galleries round the top for the spectators, the ground space down below, beneath the clear sky, is unoccupied. In the middle of this place a large bear on a long rope was bound to a stake, then a number of great English mastiffs were brought in and shown first to the bear, which they afterwards baited one after another: now the excellence and fine temper of such mastiffs was evinced, for although they were much struck and mauled by the bear, they did not give in, but had to be pulled off by sheer force, and their muzzles forced open with long sticks to which a broad ironpiece was attached at the top. The bears' teeth were not sharp so they could not injure the dogs; they have them broken short. When the first mastiffs tired, fresh ones were brought in to bait the bear.

When the first bear was weary, another one was supplied and fresh dogs to bait him, first one at a time, then more and more as it lasted, till they had overpowered the bear, then only did they come to its aid. This second bear was very big and old, and kept the dogs at bay so artfully with his paws that they could not score a point off him until there were more of them. When this bear was tired, a large white powerful bull was brought in, and likewise bound in the centre of the theatre, and one dog only was set on him at a time, which he speared with his horns and tossed in such masterly fashion, that they could not get the better of him, and as the dogs fell to the floor again, several men held the sticks under them to break their fall, so that they would not be killed. Afterwards more dogs were set on him, but could not down him. Then another powerful bear was fetched and baited by six or seven dogs at a time, which attacked him bravely on all sides, but could not get the better of him because of his thick pelt.

Lastly they brought in an old blind bear which the boys hit with canes and sticks; but he knew how to untie his leash and he ran back to his stall.

A Fishmarket, 1599, Thomas Platter

AT THE FISHMARKET, in a long street, I saw a quantity of pike up for sale; they are very fond of this . . . and feed it with needle-fish (*aiguilles*), eels, and other tiny fish. And I noticed that each of these fishermen and fishwives kept a copper or brass needle and thread in the tub, with a sharp knife. And when the purchasers desired a pike the salesmen and saleswomen slit open its belly at their bidding, placing the guts on their hands to show whether the pike was sufficiently fat, and then sewed it up again: if the pike proved fat enough, then the purchaser took it, but if the guts looked thin and poor the fishmonger kept it, throwing it back into the basin among the tenches, against which they rub themselves and recover enough to keep fresh for at least another week, in fact according to them, fish could keep fresh for some months. Indeed, they kept tench ready in the fish tanks with the pike, so that they would get used to them; all this I witnessed in London with my own eyes, nor is it otherwise.

Elizabethan London:
The Oath of Every Freeman, 1580

Anonymous

*Y*E SHALL SWEAR that ye shall be good and true to our sovereign Lady. Queen Elizabeth, etc., and to the heirs of our said sovereign Lady the Queen. Obeisant and obedient ye shall be to the Mayor and to the ministers of this City. The franchises and customs thereof ye shall maintain and this City keep harmless in that that in you is.

Ye shall be contributory to all manner of charges within this City, as summons, watches, contributions, tasks, tallages, lot and scot, and all other charges, bearing your part as a freeman ought to do.

Ye shall colour no foreign's goods whereby the Queen might lose her customs or advantages.

Ye shall know no foreign to buy or sell any merchandise within the City or the franchise thereof, but ye shall warn the Chamberlain thereof, or some minister of the chamber.

Ye shall emplead or sue no free man out of this City whiles ye may have right and law within this same City.

Ye shall take none apprentice but if he be free born, that is to say, no bond man's son, and for no less term than for seven years. Within the first year ye shall cause him to be enrolled, and at his term's end ye shall make him free of this City, if he have well and truly served you.

Ye shall also keep the Queen's peace in your person; ye shall know no gatherings, conventicles, nor conspiracies made against the Queen's peace, but ye shall warn the Mayor thereof, or let it to your power.

All these points and articles ye shall well and truly keep, according to the laws and custom of this City to your power. So God you help, and by the holy contents of this Book.

In 1580 Elizabeth also required the citizens of London to desist from building more houses: 'The Queen's majesty, perceiving the state of the City of London ... and the suburbs ... to increase daily by access of people to inhabit in the same ... doth charge and straightly command all manner of persons of what quality soever they be, to desist and forbear from any new buildings of any house or tenement within three miles from any of the gates of said City of London ... and to forbear from letting, or setting, or suffering any more families than one only to be placed or to inhabit ... in any house that heretofore hath been inhabited.'

The injunction was ignored. The tide of people drifting to London for work and for good times was unstoppable.

Riots, Puritans and Shakespeare: Theatre-going, 1584–1613

William Fleetwood, the Lord Mayor and Aldermen, and Thomas Platter

Until the Elizabethan age, plays were performed in the open air or in the yards of inns. In 1576 the actor James Burbage erected the first purpose-built playhouse ('The Theatre') in Shoreditch. From then until Elizabeth's death in 1603, ten more theatres opened in London – all of them in suburbs and sanctuaries outside the control of the city elders, who viewed the playhouse as the foundry of vice.

The Theatre certainly attracted a raucous crowd. On 18 June 1584 William Fleetwood, City Recorder, reported:

I RETURNED TO LONDON and found all the wards full of watchers, the cause thereof was for that very near the Theater or Curtain at the time of the plays there lay a prentice sleeping upon the grass and one Challes alias Grostock did turn upon the toe upon the belly of the same prentice, whereupon the apprentice start up and after words they fell to plain blows. The company increased of both sides to the number of five hundred at the least. This Challes exclaimed and said that he was a gentleman and that the apprentice was but a rascal, and some there were little better than rogues that took upon them the name of gentlemen, and said the prentices were but the scum of the world. Upon these troubles the prentices began the next day being Tuesday to make mutinies and assemblies, and did conspire to have broken the prisons and to have taken forth the prentices that were imprisoned, but my lord and I having intelligence thereof apprehended four or five of the chief conspirators, who are in Newgate and stand indicted of their lewd demeanours.

Upon Wednesday one Browne a serving-man in a blue coat, a shifting fellow, having a perilous wit of his own, intending a spoie [?] if he could have brought it to pass, did at Theater door quarrel with certain poor boys, handicraft prentices, and struck some of them and lastly he with his sword wounded and maimed one of the boys upon the left hand, whereupon there assembled near a thousand people. This Browne did very cunningly convey himself away, but by chance he was taken after and brought to Mr. Humphrey Smith, and because no man was able to charge him he dismissed him. And after this Browne was brought before Mr. Young, where he used himself so cunningly and subtly, no man being there to charge him, that there also he was dismissed. And after I sent a warrant for him, and the constables with the deputy at the Bell in Holborn found him in a parlour fast locked in; and he would not obey the warrant, but by the mean of the host he was conveyed away; and then I sent for the host and caused him to appear at Newgate at the sessions oyer and determiner, where he was committed until he brought forth his guest. The next day after he brought him forth and so we indicted him for his misdemeanour. This Browne is a common cozener, a thief and a horse stealer, and coloured all his doings here about this town with a suit that he hath in the law against a brother of his in Staffordshire. He resteth now in Newgate.

The Lord Mayor and aldermen made repeated efforts to have the theatres closed down. On 28 July 1597 they petitioned the Privy Council:

TO THE PRIVY COUNCIL:

Our humble duties remembered to your good Lords and the rest. We have signified to your Honours many times heretofore the great inconvenience which we find to grow by the common exercise of stage-plays. We presumed to do so, as well in respect of the duty we bear towards her Highness for the good government of this her city, as for conscience sake, being persuaded (under correction of your Honours' judgment) that neither in polity nor in religion they are to be suffered in a Christian commonwealth, specially being of that frame and matter as usually they are, containing nothing but profane fables, lascivious matters, cozening devices, and scurrilous behaviours, which are so set forth as that they move wholly to imitation and not to the avoiding of those faults and vices which they represent. Among other inconveniences it is not the least that they give opportunity to the refuse sort of evil-disposed and ungodly people that are within and about this city to assemble themselves and to make their matches for all their lewd and ungodly practices; being as heretofore we have found by the examination of divers apprentices and other servants who have confessed unto us that the said stage-plays were the very places of their rendezvous, appointed by them to meet with such other as were to join with them in their designs and mutinous attempts, being also the ordinary places for masterless men to come together and to recreate themselves. For avoiding whereof we are now again most humble and earnest suitors to your honours to direct your letters as well to ourselves as to the justices of peace of Surrey and Middlesex for the present stay and final suppressing of the said stage-plays, as well at the Theater, Curtain and Bankside as in all other places in and about the city; whereby we doubt not but the opportunity and the very cause of many disorders being taken away, we shall be more able to keep the worse sort of such evil and disordered people in better order than heretofore we have been. And so most humbly we take our leaves. From London the 28th of July 1597.

1. They are a special cause of corrupting their youth, containing nothing but unchaste matters, lascivious devices, shifts of cozenage, and other lewd and ungodly practices, being so as that they impress the very quality and corruption of manners which they represent, contrary to the rules and art prescribed for the making of comedies even among the heathen, who used them seldom and at certain set times, and not all the year long as our manner is. Whereby such as frequent them, being of the base and refuse sort of people or such young gentlemen as have small regard of credit or conscience, draw the same into imitation and not to the avoiding the like vices which they represent.

2. They are the ordinary places for vagrant persons, masterless men, thieves, horse-stealers, whoremongers, cozeners, coney-catchers, contrivers of treason and other idle and dangerous persons to meet together and to make their matches to the great displeasure of Almighty God and the hurt and annoyance of her Majesty's people; which cannot be prevented nor discovered by the governors of the city for that they are out of the city's jurisdiction.

3. They maintain idleness in such persons as have no vocation, and draw apprentices and other servants from their ordinary works and all sorts of people from the resort unto sermons and other Christian exercises to the great hindrance of trades and profanation of religion established by her Highness within this realm.

4. In the time of sickness it is found by experience that many, having sores and yet not heart-sick, take occasion hereby to walk abroad and to recreate themselves by hearing a play. Whereby others are infected, and themselves also many things miscarry.

In truth, the court tended to enjoy the new-fangled entertainment that was theatre and extended it its protection. And so Elizabeth's London became the London of Jonson, Marlowe and Shakespeare.

William Shakespeare (1564–1616) was born in Stratford-upon-Avon and came to London in 1590, where he joined the Lord Chamberlain's Men as actor and playwright. In 1598 he became one of the landlords of the newly-erected Globe Theatre on Bankside.

Thomas Platter from Basel attended a performance of Shakespeare's *Julius Caesar* in 1599:

AFTER DINNER ON the 21st of September, at about two o'clock, I went with my companions over the water, and in the strewn roof-house saw the tragedy of the first Emperor Julius with at least fifteen characters very well acted. At the end of the comedy they danced according to their custom with extreme elegance. Two in men's clothes and two in women's gave this performance, in wonderful combination with each other. On another occasion, I also saw after dinner a comedy, not far from our inn, in the suburb; if I remember right, in Bishopsgate. Here they represented various nations, with whom on each occasion an Englishman fought for his daughter, and overcame them all except the German, who won the daughter in fight. He then sat down with him, and gave him and his servant strong drink, so that they both got drunk, and the servant threw his shoe at his master's head and they both fell asleep. Meanwhile the Englishman went into the tent, robbed the German of his gains, and thus he outwitted the German also. At the end they danced very elegantly both in English and in Irish fashion. And thus every day at two o'clock in the afternoon in the city of London two and sometimes three comedies are performed, at separate places, wherewith folk make merry together, and whichever does best gets the greatest audience. The places are so built, that they play on a raised platform, and every one can well see it all. There are, however, separate galleries and there one stands more comfortably and moreover can sit, but one pays more for it. Thus anyone who remains on the level standing pays only one English penny: but if he wants to sit, he is let in at a further door, and there he gives another penny. If he desires to sit on a cushion in the most comfortable place of all, where he not only sees everything well, but can also be seen, then he gives yet another English penny at another door. And in the pauses of the comedy food and drink are carried round amongst the people, and one can thus refresh himself at his own cost.

The comedians are most expensively and elegantly apparelled, since it is customary in England, when distinguished gentlemen or knights die, for nearly the finest of their clothes to be made over and given to their servants, and as it is not proper for them to wear such clothes but only to imitate them, they give them to the comedians to purchase for a small sum.

What they can thus produce daily by way of mirth in the comedies, every one knows well, who has happened to see them acting or playing ...

With such and many other pastimes besides the English spend their time; in the comedies they learn what is going on in other lands, and this happens without alarm, husband and wife together in a familiar place, since for the most part the English do not much use to travel, but are content ever to learn of foreign matters at home, and ever to take their pastime.

The Globe burnt down on 29 June 1613 during a performance of the Bard's *Henry VIII*; Sir Henry Wotton was there:

NOW TO LET matters of state sleep, I will entertain you at the present with what has happened this week at the Bank's side. The King's players had a new play, called *All is True*, representing some principal pieces of the reign of Henry VIII, which was set forth with many extraordinary circumstances of pomp and majesty, even to the matting of the stage; the Knights of the Order with their Georges and garters, the Guards with their embroidered coats, and the like: sufficient in truth within a while to make greatness very familiar, if not ridiculous. Now, King Henry making a masque at the Cardinal Wolsey's house, and certain chambers being shot off at his entry, some of the paper, or other stuff, wherewith one of them was stopped, did light on the thatch, where being thought at first but an idle smoke, and their eyes more attentive to the show, it kindled inwardly, and ran round like a train, consuming within less than an hour the whole house to the very grounds. This was the fatal period of that virtuous fabric, wherein yet nothing did perish but wood and straw, and a few forsaken cloaks; only one man had his breeches set on fire, that would perhaps have broiled him, if he had not by the benefit of a provident wit put it out with bottle ale.

The Globe was rebuilt almost immediately and stood until the Puritan Commonwealth, when all London's theatres were closed down.

Queen Elizabeth at Greenwich, c. 1596
Paul Hentzner

Hentzner was a German visitor to London.

ELIZABETH, THE REIGNING Queen of England, was born at the royal palace of Greenwich, and here she generally resides, particularly in summer, for the delightfulness of its situation. We were admitted by an order, which Mr Rogers had procured from the Lord Chamberlain, into the presence-chamber hung with rich tapestry, and the floor, after the English fashion, strewed with hay, through which the Queen commonly passes on her way to chapel. At the door stood a gentleman dressed in velvet, with a gold chain, whose office was to introduce to the Queen any person of distinction that came to wait on her. It was Sunday, when there is usually the greatest attendance of nobility. In the same hall were the Archbishop of Canterbury, the Bishop of London, a great number of counsellors of state, officers of the crown, and gentlemen, who waited the Queen's coming out, which she did from her own apartment when it was time to go to prayers, attended in the following manner:–

First went gentlemen, barons, earls, knights of the Garter, all richly dressed and bareheaded; next came the Lord High Chancellor of England, bearing the seals in a red silk purse, between two, one of whom carried the royal sceptre, the other the sword of state in a red scabbard, studded with golden fleur-de-lis, the point upwards; next came the Queen, in the 65th year of her age (as we were told), very majestic; her face oblong, fair but wrinkled; her eyes small, yet black and pleasant; her nose a little hooked, her lips narrow, and her teeth black (a defect the English seem subject to, from their too great use of sugar); she had in her ears two pearls with very rich drops; her hair was of an auburn colour, but false; upon her head she had a small crown, reported to be made of some of the gold of the celebrated Luneburg table; her bosom was uncovered, as all the English ladies have it till they marry; and she had on a necklace of exceeding fine jewels; her hands were slender, her fingers rather long, and her stature neither tall nor low; her air was stately, her manner of speaking mild and obliging. That day she was dressed in white silk, bordered with pearls of the size of beans, and over it a mantle of black silk shot with silver threads; her train was very long, the end of it borne by a marchioness; instead of a chain, she had an oblong collar of gold and jewels. As she went along in all this state and magnificence, she spoke very graciously, first to one, then to another (whether foreign ministers, or those who attend for different reasons), in English, French and Italian; for besides being well skilled in Greek, Latin and the languages I have mentioned, she is mistress of Spanish, Scotch and Dutch. Whoever speaks to her, it is kneeling; now and then she raises some with her hand. While we were there, William Slawata, a Bohemian baron, had letters to present to her; and she, after pulling off her glove, gave him her right hand to kiss, sparkling with rings and jewels – a mark of particular favour. Wherever she turned her face as she was going along, everybody fell down on their knees. The ladies of the court followed next to her, very handsome and well-shaped, and for the most part dressed in white. She was guarded on each side by the gentlemen pensioners, fifty in number, with gilt halberds. In the ante-chapel, next the hall where we were, petitions were presented to her, and she received them most graciously, which occasioned the acclamation of *God save the Queue Elizabeth!* She answered it with *I thancke you myn good peupel.* In the chapel was excellent music; as soon as it and the service were over, which scarcely exceeded half-an-hour, the Queen returned in the same state and order, and prepared to go to dinner. But while she was still at prayers, we saw her table set out with the following solemnity:–

A gentleman entered the room bearing a rod, and along with him another who had a table-cloth, which after they had both knelt three times, with the utmost veneration, he spread upon the table, and after kneeling again they both retired. Then came two others, one with the rod again, the other with a salt-cellar, a plate and bread; when they had knelt as the others had done, and placed what was brought upon the table, they too retired with the same ceremonies performed by the first. At last came an unmarried lady of extraordinary beauty (we were told that she was a countess) and along with her a married one, bearing a tasting-knife; the former was dressed in white silk, who, when she had prostrated herself three times, in the most graceful manner, approached the table and rubbed the plates with bread and salt with as much awe as if the Queen had been present. When they had waited there a little while, the yeomen of the guard entered, bareheaded, clothed in scarlet, with a golden rose upon their backs, bringing in at each turn a course of twenty-four dishes, served in silver, most of it gilt; these dishes were received by a gentleman in the same order as they were brought and placed upon the table, while the lady-taster gave to each of the guard a mouthful to eat of the particular dish he had brought, for fear of any poison. During the time that this guard, which consists of the tallest and stoutest men that can be found in all England, 100 in number, being carefully selected for this service, were bringing dinner, twelve trumpets and two kettle-drums made the hall ring for half-an-hour together. At the end of all this ceremonial, a number of unmarried ladies appeared, who with particular solemnity lifted the meat off the table, and conveyed it into the Queen's inner and more private chamber, where after she had chosen for herself, the rest goes to the ladies of the court. The Queen dines and sups alone with very few attendants; and it is very seldom that any body, foreigner or native, is admitted at that time, and then only at the intercession of some distinguished personage.

~~~

The Torturing of a Jesuit Priest in the Tower of London, April 1597
Father John Gerard

Gerard was a Jesuit priest; in Elizabeth's England, Roman Catholics, due to their allegiance to Rome, were more than religious dissidents – they were enemies of the state.

O N THE THIRD day the warder came to my room straight from his dinner. Looking sorry for himself, he said the Lords Commissioners had arrived with the Queen's Attorney-General and that I had to go down to them at once.

'I am ready,' I said, 'but just let me say an *Our Father* and *Hail Mary* downstairs.'

He let me go, and then we went off together to the Lieutenant's lodgings inside the walls of the Tower. Five men were there waiting for me, none of whom, except Wade, had examined me before. He was there to direct the charges against me ...

'You say,' said the Attorney-General, 'you have no wish to obstruct the Government. Tell us, then, where Father Garnet is. He is an enemy of the state, and you are bound to report on all such men.'

'He isn't an enemy of the state,' I said ... 'But I don't know where he lives, and if I did, I would not tell you.'

'Then we'll see to it that you tell us before we leave this place.'

'Please God you won't,' I answered.

Then they produced a warrant for putting me to torture. They had it ready by them and handed it to me to read. (In this prison a special warrant is required for torture.)

I saw the warrant was properly made out and signed, and then I answered: 'With God's help I shall never do anything which is unjust or act against my conscience or the Catholic faith. You have me in your power. You can do with me what God allows you to do – more you cannot do.'

Then they began to implore me not to force them to take steps they were loath to take. They said they would have to put me to torture every day, as long as my life lasted, until I gave them the information they wanted.

'I trust in God's goodness,' I answered, 'that He will prevent me from ever committing a sin such as this – the sin of accusing innocent people. We are all in God's hands and therefore I have no fear of anything you can do to me.'

This was the sense of my answers, as far as I can recall them now.

We went to the torture-room in a kind of solemn procession the attendants walking ahead with lighted candles.

The chamber was underground and dark, particularly near the entrance. It was a vast place and every device and instrument of human torture was there. They pointed out some of them to me and said I would try them all. Then they asked me again whether I would confess.

'I cannot,' I said.

I fell on my knees for a moment's prayer. Then they took me to a big upright pillar, one of the wooden posts which held the roof of this huge underground chamber. Driven into the top of it were iron staples for supporting heavy weights. Then they put my wrists into iron gauntlets and ordered me to climb two or three wicker steps. My arms were then lifted up and an iron bar was passed through the rings of one gauntlet, then through the staple and rings of the second gauntlet. This done, they fastened the bar with a pin to prevent it slipping, and then, removing the wicker steps one by one from under my feet, they left me hanging by my hands and arms fastened above my head. The tips of my toes, however, still touched the ground, and they had to dig away the earth from under them. They had hung me up from the highest staple in the pillar and could not raise me any higher, without driving in another staple.

Hanging like this I began to pray. The gentlemen standing around asked me whether I was willing to confess now.

'I cannot and I will not,' I answered.

But I could hardly utter the words, such a gripping pain came over me. It was worst in my chest and belly, my hands and arms. All the blood in my body seemed to rush up into my arms and hands and I thought that blood was oozing from the ends of my fingers and the pores of my skin. But it was only a sensation caused by my flesh swelling above the irons holding them. The pain was so intense that I thought I could not possibly endure it, and added to it, I had an interior temptation. Yet I did not feel any inclination or wish to give them the information they wanted. The Lord saw my weakness with the eyes of His mercy, and did not permit me to be tempted beyond my strength. With the temptation He sent me relief. Seeing my agony and the struggle going on in my mind, He gave me this most merciful thought: the utmost and worst they can do is to kill you, and you have often wanted to give your life for your Lord God. The Lord God sees all you are enduring – He can do all things. You are in God's keeping. With these thoughts, God in His infinite goodness and mercy gave me the grace of resignation, and with a desire to die and a hope (I admit) that I would, I offered Him myself to do with me as He wished. From that moment the conflict in my soul ceased, and even the physical pain seemed much more bearable than before, though it must, in fact, I am sure, have been greater with the growing strain and weariness of my body . . .

Sometime after one o'clock, I think, I fell into a faint. How long I was unconscious I don't know, but I think it was long, for the men held my body up or put the wicker steps under my feet until I came to. Then they heard me pray and immediately let me down again. And they did this every time I fainted – eight or nine times that day – before it struck five . . .

A little later they took me down. My legs and feet were not damaged, but it was a great effort to stand upright . . .

❧ ❧ ❧

The Diary of a Tourist, 5 July 1598
Baron Waldstein

Waldstein was a Moravian aristocrat who travelled widely in sixteenth-century Europe. The population of London at the time of the baron's visit was between 150,000 and 200,000.

WE THEN WENT on into the nearby palace, the royal residence known as Whitehall, i.e. the White Hall. It is truly majestic, bounded on the one side by a park which adjoins another palace which is called St. James's, and on the other side by the Thames, and it is a place which fills one with wonder, not so much because of its great size as because of the magnificence of its bed-chambers and living rooms which are furnished with the most gorgeous splendour.

First you come to a vast hall which leads through into a very large walled garden where they keep deer and all kinds of other animals. We then went to see the rooms, every one of them furnished and arranged with perfect taste and elegance, with all sorts of statues and pictures to add to their beauty. There is a bust of Attila, King of the Huns, and a circular table made of some foreign wood decorated in gold. There is a picture of a cripple being carried on a blind man's shoulders with the lines:

> *Loripedem sublatum humeris fert lumine captus*
> *Et socii haec oculis munera retribuit,*
> *Quo caret alteruter concors hic praestat uterque*
> *Mutuat hic oculos, mutuat ille pedes.*
> *Mutuum auxilium.*

There is the meeting of the Emperor Maximilian I and Henry VIII near Tournai and Therouanne; King Henry VIII's entry into – and his magnificent display at – Boulogne when he had made preparations to receive the King of France there, done in two pictures; a portrait of Edward VI in 1546 at the age of nine – note the artist's ingenuity in perspective; a map of Boulogne; an extremely well-painted portrait of that Earl of Mountjoy who has just been sent to Ireland; the Papal battle in which King Francis I of France was taken prisoner by the army of Charles V in 1524; the battle of Maximilian I and Pope Julius II with Louis XII of France before Ravenna on Easter Day 1512, where 23 thousand men lost their lives; and a genealogical table of the Kings of England. There is a large looking-glass with a silk cover; a most beautifully painted picture on glass showing 36 incidents of Christ's Passion; a portrait of a woman, a goldsmith's wife, of such loveliness that she is said to have been Henry VIII's mistress. Portraits of Henry VIII King of England, Louis XII King of France, Richard II, Elizabeth Queen of Transylvania, widow of Charles XII of France, Julius Caesar, and Charles Duke of Burgundy. There are three globes; there is a ship made of gold and silver, which has its awning woven of pure silk and gold thread.

Another room has a picture of the battle against the Saracens in Piedmont, and the siege of Malta. There are also some very rich hangings.

A portrait here shows Queen Elizabeth when she was still young, in the dress which she wore when going to attend Parliament; there is a sundial in the form of an elephant; and an organ (in their language they call it 'an instrument') made of mother-of-pearl with the following verses inscribed on it:

Anglica nunc plantas, plantas et Hibernia proles
Orphei variis organa tange modis.

Reginae laudes celeres modo ferto per aures,
Subvertit nostras altra Maria lues.

One of the paintings is a very lifelike representation of plums, cherries, pears, and similar kinds of fruit. There is also a rectangular table with a marble sphere on it.

In one very fine gallery or dining-hall can be seen: a mother-of-pearl bookrest; a sundial in the form of a monkey; portraits of the Prince of Orange, of Elizabeth the daughter of King Henry II of France who married King Philip of Spain, of Mary Queen of Hungary and Regent of Belgium. In addition to these are: the Duke of Savoy with his wife, his son Philibert Emmanuel, Charles V and his Queen, a painting of the story of Scaevola before Porsena King of the Etruscans, and Edward VI at the age of twelve, with the verses:

Parvule patrissa patriae virtutis et Heros
Esto, nihil majus maximus orbis habet.
Gnatum vix possunt coelum et natura dedisse
Huius quem patris victus honoris honos.
Aequato tantum tanti tu facta parentis
Vota hominum vix quo progrediantur habent.
Vincito vicisti quot reges priscus adorat
Orbis, nec te: qui vincere possit erit.

There are maps of the Duchy of Parma, and also of Britain, both done in needlework: and a picture which shows Juno, Pallas Athene, and Venus, together with Queen Elizabeth. Beneath it are the lines:

Juno potens sceptris, et mentis acumine Pallas
Et roseo Veneris fulget in ore decus:
Adfuit ELISABETH, Juno perculsa refugit,
Obstupuit Pallas, erubuitque Venus.

In this same room see the Description of the New World on two boards with maps of the same parts of the New World alongside, printed in the reign of King Henry VII of England. There is also a diagram like an astrolabe which calculates the rising and setting of the sun. See also another board hanging here on which one can read the following story:

A certain king, seeing a revolution taking place in the kingdom, called in some Philosophers to discover the reason for this revolution. After hearing them he commanded that their opinions should, each one of them, be inscribed upon the City Gate.

The first Philosopher said:

$$
\left.\begin{array}{l}\text{Might}\\\text{Day}\\\text{Flight}\end{array}\right\}\text{is}\left\{\begin{array}{l}\text{Right}\\\text{Night}\\\text{Fight}\end{array}\right\}\text{therefore}\left\{\begin{array}{l}\text{the Realm}\\\text{the Land}\\\text{the Realm}\end{array}\right\}\text{is without}\left\{\begin{array}{l}\text{Law}\\\text{a Path}\\\text{Hounour}\end{array}\right.
$$

The second Philosopher said:

$$
\left.\begin{array}{l}\text{One}\\\text{Friend}\\\text{Evil}\end{array}\right\}\text{is}\left\{\begin{array}{l}\text{Two}\\\text{Foe}\\\text{Good}\end{array}\right\}\text{therefore}\left\{\begin{array}{l}\text{the Realm}\\\text{the Realm}\\\text{the Land}\end{array}\right\}\text{is without}\left\{\begin{array}{l}\text{Truth}\\\text{Trust}\\\text{Reverence}\end{array}\right.
$$

The third philosopher said:

$$
\left.\begin{array}{l}\text{Opinion permits licentiousness}\\\\\text{The tax collector is dishonest}\\\\\text{The jackdaw is an eagle}\end{array}\right\}\text{therefore}\left\{\begin{array}{l}\text{the Realm desires anarchy}\\\\\text{the Land is poverty-stricken}\\\\\text{there is no wisdom in the country}\end{array}\right.
$$

The fourth Philosopher said:

$$\left.\begin{array}{l}\text{Caprice}\\\text{Money}\\\text{God}\end{array}\right\} \text{is} \left\{\begin{array}{l}\text{Counsellor}\\\text{Judge}\\\text{Dead}\end{array}\right\} \text{therefore} \left\{\begin{array}{l}\text{the Land is ill-governed}\\\text{the Land is ill-guided}\\\text{the Realm abounds in evils}\end{array}\right.$$

Somewhere else was written, 'There are three things which destroy the sovereignty of Rome: Hidden Hatred, Youthful Counsel, Self-Interest.'

In another place we saw a sunshade of the Queen's, made of silver and of silk, and also the Queen's couch which is woven with gold and silver thread; the same place has gorgeous mother-of-pearl caskets covered with pure silk, the Queen's chair with silken cushions, and a number of other fine cushions on the couch. The Queen's bed-chamber has rich tapestries all around: The adjoining room is reserved for the Queen's bath: the water pours from oyster shells and different kinds of rock. In the next room there is an organ on which two persons can play duets, also a large chest completely covered in pure silk, and a clock which plays tunes by striking on bells.

The next room to this was the one where the Queen keeps her books, some of which she wrote herself. Among them there was one which she dedicated to her father as follows:

A treshault et trespuissant et redouble Prince Henry 8 de ce nom Roy l'Angleterre, de France, et d'Irlande, defenseur de la foy, Elisabeth sa tres humble fille, rend salut et devot obedience.

The title-page of another book reads:

Colloque tres familier entre deux personnages c'est a sçavoir Aulus et Barbatus diviser ensemble des articles de nostre foy Chrestienne, extraict des oeuvres d'Erasmi de Roterodam.

We also saw here some prayers of Queen Catherine (the mother of Mary) which had been translated from English into Latin by Elizabeth.

On leaving here we came to a long majestic gallery where various knights have their shields displayed, painted with their devices. [...]

From here we were taken into a large and lofty banqueting hall which the Queen suddenly arranged to be put up within 20 days when she was expecting the visit of a prince of France.

In another room Henry VII and VIII and their wives are painted. With the marriage of Henry VIII [i.e. Henry VII] to Elizabeth of York the two roses, i.e. the red and the white, are said to have grown together, for it was the King's purpose that in this marriage the struggles between the families of Lancaster and of York should come to an end. The following lines can be read here:

> *Si iuvat Heroum claras vidisse figuras,*
> *Specta has: maiores nulla tabella tulit.*
> *Certamen magnum, lis, quaestio magna: paterne*
> *Filius an vincat, vicit uterque quidem?*
> *Ipse suos hostes patriaeque incendia soepe*
> *Sustulit, et pacem civibus usque dedit;*
> *Filius ad maiora quidem prognatus, ab aulis*
> *Submovet indignos, sustituitque probos.*
> *Certe virtuti Paparum audacia cessit,*
> *Henrico octavo sceptra gerente manu.*
> *Reddita relligio est isto regnante, DElque*
> *Dogmata ceperunt esse in honore suo.*

Here too they show the rock where a hermit used to live, divided into cells for him.

In another room there is a picture of a woman of Greek

origin whom a London procurer brought from Greece, and who is still living. There is also a picture of the battle between Charles V and the Protestants, and a further room has a portrait of Anthony of Francktrue, whose bones are preserved at Helmstadt. There are some fine Indian beds of white and multi-coloured silk, and also a collection of small boxes and caskets made of tortoise shell.

There is a view from the window here of a most lovely garden: it has a number of pillars with figures of animals on them; in the centre is a fountain, and water from it, squirting up through concealed pipes, soaks people standing near. Beyond the grounds of this royal residence there is another palace; it contains a rib bone from a most enormous whale which is well worth seeing.

Among the other sights on the tourist trail followed by Waldstein were the Tower of London, St Paul's Cathedral, the Royal Exchange and Lambeth Palace. He was also much taken with London Bridge: '. . . an amazingly skilful construction of solid stonework with 19 arches; it has extremely fine buildings all along it like a street . . . fixed to one of them can still be seen the heads of a number of earls and other noblemen who have been executed for treason.'

The Gunpowder Plot, 5 November 1605
Sir Edward Hoby

Elizabeth I, 'Gloriana', died on 24 March 1603 and was succeeded by James VI of Scotland, who sat on the English throne as James I.

His brazen homosexuality, his profligacy, his coarseness ('his fingers ever ... fiddling about his cod-piece', observed one courtier) disgusted many of his new subjects. The Catholics, who might have been sympathetic to his claim to the divine right to rule, loathed James for retaining the penal laws against them.

The Gunpowder Plot was a Catholic conspiracy to blow up James and Parliament. A warning given to Lord Monteagle foiled the plot and led to the arrest of the plotters.

O N THE 5TH of November we began our Parliament, to which the King should have come in person, but refrained, through a practice but that morning discovered. The plot was to have blown up the King at such time as he should have been set in his royal throne, accompanied by his children, Nobility and Commons and ... with all Bishops, Judges and Doctors, at one instant and blast to have ruined the whole estate and kingdom of England. And for the effecting of this there was placed under the Parliament house, where the king should sit, some 30 barrels of gunpowder, with great store of wood, faggots and bars of iron ...

... In a vault under the parliament chamber before spoken of one Johnson was found with one of these close lanterns preparing the train against the next morrow, who, being after brought into the galleries of the court, and there demanded if he were not sorry for his so foul and heinous a treason, answered that he was sorry for nothing but that the act was not performed. Being replied unto him that no doubt there had been a number in that place of his own religion, how in conscience he could do them hurt, he answered a few might well perish to have the rest taken away. Others telling him that he should die a worse death than he that killed the Prince of Orange, he answered that he could bear it as well; and oftentimes repeated that he should have merited pardon if he had performed it ...

When he was brought into the King's presence, the King asked him how he could conspire so hideous a treason against his children and so many innocent souls which never offended him? He answered that it was true, but a dangerous disease required a desperate remedy. He told some of the Scots that his intent was to have blown them back into Scotland.

The Attempted Arrest of the Five Members, 4 January 1642

John Rushworth

The reign of Charles I, which began in 1625, was dominated by constitutional, religious and fiscal struggles between Crown and Parliament. London sided with the latter. The Stuarts, after all, disenchanted nearly every section of the city's populace: their madcap money schemes alienated city merchants and put the merchants' employees out of work; the Stuarts' taste for autocracy ran headlong into London's advances towards local democracy (by the 1640s, the city could boast of having over 3,000 elected officials); the Stuarts crypto-Catholicism was anathema to the 'godly' Puritans, who made up a loud and articulate minority in the city.

In 1641 anti-Stuart sentiment spilled on to the streets, whipped up by Puritan preachers and masters. Gangs of unemployed mariners marched around Whitehall shouting abuse against the royal family, apprentices opposed to episcopalism rampaged through Westminster Abbey. Meanwhile, the parish churches in the capital were cleansed of popish influences. Nehemiah Wallington, a God-fearing Puritan turner, was ecstatic:

*O*N THE BEGINNING of October, 1641, at Leonard's, Eastcheap, being our church, the idol in the wall was cut down, and the superstitious pictures in the glass was [sic] broken in pieces, and the superstitious things and prayers for the dead in brass were picked up. Broken, and the picture of the Virgin Mary on the branches of candlesticks was broken. And some of those pieces of broken glass I have, to keep for a remembrance to show to the generation to come what God hath done for us, to give us such a reformation that our forefathers never saw the like; His name ever have the praise!

Despite the whiff of revolution in the air Charles I believed that the city would support him when he launched a coup against Parliament by seeking the arrest of five dissident MPs. John Rushworth was secretary to the House of Commons.

... THE SAID five accused Members this day *after dinner* came into the House, and did appear according to the special Order and Injunction of the House laid upon them yesterday, to give their attendance upon the House, *de die in diem* and their appearance was entred in the Journal.

They were no sooner sate in their places, but the House was informed by one Captain *Langrish*, lately an Officer in Arms in *France*, that he came from among the Officers, and souldiers at *White Hall*, and understanding by them, that his Majesty was coming with a Guard of Military Men, Commanders and Souldiers, to the House of Commons, he passed by them with some difficulty to get to the House before them, and sent in word how near the said Officers and Souldiers were come; Whereupon a certain Member of the House having also private Intimation from the Countess of *Carlile*, Sister to the Earl of *Northumberland*, that endeavours would be used this day to apprehend the five Members, the House required the five Members to depart the House forthwith, to the end to avoid Combustion in the House, if the said Souldiers should use Violence to pull any of them out. To which Command of the House, four of the said Members yielded ready Obedience, but Mr. *Stroud* was obstinate, till Sir *Walter Earle* (his ancient acquaintance) pulled him out by force, the King being at that time entring into the *New Pallace-yard*, in *Westminster*. And as his Majesty came through *Westminster Hall*, the Commanders, Reformadoes, &c. that attended him, made a Lane on both sides the Hall (through which his Majesty passed and came up the Stairs to the House of Commons) and stood before the Guard of Pentioners, and Halberteers, (who also attended the King Person,) and the door of the House of Commons being thrown open, his Majesty entred the House, and as he passed up towards *the Chair* he cast his eye on the Right-hand near the Bar of the House, where Mr. *Pym* used to sit, but his Majesty not seeing him there (knowing him well) went up to the Chair, and said, 'By your leave, (Mr. Speaker) I must borrow your Chair a little,' whereupon the Speaker came out of the Chair, and his Majesty stept up into it, after he had stood in the Chair a while, casting his Eye upon the Members as they stood up *uncovered*, but could not discern any of the five Members to be there, nor indeed were they easie to be discerned (had they been there) among so many bare Faces all standing up together.

Then his Majesty made this Speech,

'Gentlemen,

I Am sorry for this occasion of coming unto you: Yesterday I sent a Serjeant at Arms upon a very Important occasion to apprehend some that by my command were accused of High Treason, whereunto I did expect Obedience and not a Message. And I must declare unto you here, that albeit, no King that ever was in *England*, shall be more careful of your Priviledges, to maintain them to the uttermost of his power then I shall be; yet you must know that in Cases of Treason, no person hath a priviledge. And therefore I am come to know if any of these persons that were accused are here: For I must tell you Gentlemen, that so long as these persons that I have accused (for no slight Crime but for Treason) are here, I cannot expect that this House will be in the Right way that I do heartily wish it: Therefore I am come to tell you that I must have them wheresoever I find them. Well since I see all the Birds are Flown, I do expect from you, that you shall send them unto me, as soon as they return hither. But I assure you, in the word of a King, I never did intend any Force, but shall proceed against them in a legal and fair way, for I never meant any other.

And now since I see I cannot do what I came for, I think this no unfit occasion to repeat what I have said formerly, That whatsoever I have done in favour, and to the good of my Subjects, I do mean to maintain it.

I will trouble you no more, but tell you I do expect as soon as they come to the House, you will send them to me; otherwise I must take my own Course to find them.'

When the King was looking about the House, the Speaker standing below by the Chair, his Majesty ask'd him, whether any of these persons were in the House? Whether he saw any of them? and where they were? To which the Speaker falling on his Knee, thus Answered.

'*May it please your Majesty,* I Have neither Eyes to see, nor Tongue to speak in this place, but as the House is pleased to direct me, whose Servant I am here, and humbly beg your Majesties Pardon, that I cannot give any other Answer than this, to what your Majesty is pleased to demand of me.'

The King having Concluded his Speech, went out of the House again which was in great disorder, and many Members cried out, aloud so as he might hear them, 'Priviledge! Priviledge!' and forthwith Adjourned till the next Day at One of the Clock . . .

The five members took refuge in the Puritan stronghold of Coleman Street. When Charles entered the city to demand that the five MPs be handed over he was greeted by throngs of citizens shouting 'Privilege of Parliament! Privilege of Parliament!' Fearing for the safety of himself and his family, Charles left London by coach on 10 January.

Over the next weeks royal power in the city was extinguished. Pro-Parliamentarians seized control of the Common Council and the Trained Bands, the city's militia. The right of the aldermen to veto Common Council decisions was abolished. In August 1642 the royalist Lord Mayor, Gurney, was thrown in the Tower. The citizens of London armed themselves for war.

They were sensible to so do, for on 22 August 1642 Charles raised his standard at Nottingham, effectively declaring war on his own country – especially its rebellious capital.

London, it might be said, won the Civil War for Parliament. It was the City's coffers that paid for Parliament's army, it was the city's streets and churches which provided that army's staunchest, most militant soldiers. The mere sight of the City's Trained Bands massed at Turnham Green on 13 November 1642 was enough to cause Charles to abandon a march on the capital, while the expedition by 'London's Brave Boys' to raise the siege of Gloucester in 1643 turned the course of war.

Furious at the loss of Gloucester, the Royalists tore into the Londoners as they made their way homewards.

The Battle of Newbury: Sergeant Henry Foster in Action, 20 September 1643

Sergeant Henry Foster, Red Regiment of the Trained Bands of the City of London

THE NEXT MORNING, September 20, very early before day, we had drawn up all our army in their several regiments and marched away by break of day; and then advancing towards the enemy with most cheerful and courageous spirits. The Lord Robartes' soldiers had begun to skirmish with them before we came up to the enemy; which we hearing, put us to a running march till we sweat again, hastening to their relief and succour.

When we were come up into the field, our two regiments of the trained bands were placed in open campania [level country] upon the right wing of the whole army. The enemy had there planted eight pieces of ordnance, and stood in a great body of horse and foot, we being placed right opposite against them and far less than twice musket shot distance from them. They began their battery against us with their great guns, above half an hour before we could get any of our guns up to us. Our gunners dealt very ill with us, delaying to come up to us. Our noble Colonel Tucker fired one piece of ordnance against the enemy, and aiming to give fire the second time was shot in the head with a cannon bullet from the enemy. The Blue regiment of the trained bands stood upon our right wing, and behaved themselves most gallantly. Two regiments of the King's horse which stood upon their right flank afar off, came fiercely upon them and charged them two or three times, but were beat back with their musketeers, who gave them a most desperate charge and made them fly.

This day our whole army wore green boughs in their hats to distinguish us from our enemies; which they perceiving one regiment of their horse had got green boughs and rid up to our regiments crying, 'Friends! friends!' but we let fly at them and made many of them and their horses tumble, making them fly with a vengeance. The enemy's cannon did play most against the Red regiment of trained bands; they did some execution amongst us at the first, and were somewhat dreadful when men's bowels and brains flew in our faces. But blessed be God that gave us courage, so that we kept our ground and after a while feared them not. Our ordnance did very good execution upon them, for we stood at so near a distance upon a plain field that we could not lightly miss one another. We were not much above half our regiments in this place; for we had sixty files of musketeers drawn off for the forlorn hope, who were engaged against the enemy in the field upon our left flank.

Where most of the regiments of the army were in fight they had some small shelter of the hedges and banks, yet had a very hot fight with the enemy and did good execution, and stood to it as bravely as ever men did. When our two regiments of the trained bands had thus played against the enemy for the space of three hours, or thereabouts, our Red regiment joined to the Blue which stood a little distance from us upon our left flank, where we gained the advantage of a little hill, which we maintained against the enemy half an hour. Two regiments of the enemy's foot fought against us all this while to gain the hill, but could not. Then two regiments of the enemy's horse, which stood upon our right flank, came fiercely upon us and so surrounded us that we were forced to charge upon them in the front and rear, and both flanks, which was performed by us with a great deal of courage and undauntedness of spirit, insomuch that we made a great slaughter among them and forced them to retreat. But presently the two regiments of the enemy's foot in this time gained the hill, and came upon us before we could well recover ourselves, that we were glad to retreat a little way into the field, till we had rallied up our men and put them into their former posture, and then came on again.

If I should speak any thing in the praise and high commendations of these two regiments of the trained bands, I should rather obscure and darken the glory of that courage and valour God gave unto them this day. They stood like so many stakes against the shot of the cannon, quitting themselves like men of undaunted spirits, even our enemies themselves being judges. It might be expected that something should be spoken of the noble and valiant service performed by the rest of the regiments of the army both horse and foot; but their courage and valour itself speaks, which was performed by them that day, our men fighting like lions in every place, the great slaughter made amongst the enemies testifies.

My noble and valiant Captain George Massie, who was with the forlorn hope, received a shot in the back from the enemy, of which wound he is since dead. This 20 September we lost about sixty or seventy men in our Red regiment of the trained bands, besides wounded men, we having the hottest charge from the enemy's cannon of any regiment in the army. Also that worthy and valiant gentleman Captain Hunt was slain in this battle, whose death is much lamented. These two poor regiments were the very objects of the enemy's battery that day and they have since made their boast of it. It is conjectured by most, that the enemy lost four for one. Seventy chief commanders were slain on their side. This is most certain, that they did acknowledge themselves to be beaten. It is credibly informed by those that were this day in the King's army, that the King himself brought up a regiment of foot and another of horse into the field, and gave fire to two pieces of ordnance, riding up and down all that day in a soldier's grey coat.

The next day I viewed the dead bodies. There lay about one hundred stripped naked in that field where our two regiments stood in battalia. This night the enemy conveyed away about thirty cart loads of maimed and dead men, as the town-people credibly reported to us, and I think they might have carried away twenty cart loads more of their dead men the next morning. They buried thirty in one pit. Fourteen lay dead in one ditch. This battle continued long. It begun about six o'clock in the morning and continued till past twelve o'clock at night. In the night the enemy retreated to the town of Newbury and drew away all their ordnance. We were in great distress for water or any accommodation to refresh our poor soldiers, yet the Lord himself sustained us that we did not faint under it. We were right glad to drink in the same water where our horses did drink, wandering up and down to seek for it. Our word this day was 'Religion', their's was 'Queen Mary' in the field.

After beating off the Royalist assault, the Trained Bands marched home to a heroes' welcome. Foster recalled:

THE LORD MAYOR together with the aldermen of the City met us at Temple-bar and entertained us joyfully, many thousands bidding us welcome home and blessing God for our safe return. Thus God that called forth to do his work brought us through many straits, delivered us from the rage and insolency of our adversaries, made them turn their backs with shame, giving us victory, and causing us to return home joyfully.

❧ ❧ ❧

The Execution of Charles I, 30 January 1649
Philip Henry

Defeated in the Civil War in 1646 Charles I surrendered to
Parliament, only to spend the next two years scheming to get
his crown back. Another round of civil war followed, which saw
Charles Stuart once again beaten. This time Parliament's army
demanded the royal head. Philip Henry, an undergraduate at
Oxford, was on leave in London at the time of the execution of
the king at Whitehall.

A T THE LATER end of the year 1648 I had leave to
goe to london to see my Father, & during my stay
there at that time at Whitehal it was that I saw the
Beheading of King Charles the first; He went by our door on
Foot each day that hee was carry'd by water to Westminster,
for he took Barge at Gardenstayres where we liv'd & once he
spake to my Father & sayd Art thou alive yet!' On the day of
his execution, which was Tuesday, Jan. 30, I stood amongst the
crowd in the street before Whitehal gate, where the scaffold
was erected, and saw what was done, but was not so near as to
hear any thing. The Blow I saw given, & can truly say with a
sad heart; at the instant whereof, I remember well, there was
such a Grone by the Thousands then present, as I never heard
before & desire I may never hear again. There was according
to Order one Troop immediately marching from-wards
charing-cross to Westm^r & another from-wards Westm^r to

charing-cross purposely to masker the people, & to disperse & scatter them, so that I had much adoe amongst the rest to escape home without hurt.

Interregnal London saw the flowering of an exotic array of political and religious sects, amongst them the Ranters.

Ranters, 1651
John Taylor

I HAVE A RECITALL of the Names and opinions of many wicked and detestable Heretiques, Heresies, and blasphemous wretches, but that I will not hold my Reader in too long and tedious suspence, Therefore I will now proceed to the matter intended, and promised in the Front and Title of this Book.

About the tenth or twelfth of May 1651. there were apprehended and taken in an unlawfull Assembly these persons following

Thomas Kerbye,	*Elizabeth Sorrell*	Widdow,
Thomas Tidford,	*Elizabeth Sorrell*	junior.
Anne Burrell,	*Mary Vanlopp.*	

These were brought before the Eight Worshipful *Laurence Whitaker* Esq; (judiciall Justice of the Peace and Quorum, for

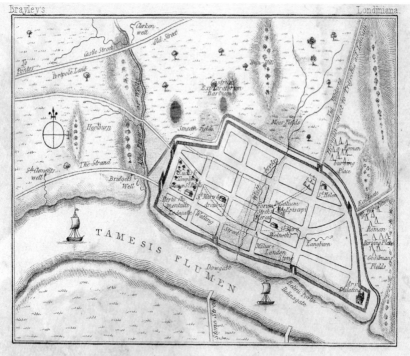

LONDINIUM AUGUSTA.

(above) A map of Londinium. The Roman city extended to 326 acres, and along the grid of straight roads lived as many as 90,000 people.

(left) The first known view of London, printed in 1500 to adorn a book of poems by the Duc d'Orléans, a prisoner of war in the Tower.

(*above*) Watt Tyler, leader of the 1381 Peasants' Revolt, is slain at Smithfield by London Mayor, Sir William Walworth.

(*left*) Sir Richard 'Dick' Whittington, merchant and thrice Mayor of London, pictured with his legendary cat.

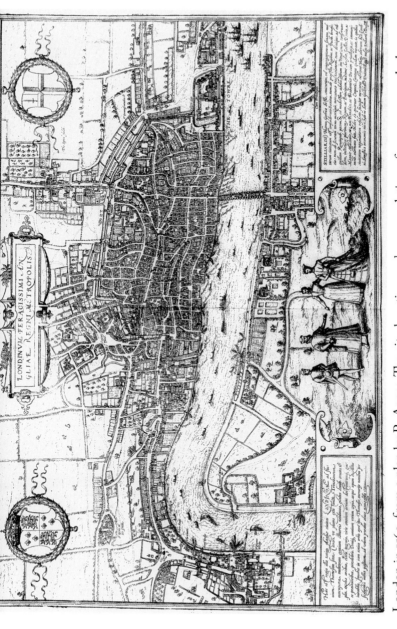

London in 1560, from a plan by R. Aggas. The city, bursting under a population of 200,000 people, has outstripped its Roman bounds to spread into a necklace of suburbs.

(above) The execution of King Charles I, 1649, at Whitehall, then a royal palace. Executions were a favourite entertainment for Londoners for centuries.

(below) The Great Fire of 1666 destroyed 13,000 buildings and was only one of several disasters to engulf Restoration London.

facing page
(top) During the Great Frost of 1683–4 shopping booths were set up on the frozen Thames, which iced over regularly until embankments built in the Victorian era narrowed the river and caused it to run faster.

(bottom) Covent Garden in the early nineteenth century.

(above) St Paul's Cathedral, erected by Sir Christopher Wren as 'an ornament to His majesty's most excellent reign, to the Church of England and to the Great City'.

(above) A London coffee house. London's first coffee house was opened in St Michael's Alley, Cornhill, in 1652.

(right) Hogarth's *Gin Lane* as described on page 211.

The Burning & Plundering of Newgate & Setting the Felons at Liberty by the Mob.

Published 1 July 1780 by Fielding & Walker, Pater-Noster-Row.

(above) The mob storm Newgate Prison during the anti-Catholic riots led by Lord Gordon in 1780.

the County of *Middlesex*) he did examine the said parties, and found their opinions to be so blasphemous, and damnable Heretical, that it amazeth me with horrour to write them, and I am sure it will strike terrour and astonishment into the hearts of any true Christian, either to read or hear it. They are tearmed, or called by the name of *Ranters*, and their Opinions they affirmed to bee as followeth.

They said that they did beleeve that one *John Robins* is God the Father, and Father of our Lord *Jesus Christ*, and that the Childe which is yet unborn and now in the womb of *Joan Robins*, (the wife of the aforesaid *John*) shall bee the Saviour of all those that shall be saved, both in this world and in the world to come; And that *Cain* (who murthered his Brother *Abel*) was the third person in the Trinity. And that all those that do deny it, do deny their own salvation.

They beleeve also that the said *John Robins* had power to raise the dead.

This was all which they acknowledged to be the grounds and principles of their Faith and Religion, for the which detestable and execrable Blasphemies, they were all six committed Prisoners to the Gate-house at *Westminster*, and there they doe remaine till some course of Law and Justice may order them according to their demerits.

✣ ✣ ✣

A Whale in the Thames, 3 June 1658
John Evelyn

John Evelyn was an Admiralty official.

A LARGE WHALE WAS taken betwixt my land butting on the Thames and Greenwich, which drew an infinite concourse to see it, by water, coach and on foot, from London and all parts. It appeared first below Greenwich at low water, for at high water it would have destroyed all the boats, but lying now in shallow water encompassed with boats after a long conflict it was killed with a harping iron (*harpoon*), struck in the head, out of which spouted blood and water by two tunnels, and after an horrid groan it ran quite on shore and died. Its length was fifty-eight foot, height sixteen; black-skinned like coach leather, very small eyes, great tail, only two small fins, a picked (*tapering*) snout, and a mouth so wide that divers men might have stood upright in it; no teeth, but sucked the slime only as through a grate of that bone which we call whalebone; the throat yet so narrow as would not have admitted the least of fishes. The extremes of the cetaceous bones hang downwards from the upper jaw, and was hairy towards the ends and bottom within side: all of it prodigious, but in nothing more wonderful than that an animal of so great a bulk should be nourished only by slime through those grates.

The Restoration: The Arrival of Charles II in London, 29 May 1660

Anonymous

The inability of the Republic to survive without Oliver Cromwell caused the army to invite the Stuarts – in the person of Charles I's eldest son, Charles II – back onto the throne of England. The alternative was anarchy. London itself had tired of the excesses of the Commonwealth – the closing down of the theatres and the banning of the celebration of Christmas being particularly irksome – and of footing the bill for its wars.

At the time of his invitation to take the throne Charles was in exile in the Netherlands. After landing at Dover, he proceeded to London.

O N TUESDAY, MAY the 29th (which happily fell out to be the anniversary of his majesty's birth-day) he set forth of Rochester in his coach; but afterwards took horse on the farther side of Black-heath, on which spacious plain he found divers great and eminent troops of horse, a most splendid and glorious equipage; and a kind of rural triumph, expressed by the country swains, in a Morrice-dance, with the old musick of taber and pipe, which was performed with all agility and chearfulness imaginable ...

In this order proceeding towards London, there were placed in Deptford, on his right hand (as he passed through the town) above an hundred proper maids, clad all alike, in white garments, with scarfs about them; who, having prepared many flaskets covered with fine linnen, and adorned with rich scarfs and ribbands, which flaskets were full of flowers and sweet herbs, strowed the way before him as he rode.

From thence passing on, he came to St. George's Fields in Southwark, where the lord mayor and aldermen of London, in their scarlet, with the recorder, and other city council, waited for him in a large tent, hung with tapestry; in which they had placed a chair of state, with a rich canopy over it. When he came thither, the lord mayor presented him with the city sword, and the recorder made a speech to him; which being done, he alighted, and went into the tent, where a noble banquet was prepared for him ...

In ... magnificent fashion his majesty entered the borough of Southwark, about half an hour past three of the clock in the afternoon; and, within an hour after, the city of London at the Bridge; where he found the windows and streets exceedingly thronged with people to behold him; and the walls adorned with hangings and carpets of tapestry and other costly stuff; and in many places sets of loud musick; all the conduits, as he passed, running claret wine; and the several companies in their liveries, with the ensigns belonging to them; as also the trained bands of the city standing along the streets as he passed, welcoming him with joyful acclamations.

And within the rails where Charing-cross formerly was, a stand of six-hundred pikes, consisting of knights and gentlemen, as had been officers of the armies of his majesty of blessed memory; the truly noble and valiant Sir John Stowell, Knight of the honourable Order of the Bath, a person famous for his eminent actions and sufferings, being in the head of them.

From which place, the citizens, in velvet coats and gold chains, being drawn up on each hand, and divers companies of foot soldiers; his majesty passed betwixt them, and entered White-hall at seven of the clock, the people making loud shouts, and the horse and foot several vollies of shot, at this his happy arrival. Where the house of lords and commons of parliament received him, and kissed his royal hand. At the same time likewise the Reverend Bishops of Ely, Salisbury, Rochester, and Chichester, in their episcopal habits, with divers of the long oppressed orthodox clergy, met in that royal chapel of king Henry the Seventh, at Westminster; there also sung *Te Deum*, &c. in praise and thanks to Almighty God, for this his unspeakable mercy, in the deliverance of his majesty from many dangers, and so happily restoring him to rule these kingdoms, according to his just and undoubted right.

London had high hopes for the 'Merrie Monarch'. He was fun-loving and urbane; he licensed playhouses and chartered the Royal Society of London for Improving Natural Knowledge. More, Charles was a political realist and understood that his monarchy was constrained by London, the coffer of the nation and the site of Parliament.

Charles II's reign, alas, turned out to be a procession of tragedies, beginning with a personal one:

Notices for a Lost Dog, 21–8 June 1660
Charles II

Charles II was a noted dog-lover. These advertisements for a lost dog were placed anonymously by the king in successive issues of the weekly *Mercurius Publicus*.

A SMOOTH BLACK DOG, less than a Greyhound, with white under his breast, belonging to the King's Majesty, was taken from Whitehal, the eighteenth day of this instant June, or thereabout. If any one can give notice to John Ellis, one of his Majesties Servants, or to his Majesties Back-Stayrs, shal be well rewarded for their labour.

WE MUST CALL upon you again for a Black Dog between a Greyhound and a Spaniel, no white about him onely a streak on his Brest and his Tayl a little bobbed. It is His Majesties own Dog, and doubtles was stoln, for the Dog was not born nor bred in England, and would never forsake his Master. Whosoever findes him may acquaint any at Whitehal, for the Dog was better known at Court than those who stole him. Will they never leave robbing His Majesty? Must he not keep a Dog? This Dog's place (though better than some imagine) is the only place which nobody offers to beg.

Journal of the Plague Year, 1665
Samuel Pepys

The Great Plague began in London in late 1664 in the parish of St Giles. Like previous visitations of the bubonic pestilence, it was carried by the black rat, *rattus rattus*. The sheer cold of the first months of 1665 prevented the infection spreading, but with the warmth of spring the bills of mortality began to climb. Come summer the plague had the city in its grip. Although the city authorities now understood that the plague was spread by contagion rather than the 'miasma' (foul gases) arising from refuse, they were unable to implement their policy of isolating the sick in their houses (complete with a red cross on the door and the incantation 'Lord have mercy upon us') because the sick often escaped incarceration. Or friends and family, taking pity, visited them. Samuel Pepys, like London's other assiduous seventeenth-century diarist John Evelyn, was an Admiralty official. Pepys wrote his diary in code, largely so that his wife did not discover his peccadilloes.

Pepys stayed in London and Greenwich throughout the plague year.

DIARY MAY 24TH 1665. To the Coffee-house with Creed, where I have not been a great while, where all the newes is of the Dutch being gone out, and of the plague growing upon us in this towne; and of remedies against it: some saying one thing, some another.

7th. Much against my will, I did in Drury Lane see two or three houses marked with a red cross upon the doors, and 'Lord have mercy upon us' writ there; which was a sad sight to me, being the first of the kind that, to my remembrance, I ever saw. It put me into an ill conception of myself and my smell, so that I was forced to buy some roll-tobacco to smell to and chaw, which took away the apprehension.

15th. The towne grows very sickly, and people to be afeard of it; there dying this last week of the plague 112, from 43 the week before, whereof but [one] in Fanchurch-streete, and one in Broad-streete, by the Treasurer's office.

29th. Up by water to White Hall, where the Court full of waggons and people ready to go out of towne.

July 5th. Up, and advised about sending of my wife's bedding and things to Woolwich, in order to her removal thither. In the afternoon I ... walked round to White Hall, the Parke being quite locked up. Grieved in my heart to part with my wife. Late home and to bed, very lonely.

29th. At noon to dinner, where I hear that my Will [his servant] is come in thither and laid down upon my bed, ill of the headake, which put me into extraordinary fear; and I studied all I could to get him out of the house, and set my people to work to do it without discouraging him.

30th (Lord's day). Will was with me to-day, and is very well again. It was a sad noise to hear our bell to toll and ring so often to-day, either for deaths or burials; I think five or six times.

August 15th. It was dark before I could get home, and so land at Church-yard stairs, where, to my great trouble, I met a dead corps of the plague, in the narrow ally just bringing down a little pair of stairs. But I thank God I was not much disturbed at it. However, I shall beware of being late abroad again.

31st. In the City died this week 7,496 and of them 6,102 of the plague. But it is feared that the true number of the dead, this week is near 10,000; partly from the poor that cannot be taken notice of, through the greatness of the number, and partly from the Quakers and others that will not have any bell ring for them.

September 3rd (Lord's day). Up; and put on my coloured silk suit very fine, and my new periwigg, bought a good while since, but durst not wear, because the plague was in Westminster when I bought it; and it is a wonder what will be the fashion after the plague is done, as to periwiggs, for nobody will dare to buy any haire, for fear of the infection, that it had been cut off of the heads of people dead of the plague.

October 16th. I walked to the Tower; but, Lord! how empty the streets are and melancholy, so many poor sick people in the streets full of sores; and so many sad stories overheard as I walk, every body talking of this dead, and that man sick, and so many in this place, and so many in that. And they tell me that, in Westminster, there is never a physician and but one apothecary left, all being dead; but that there are great hopes of a great decrease this week: God send it!

November 15th. The plague, blessed be God! is decreased 400; making the whole this week but 1300 and odd; for which the Lord be praised!

December 22nd. The weather hath been frosty these eight or nine days, and so we hope for an abatement of the plague the next weeke, or else God have mercy upon us! for the plague will certainly continue the next year if it do not.

25th (Christmas-day). To church in the morning, and there saw a wedding in the church, which I have not seen many a day; and the young people so merry one with another, and strange to see what delight we married people have to see these poor fools decoyed into our condition, every man and woman gazing and smiling at them.

31st (Lord's day). Thus ends this year ... now the plague is abated almost to nothing. My whole family hath been well all this while, and all my friends I know of, saving my aunt Bell, who is dead, and some children of my cozen Sarah's, of the plague. But many of such as I know very well, dead; yet, to our great joy, the town fills apace, and shops begin to be open again.

By the time the effect of the Plague diminished in February 1666, some 70,000 Londoners had died. Thereafter the Plague disappeared from the city, indeed from Western Europe as a whole, possibly because the rats themselves acquired immunity.

The Great Fire, 2–7 September 1666
John Evelyn

After plague, fire visited the city. At around 2 a.m. on 2 September 1666 flames broke out in the house of Farryner, the king's baker, in Pudding Lane. Named for offal ('puddinges and the other filth of Beastes') rather than desserts, Pudding Lane was one of the city's narrowest streets, barely more than a cart's width across.

2ND SEPTEMBER. THIS fatal night ... began the deplorable fire, near Fish-street, in London.

3rd. I had public prayers at home. The fire continuing, after dinner, I took coach with my wife and son, and went to the Bankside in Southwark, where we beheld that dismal spectacle, the whole city in dreadful flames near the waterside; all the houses from the Bridge, all Thames-street, and upwards towards Cheapside, down to the Three Cranes, were now consumed; and so returned, exceeding astonished what would become of the rest.

The fire having continued all this night (if I may call that night which was light as day for ten miles round about, after a dreadful manner), when conspiring with a fierce eastern wind in a very dry season, I went on foot to the same place; and saw the whole south part of the City burning from Cheapside to the Thames, and all along Corn-hill (for it likewise kindled back against the wind as well as forward), Tower-street, Fenchurch-street, Gracious-street, and so along to Baynard's Castle, and was now taking hold of St. Paul's church, to which the scaffolds contributed exceedingly. The conflagration was so universal, and the people so astonished, that, from the beginning, I know not by what despondency, or fate, they hardly stirred to quench it; so that there was nothing heard, or seen, but crying out and lamentation, running about like distracted creatures, without at all attempting to save even their goods; such a strange consternation there was upon them, so as it burned both in breadth and length, the churches, public halls, Exchange, hospitals, monuments, and ornaments; leaping after a prodigious manner, from house to house, and street to street, at great distances one from the other. For the heat, with a long set of fair and warm weather, had even ignited the air, and prepared the materials to conceive the fire, which devoured, after an incredible manner, houses, furniture, and every thing. Here, we saw the Thames covered with goods floating, all the barges and boats laden with what some had time and courage to save, as, on the other side, the carts, &c., carrying out to the fields, which for many miles were strewed with moveables of all sorts, and tents erecting to shelter both people and what goods they could get away. Oh, the miserable and calamitous spectacle! such as haply the world had not seen since the foundation of it, nor can be outdone till the universal conflagration thereof. All the sky was of a fiery aspect, like the top of a burning oven, and the light seen above forty miles round-about for many nights. God grant mine eyes may never behold the like, who now saw above 10,000 houses all in one flame! The noise and cracking and thunder of the impetuous flames, the shrieking of women and children, the hurry of people, the fall of towers, houses, and churches, was like a hideous storm; and the air all about so hot and inflamed, that at the last one was not able to approach it, so that they were forced to stand still, and let the flames burn on, which they did, for near two miles in length and one in breadth. The clouds also of smoke were dismal, and reached, upon computation, near fifty miles in length. Thus, I left it this afternoon burning, a resemblance of Sodom, or the last day. It forcibly called to my mind that passage – *non enim hic habemus stabilem civitatem*: the ruins resembling the picture of Troy. London was, but is no more! Thus, I returned.

4th September. The burning still rages, and it is now gotten as far as the Inner Temple. All Fleet-street, the Old Bailey, Ludgate-hill, Warwick-lane, Newgate, Paul's-chain, Watling-street, now flaming, and most of it reduced to ashes; the stones of Paul's flew like grenados, the melting lead running down the streets in a stream, and the very pavements glowing with fiery redness, so as no horse, nor man, was able to tread on them, and the demolition had stopped all the passages, so that no help could be applied. The eastern wind still more impetuously driving the flames forward. Nothing but the Almighty power of God was able to stop them; for vain was the help of man.

5th. It crossed towards Whitehall; but oh! the confusion there was then at that Court! It pleased his Majesty to command me, among the rest, to look after the quenching of Fetter-lane end, to preserve (if possible) that part of Holborn, whilst the rest of the gentlemen took their several posts, some at one part, and some at another (for now they began to bestir themselves, and not till now, who hitherto had stood as men intoxicated, with their hands across), and began to consider that nothing was likely to put a stop but the blowing up of so many houses as might make a wider gap than any had yet been made by the ordinary method of pulling them down with engines. This some stout seamen proposed early enough to have saved near the whole City, but this some tenacious and avaricious men, aldermen, &c., would not permit, because their houses must have been of the first. It was, therefore, now commended to be practised; and my concern being particularly for the

Hospital of St. Bartholomew, near Smith-field, where I had many wounded and sick men, made me the more diligent to promote it; nor was my care for the Savoy less. It now pleased God, by abating the wind, and by the industry of the people, when almost all was lost infusing a new spirit into them, that the fury of it began sensibly to abate about noon, so as it came no farther than the Temple westward, nor than the entrance of Smithfield, north: but continued all this day and night so impetuous towards Cripplegate and the Tower, as made us all despair. It also brake out again in the Temple; but the courage of the multitude persisting, and many houses being blown up, such gaps and desolations were soon made, as, with the former three days' consumption, the back fire did not so vehemently urge upon the rest as formerly. There was yet no standing near the burning and glowing ruins by near a furlong's space.

7th. I went this morning on foot from Whitehall as far as London Bridge, through the late Fleet-street, Ludgate-hill by St. Paul's, Cheapside, Exchange, Bishopsgate, Aldersgate, and out to Moorfields, thence through Corn-hill, &c., with extraordinary difficulty, clambering over heaps of yet smoking rubbish, and frequently mistaking where I was: the ground under my feet so hot, that it even burnt the soles of my shoes. In the meantime, his Majesty got to the Tower by water, to demolish the houses about the graff, which, being built entirely about it, had they taken fire and attacked the White Tower, where the magazine of powder lay, would undoubtedly not only have beaten down and destroyed all the bridge, but sunk and torn the vessels in the river, and rendered the demolition beyond all expression for several miles about the country.

At my return, I was infinitely concerned to find that goodly Church, St. Paul's – now a sad ruin, and that beautiful portico (for structure comparable to any in Europe, as not long before repaired by the late King) now rent in pieces, flakes of large stones split asunder, and nothing remaining entire but the inscription in the architrave, showing by whom it was built, which had not one letter of it defaced! It was astonishing to see what immense stones the heat had in a manner calcined, so that all the ornaments, columns, friezes, capitals, and projectures of massy Portland stone, flew off, even to the very roof, where a sheet of lead covering a great space (no less than six acres by measure) was totally melted. The ruins of the vaulted roof falling, broke into St. Faith's, which being filled with the magazines of books belonging to the Stationers, and carried thither for safety, they were all consumed, burning for a week following. It is also observable that the lead over the altar at the east end, was untouched, and among the divers monuments the body of one bishop remained entire. Thus lay in ashes that most venerable church, one of the most ancient pieces of early piety in the Christian world, besides near one hundred more. The lead, iron-work, bells, plate, &c., melted, the exquisitely wrought Mercers' Chapel, the sumptuous Exchange, the august fabric of Christ Church, all the rest of the Companies' Halls, splendid buildings, arches, entries, all in dust; the fountains dried up and ruined, whilst the very waters remained boiling; the voragos of subterranean cellars, wells, and dungeons, formerly warehouses, still burning in stench and dark clouds of smoke; so that in five or six miles traversing about I did not see one load of timber unconsumed, nor many stones but what were calcined white as snow.

The people, who now walked about the ruins, appeared like men in some dismal desert, or rather, in some great city laid waste by a cruel enemy; to which was added the stench that came from some poor creatures' bodies, beds, and other combustible goods. Sir Thomas Gresham's statue, though fallen from its niche in the Royal Exchange, remained entire, when all those of the Kings since the Conquest were broken to pieces. Also the standard in Cornhill, and Queen

Elizabeth's effigies, with some arms on Ludgate, continued with but little detriment, whilst the vast iron chains of the City-streets, hinges, bars, and gates of prisons, were many of them melted and reduced to cinders by the vehement heat. Nor was I yet able to pass through any of the narrow streets, but kept the widest; the ground and air, smoke and fiery vapour, continued so intense, that my hair was almost singed, and my feet unsufferably surbated. The bye-lanes and narrow streets were quite filled up with rubbish; nor could one have possibly known where he was, but by the ruins of some Church, or Hall, that had some remarkable tower, or pinnacle remaining.

I then went towards Islington and Highgate, where one might have seen 200,000 people of all ranks and degrees dispersed, and lying along by their heaps of what they could save from the fire, deploring their loss; and, though ready to perish for hunger and destitution, yet not asking one penny for relief, which to me appeared a stranger sight than any I had yet beheld.

Some 13,000 buildings were destroyed by the Fire, among them St Paul's Cathedral, 87 parish churches, the Guildhall, the Royal Exchange and 52 company halls. Effectively, the medieval city of London had disappeared into thick smoke.

The *anni horribiles* continued:

The Dutch in the Thames, June 1667
John Evelyn

A low point in London's history and Charles II's reign: the Dutch, with whom England had been at war on and off since the Protectorate, penetrate the Thames.

There was good reason for Holland's enmity towards London. Courtesy of Cromwell making England safe for capitalism, the city now threatened to eclipse Amsterdam as master of the new world economic order.

JUNE 8. TO London, alarm'd by the Dutch, who were fallen on our fleete at Chatham, by a most audacious enterprise entering the very river with part of their fleete, doing us not only disgrace, but incredible mischiefe in burning severall of our best men of warr lying at anker and moor'd there, and all this thro' our unaccountable negligence in not setting out our fleete in due time. This alarms caus'd me, fearing ye enemie might venture up ye Thames even to London, (which they might have don with ease, and fir'd all ye vessells in ye river to,) to send away my best goods, plate, &c. from my house to another place. The alarme was so great that it put both Country and Citty into paniq, feare and consternation, such as I hope I shall never see more; every body was flying, none knew why or whither. Now there were land forces dispatch'd with the Duke of Albemarle, Lord Middleton, Prince Rupert, and the Duke, to hinder ye Dutch coming to Chatham, fortifying Upnor Castle, and laying chaines and booms; but ye resolute enemy brake through all, and set fire on our ships, and retreated in spight, stopping up the Thames, the rest of their fleete lying before the mouth of it.

June 14. I went to see the work at Woolwich, a battery to prevent them coming up to London, which Pr. Rupert commanded, and sunk some ships in the river.

June 17. This night about 2 o'clock some chipps and combustible matter prepar'd for some fire-ships taking flame in Deptford yard, made such a blaze, and caus'd such an uproar in ye Tower, it being given out that the Dutch fleete was come up and had landed their men and fir'd the Tower, as had like to have don more mischiefe before people would be persuaded to the contrary and believe the accident. Every body went to their arms. These were sad and troublesome times!

June 24. The Dutch fleet still continuing to stop up the river, so as nothing could stir out or come in, I was before ye Council, and commanded by his Ma^{ty} to go with some others and search about the environs of the citty, now exceedingly distress'd for want of fuell, whether there could be any peate or turfe found fit for use. The next day I went and discover'd enough, and made my report that there might be found a greate deale; but nothing further was don in it.

June 28. I went to Chatham, and thence to view not onely what mischiefe the Dutch had don, but how triumphantly their whole fleete lay within the very mouth of Thames, all from ye North fore-land, Margate, even to ye buoy of the Nore – a dreadfule spectacle as ever Englishmen saw, and a dishonour never be wip'd off!

At least the debacle of the Dutch invasion stimulated the birth of the Royal Navy. In the event, nothing could hold back London's future as the City of Capitalism. The foundation of the Bank of England – the beginning of the modern banking system – in 1693 only ratified it.

❧ ❧ ❧

A Visit to a Gaming House, 1 January 1668
Samuel Pepys

B Y AND BY I met with Mr Brisband, and having it in my mind this Christmas to go to see the manner of the gaming at the Groome-Porter's, I did tell Brisband of it, and he did lead me thither: where, after staying an hour, they begun to play at about eight at night, where to see how differently one man took his losing from another, one cursing and swearing, and another only muttering and grumbling to himself, a third without any apparent discontent at all; to see how the dice will run good luck in one hand for half an hour together, and another have no good luck at all; to see how easily here, where they play nothing but guinnys, a £100 is won or lost; to see two or three gentlemen come in there drunk, and putting their stock of gold together, one 22 pieces, the second 4, and the third 5 pieces, and these to play one with another, and forget how much each of them brought, but he that brought the 22 thinks that he brought no more than the rest; to see the different humours of gamesters to change their luck when it is bad, how ceremonious they are as to call for new dice, to shift their places, to alter their manner of throwing, and that with great industry, as if there was anything in it; to see how some old gamesters that have no money now to spend as formerly do come and sit and look on as among others, Sir Lewis Dives, who was here, and hath been a great gamester in his time; to hear their cursing and damning to no purpose, as one man being to throw a seven if he could, and failing to do it after a great many throws cried he would be damned if ever he flung seven more while he lived, his despair of throwing it being so great, while others did it as their luck served almost every throw; to see how persons of the best quality do here sit down and play with people of any, though meaner; and to see how people in ordinary clothes shall come hither and play away 100, or 2 or 300 guinnys, without any kind of difficulty; and lastly, to see the formality of the groome-porter, who is their judge of all disputes in play and all quarrels that may arise therein, and how his under-officers are there to observe true play at each table, and to give new dice, is a consideration I never could have thought had been in the world, had I not now seen it. And mighty glad I am that I did see it, and it may be will find another evening before Christmas be over to see it again, when I may stay later, for their heat of play begins not till about eleven or twelve o'clock; which did give me another pretty observation of a man, that did win mighty fast when I was there. I think he won £100 at single pieces in a little time. While all the rest envied him his good fortune he cursed it, saying, 'A pox on it, that it should come so early upon me, for this fortune two hours hence would be worth something to me, but then, God damn me, I shall have no such luck.' This kind of prophane, mad entertainment they give themselves. And so I, having enough for once, refusing to venture, though Brisband pressed me hard, and tempted me with saying that no man was ever known to lose the first time, the devil being too cunning to discourage a gamester; and he offered me also to lend me ten pieces to venture, but I did refuse, and so went away, and took coach and home about 9 or 10 at night.

Highway Robbery, 11 May 1674
John Verney

ETWEENE 7 & 8 aclock, 5 or more horsmen dogd ye Duke of Ormond, who went home by ye way of Pal-mal & soe up James' Street & just as his coach came to ye upper end thereof, on of them clapt a pistoll to his coachman that if eyther he spoke or drove he was a dead man, the rest alighted & comanded him out of ye coach; he told them that if it were his money they should have it, soe they puld him out of ye coach, forct him on horsback behind one of them, & away they carried him, my Ld havinge recollected himself that he had gone about 30 paces as he ghessed (& as he told me himself for I went yesterday morninge to see him) & finding he was hinmost, his foreman havinge his sword & bridle in one hand, & his pistoll in ye other wrested ye pistoll out of his hand, & threw ye fellow downe, fell with him & upon him, & gott his sword & gott loose of them not with out some other hazards one pistoll beinge shott att him & two more fired. He is bruised in his ey, & a knock over the pate with a pistoll as he ghessed, & a small cutt in his head, after all which he is like I thank God to doe well. This makes all ye towne wonder, if money had beene their designe they might have had it, if his life, they might have had it alsoe. Some think & conjecture only, that their malice & spite was such that they would have carried him to Tiburne, & have hanged him there. They cannot Imagine whom to suspect for it. The horse they left behind. It was a chestnutt, with a bald face, & a white spott on his side. He that was dismounted gott off in ye dark & crowd.

The expansion of stagecoach travel gave men 'on the Accompt' their golden age.

Lanes and commons around the capital became infested with highwaymen. A century after the Duke of Ormond's mugging, Sir John Fielding, the blind magistrate and half-brother to the novelist Henry Fielding, reported to Charles Jenkinson, the secretary to the Treasury:

Sir John Fielding to Mr. Jenkinson.
Bow Street, June 28, 1764.

SIR JOHN FIELDING presents his respectful compliments to Mr. Jenkinson; thought it his indispensable duty to his country to transmit to him the enclosed account of robberies committed since Monday night last, and to acquaint him that in consequence of these repeated informations, he last night sent a foot patrole consisting of a peace officer and three assistants, into the fields near Tyburn and Tottenham Court Roads, to search the ditches where footpads have lately infested, that before they got out of the coach which carried them to the spot, they narrowly escaped being murdered, by three footpads, who without giving them the least notice fired two pistols immediately into the coach, but thank God without effect; two of them were afterwards taken, though not before one of them was dangerously wounded; all which circumstances might, I am convinced, have been prevented. There is nothing I so sincerely lament as the want of an opportunity of convincing Mr. Grenville of the amazing importance of the police to Government; for notwithstanding his most laudable resolution not to lay any permanent expense on the Crown that can be avoided, yet I am sure that he will never spare any necessary expense where public good is the object. For my part I can only propose and inform, which I shall always do most faithfully; but, injustice to myself, cannot conclude this letter without assuring you that your manner of behaviour to me the other morning gave me much real concern, it being totally different from any that I have ever received from any person, in any department whatever, on whom I have been obliged to attend, in consequence of my miserable employ. However, I still hope, that time will convince you how little I deserve the most distant diffidence. Your sincere friend and the public's faithful servant,

JOHN FIELDING.

Account of Robberies committed –

1. Christopher Pratt, driver of Mr. Stanton's waggon of Market Harborough, with the Bedford and Huntingdon waggoners robbed on Finchley Common on Friday night by two footpads, who beat and wounded them much.

2. Francis Walker, master coachman, of Nag's Head Yard, Oxford Road, drives No. 325, robbed on Tuesday night by two or three footpads near Paddington, of his own watch and money; and two ladies of their purses.

3. Mr. Taylor of King Street, Golden Square, brewer, in company with another gentleman, robbed the same night near Gunnersbury House, by a single highwayman.

4. The Honourable Mrs. Grey, robbed the same night near Sion House, by a highwayman.

5. Mr. Kearr, whipmaker of the Mews, with three other gentlemen in post-chaises, all robbed the same night near Turnham Green, by a highwayman.

6. Mr. Jackson, of Great Queen Street, robbed in one of the Hampstead stages, near Kentish Town, by a single highwayman, on Monday night.

7. The Bath and Bristol coaches on Hounslow Heath, Tuesday night.

8.   Mr. Rosser, near Islington, last night, of his gold watch,
      by two footpads.

Casanova on visiting London was given sensible advice: 'We
English always carry two purses on our journeys, a small one for
the robbers and a large one for ourselves.'

≫ ≫ ≫

London Arisen from the Ashes: Wren Rebuilds St Paul's Cathedral, 1675–1710
Daniel Defoe

After the Great Fire of 1666, several grand designs for London's
redevelopment were put forward, among them one from Dr
Christopher Wren, a professor of astronomy, for continental
boulevards radiating from London Bridge. Alas, any scheme
for orderly grids and roads stumbled on the impossibility of
purchasing the necessary plots of land, and the city conspicuously
failed to redevelop along elegant, geometric designs. Within
three years of the fire, some 2,800 houses had been erected,
almost all of them along the traditional arteries.

Wren may not have got his continental boulevards but, as
one of the commissioners charged with the reconstruction of
London, he did ensure that it was fashioned from brick and
stone instead of timber. He also designed and supervised the
construction of 52 churches, 36 company halls, 2 great hospitals

for retired or injured servicemen (the Royal Chelsea and the Greenwich Royal Hospital), the Royal Exchange, the Theatre Royal and, the crowning glory, St Paul's Cathedral.

Wren received the Royal Warrant to build St Paul's in May 1675. Thirty-five years later the cathedral was completed, by which time Wren himself was 78.

Daniel Defoe, novelist and journalist, was born in Stoke Newington. This account of St Paul's Cathedral and its construction is from *A Tour Thro' the Whole Island of Great Britain Divided into Circuits or Journies.*

THE BEAUTY OF all the Churches in the City, and of all the Protestant Churches in the World, is the Cathedral of St. *Paul*'s; a Building exceeding Beautiful and Magnificent; tho' some Authors are pleased to expose their Ignorance, by pretending to find Fault with it: 'Tis easy to find Fault with the Works even of God himself, when we view them in the Gross, without regard to the particular Beauties of every Part separately considered, and without searching into the Reason and Nature of the Particulars; but when these are maturely inquired into, viewed with a just Reverence, and considered with Judgment, then we fly out in due Admirations of the Wisdom of the Author from the Excellency of his Works

The vast Extent of the Dome, that mighty Arch, on which so great a Weight is supported (meaning the upper Towers or Lanthorn of Stone Work Seventy Feet high) may well account for the Strength of the Pillars and Butments below; yet those common Observers of the superficial Parts of the Building, complain, that the Columns are too gross, that the Work looks heavy, and the lower Figures near the Eye are too large, as if the *Dorick* and the *Attick* were not each of them as beautiful in their Place as the *Corinthian*.

The Wise Architect, like a compleat Master of his Business, had the Satisfaction, in his Lifetime, of hearing those ignorant Reprovers of his Work confuted, by the Approbation of the best Masters in Europe; and the Church of St. *Peter*'s in *Rome*, which is owned to be the most finished Piece in the World, only exceeds St. *Paul*'s in the Magnificence of its inside Work; the Painting, the Altars, the Oratories, and the Variety of its Imagery; Things, which, in a Protestant Church, however ornamental, are not allowed of.

If all the Square Columns, the great Pillasters, and the Flat Pannel Work, as well within as without, which they now alledge are too heavy and look too gross, were filled with Pictures, adorned with Carved Work and Gilding, and crowded with adorable Images of the Saints and Angels, the kneeling Crowd would not complain of the Grossness of the Work; but 'tis the Protestant Plainness, that divesting those Columns, &c. of their Ornaments, makes the Work, which in itself is not so large and gross as that of St *Peter*'s, be called gross and heavy; whereas, neither by the Rules of Order, or by the Necessity of the Building, to be proportioned and sufficient to the Height and Weight of the Work, could they have been less, or any otherwise than they are.

Nay, as it was, those Gentlemen who in Parliament opposed Sir *Christopher Wren*'s Request, of having the Dome covered with Copper, and who moved to have had the Lanthorn on the Top made shorter, and built of Wood; I say, those Gentlemen pretending Skill in the Art, and offering to reproach the Judgment of the Architect, alledged, That the Copper and the Stone Lanthorn would be too heavy, and that the Pillars below would not support it.

To which Sir *Christopher* answered, That he had sustained the Building with such sufficient Columns, and the Buttment was every where so good, that he would answer for it with his Head, that it should bear the Copper Covering and the

Stone Lanthorn, and Seven Thousand Ton weight laid upon it more than was proposed, and that nothing below should give way, no not One half quarter of an Inch; but that, on the contrary, it should be all the firmer and stronger for the Weight that should be laid on it; adding, That it was with this View that the Work was brought up from its Foundation, in such manner, as made common Observers rather think the First Range of the Buildings too gross for its upper Part; and that, if they pleased, he would undertake to raise a Spire of Stone upon the whole, a Hundred Foot higher than the Cross now stands.

When all these Things are considered complexly, no Man that has the least Judgment in Building, that knows any Thing of the Rules of Proportion, and will judge impartially, can find any Fault in this Church; on the contrary, those excellent Lines of Mr *Dryden*, which were too meanly applied in Allegory to the Praise of a paltry Play, may be, with much more Honour to the Author, and Justice to this Work, be applied here to St. *Paul's* Church.

> *Strong* Dorick *Pillars form the Base,*
> Corinthian *fills the upper Space;*
> *So all below is Strength, and all above is Grace.*

Sir *Christopher's* Design was, indeed, very unhappily baulked in several Things at the beginning, as well in the Situation as in the Conclusion of this Work, which, because very few may have heard of, I shall mention in Publick, from the Mouth of its Author.

1. In the Situation: He would have had the Situation of the Church removed a little to the *North*, that it should have stood just on the Spot of Ground which is taken up by the Street called *Pater-noster-Row*, and the Buildings on either Side; so that the *North* Side of the Church should have stood

open to the Street now called *Newgate-street*, and the *South* Side, to the Ground on which the Church now stands.

By this Situation, the *East* End of the Church, which is very beautiful, would have looked directly down the main Street of the City, *Cheapside*; and for the *West* End, *Ludgate* having been removed a little North, the main Street called *Ludgate-street* and *Ludgate-Hill*, would only have sloped a little *W. S. W.* as they do now irregularly Two Ways, one within, and the other without the Gate, and all the Street beyond *Fleet-Bridge* would have received no Alteration at all.

By this Situation, the common Thorough-fare of the City would have been removed at a little farther Distance from the Work, and we should not then have been obliged to walk just under the very Wall as we do now, which makes the Work appear quite out of all Perspective, and is the chief Reason of the Objections I speak of; whereas, had it been viewed at a little Distance, the Building would have been seen infinitely to more Advantage.

Had Sir *Christopher* been allowed this Situation, he would then, also, have had more Room for the Ornament of the *West* End, which, tho' it is a most beautiful Work, as it now appears, would have been much more so then, and he would have added a Circular Piazza to it, after the Model of that at *Rome*, but much more Magnificent, and an Obelisk of Marble in the Center of the Circle, exceeding any Thing that the World can now shew of its kind, I mean of Modern Work.

But the Circumstance of Things hindered this Noble Design, and the City being almost rebuilt before he obtained an Order and Provision for laying the Foundation; he was prescribed to the narrow Spot where we see it now stands, in which the Building, however Magnificent in itself, stands with infinite Disadvantage as to the Prospects of it; the Inconveniencies of which was so apparent when the Church was finished, that Leave was at length, tho' not without difficulty, obtained, to pull down one whole Row of Houses on the *North* Side of the Body of the Church, to make Way for the Ballister that surrounds the Cimetry or Church-yard, and, indeed, to admit the Light into the Church, as well as to preserve it from the Danger of Fire.

Another Baulk which, as I said, Sir *Christopher* met with, was in the Conclusion of the Work, namely, the covering of the Dome, which Sir *Christopher* would have had been of Copper double Gilded with Gold; but he was overruled by *Party*, and the City thereby, deprived of the most glorious Sight that the World ever saw, since the Temple of *Solomon*.

Yet with all these Disadvantages, the Church is a most regular Building, Beautiful, Magnificent, and beyond all the Modern Works of its Kind in *Europe*, St. *Peter*'s at *Rome*, as above, only excepted.

It is true, St. *Peter*'s, besides its Beauty in Ornament and Imagery, is beyond St. *Paul*'s in its Dimensions, is every way larger; but it is the only Church in the World that is so; and it was a merry Hyperbole of Sir *Christopher Wren*'s, who, when some Gentlemen in Discourse compared the Two Churches, and in Compliment to him, pretended to prefer St. *Paul*'s, and when they came to speak of the Dimensions, suggested, that St. *Paul*'s was the biggest: *I tell you*, says Sir *Christopher*, *you might set it in St. Peter's, and look for it a good while, before you could find it.*

Having thus spoken of the City and adjacent Buildings of *London*, and of the Particulars which I find chiefly omitted by other Writers, I have not Room here to enter into all the Articles needful to a full Description: However, I shall touch a little at the Things most deserving a Stranger's Observation.

The Great Frost, 1683–4
John Evelyn

27 DECEMBER 1683. I went to visit Sir John Chardin, a French gentleman who had travelled three times by land into Persia, and had made many curious researches in his travels, of which he was now setting forth a relation. It being in England this year one of the severest frosts that had happened of many years, he told me the cold in Persia was much greater, the ice of an incredible thickness . . .

1 January 1684. The weather continuing intolerably severe, streets of booths were set up upon the Thames. The air was so very cold and thick, as of many years there had not been the like . . .

6 January. The river quite frozen.

9 January. I went across the Thames on the ice, now become so thick as to bear not only streets of booths, in which they roasted meat, and had divers shops of wares quite across as in a town, but coaches, carts and horses passed over. So I went from Westminster stairs to Lambeth, and dined with the archbishop . . . After dinner and discourse with his grace till evening prayers Sir George Wheeler and I walked over the ice from Lambeth stairs to the horse ferry . . .

16 January. The Thames was filled with people and tents selling all sorts of wares as in the city.

24 January. The frost continuing more and more severe, the

Thames before London was still planted with booths in formal streets, all sorts of trades and shops furnished and full of commodities, even to a printing press, where the people and ladies took a fancy to have their names printed, and the day and year set down when printed on the Thames. This humour took so universally that it was estimated the printer gained £5 a day for printing a line only at sixpence a name, besides what he got by ballads, &c. Coaches plied from Westminster to the Temple, and from several other stairs to and fro, as in the streets; sleds, sliding with skates, a bull-baiting, horse and coach races, puppet-plays and interludes, cooks, tippling and other lewd places, so that it seemed to be a bacchanalian triumph or carnival on the water, whilst it was a severe judgment on the land, the trees not only splitting as if lightning-struck, but men and cattle perishing in divers places, and the very seas so locked up with ice that no vessels could stir out or come in; the fowls, fish and birds and all our exotic plants and greens universally perishing. Many parks of deer were destroyed, and all sorts of fuel so dear that there were great contributions to preserve the poor alive.

Nor was this severe weather much less intense in most parts of Europe, even as far as Spain and the most southern tracts. London, by reason of the excessive coldness of the air hindering the ascent of the smoke, was so filled with the fuliginous steam of the sea-coal that hardly could one see across the streets; and this, filling the lungs with its gross particles, exceedingly obstructed the breast, so as one could scarcely breathe. Here was no water to be had from the pipes and engines, nor could the brewers and divers other tradesmen work, and every moment was full of disastrous accidents.

4 February. I went to Sayes Court to see how the frost had dealt with my garden, where I found many of the greens and rare plants utterly destroyed, the oranges and myrtles very sick, the rosemary and laurels dead to all appearance, but the cypress likely to endure it.

5 February. It began to thaw, but froze again. My coach crossed from Lambeth to the horse ferry at Millbank, Westminster. The booths were almost all taken down, but there was first a map or landscape cut in copper representing all the manner of the camp, and the several actions, sports and pastimes thereon, in memory of so signal a frost . . .

8 February. The weather was set in to an absolute thaw and rain, but the Thames still frozen.

10 February. After eight weeks missing the foreign posts there came abundance of intelligence from abroad.

The Great Frost of 1683–4 was by no means the only time the Thames froze solid. Henry VIII crossed the river on horseback in 1537 to reach Greenwich Palace, while in 1564 football was played mid-river. In January 1679 the freezing of the Thames prevented the extraction of water to douse a fire that broke out in the Middle and Inner Temples. The last frost fair on the Thames was in 1814 – the embankments built by the Victorians, which caused the river to become narrower, deeper and faster, made it nigh impossible for the Thames to ice over.

Cockfighting, 18 June 1710
Zacharias von Uffenbach

Cockfighting was one of the oldest blood sports beloved of
Londoners, popular across the social spectrum.

IN THE AFTERNOON we went to see the cock-fighting.
This is a sport peculiar to the English, which, however
great the pleasure this nation takes in it, seems very
foolish to foreigners. A special building has been erected for it
near 'Gray's Inn'. When there is to be a fight, printed bills are
carried round and sometimes invitations to fanciers appear in
the news-sheets as well as the amount of the wagers and the
number and species of cocks that are to fight. The building is
round like a tower and inside it is just like a 'theatrum
anatomicum' as all round it there are benches in tiers, on
which the spectators sit. In the middle is a round table covered
with mats, on which the cocks have to fight. When it is time
to begin the persons appointed to do so bring in the cocks
hidden in two sacks and then, before they have seen the birds,
everyone starts to shout their wagers. The people, gentlefolk
as well as commoners (they all sit together), act like madmen
and go on raising the odds to twenty guineas and more. As
soon as one of the bidders calls 'done' . . ., the other is held to
his bargain. Then the cocks are taken out of the sacks and
fitted with silver spurs, . . . As soon as the cocks appear, the
shouts grow even louder and the betting is continued. When
they are put on to the table, some attack at once while others
run away from the rest and, as we ourselves saw, try in their
fright to jump down from the table among the crowd; they
are then however thrown back with loud cries (especially from

those who have put their money on the lively cocks which chase the others) and are thrust at each other until they get angry. Then one should just see how they peck at each other, and especially how they hack with their spurs. Their combs bleed quite horribly and they often slit each other's crop and abdomen with the spurs. There is nothing so amusing as when one cock seems quite exhausted and there are great shouts of joy and terrific bets and then, though he seemed quite done for, he suddenly recovers and masters the other. When one of the two is dead, the victor never fails to start crowing and jumping on the other and it often happens that they sing their song of triumph before victory is assured and the other wins after all. Sometimes when both are exhausted and neither will attack the other again, they are removed and others take their place; in this case the wagers are cancelled. But if one of them wins those who put their money on the loser have to pay immediately, so that an ostler in his apron often wins several guineas from a lord. If a man has made a bet and is unable to pay he is made, as a punishment, to sit in a basket tied to the ceiling and is drawn up in it amidst mighty laughter. The people become as heated about their wagers as the cocks themselves.

Not for another 100 years did Londoners lose their appetite for cockfighting: cockpits were banned in 1833. Bear-baiting and bull-baiting had already been outlawed. New – but bloodless – sports featuring animals took their place: there was horse-racing at Epsom and, later, greyhound racing at White City.

Making Hay in Chelsea, 19 May 1711
Jonathan Swift

D O YOU KNOW that about our town we are mowing already and making hay, and it smells so sweet as we walk through the flowery meads; but the hay-making nymphs are perfect drabs, nothing so clean and pretty as farther in the country. There is a mighty increase of dirty wenches in straw hats since I [first] knew London.

❧ ❧ ❧

The Mohock Club, March 1712
Lady Strafford

The Mohock Club was a street gang whose speciality was stabbing and slashing innocent passers-by.

M AR. 11, 1712:– ... Here is nothing talked about but men that goes in partys about the street and cuts people with swords or knives, and they call themselves by som hard name that I can nethere speak nor spell; but a Satturday night coming from the opera they assalted Mr. Davenant and drew their swords upon him, but he took won of them and sent to the round house, but 'tis thought 'twas sombody that would have been known and they gave mony and made their escape, but what was the great jest about town was they said they had cut of his head of hare.

March. 14, 1712:– ... I am very much frighted with the fyer, but much more with a gang of Devils that call themselves Mohocks; they put an old woman into a hogshead, and rooled her down a hill, they cut some nosis, others hands, and several barbarass tricks, without any provocation. They are said to be young gentlemen, they never take any mony from any; instead of setting fifty pound upon the head of a highwayman, sure they would doe much better to sett a hundred upon thear heads.

Handel's Water Music, 17 July 1717
Daily Courant

Handel, born in Saxony, was naturalized as an Englishman in 1727.

*O*N WEDNESDAY EVENING at about eight the King took water at Whitehall in an open barge ... and went up the river towards Chelsea. Many other barges with persons of quality attended, and so great a number of boats, that the whole river in a manner was covered. A City Company's barge was employed for the music, wherein were fifty instruments of all sorts, who played all the way from Lambeth, while the barges drove with the tide without rowing as far as Chelsea, the finest symphonies, composed express for this occasion by Mr. Hendel, which His Majesty liked so well that he caused it to be played over three times in going and returning. At eleven His Majesty went ashore at Chelsea, where a supper was prepared, and then there was another very fine consort of music, which lasted till two, after which His Majesty came again into his barge and returned the same way, the music continuing to play until he landed.

The *Daily Courant* was founded in 1702, one of a slew of newspapers prompted into life by the latest London fashion for the literate: going to the coffee-house.

Coffee-houses, c. 1722–5
John Macky and César de Saussure

Coffee-houses, which sold the new exotic beverages of coffee and tea, opened in London in the early 1650s. They were distinct from chocolate houses only in the refreshment offered; both types of house became places for philosophizing as well as for pleasure, which caused governments to fear and even suppress them. To no avail. The craze for coffee-houses was insuppressible and by the early eighteenth century there were over 2,000 of them in London.

John Macky, a Scottish visitor to London, recorded the West End coffee-houses:

I AM LODGED IN a street called Pall Mall, the ordinary residence of all strangers, because of its vicinity to the King's Palace, the park, the Parliament House, the Theatres and the Chocolate and Coffee Houses, where the best company frequent. If you would know our manner of living, 'tis thus: We rise by nine, and those that frequent great men's Levees find entertainment at them till eleven. About twelve the Beau Monde assembles at several Coffee or Chocolate Houses, the best of which are the Cocoa-Tree and White's Chocolate Houses, St James's, the Smyrna, Mrs Rochford's and the British Coffee-houses, and all these are so near one another that in less than an hour you see the company of them all. We are carried to these places in chairs (or Sedans) which are here very cheap, a guinea a week or shilling per hour, and your chairmen serve you for porters to run errands as your gondoliers do at Venice.

If it be fine weather, we take a turn in the Park till two,

when we go to Dinner; and if it be dirty, you are entertained at Picket or Basset [card games] at White's, or you must talk politicks at the Smyrna and St James's. I must not forget to tell you, that the Parties have their different places, where, however a stranger is always well received; but a Whig will no more go to the Cocoa-Tree or Ozinda's than a Tory will be seen at the Coffee-House of St James's.

White's Chocolate House became White's Club, the most aristocratic (and the oldest) of London's gentlemen's clubs. The tendency of like-minded Londoners to congregate in the same coffee-house extended to business as well as to politics: Dr Johnson and Sir Joshua Reynolds founded the Literary Club at the Turk's Head in Soho (which incidentally took its name from the 'So-hoe' cry of huntsmen in the days when the area was open field), while shipping insurers met at Lloyds, where they eventually founded the insurance market.

César de Saussure, a Swiss Protestant, noted that the coffee-houses were often rudimentary:

IN LONDON THERE are a great number of coffee-houses, most of which, to tell the truth, are not over clean or well furnished, owing to the quantity of people who resort to these places and because of the smoke, which would quickly destroy good furniture. Englishmen are great drinkers. In these coffee-houses you can partake of chocolate, tea, or coffee, and of all sorts of liquors, served hot; also in many places you can have wine, punch, or ale ... What attracts enormously in these coffee-houses are the gazettes and other public papers. All Englishmen are great newsmongers. Workmen habitually begin the day by going to coffee-rooms in order to read the latest news. I have often seen shoeblacks and other persons of that class club together to purchase a farthing paper . . . Some coffee-houses are a resort for learned scholars and for wits; others are the resort of dandies or of politicians, or again of professional newsmongers.

In the Georgian century, London became pleasured. London's place as the greatest port in Britain and the City's role as the globe's financial hub ensured that easy money sloshed around, along with the free time to enjoy it. Materialistic values waxed, religion waned.

John Wesley Stoned, *12 September 1742*

Wesley, the founder of Methodism, began preaching in London in 1738.

I WAS DESIRED TO preach in an open place, commonly called the Great Gardens, lying between Whitechapel and Coverlet Fields, where I found a vast multitude gathered together. Taking knowledge that a great part of them were little acquainted with the things of God, I called upon them in the words of our Lord, 'Repent ye, and believe the gospel.' Many of the beasts of the people laboured much to disturb those who were of a better mind. They endeavoured to drive in a herd of cows among them; but the brutes were wiser than their masters. They then threw whole showers of stones, one of which struck me between the eyes: but I felt no pain at all; and, when I had wiped away the blood, went on testifying with a loud voice that God hath given to them that believe 'not the spirit of fear, but of power, and of love, and of a sound mind'. And, by the spirit which now appeared through the whole congregation, I plainly saw what a blessing it is when it is given us, even in the lowest degree, to suffer for His name's sake.

Wesley's evangelical style helped the Methodists partially buck the trend towards religious non-observance, for they found an ear amongst thrifty tradespeople – the sort who, a century before, had provided the backbone of Puritanical London. The Anglican Church, meanwhile, found itself with 100 churches inside the city walls while the capital's population was increasingly living outside the self-same walls in new, godless communities.

Many of those hung at Tyburn (near present-day Marble Arch) were from the teeming extra-mural settlements of St Giles, Southwark, Smithfield and Whitechapel.

A Hanging at Tyburn, c. 1745
Samuel Richardson

Executions at Tyburn were a public spectacle, attended by as many as 80,000 people.

DEAR BROTHER,
I have this day been satisfying a curiosity, I believe natural to most people, by seeing an execution at Tyburn: The sight has had an extraordinary effect upon me, which is more owing to the unexpected oddness of the scene, than the affecting concern which is unavoidable in a thinking person, at a spectacle so awful, and so interesting, to all who consider themselves of the same species with the unhappy sufferers.

That I might the better view the prisoners, and escape the pressure of the mob, which is prodigious, nay, almost incredible, if we consider the frequency of these executions in London, which is once a month; I mounted my horse, and accompanied the melancholy cavalcade from Newgate to the fatal tree. The criminals were five in number. I was much disappointed at the unconcern and carelessness that appeared in the faces of three of the unhappy wretches: The countenances of the other two were spread with that horror and despair which is not to be wonder'd at in men whose period of life is so near, with the terrible aggravation of its being hastened by their own voluntary indiscretion and misdeeds. The exhortation spoken by the bell-man, from the wall of St Sepulchre's churchyard, is well intended; but the noise of the officers, and the mob, was so great, and the silly curiosity of people climbing into the cart to take leave of the criminals, made such a confused noise, that I could not hear the words of the exhortation when spoken; tho' they are as follow:

'All good people pray heartily to God for these poor sinners, who now are going to their deaths; for whom this great bell doth toll.

'You that are condemned to die, repent with lamentable tears. Ask mercy of the Lord for the salvation of your own souls, thro' the merits, death, and passion, of Jesus Christ, who now sits at the right-hand of God, to make intercession for as many of you as penitently return unto him.

'*Lord have mercy upon you! Christ have mercy upon you!*' – which last words the bell-man repeats three times.

All the way up Holborn the crowd was so great, as, at every twenty or thirty yards, to obstruct the passage; and wine, notwithstanding all the good order against that practice, was brought the malefactors, who drank greedily of it, which I thought did not suit well with their deplorable circumstances: After this, the three thoughtless young men, who at first seemed not enough concerned, grew most shamefully daring and wanton; behaving themselves in a manner that would have been ridiculous in men in any circumstance whatever: They swore, laugh'd, and talked obscenely; and wish'd their wicked companions good luck, with as much assurance as if their employment had been the most lawful.

At the place of execution, the scene grew still more shocking; and the clergyman who attended was more the subject of ridicule, than of their serious attention. The psalm was sung amidst the curses and quarrelling of hundreds of the most abandon'd and profligate of mankind: Upon whom (so stupid are they to any sense of decency) all the preparation of the unhappy wretches seems to serve only for the subject of a barbarous kind of mirth, altogether inconsistent with humanity. And as soon as the poor creatures were half-dead, I was much surprised, before such a number of peace-officers, to see the populace fall to haling and pulling the carcases with so much earnestness, as to occasion several warm rencounters, and broken heads. These, I was told, were the friends of the persons executed, or such as, for the sake of tumult, chose to appear so, and some persons sent by private surgeons to obtain bodies for dissection. The contests between these were fierce and bloody, and frightful to look at: so that I made the best of my way out of the crowd, and, with some difficulty, rode back among a large number of people, who had been upon the same errand with myself. The face of every one spoke a kind of mirth, as if the spectacle they had beheld had afforded pleasure instead of pain, which I am wholly unable to account for.

In other nations, common criminal executions are said to be little attended by any beside the necessary officers, and the mournful friends, but here, all was hurry and confusion, racket and noise, praying and oaths, swearing and singing psalms; I am unwilling to impute this difference in our own from the practice of other nations, to the cruelty of our natures; to which, foreigners, however, to our dishonour, ascribe it. In most instances, let them say what they will, we are humane beyond what other nations can boast; but in this, the behaviour of my countrymen is past my accounting for; every street and lane I passed through, bearing rather the face of a holiday, than of that sorrow which I expected to see, for the untimely deaths of five members of the community.

One of their bodies was carried to the lodging of his wife, who not being in the way to receive it, they immediately hawked it about to every surgeon they could think of, and when none would buy it, they rubb'd tar all over it, and left it in a field hardly cover'd with earth.

This is the best description I can give you of a scene that was no way entertaining to me, and which I shall not again take so much pains to see. I am, dear brother,

The disorderly behaviour of the mob at Tyburn increasingly concerned the city authorities, who in 1783 switched the place of execution to Newgate. The mob simply gathered there instead.

~~~

Earthquake, 11 March 1750
Horace Walpole

Horace Walpole was the consummate man of letters: his correspondence to Madame du Deffand alone ran to over 1,500 epistles. His conversion of a humble coachman's cottage in Twickenham into the faux castle of Strawberry Hill ushered in the Gothic revival in the arts. Walpole's father, Robert, was Britain's first prime minister.

*I*N THE NIGHT between Wednesday and Thursday last (exactly a month since the first shock), the earth had a shivering fit between one and two; but so slight that, if no more had followed, I don't believe it would have been noticed. I had been awake, and had scarce dozed again – on a sudden I felt my bolster lift up my head; I thought somebody was getting from under my bed, but soon found it was a strong earthquake, that lasted near half a minute, with a violent vibration and great roaring. I rang my bell; my servant came in, frightened out of his senses: in an instant we heard all the windows in the neighbourhood flung up. I got up and found people running into the streets, but saw no mischief done: there has been some; two old houses flung down, several chimneys, and much chinaware. The bells rung in several houses. Admiral Knowles, who has lived long in Jamaica, and felt seven there, says this was more violent than any of them: Francesco prefers it to the dreadful one at Leghorn. The wise say, that if we have not rain soon, we shall certainly have more. Several people are going out of town, for it has nowhere reached above ten miles from London: they say, they are not frightened, but that it is such fine weather, 'Lord! one can't help going into the country!' The only visible effect it has had, was on the Ridotto, at which, being the following night, there were but four hundred people. A parson, who came into White's the morning of earthquake the first, and heard bets laid on whether it was an earthquake or the blowing up of powder mills, went away exceedingly scandalized, and said, 'I protest, they are such an impious set of people, that I believe if the last trumpet was to sound, they would bet puppet-show against Judgment.'

※ ※ ※

Gin Lane, 1751 (see Plate 12)

William Hogarth

Gin, from the French *genièvre*, meaning juniper, was initially lauded by all and sundry since it distilled down the nation's corn surplus. So cheap did gin become that sellers could boast of it: 'Drunk for a penny, dead drunk for two pence.' By the mid-1700s London was gripped by a gin-drinking plague; every eleventh house in the capital was retailing the spirit. William Hogarth's famous illustration *Gin Lane* scarcely exaggerates the dangers of the gin-craze: whilst offering the poor temporary oblivion from realities of urban life, it also caused them to be feckless and violent. A campaign by the College of Physicians, London magistrates and concerned citizens to curb spirit-drinking resulted in the Gin Act of 1751, which increased the duties on spirits. The gin-craze gradually subsided and London returned to being a city of ale and wine drinkers.

Man About Town: A Rake's Progress, 25 November 1762–4 June 1763

James Boswell

The eldest son of the eighth Laird of Auchinleck (pronounced 'Affleck' for those who care to know), Boswell fled to London in 1760, aged 20, where he turned Catholic. As an antidote to this perceived religious fervour, a family friend encouraged the boy into libertinism – with wildly successful result:

THURSDAY 25 NOVEMBER.

I WENT TO LOVE's and drank tea. I had now been some time in town without female sport. I determined to have nothing to do with whores, as my health was of great consequence to me. I went to a girl with whom I had an intrigue at Edinburgh, but my affection cooling, I had left her. I knew she was come up. I waited on her and tried to obtain my former favours, but in vain. She would by no means listen. I was really unhappy for want of women. I thought it hard to be in such a place without them. I picked up a girl in the Strand; went into a court with intention to enjoy her in armour. But she had none. I toyed with her. She wondered at my size, and said if I ever took a girl's maidenhead, I would make her squeak. I gave her a shilling, and had command enough of myself to go without touching her. I afterwards trembled at the danger I had escaped. I resolved to wait cheerfully till I got some safe girl or was liked by some woman of fashion.

The Louisa referred to by Boswell in his journal entry below was Mrs Lewis, an actress with the Convent Garden Theatre.

WEDNESDAY 12 JANUARY.

We supped cheerfully and agreeably and drank a few glasses, and then the maid came and put the sheets, well aired, upon the bed. I now contemplated my fair prize. Louisa is just twenty-four, of a tall rather than short figure, finely made in person, with a handsome face and an enchanting languish in her eyes. She dresses with taste. She has sense, good humour, and vivacity, and looks quite a woman in genteel life. As I mused on this elevating subject, I could not help being somehow pleasingly confounded to think that so fine a woman was at this moment in my possession, that without any motives of interest she had come with me to an inn, agreed to be my intimate companion, as to be my bedfellow all night, and to permit me the full enjoyment of her person.

When the servant left the room, I embraced her warmly and begged that she would not now delay my felicity. She declined to undress before me, and begged I would retire and send her one of the maids. I did so, gravely desiring the girl to go up to Mrs. Digges [Lewis' cover name]. I then took a candle in my hand and walked out to the yard. The night was very dark and very cold. I experienced for some minutes the rigours of the season, and called into my mind many terrible ideas of hardships, that I might make a transition from such dreary thoughts to the most gay and delicious feelings. I then caused make a bowl of negus, very rich of the fruit, which I caused be set in the room as a reviving cordial.

I came softly into the room, and in a sweet delirium slipped into bed and was immediately clasped in her snowy arms and pressed to her milk-white bosom. Good heavens, what a loose did we give to amorous dalliance! The friendly curtain of darkness concealed our blushes. In a moment I felt myself animated with the strongest powers of love, and, from my dearest creature's kindness, had a most luscious feast. Proud of my godlike vigour, I soon resumed the noble game. I was in full glow of health. Sobriety had preserved me from effeminacy and weakness, and my bounding blood beat quick and high alarms. A more voluptuous night I never enjoyed. Five times was I fairly lost in supreme rapture. Louisa was madly fond of me; she declared I was a prodigy, and asked me if this was not extraordinary for human nature. I said twice as much might be, but this was not, although in my own mind I was somewhat proud of my performance. She said it was what there was no just reason to be proud of. But I told her I could not help it. She said it was what we had in common with the beasts. I said no. For we had it highly improved by the pleasures of sentiment. I asked her what she thought enough. She gently chid me for asking such questions, but said two times. I mentioned the Sunday's assignation, when I was in such bad spirits, told her in what agony of mind I was, and asked her if she would not have despised me for my imbecility. She declared she would not, as it was what people had not in their own power.

She often insisted that we should compose ourselves to sleep before I would consent to it. At last I sunk to rest in her arms and she in mine. I found the negus, which had a fine flavour, very refreshing to me. Louisa had an exquisite mixture of delicacy and wantonness that made me enjoy her with more relish. Indeed I could not help roving in fancy to the embraces of some other ladies which my lively imagination strongly pictured. I don't know if that was altogether fair. However, Louisa had all the advantage. She said she was quite fatigued and could neither stir leg nor arm. She begged

I would not despise her, and hoped my love would not be altogether transient. I have painted this night as well as I could. The description is faint; but I surely may be styled a Man of Pleasure.

Boswell's tryst with Mrs Lewis resulted in the contraction of gonorrhoea.

FRIDAY 25 MARCH.

As I was coming home this night, I felt carnal inclinations raging through my frame. I determined to gratify them. I went to St. James's Park, and, like Sir John Brute, picked up a whore. For the first time did I engage in armour, which I found but a dull satisfaction. She who submitted to my lusty embraces was a young Shropshire girl, only seventeen, very well-looked, her name Elizabeth Parker. Poor being, she has a sad time of it.

THURSDAY 31 MARCH.

At night I strolled into the Park and took the first whore I met, whom I without many words copulated with free from danger, being safely sheathed. She was ugly and lean and her breath smelt of spirits. I never asked her name. When it was done, she slunk off. I had a low opinion of this gross practice and resolved to do it no more. I went and sat a while with Webster.

SATURDAY 4 JUNE.

It was the King's birthnight, and I resolved to be a blackguard and to see all that was to be seen. I dressed myself in my second-mourning suit, in which I had been powdered many

months, dirty buckskin breeches and black stockings, a shirt
of Lord Eglinton's which I had worn two days, and little
round hat with tarnished silver lace belonging to a disbanded
officer of the Royal Volunteers. I had in my hand an old
oaken stick battered against the pavement. And was not
I a complete blackguard? I went to the Park, picked up a
low brimstone, called myself a barber and agreed with her
for sixpence, went to the bottom of the Park arm in arm,
and dipped my machine in the Canal and performed most
manfully. I then went as far as St. Paul's Church-yard,
roaring along, and then came to Ashley's Punch-house and
drank three threepenny bowls. In the Strand I picked up a
little profligate wretch and gave her sixpence. She allowed
me entrance. But the miscreant refused me performance. I
was much stronger than her, and *volens nolens* pushed her
up against the wall. She however gave a sudden spring from
me; and screaming out, a parcel of more whores and soldiers
came to her relief. 'Brother soldiers,' said I, 'should not a
half-pay officer r—g—r for sixpence? And here has she used
me so and so.' I got them on my side, and I abused her in
blackguard style, and then left them. At Whitehall I picked
up another girl to whom I called myself a highwayman and
told her I had no money and begged she would trust me. But
she would not. My vanity was somewhat gratified tonight
that, notwithstanding of my dress, I was always taken for a
gentleman in disguise. I came home about two o'clock, much
fatigued.

Occasionally Boswell took of the pleasures of the mind, as well
as of the flesh. He precociously struck up a friendship with the
lexicologist Dr Johnson, whom Boswell found living in a 'literary
state, very solemn and very slovenly' in the Inner Temple.

   Like so many Georgian Londoners, Samuel Johnson was

not born within the sound of Bow Bells, but was a hick 'gone up to town', part of that population trend which saw London grow from 575,000 souls in 1700 to a million in 1800. Often Johnson vilified the monstrous metropolis, complaining, like the anonymous author of the fourteenth-century 'London Lickpenny' of its materialism:

FOR WHO WOULD leave, unbrib'd, *Hibernia*'s Land,
Or change the Rocks of Scotland for the *Strand*?
  Here Malice, Rapine, Accident, conspire,
  And now a Rabble rages, now a Fire:
There Ambush here relentless Ruffians lay,
And here the fell Attorney prowls for Prey:
Here falling Houses thunder on your Head,
  And here a female Atheist talks you dead.

Usually, though, Johnson loved not loathed London, famously telling Boswell, 'You find no man at all intellectual who is willing to leave London. No, sir, when a man is tired of London, he is tired of life; for there is in London all that life can afford.'

Visitors assented. They wondered at London's sheer size, its busyness and its imposing buildings and boulevards. The German traveller J.W. von Archenholz found in the West End that 'the houses are mostly new and elegant; the squares are superb, the streets straight and open.' The first London square, Bloomsbury, was laid out in the 1660s but it was in the Georgian century that the London square became so desirable a residential location.

The West End squares confirmed the polarity between the London rich and the London poor. They no longer lived side by side – the rich went west (predominantly) and left the poor behind in teeming ghettoes. The Georgians coined the word 'slum' for such places.

Crowded and excluded London found its voice in riot.

ᴣᴣ ᴣᴣ ᴣᴣ

Wilkes and the Mob, March 1768
Horace Walpole

Born in Clerkenwell, the son of a rich distiller, the politician John Wilkes was famously quick-witted. An elector once blustered to him 'Vote for you, Sir! I'd sooner vote for the Devil.' 'But in case your friend should not stand?' asked Wilkes.

In and out of Parliament Wilkes steadfastly attacked George III's chief minister, Lord Bute, and opined in 1763 that the Royal Speech was libellous. The House of Commons sought to prosecute and expel Wilkes but ultimately gave up. Posterity considers Wilkes to have established the right of every constituency to return the member of its choice. He called himself the 'friend of liberty'. He was certainly the darling of the London mob.

E [WILKES] STOOD for the City of London, and was the last on the poll of seven candidates, none but the mob, and most of them without votes, favouring him. He then offered himself to the County of Middlesex. The election came on last Monday. By five in the morning a very large body of Weavers etc, took possession of Piccadilly, and the roads and turnpikes leading to Brentford, and would suffer nobody to pass without blue cockades, and papers inscribed, 'No. 45, Wilkes and Liberty'. They tore to pieces the coaches of Sir W. Beauchamp Proctor, and Mr. Cooke, the other candidates, though the latter was not there, but in bed with the gout, and it was with difficulty that Sir

William and Mr. Cooke's cousin got to Brentford. There, however, lest it should be declared a void election, Wilkes had the sense to keep everything quiet. But, about five, Wilkes, being considerably ahead of the other two, his mob returned to town and behaved outrageously. They stopped every carriage, scratched and spoilt several with writing all over them 'No. 45', pelted, threw dirt and stones, and forced everybody to huzza for Wilkes. I did but cross Piccadilly at eight, in my coach, with a French monsieur d'Angeul, whom I was carrying to Lady Hertford's; they stopped us, and bid us huzza. I desired him to let down the glass on his side, but, as he was not alert, they broke it to shatters. At night they insisted, in several streets, on houses being illuminated, and several Scotch refusing, had their windows broken. Another mob rose in the City, and Harley, the present Mayor, being another Sir William Walworth, and having acted formerly and now with great spirit against Wilkes, and the Mansion House not being illuminated, and he out of town, they broke every window, and tried to force their way into the House. The Trained Bands were sent for, but did not suffice. At last a party of guards, from the Tower, . . . dispersed the tumult. At one in the morning a riot began before Lord Bute's house, in Audley Street, though illuminated. They flung two large flints into Lady Bute's chamber, who was in bed, and broke every window in the house. Next morning, Wilkes and Cooke were returned members. The day was very quiet, but at night they rose again, and obliged almost every house in town to be lighted up, even the Duke of Cumberland's and Princess Amelia's.

The Lord Mayor's Banquet, 1768
William Hickey

THE 9TH BEING the Lord Mayor's day, I arrayed myself in my full suit of velvet. Alderman Woolridge called at my father's and conveyed me in his chariot to Guildhall at half-past four o'clock; about half an hour after which the procession arrived from Westminster. At six, we sat down to a profusion of turtle and venison, followed by all the etceteras of French cookery, with splendid dessert of pines, grapes, and other fruits. I was seated between Mrs Healy, sister to Wilkes, and Lord Lewisham, eldest son of the Earl of Dartmouth. Mrs Healy almost enveloped me in her immense hoop, but was vastly attentive to me, whom she perceived to be a stranger, ordering one of her servants to wait upon me, and naming to me the different persons who sat at the same table, amongst whom were most of the great officers of state, the Lord Chancellor, judges, and Master of the Rolls. The heat from the crowd assembled and immense number of lights was disagreeable to all, to many quite oppressive and distressing.

The Lord Mayor's table, at which I was, and nearly opposite his Lordship, was less so than other parts of the hall, from being considerably elevated above the rest. The wines were excellent, and the dinner the same, served, too, with as much regularity and decorum as if we had been in a private house; but far different was the scene in the body of the hall, where, in five minutes after the guests took their stations at the tables, the dishes were entirely cleared of their contents, twenty hands seizing the same joint or bird, and literally tearing it to pieces. A more determined scramble could not be; the roaring and noise was deafening and hideous, which increased as the liquor operated, bottles and glasses flying across from side to side without intermission. Such a bear garden altogether I never beheld, except my first visit to Wetherby's, which it brought very forcibly to my recollection.

This abominable and disgusting scene continued till near ten o'clock, when the Lord Mayor, Sheriffs, the nobility, etc., adjourned to the ball and card rooms, and the dancing commenced. Here the heat was no way inferior to that of the hall, and the crowd so great there was scarce a possibility of moving. Rejoiced, therefore, was I upon Alderman Woolridge's saying he would take me home whenever I wished it; I eagerly answered, 'This moment, if you please.' He thereupon took me through some private apartments and down a flight of stairs to a door opening into a back lane where his carriage was ready, into which we stepped without the smallest difficulty or impediment, and were driven home. Completely exhausted, I retired to bed, perfectly satisfied with having once partaken of a Lord Mayor of London's feast.

The Gordon Riots, 6 June 1780

Ignatius Sancho

Lord George Gordon was the head of a 50,000-strong mob that marched on Parliament demanding the repeal of a 1778 Act granting Catholics civil liberties. The worst riots in the capital's history followed. It was less popery the mob objected to than Irish navvies, who were deemed to be lowering wages.

The black Londoner Ignatius Sancho, society grocer and friend of David Garrick and Laurence Sterne, observed the riots from his window in Charles Street:

Charles Street, June 6th 1780

DEAR AND MOST Respected Sir,
In the midst of the most cruel and ridiculous confusion, I am now set down to give you a very imperfect sketch of the maddest people that the maddest times were ever plagued with [. . .]. There is at this present moment at least a hundred thousand poor, miserable, ragged rabble, from twelve to sixty years of age, with blue cockades in their hats, besides half as many women and children, all parading the streets, the Bridge, the Park, ready for any and every mischief. Gracious God, what's the matter now? I was obliged to leave off, the shouts of the mob, the horrid clashing of swords, and the clutter of a multitude in swiftest motion drew me to the door where every one in the street was employed in shutting up shop. It is now just five o'clock, the ballad-mongers are exhausting their musical talents with the downfall of Popery, Sandwich and North. Lord Sandwich narrowly escaped with life about an hour since; the mob seized his chariot going to the House, broke his glasses, and in

struggling to get his Lordship out they somehow have cut his face. The Guards flew to his assistance, the light horse scoured the road, got his chariot, escorted him from the coffee-house where he had fled for protection, to his carriage, and guarded him bleeding very fast home. This, this is liberty! genuine British Liberty! This instant about two thousand liberty boys are swearing and swaggering by with large sticks, thus armed in hopes of meeting with the Irish chairmen and labourers. All the Guards are out and all the horse, the poor fellows are just worn out for want of rest, having been on duty ever since Friday. Thank heaven, it rains. May it increase so as to send these wretches safe to their homes, their families and wives. About two this afternoon a large party took it into their heads to visit the King and Queen and entered the Park for that purpose, but found the Guard too numerous to be forced and after some useless attempts gave it up. It is reported the House will either be prorogued or parliament dissolved this evening, as it is in vain to think of attending any business while this anarchy lasts.

I cannot but felicitate you, my good friend, upon the happy distance you are placed from our scene of confusion. May foul Discord and her cursed train never approach your blessed abode! Tell Mrs S ..., her good heart would ache did she see the anxiety, the woe, in the faces of mothers, wives, and sweethearts, each equally anxious for the object of their wishes, the beloved of their hearts. Mrs Sancho and self both cordially join in love and gratitude and every good wish, crowned with the peace of God, which passeth all understanding &c.

I am, dear Sir,
Yours ever by inclination,
Ign. Sancho.

Postscript,

The Sardinian Ambassador offered 500 guineas to the rabble to save the painting of our Saviour from the flames, and 1000 guineas not to destroy an exceeding fine organ. The gentry told him they would burn him if they could get at him, and destroyed the picture and organ directly. I am not sorry I was born in Afric. I shall tire you, I fear, and if I cannot get a frank, make you pay dear for bad news. There is about a thousand mad men armed with clubs, bludgeons and crows, just now set off for Newgate, to liberate, they say, their honest comrades. I wish they do not some of them lose their lives of liberty before morning. It is thought by many who discern deeply that there is more at the bottom of this business than merely the repeal of an act which has yet produced no bad consequences, and perhaps never might. I am forced to own that I am for universal toleration. Let us convert by example, and conquer by our meekness and brotherly love.

Eight o'clock. Lord George Gordon has this moment announced to my Lords the mob that the Act shall be repealed this evening. Upon this, they gave a hundred cheers, took the horses from his hackney-coach, and rolled him full jollily away. They are huzzaing now ready to crack their throats.

Huzzah.

Since any authority figure deemed to be against the Mob was likely to have his home set upon, few magistrates could be found to oppose the terror. Order was only restored when George III sent the troops in. They shot, by government admittance, nearly 300 rioters. If the victims of mob fires, house-razings, and assaults are added in, the Gordon Riots left around 850 dead behind them.

The list of the dead includes 21 rioters hanged at the site of their outrages. Lord Gordon employed the slick skills of the famed lawyer Thomas Erskine and was acquitted of treason. He later died in Newgate Prison nonetheless, while serving a sentence for libelling Marie Antoinette.

<center>~~~</center>

Ranelagh Pleasure Gardens, 12 June 1782

Karl Philipp Moritz

Ranelagh Pleasure Gardens opened in Chelsea in 1742, eclipsing the rival and cheaper gardens at Vauxhall. Ranelagh's chief attraction was the Rotunda, with its orchestra in the centre and tiered boxes around – save for that Ranelagh offered the same fare as the city's other pleasure gardens: dancing, tableaux, refreshments (Ranelagh's half a crown entrance fee included punch and coffee), promenading and discreet corners for courting.

OFTEN AS I had heard Ranelagh spoken of, I had yet formed only an imperfect idea of it. I supposed it to be a garden somewhat different from that of Vauxhall; but, in fact, I hardly knew what I thought of it. Yesterday evening I took a walk, in order to visit this famous place of amusement; but I missed my way and got to Chelsea; where I met a man with a wheelbarrow, who not only very civilly showed me the right road, but also conversed with me the whole of the distance, which we walked together. And finding, on inquiry, that I was a subject of the King of Prussia, he desired me, with much eagerness, to relate to him some anecdotes concerning that mighty monarch.

At length I arrived at Ranelagh; and having paid my half-crown, on entrance, I soon inquired for the garden door, and it was readily shown to me; when, to my infinite astonishment, I found myself in a poor, mean-looking, and ill-lighted garden, where I met but few people. I had not been here long before I was accosted by a young lady, who also was walking there, and who, without ceremony, offered me her arm, asking me why I walked thus solitarily? I now concluded, this could not possibly be the splendid, much-boasted Ranelagh; and so, seeing not far from me a number of people entering a door, I followed them, in hopes either to get out again, or to vary the scene.

But it is impossible to describe, or indeed to conceive, the effect it had on me, when, coming out of the gloom of the garden, I suddenly entered a round building, illuminated by many hundred lamps; the splendour and beauty of which surpassed everything of the kind I had ever seen before. Everything seemed here, to be round: above, there was a gallery, divided into boxes; and in one part of it an organ with a beautiful choir, from which issued both instrumental and vocal music. All around, under this gallery, are handsome painted boxes for those who wish to take refreshments: the floor was covered with mats; in the middle of which are four high black pillars; within which there are neat fire places for preparing tea, coffee, and punch: and all around also there are placed tables, set out with all kinds of refreshments. Within these four pillars, in a kind of magic rotundo, all the *beau-monde* of London move perpetually round and round.

I at first mixed with this immense concourse of people, of all sexes, ages, countries, and characters: and I must confess, that the incessant change of faces, the far greater number of which were strikingly beautiful, together with the illumination, the extent and majestic splendour of the place, with the continued sound of the music, makes an inconceivably delightful impression on the first entering the building. Thus I spent here some hours in the night, in a continual variation of entertainment; when the crowd now all at once began to lessen, and I also took a coach and drove home.

By the new century, however, Ranelagh and the other pleasure gardens had sunk into seediness and disrepute. Ranelagh closed its gates for ever in 1804.

ℒ ℒ ℒ

London Hospitals, 1788
John Howard

The London Hospital in Whitechapel Road

THIS SPACIOUS BUILDING is for the reception and relief of sick and wounded seamen &c. It consists of 18 wards; but now 7 only are occupied ... The wards in general are 20 feet wide, and 12 high, and each contains about 18 beds, which have no testers ... The passages, which are 8 feet wide, are dark. There are no cisterns for water: the vaults are often offensive. In this, and our other hospitals, medical and chirurgical patients are together. Here the middle floor is occupied by the women, and the lower and upper floors by the men. Would it not be better if the men were on one side of the house, and the women on the other? I could wish that there were two wards appropriated to Jew patients, as they must almost starve, on their scanty allowance of bread and beer, with only 2½d. a day ... In a dirty room in the cellar there is a cold and a hot bath, which seem to be seldom used. The wards were not dirty, but the house has not been whitewashed for some years; nor has it, within or without, the appearance of neatness. Patients are generously admitted without any fee or reward to nurses &c. nor is any security required for the expense of burial or removal; but for parish poor and soldiers, 4d. per day must be paid for their subsistence. All accidents, whether recommended or not, are received at any hour of the day or night. Here is a large chapel, in which divine service is performed twice every Sunday; and prayers are read three days in the week.

The patients' diet I disapprove of; as, their *common diet* is 8 oz. of meat *every* day for dinner; and for supper, broth 6 days in the week. No *vegetables*, and only 12 oz. of bread a day. The *middle diet* is 4 oz. of meat every day for dinner; and for supper, a pint of broth or panado. No *vegetables*, and only 8 oz. of bread. The breakfast for every day, of those patients that are on *common* diet, is one pint of milk pottage or water-gruel. Those on the *middle* diet, one pint of panado or water-gruel. The drink of the former is three pints of beer in summer and one quart in winter. Of the latter one pint of beer every day. Sept. 15th 1788, Patients 120. By a letter received lately, I am informed that the committee are exerting themselves, and making several improvements in this hospital.

St. Bartholomew's Hospital in Smithfield

The wards of this hospital, which are 3 sides of a spacious quadrangle, are on the ground floor and 3 stories above. The wards . . . were clean and not offensive, except the men's 4 foul wards, which are on the uppermost storey, and had not one window open. The 2 foul wards for women were clean and fresh. The wards are lofty, 22 feet wide, and in each were about 15 beds. The bedsteads are wood, and their testers, though lofty, are a harbour for dust and lumber. The beds were not crowded, and the wards were quiet. The staircases are wide; the landing places spacious; and the windows were open. The diet of the patients is nearly the same as in the London Hospital . . . To each ward there is a sister and a nurse; the former has a room adjoining, but no window into her ward. Fees are taken for the admission of patients: for clean patients 2s. *viz.* 1s. for the sister, 6d. to the nurse, 6d. to the beadle; for foul patients £1. 5s. 8d., *viz.* 5s. for flannels, 18s. 8d. for 2 month's subsistence at 4d. per day: 2s. ward dues. Every patient must deposit 17s. 6d. for a burial fee, or a housekeeper give security; except in case of sudden accidents. Sept. 19th 1788, Patients 428.

The Middlesex Hospital in Marylebone

This hospital . . . consists of 16 wards, of which only 4 are occupied, the funds being very low. The rooms are close and dirty, except one . . . The bedsteads and wooden testers are old: the house wants whitewashing, and the whole has an air of poverty . . . Sept. 16th 1788, Patients 70.

St. Thomas's Hospital in Southwark

Some of the wards in this hospital are only 18 feet wide: the bedsteads are iron and very properly detached from the walls: there are no testers, but semicircular irons for the curtains in winter. The wards were fresh and clean, except the 3 foul wards, in which were 53 men and 27 women: these were very offensive and had not a window open. There were no water closets. The bread was excellent ... I am sorry to find such great quantities of beer brought from public houses into this and other hospitals. Here and at Guy's, the patients easily get out, there being no proper attention to the gates, so that the adjoining gin-shops often prevent the efficacy of medicine and diet. Sept 17th 1788, Patients 440.

Guy's Hospital in Southwark

... The wards in this hospital are in general too low: the height of some is only 9½ feet. In several of the old wards (each containing about 30 beds) the beds and testers are wood, and infested with bugs. In the new wards, which were clean and fresh, are iron bedsteads and hair beds ... The window at the upper end of each of these wards opens from the ceiling to the floor ... The water closets in the new wards are of the *best* construction, and *not* in the least *offensive*; for by opening the door, water is turned into them ... Here are excellent baths, in clean and neat rooms ... Sept. 17th 1788, Patients 304.

The Westminster Hospital in James's Street

... For the relief of the sick and needy from all parts; with an establishment for incurables ... The beds parallel and close to the walls, with wooden testers . . . the walls dirty . . . Sept. 24th 1788, Patients 71, and 14 incurables.

St. George's Hospital for Sick and Lame at Hyde Park Comer

. . . Here are three large, and three small wards for men; and the same number for women: the lower wards are for accidents. The wards . . . are too close . . . all the windows being shut . . . A good garden . . . Sept. 22nd 1788, Patients 150.

The British Lying-in Hospital, in Brownlow Street, for the Reception of Married Women

Here are 6 wards, and in each 6 beds. The wards were clean and quiet: provision good: kitchen and pantry clean. This is a good institution, and proper attention is paid to the patients; who continue here 3 weeks after they are delivered . . . Here *female* pupils are instructed in the art of midwifery, and after residing 4 or 6 months, receive certificates of their ability to practise . . . Women delivered and discharged from 31 Dec. 1786 to 31 Dec. 1787, 550. Died 7. Total 557.

The City of London Lying-in Hospital in the City Road, for Married Women

Here are 8 wards . . . 6 only are occupied, each containing 8 beds. The wards and beds were clean . . . Sept. 23rd 1788, Women 36.

The Lock Hospital near Hyde Park Corner, for the Relief of Venereal Patients Only

Here are 3 wards for men and 3 for women . . . Sept. 22nd 1788, Men 36, Women 28.

Bethlem Hospital in Moorfields, for the Care of Lunatics, and the Reception of Incurables

The committee room and apartments for the stewards &c. are in the centre; and in long galleries and wings on either side, are the rooms for the patients. The size of these rooms is 12 feet by 8 feet 10 inches, and 12 feet 10 inches high . . . On the 4 floors there are about 270 rooms: these were quite clean and not offensive, though the house is old and wants whitewashing . . . The patients communicate with one another from the top to the bottom of the house, so that there is no separation of the calm and quiet from the noisy and turbulent, except those who are chained in their cells. To each side of the house there is only one vault: very offensive . . .

There are sitting rooms with fireplaces properly guarded with iron – a cold bath and airing grounds for each sex – *no chapel* – bread allowance to patients 1 lb. a day . . . Visitors are admitted by a governor's ticket, only on Mondays and Wednesdays, between the hours of 10 and 12. Sept. 26th 1788, Men 133, Women 139.

St. Luke's Hospital for Lunatics in Old Street Road

This spacious building was first occupied on new year's day 1786 . . . Here are on each of the three floors, three long galleries and wings ... In each gallery there are 32 cells ... very clean and not offensive ... Two sitting rooms in each gallery, one for the quiet, the other for the turbulent; but I could wish that the noisy and turbulent were in a separate part of the house ... Sept. 25 1788, men 54, women 108.

I shall beg leave to subjoin a few general observations concerning defects in the London Hospitals ...

The securities and fees required at admission into many of the hospitals bear hard upon the poor, and absolutely exclude many of those who have the greatest occasion for charitable relief. The nurses' fees in particular open a door to many impositions. The visits of Governors are too often only a matter of form, the visitor hurrying out of an offensive room, and readily acquiescing in the reports of nurses etc. Hence I apprehend, many instances of neglect in surgeons and their dressers, as well as other officers, go unnoticed. I have never found any clergyman administering consolation to the sick; and prayers are usually attended by very few. Whitewashing the wards is seldom or never practised; and injurious prejudices against washing floors, and admitting fresh air, are suffered to operate. Bathing, either hot or cold, is scarcely ever used; I suppose, because it would give trouble to the attendants. There are no convalescent wards or sitting rooms, so that patients are often turned out very unfit for work, or the common mode of living. The admission of great quantities of beer for the patients from ale-houses, by alleged, or pretended orders from the faculty, is a great and growing evil. Every *proper* article of diet should be provided by the hospital, and *no other*, on any account, be admitted. It is a pity that for want of these circumstances, such noble institutions should be rendered of much less public utility, than was intended by their generous founders and supporters.

'The Rage for Building':
The Growth of London, 8 June 1791
Horace Walpole

THE DUKE OF St. Albans has cut down all the brave old trees at Hanworth, and consequently reduced his park to what it issued from – Hounslow-heath: nay, he has hired a meadow next to mine, for the benefit of embarkation; and there lie all the good old corpses of oaks, ashes, and chestnuts, directly before your windows, and blocking up one of my views of the river! but so impetuous is the rage for building, that his Grace's timber will, I trust, not annoy us long. There will soon be one street from London to Brentford; ay, and from London to every village ten miles round! Lord Camden has just let ground at Kentish Town for building fourteen hundred houses – nor do I wonder; London is, I am certain, much fuller than ever I saw it. I have twice this spring been going to stop my coach in Piccadilly, to inquire what was the matter, thinking there was a mob – not at all; it was only passengers.

London: A Georgian Poet's View, 1794

William Blake

To some, Georgian London was a miracle; to others it was monster, a Babylon on the Thames. Blake, himself a Cockney, looked around the city and saw only the alienation of man and the loss of natural innocence. Blake thus prefigured the Romantic movement – the opium of the metropolis' culturati in the next century.

I WANDER THRO' each charter'd street,
Near where the charter'd Thames does flow,
And mark in every face I meet
Marks of weakness, marks of woe.

In every cry of every Man,
In every Infant's cry of fear,
In every voice, in every ban,
The mind-forg'd manacles I hear.

How the Chimney-sweeper's cry
Every black'ning Church appalls;
And the hapless Soldier's sigh
Runs in blood down Palace walls.

But most thro' midnight streets I hear
How the youthful Harlot's curse
Blasts the new born Infant's tear,
And blights with plagues the Marriage hearse.

Mr Whitbread's Brewery, c. 1800
Johanna Schopenhauer

Brewing was a brobdingnagian business in Georgian London, one dominated by the firms of Perkins' in Southwark, Truman Hanbury and Buxton in Spitalfields, Charrington's in Mile End Road, Watney's in Pimlico and Whitbread's in Chiswell Street.

WHAT PREPARATIONS TO make a jar of porter! What commotion, what cranking and rattling of machinery! Beer barrels larger than a house in the Highlands! Cooling vats as wide as an ocean! Mr Whitbread's brewery would seem worthy to brew the invigorating infusion for Odin's heroes in Valhalla.

But to be serious, this brewery really is one of London's most important sights. The old King once visited it and took breakfast in the brew-house, an occasion which cost the owner some fifteen hundred pounds. The English satirist, Peter Pindar, endeavoured, in his 'Instructions to a Celebrated Laureate', to persuade the official poet to record this famous event in verse. Among other things the King asked Mr Whitbread how many barrels he owned, to which that gentleman replied: 'Laid closely together lengthwise, they might well stretch from London to Windsor.' Windsor lies 22 miles from London but, in view of the size of this huge establishment, Mr Whitbread's assertion does not seem all that impossible.

A steam-engine, situated in the basement, is the mainspring of this whole immense enterprise, and is the cleanest, simplest and least noisy we have ever seen. It has been calculated that it does the work of seventy horses, working day and night. Initially it supplies the necessary water, and carries the ready beer through subterranean channels across the road, into another building, where it is put into barrels. It brings these barrels, ready for loading, from the cellar. It grinds the malt, stirs it in the 20-feet deep vats and then transports it, with the help of a screw-like contrivance, up to the very top of the building. There, are found the very large but shallow tanks, only a few inches deep, which are used for cooling the beer. We were assured they would cover five English acres. The porter only needs to stand in them for six hours to be completely cold.

While everything in this vast establishment gives the impression of extreme cleanliness and order, working with apparent ease, every day something new has to be invented to improve what already seems to be perfect. Great stress is placed on the saving of fuel required by the three large vats, each containing five hundred barrels. The brewery employs two hundred workmen and eighty extraordinarily large horses. These are perhaps the biggest animals of their kind in existence and the shoes of one, which had to be put down because of illness, weighed 24 pounds. They are surely the giants of their breed.

In a building, higher and bigger than a church, stand forty-nine large barrels in which the beer is stored until it is decanted into smaller ones for distribution. Through remaining in the larger containers for a while, the quality is said to improve greatly. If Diogenes had the good fortune to live in a barrel of such size, the philosopher could easily have entertained twelve people at a round table and still had room for a pretty little boudoir for himself. The largest of these barrels has a kind of gallery at the top with a stair leading up to it. It is 27 feet high and has a diameter of 22 feet. It is hooped from top to bottom with iron bands at intervals of 6 inches. Towards the bottom the bands are very close to one another. All the barrels are made of strong oak and several contain 3,500 ordinary barrels. The famous barrel at Heidelberg would lose its place of honour in this company.

When we finally left the brewery, we felt somewhat intoxicated from the smell of the beer, in fact the atmosphere made one feel that one might be able to live on air. The men employed there, however, did not look at all as if they were willing to experiment in that way.

✗ ✗ ✗

Shooting Under London Bridge in a Boat, 12 July 1810
Louis Simond

JULY 12 [. . .] I have already mentioned certain basins, or docks, situated below London, into which whole fleets of merchantmen are laid up under lock and key. We provided ourselves with a letter of introduction for the Captain of the West-India docks, and taking a boat at the Whitehall Stairs, towards the latter part of the ebbing tide, we descended swiftly through the whole length of the town. The Adelphi and Somerset House, on the left, looked extremely well; the latter indeed magnificent, with the same black and white stains as at St Paul's, and on all other stone buildings in London; it has a singular effect, and not a bad one. The bridge opposite Somerset House is just begun; it will be only the fourth bridge, and not enough for this overgrown town. Paris has six or seven bridges. Blackfriars bridge is decaying rapidly. The stones are too soft, and scale off near the water's edge. The ornamental columns at each pier will not stand many years. It is a very handsome bridge. From all parts of the river the head and shoulders of St Paul's tower over every thing else, and its bright dome reflects the rays of the sun, invisible to the inhabitants of the busy world around its base, enveloped as they are in their own atmosphere of smoke. Not far from it the monument rears its bold and light form in just proportions. And farther down, the old tower of London, which although without beauty in itself, sets off the dull mass of private buildings. Nothing can well be uglier than London bridge; every arch is of a size different from its next neighbour; there are more solid than open parts; it is in fact like a thick wall, pierced with small unequal holes here and there, through which the current, dammed up by this clumsy fabric, rushes with great velocity, and in fact takes a leap, the difference between high and low water being upwards of 15 feet. Passengers are generally landed above, and taken up below the bridge; but being desirous of trying this little Niagara, which cannot be very dangerous, since so many boats pass it every day in safety, and being quite sure of reaching the shore by swimming, I remained with the boatman. He took the third arch, placed his boat in a direct line, then rested on his oars. The boat shot along an inclined plane, through the narrow hole, not 20 feet wide I believe, – ascended a little, then descended an abrupt step, – the prow straight down, – and up again in a moment – lifting some water into the boat, which turned several times round in the eddy below the bridge, before it got into the straight current. I am astonished this fall, repeated twice a-day for some hours, has not undermined the bridge long ago.

Below London bridge, the Thames begins to assume the appearance of a sea port. You see shipping at anchor on both sides, many Dutch, Danes, and Swedes, with licences, I suppose, and many Americans; two or three seventy-fours on the stocks, and some East Indiamen; Admiral de Winter's ship afloat, dismantled. We soon found ourselves in a crowd of boats, very gaily attired, full of rowers, and in great activity. It was a rowing match, – they appeared ready to start, and we took our station among the spectators. A shot fired was the signal. Three very light boats like the one we were in, 20 feet long, – 4½ feet beam, – 16 inches deep, – the greatest breadth in the middle, – sharp, fore and aft, like a shuttle, – clinker built, – one man in each, with sculls. One of the champions was orange all over, – the other yellow, – the third red. In a few minutes there was a great cry of Foul! foul! answered equally loud with Fair! fair! The friends on both sides interfered and stopped the boats. What it was exactly we could not make out, some nice point no doubt, as there was much vehement argumentation on both sides; but, apparently, without abuse or quarrelling, things were adjusted and the race resumed. The contending oarsmen passed very swiftly by us, straining every nerve, amidst shouts and acclamations. We saw them turn half-a mile above, around a large boat stationed there for the purpose, decorated with streamers, and covered with the *beau sexe* all in white. The orange man, who had the lead at first, seemed now to be overtaken by the red, – the yellow far behind. Returning, they soon passed us again, on the other side, followed by a fleet of boats, and were out of sight in a few minutes, down the river: – a band of music playing all the while.

The Season: Jane Austen's Party, April 1811

Jane Austen

By the Regency era, travelling up to London for 'the season' was an ingrained habit of the aristocracy and gentry. The season lasted four months, starting from New Year. For the season of 1811 Jane Austen stayed at her brother's house in Sloane Street.

*O*UR PARTY WENT extremely well ... The rooms were dressed up with flowers &c, & looked very pretty. – A glass for the Mantlepiece was lent, by the Man who is making their own. Mr Egerton & Mr Walter came at ½ past 5, & the festivities began with a p^r of very fine Soals ... At ½ past 7 arrived the Musicians in two Hackney coaches, & by 8 the lordly Company began to appear ... The Draw^g room being soon hotter than we liked, we placed ourselves in the connecting Passage, which was comparatively cool, & gave us all the advantage of the Music at a pleasant distance, as well as that of the first view of every new comer. – I was quite surrounded by acquaintance, especially Gentlemen ... I had as much upon my hands as I could do ... We were all delight & cordiality of course. Miss M. seems very happy, but has not beauty enough to figure in London. – Including everybody we were 66 – which was considerably more than Eliza was expecting ... The Music was extremely good ... It opened with (tell Fanny) 'Prike pe Parp pin Praise pof Prapella' [Jane and her niece Fanny created a nonsense language] – ...

Between the Songs were Lessons on the Harp, or Harp &
Piano Forte together ... There was one female singer, a short
Miss Davis all in blue, whose voice was said to be very fine
indeed; & all the Performers gave great satisfaction by doing
what they were paid for, & giving themselves no airs. – No
amateur could be persuaded to do anything. – The House was
not clear till after 12 ...

Austen's greatest pleasure during her capital sojourns was
shopping. She was not alone. Conspicuous consumption was
the order of the age, and was satisfied by the foundation of
high-end ('quality') emporiums that would become household
names: William Fortnum (joined by his friend Hugh Mason)
opened a grocery shop in 1707; William Hamley founded a toy
shop in 1760; James Christie opened his auction room in Pall
Mall in 1766, while John Hatchard opened his bookseller's in
1797.

The most fashionable shopping street in late Georgian
London was Regent Street, designed by John Nash, which also
had the advantage of, in Sir John Summerson's famous phrase,
'damming up Soho'. In effect, Regent Street divided the upper-
class West End from the regions where the poor lived.

Although Nash's wish to remodel the city in an orderly
fashion stumbled on the old problem of property rights, he
succeeded in bringing more elegance to the West End. As
one visitor, Prince Pückler-Muskau, noted in 1826: 'London is
extremely improved in the direction of Regent Street, Portland
Place and Regent's Park. Now for the first time, it has the air of
a seat of Government ...'

Death of a Climbing Boy, 29 March 1813
The Parliamentary Committee on Climbing Boys

From evidence presented to the Parliamentary Committee on climbing boys or 'chimney sweeps':

O N MONDAY MORNING, 29 March 1813, a chimney sweeper of the name of Griggs attended to sweep a small chimney in the brewhouse of Messrs Calvert and Co. in Upper Thames Street; he was accompanied by one of his boys, a lad of about eight years of age, of the name of Thomas Pitt. The fire had been lighted as early as 2 o'clock the same morning, and was burning on the arrival of Griggs and his little boy at eight. The fireplace was small, and an iron pipe projected from the grate some little way into the flue. This the master was acquainted with (having swept the chimneys in the brewhouse for some years), and therefore had a tile or two broken from the roof, in order that the boy might descend the chimney. He had no sooner extinguished the fire than he suffered the lad to go down; and the consequence, as might be expected, was his almost immediate death, in a state, no doubt, of inexpressible agony. The flue was of the narrowest description, and must have retained heat sufficient to have prevented the child's return to the top, even supposing he had not approached the pipe belonging to the grate, which must have been nearly red hot; this however was not clearly ascertained on the inquest, though the appearance of the body would induce an opinion that he had been unavoidably pressed against the pipe. Soon after his descent, the master, who remained on the top, was apprehensive that something had happened, and therefore desired him to come up; the answer of the boy was, 'I cannot come up, master, I must die here.' An alarm was given in the brewhouse immediately that he had stuck in the chimney, and a bricklayer who was at work near the spot attended, and after knocking down part of the brickwork of the chimney, just above the fireplace, made a hole sufficiently large to draw him through. A surgeon attended, but all attempts to restore life were ineffectual. On inspecting the body, various burns appeared; the fleshy part of the legs and a great part of the feet more particularly were injured; those parts too by which climbing boys most effectually ascend or descend chimneys, viz. the elbows and knees, seemed burnt to the bone; from which it must be evident that the unhappy sufferer made some attempts to return as soon as the horrors of his situation became apparent.

Despite the findings of the Committee, it was not until 1875 that the use of climbing boys was effectively forbidden.

Mrs Fry at Newgate, March 1822
Maria Edgeworth

Wife of the London merchant John Fry, Elizabeth Fry became a preacher for the Society of Friends in 1810. She visited Newgate Prison for women shortly afterwards, where she found 300 women and their children in abysmal conditions. She devoted the remainder of her life to penal reform.

YESTERDAY WE WENT the moment we had swallowed our breakfast – N.B. superfine green tea given to us by Mrs. Taddy, – by appointment to Newgate. The private door opened at sight of our tickets, and the great doors and the little doors, and the thick doors, and doors of all sorts, were unbolted and unlocked, and on we went through dreary but clean passages, till we came to a room where rows of empty benches fronted us. A table on which lay a large Bible. Several ladies and gentlemen entered and took their seats on benches at either side of the table, in silence.

Enter Mrs. Fry in a drab-coloured silk cloak, and plain borderless Quaker cap; a most benevolent countenance, – Guido-Madonna face, – calm, benign ... The prisoners came in, and in an orderly manner ranged themselves on the benches. All quite clean, faces, hair, caps, and hands. On a very low bench in front, little children were seated and were *settled* by their mothers. Almost all these women, about thirty, were under sentence of transportation, some few only were for imprisonment. One who did not appear was under sentence of death, – frequently women when sentenced to death become ill, and unable to attend Mrs. Fry; the others come regularly and voluntarily.

She opened the Bible, and read in the most sweetly solemn, sedate voice I ever heard, slowly and distinctly, without anything in the manner that could distract attention from the matter. Sometimes she paused to explain, which she did with great judgement, addressing the convicts, '*we* have felt; *we* are convinced'. They were very attentive, unaffectedly interested I thought in all she said, and touched by her manner. There was nothing put on in their countenances, not any appearance of hypocrisy. I studied their countenances carefully, but I could not see any which, without knowing to whom they belonged, I should have decided was bad; yet Mrs. Fry assured me that all those women had been the worst sort. She confirmed what we had read and heard, that it was by their love of their children that she first obtained influence over these abandoned women. When she first took notice of one or two of their fine children, the mothers said that if she could but save their children from the misery they had gone through in vice, they would do anything she bid them. And when they saw the change made in their children by her schooling, they begged to attend themselves. I could not have conceived that the love of their children could have remained so strong in hearts in which every other feeling of virtue had so long been dead . . .

Mrs. Fry often says an extempore prayer; but this day she was quite silent while she covered her face with her hands for some minutes: the women were perfectly silent with their eyes fixed upon her, and when she said, 'you may go', they went away *slowly*. The children sat quite still the whole time, – when one *leaned*, the mother behind set her upright . . .

There is only one being among all those upon whom she has tried to make salutary impression, on whom she could make none, – an old Jewess. She is so depraved, and so odiously dirty that she cannot be purified, body or mind; wash her and put clean clothes on, she tears and dirties them, and swarms with vermin again in twenty-four hours. I saw her in the kitchen where they were served with broth: a horrible spectacle, which haunted me the whole day and night afterwards. One eye had been put out and closed up, and the other glared with malignant passion. I asked her if she was not happier since Mrs. Fry had come to Newgate. She made no direct reply, but said, 'It is hard to be happy in a jail; if you tasted *that* broth you'd find it is nothing but dish-water.' I did taste it, and found it very good.

⅍ ⅍ ⅍

'Peelers': The Formation of the Metropolitan Police, October 1829
Sir Robert Peel

Peel's Metropolitan Police replaced the varied collection of 'thief-takers' – including the Bow Street Runners – who policed Georgian London, just as these forces had replaced the watchmen of previous eras.

Whitehall, October 10th, 1829.

MY DEAR CROKER,

Thanks for your suggestions in regard to the Metropolitan Police.

When I fixed the present rate of pay, I fixed it under an impression that it might be necessary to raise it, but I felt quite sure that it would be much easier to raise than to reduce the rate of pay. I cannot say that the short experience I have hitherto had has confirmed my first impression. I will not as yet speak decidedly on the point, but I am very far from being prepared to admit that the improvement of the situation of a common police constable by the giving him more money, would increase the efficiency of the establishment.

I have above 2000 applications for the appointment at the present rate of pay (this no doubt is a very bad test, if it were the only one). Every man who has been dismissed or has resigned, has with scarcely an exception petitioned for reinstatement. I do not again rely much upon this.

I must first consider what is the class of man I want; and secondly, will the rate of pay maintain the proper respectability of that class?

No doubt three shillings a day will not give me all the virtues under heaven, but I do not want them. Angels would be far above my work. Looking at the duties I want to be performed, I am not at all sure whether (all considerations of expense being put out of the question) three or four shillings a day will not ensure their performance in a much better manner than ten or twelve would. I have refused to employ gentlemen – commissioned officers, for instance – as superintendents and inspectors, because I am certain they would be above their work. They would refuse to associate with other persons holding the same offices who were not of equal rank, and they would therefore degrade the latter in the eyes of men.

A sergeant of the Guards at £200 a year is a better man for my purpose than a captain of high military reputation if he would serve for nothing, or if I could give him a thousand a year without entailing a fresh charge. For somewhat similar reasons, a three shilling a day man is better than a five shilling a day man.

After all, however, the real question is – how will three

shillings a day support a man? I speak as yet hesitatingly; but I have good reasons for thinking that one of my police constables, if a single man, can find out of his pay of a guinea a week: (1) lodgings, (2) medical attendance, (3) very comfortable subsistence at his mess, (4) clothing; and can, after finding these, save out of his pay ten shillings a week.

Now, I think the policy of enabling him to save more is questionable. However, the impressions under which I am at present writing are liable to be varied by further experience.

I must add to the number of the police for the present, district. I must say that it has worked much better in the first fortnight than I could have expected.

Ever most faithfully yours,

ROBERT PEEL.

William IV Rambles the Streets, 19 July 1830

Charles Greville

William IV succeeded to the throne in 1830, aged 65. A long-time sailor, he proved a most un-regal monarch, whose perambulations amidst the common hordes shocked polite society.

*J*ULY 20TH – Yesterday was a very busy day with H. Majesty, who is going much too fast, and begins to alarm his Ministers and astonish the world. In the morning he inspected the Coldstreams, dressed (for the first time in his life) in a military uniform and with a great pair of gold spurs half-way up his leg like a game-cock, although he was not to ride, for having chalk-stones in his hands he can't hold the reins. The Queen came to Lady Bathurst's to see the review and hold a sort of drawing-room, when the Ministers' wives were presented to her, and official men, to which were added Lady Bathurst's relations; everybody was undressed except the Officers. She is very ugly, with a horrid complexion, but has good manners, and did all this (which she hated) very well. She said the part as if she was acting and wished the green curtain to drop. After the review the King, with the Dukes of Cumberland, Sussex, and Gloster, and Prince George and the Prince of Prussia, and the Duchess of Cumberland's son, came in through the garden gate; the Duchess of Gloster and Princess Augusta were already there; they breakfasted and then went away, the Duke of Gloster bowing to the company while nobody was taking any notice of him or thinking about him. Nature must have been merry when she made this Prince, and in the sort of mood that certain great Artists used to exhibit in their comical caricatures; I never saw a countenance which that line in M'Flecknoe would so well describe –

And lambent dullness plays around his face.

At one there was to be a Council, to swear in Privy Councillors and Lord-Lieutenants, and receive Oxford and Cambridge Addresses. The review made it an hour later, and the Lieutenants, who had been summoned at one, and who are great, selfish, pampered aristocrats, were furious at being kept waiting, particularly Lord Grosvenor and the Duke of Newcastle, the former very peevish, the latter better humoured. I was glad to see them put to inconvenience. I never saw so full a Court, so much nobility with Academical Tag rag and bobtail. After considerable delay the King received the Oxford and Cambridge Addresses on the Throne, which (having only one throne between them) he then abdicated for the Queen to seat herself on and receive them too. She sat it very well, surrounded by the Princesses and her Ladies and household. When this mob could be got rid of the table was brought in and the Council held. The Duke was twice sworn as Constable of the Tower and Lieutenant of Hants; then Jersey and the new Privy Councillors; and then the host of Lieutenants six or seven at a time, or as many as could hold a bit of the bible. I begged the King would, to expedite the business, dispense with their kneeling, which he did, and so we got on rapidly enough; and I whispered to Jersey, who stood by me behind the King with his white wand, 'The pace is good, isn't it?' As they each kissed his hand, I told him their name or County, or both, and he had a civil word to say to everybody, inviting some to dinner, promising to visit others, reminding them of former visits, or something good-humoured; he asked

Lord Egremont's *permission* to go and live in his County, at Brighton.

All this was very well; no great harm in it; more affable, less dignified than the late King; but when this was over, and after so much fatigue, when he might very well have sat himself quietly down and rested, he must needs put on his plain cloathes and start on a ramble about the Streets, all alone too. In Pall Mall he met Watson Taylor, and took his arm and went up St. James's Street. There he was soon followed by a mob making an uproar, and when he got near White's a whore came up and kissed him. Belfast (who had been sworn in Privy Councillor in the morning), who saw this from White's, and Clinton thought it time to interfere, and came out to attend upon him. The mob increased, and always holding W. Taylor's arm, and flanked by Clinton and Belfast, who got shoved and kicked about to their inexpressible wrath, he got back to the Palace amid shouting and bawling and applause. When he got home he asked them to go in and take a quiet walk in the garden, and said, 'Oh, never mind all this; when I have walked about a few times they will get used to it, and will take no notice.' There are other stories, but I will put down nothing I do not see or hear, or hear from eye witnesses. Belfast told me this in the Park, fresh from the scene and smarting from the buffeting he had got. All the Park was ringing with it, and I told Lady Bathurst, who thought it so serious she would get Ld. B. to write to the Duke directly about it. Lord Combermere wanted to be made a Privy Councillor yesterday, but the Duke would not; he is in a sort of half-disgrace, and is not to be made yet, but will be by-and-by.

William IV died in 1837. His obituary in *The Times* noted, fairly enough, 'He was not a man of talent or of much refinement ... But he had a warm heart, and it was an English heart.'

At the time of William's passing, the population of London was about 1.5 million, making it the largest city on the planet. Tenements in slum districts known, in the vernacular of the time, as 'rookeries' teemed with people. Disease ran rife. Diphtheria, measles, smallpox and typhus were constant killers. Another contagion arrived in 1831 – another bacillus that ensured that the life expectancy of poor Londoners did not linger beyond 27 years.

✗ ✗ ✗

King Cholera, 1832
Charles Greville

17 FEBRUARY 1832

THE CHOLERA HAS produced more alertness than alarm here; in fact, at present it is a mere trifle – in three days twenty-eight persons. Nothing like the disorders which rage unheeded every year and every day among the lower orders. It is its name, its suddenness, and its frightful symptoms that terrify. The investigations, however, into the condition of the different parishes have brought to light dreadful cases of poverty and misery. A man came yesterday from Bethnal Green with an account of that district. They are all weavers, forming a sort of separate community; there they are born, there they live and labour, and there they die. They neither migrate nor change their occupation; they can do nothing else. They have increased in a ratio at variance with any principles of population, having nearly tripled in twenty years, from 22,000 to 62,000. They are for the most part out of employment, and can get none. 1,100 are crammed into the poor-house, five or six in a bed; 6,000 receive parochial relief. The parish is in debt; every day adds to the number of paupers and diminishes that of ratepayers. These are principally small shopkeepers, who are beggared by the rates. The district is in a complete state of insolvency and hopeless poverty, yet they multiply, and while the people look squalid and dejected, as if borne down by their wretchedness and destitution, the children thrive and are healthy. Government is ready to interpose with assistance, but what can Government do? We asked the man who came what could be done for them. He said 'employment', and employment is impossible . . .

IN THE MEANTIME the cholera has made its appearance in London, at Rotherhithe, Limehouse, and in a ship off Greenwich – in all seven cases. These are amongst the lowest and most wretched classes, chiefly Irish, and a more lamentable exhibition of human misery than that given by the medical men who called at the Council Office yesterday I never heard. They are in the most abject state of poverty, without beds to lie upon. The men live by casual labour, are employed by the hour, and often get no more than four or five hours' employment in the course of the week. They are huddled and crowded together by families in the same room, not as permanent lodgers, but procuring a temporary shelter; in short, in the most abject state of physical privation and moral degradation that can be imagined. We have sent down members of the Board of Health to make preparations and organize boards; but, if the disease really spreads, no human power can arrest its progress through such an Augean stable.

I APRIL 1832

I have refrained for a long time from writing down anything about the cholera, because the subject is intolerably disgusting to me, and I have been bored past endurance by the perpetual questions of every fool about it. It is not, however, devoid of interest. In the first place, what has happened here proves that 'the people' of this enlightened, reading, thinking, reforming nation are not a whit less barbarous than the serfs in Russia, for precisely the same prejudices have been shown here that were found at St. Petersburg and at Berlin. The disposition of the public was (and is) to believe that the whole thing was a humbug, and accordingly plenty of people were found to write in that sense, and the press lent itself to propagate the same idea. The disease, however, kept creeping on, the Boards of Health which were everywhere established immediately became odious, and the vestries and parishes stoutly resisted all pecuniary demands for the purpose of carrying into effect the recommendations of the Central Board or the orders of the Privy Council. In this town the mob has taken the part of the anti-cholerites, and the most disgraceful scenes have occurred. The other day a Mr. Pope, head of the hospital in Marylebone (Cholera Hospital), came to the Council Office to complain that a patient who was being removed with his own consent had been taken out of his chair by the mob and carried back, the chair broken, and the bearers and surgeon hardly escaping with their lives. Furious contests have taken place about the burials, it having been recommended that bodies should be burned directly after death, and the most violent prejudice opposing itself to this recommendation; in short, there is no end to the scenes of uproar, violence, and brutal ignorance that have gone on, and this on the part of the lower orders, for whose especial benefit all the precautions are taken, and for whose relief large sums have been raised and all the resources of charity called into activity in every part of the town.

It was not understood at the time that the cholera outbreak was caused by polluted water. This vital scientific breakthrough was made in 1854 by Dr John Snow, who noticed that those who drank from the pump in Broad Street died, while those who worked in the nearby brewery, and drank beer instead of water, did not. By then cholera had taken the lives of 30,000 Londoners.

The Opening of the London to Deptford Railway, 14 December 1837

John O' London

London's first railway was mounted on a twin-track viaduct.

THE DIRECTORS HAVING arrived at the London terminus were shown to their seats by ushers in waiting, and the band of music having taken up its positions on the roof of the carriage, the official bugler blew the signal for the start, and the train steamed off amidst the firing of cannon, the ringing of church bells, and the cheers of an excited crowd. Spa Road, the only intermediate station, was filled to excess with almost the multitude there assembled, was reached with almost the swiftness of a discharged rocket, and afterwards Deptford, where a vast concourse, in carriages and on foot, awaited the visitors, with a second band of music, which then took the place of the first on the return journey.

The journey took 14 minutes to complete.

So began the railway age, an age in which London would be broken up and remade. The construction of the railways saw whole swathes of the capital knocked down to make way for track and stations. Charles Dickens witnessed the construction of the London & Birmingham Railway line at Camden Town:

THE FIRST SHOCK of a great earthquake had, just at that period, rent the whole neighbourhood to its centre. Traces of its course were visible on every side. Houses were knocked down; streets broken through and stopped; deep pits and trenches dug in the ground; enormous heaps of earth and clay thrown up; buildings that were undermined and shaking propped by great beams of wood. Here, a chaos of carts, overthrown and jumbled together, lay topsy-turvy at the bottom of a steep unnatural hill; there confused treasures of iron soaked and rusted in something that had accidentally become a pond. Everywhere were bridges that led nowhere; thorough-fares that were wholly impassable; Babel towers of chimneys, wanting half their height; temporary wooden houses and enclosures, in the most unlikely situations; carcases of ragged tenements, and fragments of unfinished walls and arches, and piles of scaffolding and wilderness of bricks, and giant forms of cranes, and tripods straddling above nothing.

The human cost was fantastic; for just two miles of track the North London Railway company knocked down 900 houses, obliging their occupiers to relocate to already crowded slums. Crowding them still further were the tens of thousands of migrants who poured into London annually – about half of whom were Irish – to work on the railways. The poor got to live with the poor – while the railway allowed the rich to move out, to leafy villages such as Norwood and Sydenham. No longer was London a city where, irrespective of social status, people lived side-by-side. London became a place of distinctions in class and address.

Under the pressure of increased population, London broke its bounds. There was little planning. Unlike Paris, which grew within the ancient restraint of the city limits, or New York, which was hemmed in by rivers and sea, London simply sprawled where it liked, swallowing up farmland, market gardens, piggeries and villages. A little over a decade after the opening of the Deptford line, the reformers Henry Mayhew and John Binny went up in a balloon to view London from above and were aghast at its size:

IN THE OPPOSITE direction to that in which the wind was insensibly wafting the balloon, lay the leviathan Metropolis, with a dense canopy of smoke hanging over it ... It was impossible to tell where the monster city began or ended, for the buildings stretched not only to the horizon on either side, but far away into the distance ...

The railway age coincided almost exactly with the reign of the queen who would see London at its most powerful, the capital of the world.

Queen Victoria at Her Coronation, 28 June 1838

Queen Victoria

At the time of Victoria's coronation, she was 19 years old.

I WAS AWOKE AT four o'clock by the guns in the Park, and could not get much sleep afterwards on account of the noise of the people, bands, etc., etc. Got up at seven, feeling strong and well; the Park presented a curious spectacle, crowds of people up to Constitution Hill, soldiers, bands, etc. I dressed, having taken a little breakfast before I dressed, and a little after. At half past 9 I went into the next room, dressed exactly in my House of Lords costume ...

At 10 I got into the State Coach with the Duchess of Sutherland and Lord Albemarle and we began our Progress ... It was a fine day, and the crowds of people exceeded what I have ever seen; many as there were the day I went to the City, it was nothing, nothing to the multitudes, the millions of my loyal subjects, who were assembled *in every spot* to witness the Procession. Their good humour and excessive loyalty was beyond everything, and I really cannot say *how* proud I feel to be the Queen of *such* a Nation. I was alarmed at times for fear that the people would be crushed and squeezed on account of the tremendous rush and pressure.

I reached the Abbey amid deafening cheers at a little after half past eleven; I first went into a robing-room quite close to the entrance where I found my eight train-bearers ...

After putting on my mantle, and the young ladies having properly got hold of it and Lord Conyngham holding the end of it, I left the robing-room and the Procession began as is described in the annexed account, and all that followed and took place. The sight was splendid; the bank of Peeresses quite beautiful all in their robes, and the Peers on the other side. My young train-bearers were always near me, and helped me whenever I wanted anything. The Bishop of Durham stood on the side near me, but he was, as Lord Melbourne told me, remarkably *maladroit*, and never could tell me what was to take place. At the beginning of the Anthem, where I've made a mark, I retired to St. Edward's Chapel, a dark small place immediately behind the Altar, with my ladies and train-bearers – took off my crimson robe and kirtle, and put on the supertunica of cloth of gold, also in the shape of a kirtle, which was put over a singular sort of little gown of linen trimmed with lace; I also took off my circlet of diamonds and then proceeded bareheaded into the Abbey; I was then seated upon St. Edward's chair, where the Dalmatic robe was clasped round me by the Lord Great Chamberlain. Then followed all the various things; and last (of those things) the Crown being placed on my head – which was, I must own, a most beautiful impressive moment; *all* the Peers and Peeresses put on their coronets at the same instant.

My excellent Lord Melbourne, who stood very close to me throughout the whole ceremony, was *completely* overcome at this moment, and very much affected; he gave me such a kind, and I may say *fatherly* look. The shouts, which were very great, the drums, the trumpets, the firing of the guns, all at the same instant, rendered the spectacle most imposing.

London in 1838 was the world's biggest city – for the next 50 years it would grow exponentially. When Victoria died in 1901 the city's population was 4.5 million.

~~

The Condition of the Working Class in London, c. 1844

Friedrich Engels

ONDON IS UNIQUE, because it is a city in which one can roam for hours without leaving the built-up area and without seeing the slightest sign of the approach of open country. This enormous agglomeration of population on a single spot has multiplied a hundred-fold the economic strength of the two and a half million inhabitants concentrated there. This great population has made London the commercial capital of the world and has created the gigantic docks in which are assembled the thousands of ships which always cover the River Thames. I know nothing more imposing than the view one obtains of the river when sailing from the sea up to London Bridge. Especially above Woolwich the houses and docks are packed tightly together on both banks of the river. The further one goes up the river the thicker becomes the concentration of ships lying at anchor, so that eventually only a narrow shipping lane is left free in midstream. Here hundreds of steamships dart rapidly to and fro. All this is so magnificent and impressive that one is lost in admiration. The traveller has good reason to marvel at England's greatness even before he steps on English soil.

It is only later that the traveller appreciates the human suffering which has made all this possible. He can only realise the price that has been paid for all this magnificence after he has tramped the pavements of the main streets of London for some days and has tired himself out by jostling his way through the crowds and by dodging the endless stream of coaches and carts which fills the streets. It is only when he has visited the slums of this great city that it dawns upon him that the inhabitants of modern London have had to sacrifice so much that is best in human nature in order to create those wonders of civilisation with which their city teems. The vast majority of Londoners have had to let so many of their potential creative faculties lie dormant, stunted and unused in order that a small, closely knit group of their fellow citizens could develop to the full the qualities with which nature has endowed them. The restless and noisy activity of the crowded streets is highly distasteful, and it is surely abhorrent to human nature itself. Hundreds of thousands of men and women drawn from all classes and ranks of society pack the streets of London. Are they not all human beings with the same innate characteristics and potentialities? Are they not all equally interested in the pursuit of happiness? And do they not all aim at happiness by following similar methods? Yet they rush past each other as if they had nothing in common. They are tacitly agreed on one thing only – that everyone should keep to the right of the pavement so as not to collide with the stream of people moving in the opposite direction. No one even thinks of sparing a glance for his neighbour in the streets. The more that Londoners are packed into a tiny space, the more repulsive and disgraceful becomes the brutal indifference with which they ignore their neighbours and selfishly concentrate upon their private affairs. We know well enough that this isolation of the individual – this narrow-minded egotism – is everywhere the fundamental principle of modern society. But nowhere is this selfish egotism so blatantly evident as in the frantic bustle of the great city. The disintegration of society into individuals, each guided by his private principles and each pursuing his own aims has been pushed to its furthest limits in London. Here indeed human society has been split into its component atoms ...

Every great town has one or more slum areas into which the working classes are packed. Sometimes, of course, poverty is to be found hidden away in alleys close to the stately homes of the wealthy. Generally, however, the workers are segregated in separate districts where they struggle through life as best they can out of sight of the more fortunate classes of society. The slums of the English towns have much in common – the worst houses in a town being found in the worst districts. They are generally unplanned wildernesses of one- or two-storied terrace houses built of brick. Wherever possible these have cellars which are also used as dwellings. These little houses of three or four rooms and a kitchen are called cottages, and throughout England, except for some parts of London, are where the working classes normally live. The streets themselves are usually unpaved and full of holes. They are filthy and strewn with animal and vegetable refuse. Since they have neither gutters nor drains the refuse accumulates in stagnant, stinking puddles. Ventilation in the slums is inadequate owing to the hopelessly unplanned nature of these areas. A great many people live huddled together in a very small area, and so it is easy to imagine the nature of the air in these workers' quarters. However, in fine weather the streets are used for the drying of washing and clothes lines are stretched across the streets from house to house and wet garments are hung out on them.

We propose to describe some of these slums in detail. In London there is the well-known 'rookery' of St. Giles, which is to be demolished to make way for wide new thoroughfares. St. Giles is situated in the most densely populated part of London and is surrounded by splendid wide streets which are used by the fashionable world. It is close to Oxford Street, Trafalgar

Square and the Strand. It is a confused conglomeration of tall houses of three or four stories. The narrow, dirty streets are just as crowded as the main thoroughfares, but in St. Giles one sees only members of the working classes. The narrowness of the roads is accentuated by the presence of street markets in which baskets of rotting and virtually uneatable vegetables and fruit are exposed for sale. The smell from these and from the butchers' stalls is appalling. The houses are packed from cellar to attic and they are as dirty inside as outside. No human being would willingly inhabit such dens. Yet even worse conditions are to be found in the houses which lie off the main road down narrow alleys leading to the courts. These dwellings are approached by covered passages between the houses. The extent to which these filthy passages are falling into decay beggars all description. There is hardly an unbroken windowpane to be seen, the walls are crumbling, the door posts and window frames are loose and rotten. The doors, where they exist, are made of old boards nailed together. Indeed in this nest of thieves doors are superfluous, because there is nothing worth stealing. Piles of refuse and ashes lie all over the place and the slops thrown out into the street collect in pools which emit a foul stench. Here live the poorest of the poor. Here the worst-paid workers rub shoulders with thieves, rogues and prostitutes. Most of them have come from Ireland or are of Irish extraction. Those who have not yet been entirely engulfed in the morass of iniquity by which they are surrounded are daily losing the power to resist the demoralising influences of poverty, dirt and low environment.

St. Giles, however, is by no means the only London slum. In the vast mass of streets which make up the metropolis there are thousands of hidden alleys and passages where the houses are so bad that no one with an iota of self-respect would live in them unless forced to do so by dire poverty. Such dens of extreme poverty are often to be found close to the splendid mansions of the wealthy. Recently at a coroner's inquest an area near Portman Square – a very respectable part of London – was described as the abode of 'a large number of Irish demoralised by dirt and poverty'. In a street like Long Acre, which, although not fashionable, is still respectable, there are many cellar dwellings from which emerge into the light of day sickly children and half-starved, ragged women. In the immediate vicinity of the second most important theatre in London, that in Drury Lane, are to be found some of the worst streets in the metropolis. In Charles Street, King Street and Parker Street all the houses are crammed from cellar to roof with many poor families. In 1840, according to a report printed in the *Journal* of the Statistical Society of London, there were in the parishes of St. John and St. Margaret, Westminster, 5,366 working-class families living in 5,294 'dwellings' (if they deserve this appellation!). Altogether there were 16,176 men, women and children thrown together without distinction of age or sex. Three quarters of the families lived in a single room. It is stated in the same *Journal* – that 1,465 working-class families totalling about 6,000 persons lived under similar conditions in [the Inner Ward of] the aristocratic parish of St. George, Hanover Square. In two-thirds of the families investigated the members were packed into a single room. How shamefully do the wealthier classes exploit, under the protection of the law, these miserable slum-dwellers, who are so poor that no thief would think of trying to rob them. The following [weekly] rents are charged for accommodation in the revolting dwellings near Drury Lane which we have just described: 3s. for cellars, 4s. for a room on the ground floor, 4s. 6d. on the first floor, 4s. on the second floor, 3s. for an attic. The starving inhabitants of Charles Street pay their landlord an annual tribute of £2,000, while the 5,366 families in Westminster mentioned above together pay an annual rent of £40,000.

The largest working-class district lies in Whitechapel and Bethnal Green to the east of the Tower of London. Here live the great majority of London's workers. The Rev. G. Alston, incumbent of St. Philip's, Bethnal Green, has given the following account of conditions in his parish:

It contains 1,400 houses, inhabited by 2,795 families, comprising a population of 12,000. The space within which this large amount of population are living is less than 400 yards square, and it is no uncommon thing for a man and his wife, with four or five children, and sometimes the grandfather and grandmother, to be found living in a room from ten to twelve feet square, and which serves them for eating and working in. I believe that till the Bishop of London called the attention of the public to the state of Bethnal-green, about as little was known at the West-end of the town of this most destitute parish as the wilds of Australia or the islands of the South Seas. If we really desire to find out the most destitute and deserving, we must lift the latch of their doors, and find them at their scanty meal; we must see them when suffering from sickness and want of work; and if we do this from day to day in such a neighbourhood as Bethnal-green, we shall become acquainted with a mass of wretchedness and misery such as a nation like our own ought to be ashamed to permit. I was Curate of a parish near Huddersfield during the three years of the greatest manufacturing distress; but I never witnessed such a thorough prostration of the poor as I have seen since I have been in Bethnal-green. There is not one father of a family in ten throughout the entire district that possesses any clothes but his working dress, and that too commonly in the worst tattered condition; and with many this wretched clothing form their only covering at night, with nothing better than a bag of straw or shavings to lie upon.

This description enables us to appreciate the conditions inside these dwellings. We may add also some evidence given by public officials, who sometimes have occasion to enter the homes of the workers.

On November 16th, 1843, Mr. Carter, the coroner for Surrey, held an inquest on the body of a certain Ann Galway, who died at the age of 45. We take the following account of her home from press reports. She lived in no. 3, White Lion Court, Bermondsey Street, London, with her husband and nineteen-year-old son. The family occupied a single small room in which there were neither beds, bedding nor other furniture. She lay dead by the side of her son on a heap of feathers which practically covered her naked body, for she had neither sheet nor blanket. The feathers had stuck so fast to her that the doctor was unable to examine the body until it had been washed. The doctor found that the body was emaciated and verminous. Part of the floor in the room had been torn up and the hole used by the family as a privy.

On Monday, January 15th, 1844, two boys appeared before the magistrate at Worship Street police court, London, charged with stealing a half-cooked cow-heel from a shop. They immediately devoured their spoils as they were ravenous. The magistrate felt it necessary to enquire further into the circumstances and was given the following information by the police. The boys were brothers and their mother was a widow. Their father had served in the Army and had later been a policeman. After the death of her husband, the widow was left to struggle along as best she could with nine children. The family lived in dire poverty at no. 2, Pool's Place, Quaker

Court, Spitalfields. When visited by a policeman she was found with six of her children. They were all huddled together and the only furniture consisted of two rush-bottomed chairs with seats gone, a little table with two legs broken, one broken cup and one small dish. Hardly a spark of fire came from the hearth and in one corner lay as many rags as would fill a woman's apron. It was on these rags that the whole family slept at night. As they had no blankets they slept in the miserable tatters worn during the daytime. The wretched woman told the policeman that she had to sell her bed during the previous year in order to buy food. She had pawned her bedding with the grocer for food. Indeed everything had been sold to get bread. The magistrate made her a generous grant from the poor-box.

In February 1844 an application for assistance was made to the Marlborough Street magistrate on behalf of Theresa Bishop, a 60-year- old widow, and her 26-year-old daughter who was ill. She lived at no. 5, Brown Street, Grosvenor Square, in a little back room hardly bigger than a cupboard. The room contained no proper furniture. A *chest* was used both as table and chair, while a heap of rags in a corner served as a bed for both women. The mother earned a little money as a charwoman. Her landlord stated that she and her daughter had lived in this condition since May 1843. Gradually all their remaining possessions had been sold or pawned, but even so they had been unable to pay any rent. The magistrate allowed them 20s. out of the poor-box.

It is not, of course, suggested that all London workers are so poverty stricken as these three families. There can be no doubt that for every worker who is rendered utterly destitute by society there are ten who are better off. On the other hand it can be confidently asserted that thousands of decent and industrious families – far more deserving of respect than all the rich people in London – live under truly deplorable conditions which are an affront to human dignity. It is equally incontestable that every working man without exception may well suffer a similar fate through no fault of his own and despite all his efforts to keep his head above water.

However wretched may be the dwellings of some of the workers – who do at least have a roof over their heads – the situation of the homeless is even more tragic. Every morning fifty thousand Londoners wake up not knowing where they are going to sleep at night. The most fortunate are those who have a few pence in their pocket in the evening and can afford to go to one of the many lodging houses which exist in all the big cities. But these establishments only provide the most miserable accommodation. They are crammed full of beds from top to bottom – four, five and even six beds in a room – until there is no room for more. Each bed is filled to capacity and may contain as many as four, five or even six lodgers. The lodging house keeper allocates his accommodation to all his customers in rotation as they arrive. No attempt is made to segregate the sick and the healthy, the old and the young, the men and the women, the drunk and the sober. If these ill-assorted bed-fellows do not agree there are quarrels and fights which often lead to injuries. But if they do agree among themselves, it is even worse, for they are either planning burglaries or are engaged in practices of so bestial a nature that no words exist in a modern civilised tongue to describe them. Those who cannot afford a bed in a lodging house sleep where they can, in passages, arcades or any corner where the police and the owners are unlikely to disturb their slumbers. A few find accommodation in the shelters provided by private charitable organizations. Others sleep on benches in the parks in full view of Queen Victoria's windows. An account of these conditions may be found in a leading article of the *Times* for October 12th, 1843:

It appears from the report of the proceedings at Marlborough Street Police Office in our columns of yesterday, that there is an average number of 50 human beings, of all ages, who huddle together in the parks every night, having no other shelter than what is supplied by the trees and hollows of the embankment. Of these the majority are young girls, who have been seduced from the country by the soldiers, and turned loose on the world in all the destitution of friendless penury, and all the recklessness of early vice.

This is truly horrible. Poor there must be everywhere. Indigence will find its way and set up its hideous state in the heart of a great and luxurious city. Amid the thousand narrow lanes and by-streets of a populous metropolis there must always, we fear, be much suffering – much that offends the eye – much that lurks unseen.

But that within the precincts of wealth, gaiety, and fashion, nigh the regal grandeur of St. James's, close on the palatial splendour of Bayswater, on the confines of the old and new aristocratic quarters in a district where the cautious refinement of modern design has refrained from creating one single tenement for poverty; which seems, as it were, dedicated to the exclusive enjoyments of wealth – that there want, and famine, and disease, and vice should stalk in all their kindred horrors, consuming body by body, soul by soul!

It is, indeed, a monstrous state of things! Enjoyment the most absolute, that bodily ease, intellectual excitement, or the more innocent pleasures of sense can supply to man's craving, brought in close contact with the most unmitigated misery! Wealth, from its bright saloons, laughing – an insolently heedless laugh – at the unknown wounds of want! Pleasure, cruelly but unconsciously mocking the pain that moans below! All contrary things mocking one another – all contrary, save the vice which tempts and the vice which is tempted!

But let all men, whether of theory or of practice, remember this – that within the most courtly precincts of the richest city on GOD'S earth, there may be found, night after night, winter after winter, women – young in years – old in sin and suffering – outcasts from society – ROTTING FROM FAMINE, FILTH AND DISEASE. Let them remember this, and learn not to theorize but to act. God knows, there is much room for action now-a-days.

Reference has already been made to the shelters for the destitute. Two examples may be given to illustrate the hopeless overcrowding in these establishments. In a new Refuge for the Houseless in Upper Ogle Street [Marylebone], which has accommodation for 300, no less than 2,740 persons were given shelter for one or more nights between January 27th, and March 7th, 1844. Although it was a mild winter the number of people seeking accommodation in the shelter in Upper Ogle Street – and also in the hostels in Whitecross Street and Wapping-increased rapidly, and every night many applicants had to be refused admission. In another shelter, the Central Asylum in Playhouse Yard, the average number of persons accommodated in the first three months of 1843 amounted to 460. The total number of persons sheltered was 6,681, while the number of portions of bread distributed amounted to 96,141. Yet the committee responsible for the administration of this institution reported that only after the opening of the new Eastern Asylum had they been able to afford adequate provision for the applicants.

Benjamin Disraeli, the young Tory who would go on to become prime minister, conjured up the phrase 'Two Nations' to describe the gyre between poor and rich in Victorian England. To close the gap, the poor – for the first time – began to organize themselves politically. An early manifestation was Chartism.

❧ ❧ ❧

Chartist Demonstration, 10 April 1848
Lord John Russell

The Chartist movement, named after the People's Charter of 1838, sought universal male suffrage. In 1848 the third and final Chartist petition was brought to London.

Russell, the Prime Minister, writes to Queen Victoria, who was holidaying on the Isle of Wight:

LORD RUSSELL . . . has the honour to state that the Kennington Common Meeting [of the Chartists] has proved a complete failure.

About 12,000 or 15,000 persons met in good order. Feargus O'Connor, upon arriving upon the ground in a car, was ordered by Mr Mayne [the Commissioner of Police – ed.] to come and speak to him. He immediately left the car and came, looking pale and frightened, to Mr Mayne. Upon being told that the meeting would not be prevented, but that no procession would be allowed to pass the bridges, he expressed the utmost thanks, and begged to shake Mr Mayne by the hand. He then addressed the crowd, advising them to disperse, and after rebuking them for their folly he went off in a cab to the Home Office, where he repeated to Sir George Grey [the Home Secretary – ed.] his thanks, his fears, and his assurances that the crowd should disperse quietly. Sir George Grey said he had done very rightly, but that the force at the bridges should not be diminished.

Mr F. O'Connor – 'Not a man should be taken away. The Government have been quite right. I told the Convention that if they had been the Government they never would have allowed such a meeting.'

The last account gave the numbers as about 5,000 rapidly dispersing.

The mob was in good humour, and any mischief that now takes place will be the act of individuals; but it is to be hoped the preparations made will daunt those wicked but not brave men.

The accounts from the country are good. Scotland is quiet. At Manchester, however, the Chartists are armed, and have bad designs.

A quiet termination of the present ferment will greatly raise us in foreign countries.

Lord John Russell trusts your Majesty has profited by the sea air.

The petition was a fiasco, as was an attempted Chartist insurrection in the capital in August. Thomas Frost, a Chartist conspirator, recalled:

ON THE EVENING of the 15th of August, which was finally fixed for the outbreak, a number of men assembled at a public-house called the Orange Tree, in Orange Street, Bloomsbury, and were in feverish expectation of the signal, when an inspector of police appeared at the door of the room in which they were seated, with a drawn cutlass in his right hand, and a cocked pistol in his left. Behind him those seated opposite the door could see a dozen constables, all similarly armed. There was a movement among the party as he entered, indicative of meditated resistance or escape: but it was checked by the threat to shoot down the first who resisted, or attempted to leave the room.

Commanding each in his turn to stand up, the inspector then searched them, and afterwards the room. A sword was found under the coat of one, and the head of a pike, made to screw into a socket, under that of another. One had a pair of pistols in his pocket, and a fourth was provided with a rusty bayonet, fastened to the end of a stick. Some were without other weapons than shoemakers' knives. A pike, which no one would own, was found under a bench upon which several of the men had been sitting. All of the party were taken into custody, and marched off to the nearest police station . . .

Chartism was of no importance thereafter. Britain, for all its class tensions and for all the stresses caused by breakneck industrialization, was a remarkably stable society. London, in particular, enjoyed a rock-like solidity, since the nature of local industry, which tended to be small scale and spread out, actually worked against working-class organization.

Revolutions swept through European capital after capital in 1848. London managed a damp-squib demonstration and a risible attempted putsch, which barely anyone noticed.

Victorian London: Street Life, c. 1850
Henry Mayhew

Henry Mayhew was the author of the pioneering social study, *London Labour and the London Poor*, the first volume of which was published in 1851.

A Watercress Girl

THE LITTLE WATERCRESS girl who gave me the following statement, although only eight years of age, had entirely lost all childish ways, and was, indeed, in thoughts and manner, a woman. There was something cruelly pathetic in hearing this infant, so young that her features had scarcely formed themselves, talking of the bitterest struggles of life, with the calm earnestness of one who had endured them all. I did not know how to talk with her. At first I treated her as a child, speaking on childish subjects; so that I might, by being familiar with her, remove all shyness, and get her to narrate her life freely. I asked her about her toys and her games with her companions; but the look of amazement that answered me soon put an end to any attempt at fun on my part. I then talked to her about the parks, and whether she ever went to them. 'The parks!' she replied in wonder, 'where are they?' I explained to her, telling her that they were large open places with green grass and tall trees, where beautiful carriages drove about, and people walked for pleasure, and children played. Her eyes brightened up a little as I spoke; and she asked, half doubtingly, 'Would they let such as me go there – just to look?' All her knowledge seemed to begin and end with watercresses, and what they fetched. She knew no more of London than that part she had seen on her rounds, and believed that no quarter of the town was handsomer or pleasanter than it was at Farringdon-market or at Clerkenwell, where she lived. Her little face, pale and thin with privation, was wrinkled where the dimples ought to have been, and she would sigh frequently. When some hot dinner was offered to her, she would not touch it, because, if she ate too much, 'it made her sick,' she said; 'and she wasn't used to meat, only on a Sunday.'

The poor child, although the weather was severe, was dressed in a thin cotton gown, with a threadbare shawl wrapped round her shoulders. She wore no covering to her head, and the long rusty hair stood out in all directions. When she walked she shuffled along, for fear that the large carpet slippers that served her for shoes should slip off her feet.

'I go about the streets with water-creases, crying, "Four bunches a penny, water-creases." I am just eight years old – that's all, and I've a big sister, and a brother and a sister younger than I am. On and off, I've been very near a twelvemonth in the streets. Before that, I had to take care of a baby for my aunt. No, it wasn't heavy – it was only two months old; but I minded it for ever such a time – till it could walk. It was a very nice little baby, not a very pretty one; but, if I touched it under the chin, it would laugh. Before I had the baby, I used to help mother, who was in the fur trade; and, if there was any slits in the fur, I'd sew them up. My mother learned me to needle-work and to knit when I was about five. I used to go to school, too; but I wasn't there long. I've forgot all about it now, it's such a time ago; and mother took me away because the master whacked me, though the missus use'n't to never touch me. I didn't like him at all. What do you think? he hit me three times, ever so hard, across the face with his cane, and made me go dancing down stairs; and when mother saw the marks on my cheek, she went to blow him up, but she couldn't see him – he was afraid. That's why I left school.

'The creases is so bad now, that I haven't been out with 'em for three days. They're so cold, people won't buy 'em; for when I goes up to them, they say, "They'll freeze our bellies." Besides, in the market, they won't sell a ha'penny handful now – they're ris to a penny and tuppence. In summer there's lots, and 'most as cheap as dirt; but I have to be down at Farringdon-market between four and five, or else I can't get any creases, because everyone almost – especially the Irish – is selling them, and they're picked up so quick. Some of the saleswomen – we never calls 'em ladies – is very kind to us children, and some of them altogether spiteful. The good one will give you a bunch for nothing, when they're cheap; but the others, cruel ones, if you try to bate them a farden less than they ask you, will say, "Go along with you, you're no good." I used to go down to market along with another girl, as must be-about fourteen, 'cos she does her back hair up. When we've bought a lot, we sits down on a door-step, and ties up the bunches. We never goes home to breakfast till we've sold out; but, if it's very late, then I buys a penn'orth of pudden, which is very nice with gravy. I don't know hardly one of the people, as goes to Farringdon, to talk to; they never speaks to me, so I don't speak to them. We children never play down there, 'cos we're thinking of our living. No; people never pities me in the street – excepting one gentleman, and he says, says he, "What do you do out so soon in the morning?" but he gave me nothink – he only walked away.

'It's very cold before winter comes on reg'lar – specially getting up of a morning. I gets up in the dark by the light of the lamp in the court. When the snow is on the ground, there's creases. I bears the cold – you must; so I puts my hands under my shawl, though it hurts 'em to take hold of the

creases, especially when we takes 'em to the pump to wash 'em.
No; I never see any children crying – it's no use.'

Street Slang

This East End street language noted by Mayhew was the basis
for the famous Cockney rhyming slang. Cockney itself is derived
from Middle English 'cokeney', meaning a misshapen egg.

IN ORDER THAT I might omit nothing which will give the
student of that curious phase of London life in London
streets – the condition of the patterers – a clear understanding
of the subject, I procured the following account from an
educated gentleman: 'I had lived,' he said, 'more than a year
among the tradesmen and tramps, who herd promiscuously
together in low lodging-houses. One afternoon I was taking
tea at the same table with a brace of patterers. They eyed me
with suspicion; but, determined to know their proceedings,
I launched out the only cant word I had then learned. They
spoke of going to Chatham. Of course, I knew the place,
and asked them, "Where do you stall to in the huey?" which,
fairly translated, means, "Where do you lodge in the town?"
Convinced that I was "fly," one of them said, "We drop the
main toper (go off the main road) and slink into the crib
(house) in the back drum (street)." After some altercation with
the "mot" of the "ken" (mistress of the lodging-house) about
the cleanliness of a knife or fork, my new acquaintance began
to arrange "ground", &c., for the night's work. I got into their
confidence by degrees; and I give below a vocabulary of their
talk to each other:

Word.	Meaning.
Crabshells	Shoes.
Kite	Paper.
Nests	Varieties.
Sticky	Wax.
Toff	Gentleman.
Burerk	Lady.
Camister	Minister.
Crocus	Doctor.
Bluff	An excuse.
Balmy	Insane.
Mill Tag	A shirt.
Smeesh	A shift.
Hay-bag	A woman.
Doxy	A wife.
Flam	A lie.
Teviss	A shilling.
Bull	A crown.
Flag	An apron.

The Bird Seller

'THE LAST WHOLE day that I was at my pitch I sold nine birds, and took about 3 shillings. If I could buy birds ever so cheap, there's always such losses by their dying. I've had three parts of my young linnets die, do what I might, but not often so many. Then if they die all the food they've had is lost. There goes all for nothing the rape and flax-seed for your linnets, canary for your goldfinches, chopped eggs for your nightingales, and German paste for your sky-larks. I've made my own German paste when I've wanted a sufficient quantity. It's made of pea-meal, treacle, hog's-lard, and moss-seed. I sell more goldfinches than anything else. I used to sell a good many sparrows for shooting, but I haven't done anything that way these eight or nine years. It's a fash'nable sport still, I hear. I've reared nightingales that sung beautiful, and have sold them at 4s. a piece, which was very cheap. They often die when the time for their departure comes. A shopkeeper as supplied such as I've sold would have charged £1 a piece for them. My favouritest birds is redpoles, but they're only sold in the season.

'My customers are all working people, all of them. I sell to nobody else; I make 4s. or 5s.; I call 5 s. a good week at this time of year, when the weather suits. I lodge with a married sister; her husband's a wood-chopper, and I pay 1s. 6d a week, which is cheap, for I've no sticks of my own. If I earn 4s. there's only 2s. 6d left to live on the week through. In winter, when I can make next to nothing, and must keep my birds, it is terrible – oh, yes, sir, if you believe me, terrible!'

Under the Street: The Life of a Sewer Hunter

Sewer-hunters, or 'toshers', were among the most desperate of those seeking a living in Victorian London. They searched and panned the sewers – still, in this era, rainwater ducts – for anything saleable. Quite different from 'fermors' and 'rakers', whose occupation was the cleaning of sewers, toshers left their mark on London language: their occupation is the origin of the pejorative 'tosh'.

'I STAY'D WITH the old un a long time, and we used to git lots o' tin, specially when we'd go to work the sewers. I liked that well enough. I could git into small places where the old un couldn't, and when I'd got near the grating in the street, I'd search about in the bottom of the sewer; I'd put down my arm to my shoulder in the mud and bring up shillings and half-crowns, and lots of coppers, and plenty other things. I once found a silver jug as big as a quart pot, and often found spoons and knives and forks and every thing you can think of. Bless your heart the smell's nothink; it's a roughish smell at first, but nothink near so bad as you thinks, 'cause, you see, there's sich lots o'water always a coming down the sewer, and the air gits in from the gratings, and that helps to sweeten it a bit. There's some places, 'specially in the old sewers, where they say there's foul air, and they tells me the foul air 'ill cause instantious death, but I niver met with anythink of the kind, and I think if there was sich a thing I should know somethink about it, for I've worked the sewers, off and on, for twenty year. When we comes to a narrow-place as we don't know, we takes the candle out of the lantern and fastens it on the hend of the o, and then runs it up the sewer, and if the light stays in, we knows as there a'n't no danger. We used to go up the city sewer at Blackfriars-bridge, but that's stopped up now; it's boarded across inside. The city wouldn't let us up if they knew it, 'cause of the danger, they say, but they don't care if we hav'n't got nothink to eat nor a place to put our heads in, while there's plenty of money lying there and good for nobody. If you was caught up it and brought afore the Lord Mayor, he'd give you fourteen days on it, as safe as the bellows, so a good many on us now is afraid to wenture in. We don't wenture as we used to, but still it's done at times. There's a many places as I knows on where the bricks has fallen down, and that there's dangerous ...

'I've often seed as many as a hundred rats at once, and they're woppers in the sewers, I can tell you; them there water rats, too, is far more ferociouser than any other rats, and they'd think nothink of tackling a man, if they found they couldn't get away no how, but if they can why they runs by and gits out o' the road. I knows a chap as the rats tackled in the sewers; they bit him hawfully: you must ha' heard on it; it was him as the water-men went in arter when they heard him a shouting as they was a rowin' by. Only for the water-men the rats would ha' done for him, safe enough. Do you recollect hearing on the man as was found in the sewers about twelve year ago? – oh you must – the rats eat every bit of him, and left nothink but his bones. I knowed him well, he was a rig'lar shore-worker.

'The rats is wery dangerous, that's sartain, but we always goes three or four on us together, and the varmint's too wide awake to tackle us then, for they know they'd git off second best. You can go a long way in the sewers if you like; I don't know how far. I niver was at the end on them myself, for a cove can't stop in longer than six or seven hour, 'cause of the tide; you must be out before that's up. There's a many branches on ivery side, but we don't go into all; we go where we know, and where we're always sure to find somethink. I know a place now where there's more than two or three hundredweight of metal all rusted together, and plenty of money among it too; but its too heavy to carry it out, so it 'ill stop there I s'pose till the world comes to an end. I often brought out a piece of metal half a hundred in weight, and took it under the harch of the bridge, and broke it up with a large stone to pick out the money. I've found sovereigns and half sovereigns over and over ag'in, and three on us has often cleared a couple of pound apiece in one day out of the sewers. But we no sooner got the money than the publican had it. I only wish I'd back all the money I've guv to the publican, and I wouldn't care how the wind blew for the rest of my life . . .'

Mud-larks

THERE IS ANOTHER class who may be termed river-finders, although their occupation is connected only with the shore; they are commonly known by the name of 'mud-larks,' from being compelled, in order to obtain the articles they seek, to wade sometimes up to their middle through the mud left on the shore by the retiring tide. These poor creatures are certainly about the most deplorable in their appearance of any I have met with in the course of my inquiries. They may be seen of all ages, from mere childhood to positive decrepitude, crawling among the barges at the various wharfs along the river; it cannot be said that they are clad in rags, for they are scarcely half covered by the tattered indescribable things that serve them for clothing; their bodies are grimed with the foul soil of the river, and their torn garments stiffened up like boards with dirt of every possible description.

Among the mud-larks may be seen many old women, and it is indeed pitiable to behold them, especially during the winter, bent nearly double with age and infirmity, paddling and groping among the wet mud for small pieces of coal, chips of wood, or any sort of refuse washed up by the tide. These women always have with them an old basket or an old tin kettle, in which they put whatever they chance to find. It usually takes them a whole tide to fill this receptacle, but when filled, it is as much as the feeble old creatures are able to carry home.

The mud-larks generally live in some court or alley in the neighbourhood of the river, and, as the tide recedes, crowds of boys and little girls, some old men, and many old women, may be observed loitering about the various stairs, watching eagerly for the opportunity to commence their labours. When the tide is sufficiently low they scatter themselves along the shore, separating from each other, and soon disappear among the craft lying about in every direction. This is the case on both sides of the river, as high up as there is anything to be found, extending as far as Vauxhall-bridge, and as low down as Woolwich. The mud-larks themselves, however, know only those who reside near them, and whom they are accustomed to meet in their daily pursuits; indeed, with but few exceptions, these people are dull, and apparently stupid; this is observable particularly among the boys and girls, who, when engaged in searching the mud, hold but little converse one with another. The men and women may be passed and repassed, but they notice no one; they never speak, but with a stolid look of wretchedness they plash their way through the mire, their bodies bent down while they peer anxiously about, and occasionally stoop to pick up some paltry treasure that falls in their way.

The mud-larks collect whatever they happen to find, such as coals, bits of old-iron, rope, bones, and copper nails that drop from ships while lying or repairing along shore. Copper nails are the most valuable of all the articles they find, but these they seldom obtain, as they are always driven from the neighbourhood of a ship while being new-sheathed. Sometimes the younger and bolder mud-larks venture on sweeping some empty coal-barge, and one little fellow with whom I spoke, having been lately caught in the act of so doing, had to undergo for the offence seven days' imprisonment in the House of Correction: this, he says, he liked much better than mud-larking, for while he staid there he wore a coat and shoes and stockings, and though he had not over much to eat, he certainly was never afraid of going to bed without anything at all – as he often had to do when at liberty. He thought he would try it on again in the winter, he told me, saying, it would be so comfortable to have clothes and shoes and stockings then, and not be obliged to go into the cold wet mud of a morning.

Dog's-dung Finders

DOGS'-DUNG IS CALLED 'Pure,' from its cleansing and purifying properties.

The name of 'Pure-finders,' however, has been applied to the men engaged in collecting dogs'-dung from the public streets only, within the last 20 or 30 years. Previous to this period there appears to have been no men engaged in the business, old women alone gathered the substance, and they were known by the name of 'bunters,' which signifies properly gatherers of rags; and thus plainly intimates that the rag-gatherers originally added the collecting of 'Pure' to their original and proper vocation. Hence it appears that the bone-grubbers, rag-gatherers, and pure-finders, constituted formerly but one class of people, and even now they have, as I have stated, kindred characteristics.

The pure-finders meet with a ready market for all the dogs'-dung they are able to collect, at the numerous tanyards in Bermondsey, where they sell it by the stable-bucket full, and get from 8*d*. to 10*d*. per bucket, and sometimes 1*s*. and 1*s*. 2*d*. for it, according to its quality. The 'dry limy-looking sort' fetches the highest price at some yards, as it is found to possess more of the alkaline, or purifying properties; but others are found to prefer the dark moist quality. Strange as it may appear, the preference for a particular kind has suggested to the finders of Pure the idea of adulterating it to a very considerable extent; this is effected by means of mortar broken away from old walls, and mixed up with the whole mass, which it closely resembles; in some cases, however, the mortar is rolled into small balls similar to those found. Hence it would appear, that there is no business or trade, however insignificant or contemptible, without its own peculiar and appropriate tricks.

The pure-finders are in their habits and mode of proceeding

nearly similar to the bone-grubbers. Many of the pure-finders are, however, better in circumstances, the men especially, as they earn more money. They are also, to a certain extent, a better educated class. Some of the regular collectors of this substance have been mechanics, and others small tradesmen, who have been reduced. Those pure-finders who have 'a good connection,' and have been granted permission to cleanse some kennels, obtain a very fair living at the business, earning from 10s. to 15s. a week. These, however, are very few; the majority have to seek the article in the streets, and by such means they can obtain only from 6s. to 10s. a week. The average weekly earnings of this class are thought to be about 7s. 6d.

✒ ✒ ✒

A Visit to the Great Exhibition, 7 June 1851
Charlotte Brontë

The Great Exhibition was an unmitigated success, the pre-eminent symbol of London's place as the epicentre of the greatest empire.

Housed in Joseph Paxton's revolutionary glass house in Hyde Park, the Exhibition was opened on May Day 1851 by Queen Victoria. Inside the Great Exhibition's 19 acres of glass and iron (nicknamed by the wits at *Punch*, 'Crystal Palace'), Victoria and her subjects were treated to nearly 19,000 displays from Britain and around the world. The attendance statistics were staggering – over 6 million people visited the exhibition. One of them was the author of the recently published *Jane Eyre*:

ESTERDAY I WENT for the second time to the Crystal Palace. We remained in it about three hours, and I must say I was more struck with it on this occasion than at my first visit. It is a wonderful place – vast, strange, new, and impossible to describe. Its grandeur does not consist in one thing, but in the unique assemblage of all things. Whatever human industry has created you find there, from the great compartments filled with railway engines and boilers, with mill machinery in full work, with splendid carriages of all kinds, with harness of every description, to the glass-covered and velvet spread stands loaded with the most gorgeous work of the goldsmith and silversmith, and the carefully guarded caskets full of real diamonds and pearls worth hundreds of thousands of pounds. It may be called a bazaar or a fair, but it is such a bazaar or fair as Eastern genii might have created. It seems as if only magic could have gathered this mass of wealth from all the ends of the earth – as if none but supernatural hands could have arranged it thus, with such a blaze and contrast of colours and marvellous power of effect. The multitude filling the great aisles seems ruled and subdued by some invisible influence. Amongst the thirty thousand souls that peopled it the day I was there not one loud noise was to be heard, not one irregular movement seen; the living tide rolls on quietly, with a deep hum like the sea heard from the distance.

The Great Exhibition – whose prime supporter was Victoria's husband, Albert – was as profitable as it was popular. The proceeds were used to buy a tract of land in South Kensington, on which were later built inter alia the Victoria and Albert Museum, the Natural History Museum, the Science Museum and the Royal Albert Hall.

High Society: A Fancy-dress Ball at Buckingham Palace, 1851

Anne Thackeray Ritchie

*T*HAT WAS IN 1851, the year of the great Exhibition, and one wonderful and never-to-be-forgotten night my father took us to see some great ladies in their dresses going to the Queen's fancy-dress ball at Buckingham Palace. We drove to some big house (it was all very vague and dazzlingly indistinct in my mind). We were shown into a great empty room and almost immediately some doors were flung open, there came a blaze of light, a burst of laughing voices, and from a many-twinkling dinner-table rose a company that seemed, to our unaccustomed eyes, as if all the pictures in Hampton Court had come to life. The chairs scraped back, the ladies and gentlemen advanced together over the shining floors.

I can remember their high heels clicking on the floor; they were in the dress of the court of King Charles II, the ladies beautiful, dignified and excited. There was one, lovely and animated in yellow; I remember her pearls shining. Another seemed to us even more beautiful, as she crossed the room, all dressed in black, but she, I think, was not going to the ball; and then somebody began to say Sir Edwin Landseer had promised to rouge them and then everybody to call out for him, and then there was an outcry about his moustaches that 'really must be shaved off' for they were not in keeping with his dress.

Then, as in a dream, we went off to some other great house, Bath House perhaps, where one lady, more magnificently dressed than all the others, was sitting in a wax-lighted dressing-room and just behind her chair stood a smiling gentleman, also in court dress, whom my father knew, and he held up something in one hand and laughed, and said he must go back to the house from whence he had come and the lady thanked him and called him Sir Edwin. We could not understand who this Sir Edwin was, who seemed to be wherever we went, nor why he should put on the rouge. Then a fairy thundering chariot carried off this splendid lady and the nosegays of the hanging footman seemed to scent the air as the equipage drove off, under the covered way. Perhaps all this is only a dream, but I think it is true: for there was again a third house where we found more pictures, two beautiful alive young pictures and their mother, for whom a parcel was brought in post-haste, containing a jewel all dropping with pearls. That evening was always the nearest approach to a live fairy tale that we ever lived; and that ball more brilliant than any we ever beheld.

Karl Marx at Home, 1852

Karl Marx

Karl Marx arrived in London in 1849, one of about a thousand radical émigrés who settled there after the collapse of the European revolutions of 1848. Aside from offering freedom, London provided the unparallelled resource of the British Museum (especially its Reading Room, which opened in 1857), where Marx began the researches on political economy that would find their final expression in *Das Kapital*.

Marx lived in Soho and Kentish Town, often in penury and usually reliant on subsidy from his friend and collaborator, Friedrich Engels.

EAR ENGELS!

Your letter today dropped into a very disturbed atmosphere. My wife is ill, little Jenny is ill, little Lene has a kind of nervous fever. I could not and cannot call the doctor because I have no money for medicine. For 8–10 days I have kept the family going on bread and potatoes, and it is even doubtful whether I can get these today. That diet of course was not conducive to health in the present climatic conditions. I've written no articles for Dana because I did not have the penny to go to read newspapers. Incidentally, as soon as you've sent No. xix I'll send you a letter with my opinion on xx, a summary of this present shit.

When I was with you and you told me you'd be able to obtain for me a somewhat larger sum by the end of August I wrote and told my wife to put her mind at rest. Your letter 3–4 weeks ago indicated that there was not much hope but nevertheless some. Thus I put off all creditors until the beginning of September, who, as you know, are always only paid small fragments. Now the storm is universal.

I have tried everything but in vain. First that dog Weydemeyer cheats me of 15£. I write to Germany to Streit (because he had written to Dronke in Switzerland). The pig doesn't even reply. I turn to Brockhaus and offer him articles for *Gegenwart*, of harmless content. He declined in a very polite letter. Finally throughout last week I've been running around with an Englishman all day long because he wanted to obtain from me the discount for the bills on Dana. In vain.

The best and most desirable thing that could happen would be for my landlady to throw me out of the house. At least I would save the sum of 22£ then. But I can hardly expect her to be so obliging. Then there are the baker, the milkman, the tea fellow, the greengrocer, and an old butcher's bill. How am I to cope with all this diabolical mess? In the end, during the past 8-10 days I borrowed a few shillings and pence from Knoten, which was the last thing I wanted to do but it was necessary in order not to croak.

You will have observed from my letters that, as usual when I am in it myself and do not just hear about it from afar, I am wading through the shit with great indifference. But what's to be done? My house is a hospital, and the crisis is getting so disruptive that it compels me to give it my all-highest attention. What's to be done?

[…]

Yours, K. M.

Some London Wonders:
Gaslights, Penny Gaffs and Omnibuses, 1853
Max Schlesinger

Schlesinger was a German tourist. Like all visitors to the British capital he was overcome by its bright lights, endless traffic and diversity of entertainment.

HOLBORN IS ILLUMINATED with gas-light, but the brightest glare bursts forth exactly opposite to us. Who, in the name of all that is prudent, can the people be who make such a shocking waste of gas? They are 'Moses and Son', the great tailor and outfitters, who have lighted up the side-front of their branch-establishment. All round the outer walls of the house, which is filled with coats, vests and trousers to the roof, and which exhibits three separate side-fronts towards three separate streets, there are many thousands of gas-flames, forming branches, foliage and arabesques, and sending forth so dazzling a blaze that this fiery column of Moses is visible to Jews and Christians at the distance of half a mile, lighting up the haze which not even the clearest evening can wholly banish from the London sky. Among the fiery flowers burns the inevitable royal crown, surrounding the equally unavoidable letters V.R. To the right of these letters we have Moses and Son blessing the Queen in flaming characters of hydro-carbon: God bless the People.

What do they make this illumination for? This is not a royal birthday, or the anniversary of a great national victory. Motives of loyalty, politics or religion have nothing to do with the great illuminations executed by Messrs. Moses and

Son. The air is calm, there is not even a breath of wind; it's a hundred to one that Oxford Street and Holborn will be thronged with passengers; this is our time to attract the idlers. A heavy expense this, burning all that gas for ever so many hours, but it pays somehow.

Theatre was enormously popular in Victorian London. The annual audience for theatres in the West End was approaching 10 million. Impresarios had their heyday: Richard D'Oyly Carte made a fortune from staging the comedy operas of the tyros Gilbert and Sullivan, beginning with *Trial by Jury* at the Royalty Theatre in Soho in 1875.

Not all theatre took place in the West End, however. 'Penny Gaffs', the poor man's makeshift theatre, were staged in the East End.

WE PASS THROUGH a low door, and enter a kind of ante-chamber, where we pay a penny each. A buffet with soda-water, lemonade, apples and cakes is surrounded by a crowd of thinly-clad factory-girls, and a youthful cavalier with a paper cap is shooting at a target with a cross-bow, and after each shot he throws a farthing on the buffet. Passing through the ante-chamber and a narrow corridor, we enter the pit of the penny-theatre, a place capable of holding fifty persons. There are also galleries – a dozen of wooden benches rise in amphitheatrical fashion up to the ceiling; and, strange to say, the gentlemen sit on one side and the ladies on the other. This separation of the sexes is owing to the great refinement of feeling. The gentlemen, chiefly labourers and apprentices, luxuriate during the representation in the aroma of their 'pickwicks' [a type of cheap cigar], a weed of which we can assure the reader that it is not to be found in the Havana; but they are gallant enough to keep the only window in the house wide open.

Just as we enter we see the director, a small curly-headed man, with a red punch face, ascending the stage by means of a ladder. He makes two low bows, one for the ladies and one for the gentlemen, and delivers himself of a grand oration, to excuse some small deficiencies in his institution. At every third word he is interrupted by the cheers and remarks of the audience.

'Ladies and Gentlemen,' says he, 'I am sorry I cannot produce a prima donna to-night. Jenny Lind has sent me a message by my own submarine telegraph, asking for an extension of her leave. You would not surely shorten the honeymoon of the nightingale. Madame Sontag tells me, quite in confidence, that she is falling off, and that, although her voice is good enough for Yankee ears, she wants the courage to make her appearance before the refined public of No 17, Broad-street, London. Mlle. Wagner was at my service, cheap as any stale mackerel; but could I insult you by producing her! Would not every note have reminded you of the fact, that she values nothing in England but its copper pence. Besides, the terms that exist between myself and Mr Lumley – there are considerations – I hope you'll understand me, ladies and gentlemen? The overture is about to commence!'

The speaker vanishes through a trap-door, through which two fellows presently ascend. One is dressed up to represent an Irishman, the other wears the characteristic habiliments of a Scotch Highlander. They play some national airs, and while thus engaged strip themselves of every particle of their outer clothing and appear as American planters. Some one from below hands up a couple of straw hats, which they clap on their heads, and the metamorphosis is complete. They then go to the back of the stage and return with an unfortunate

'African'. The part is acted by no less distinguished a person than the director himself. His face is blackened, he has a woolly wig on his head, and heavy chains on his wrists and ankles; and to prevent all misunderstandings, there is pinned to his waistcoat an enormous placard, with the magic words of 'UNCLE TOM'.

The planters produce meanwhile a couple of stout whips, which instruments of torture they use in a very unceremonious manner, in belabouring the back of the slave, when all of a sudden that illustrious Negro, exclaiming 'LIBER–R–R–TY! LIBER–R–R–TY!' breaks his fetters, and turning round with great deliberation, descends into the pit. Exeunt the two planters.

Transformation:– Three forms issue from the back door; a colossal female, with a trident and a diadem of gilt paper, bearing the legend of 'BRITANNIA'; after her, a pot-bellied old gentleman, with a red nose and a spoon in his right hand, while his left holds an enormous soup-plate, with a turtle painted on the back of it.

Britannia, heaving a deep sigh, sits down on a stool, adjusts a telescope, which is very long and very dirty, and looks out upon the ocean. The gentleman with the red nose, who, of course, represents the Lord Mayor of the good City of London, kneels down at her feet, and indulges in a fit of very significant howlings and gnashings of teeth. The third person is a sailor-boy complete with a south-wester, blue jacket and wide trousers, who dances a hornpipe while Britannia sighs and the Lord Mayor howls.

Now comes the great scene of the evening! Somebody or something, diving up from the very midst of the pit, makes a rush against the stage. It is the Uncle Tom of the last scene; his face is as black and his hair as woolly as ever; but a cocked hat, a pair of red trousers and top boots, and an enormous sword, brings it home to even the dullest understanding, that this is a very dangerous person! Besides, on his back there is a placard with the inscription: 'Solouque – NAPOLEON – EMPEROR!!'

The monster bawls out 'INVASION!' while, to the great delight of the ladies and gentlemen, he bumps his head several times against the chalky cliffs of Britain, which, on the present emergency, are represented by the wooden planks of the stage. The very sailor-boy, still dancing his hornpipe, shows his contempt for so much ferocity and dullness. He greets the invader with a scornful – 'Parli-vow Frenchi?'

At this juncture, the conqueror becomes aware of the presence of the short ladder, and mounts it forthwith. The boy vents his feelings of horror and disgust in an expressive pantomime, the Lord Mayor howls louder than ever, and the gnashing of his teeth is awful to behold; but just as the invader has gained the edge of the stage, he is attacked by the sailor who, applying his foot to a part of the Frenchman's body which shall be nameless, kicks him back into the pit. The public cheer, Britannia and the Lord Mayor dance a polka, and the sailor sings 'God Save the Queen'.

The omnibus was introduced into London in 1829 by George Shillibeer. Invented in France, the omnibus was a single-deck coach that could seat about twenty passengers and was drawn by (usually) three horses abreast. By the time of Schlesinger's visit, the omnibus was the preferred method of travel about town for the middle classes. On London's crowded streets omnibus accidents were frequent.

ELEVEN AM. ONE of the wheelers of a four-horse omnibus slipped on the pavement and fell down at the foot of the Holborn-side obelisk, between Fleet-street and Ludgate-hill.

There's a stoppage. The horse makes vain endeavours to get up; there is no help for it, they must undo reins, buckles and straps to free him. But a stoppage of five minutes in Fleet-street creates a stoppage in every direction to the distance of perhaps half a mile or a mile. Leaning as we do against the railings of the obelisk, we look forwards towards St. Paul's, and back to Chancery-lane, up to Holborn on our left, and down on our right to Blackfriar's-bridge; and this vast space presents the curious spectacle of scores of omnibuses, cabs, gigs, horses, carts, brewers' drays, coal wagons, all standing still, and jammed into an inextricable fix. Some madcap of a boy attempts the perilous passage from one side of the street to the other; he jumps over carts, creeps under the bellies of horses, and, in spite of the manifold dangers which beset him, he gains the opposite pavement. But those who can spare the time or who set some store by their lives, had better wait. Besides it is pleasant to look at all this turmoil and confusion … The difficulty is soon got over. Two policemen, a posse of idle cabmen and sporting amateurs, and a couple of ragged urchins, to whom the being allowed to touch a horse is happiness indeed, have come to the rescue, loosening chains and traces, getting the horse up and putting him to again.

Fog, 1853
Charles Dickens

The first London fogs, which clung to the Thames, were God-made. By the fifteenth century sea-coal and wood fires created a pall of unnatural mist that hung almost permanently over the city. The 'Dark Age' of London fog came in the reign of Victoria when half a million coal fires, combined with putrefying matter from the sewers, caused fog so dense that it was opaque; in 1873 19 pedestrians died from walking into the Thames and other bodies of water.

LONDON. MICHAELMAS TERM lately over, and the Lord Chancellor sitting in Lincoln's Inn Hall. Implacable November weathet. As much mud in the streets, as if the waters had but newly retired from the face of the earth, and it would not be wonderful to meet a Mega-losaurus, forty feet long or so, waddling like an elephantine lizard up Holborn Hill. Smoke lowering down from chimney-pots, making a soft black drizzle, with flakes of soot in it as big as full-grown snow-flakes – gone into mourning, one might imagine, for the death of the sun. Dogs, undistinguish-able in mire. Horses, scarcely better; splashed to their very blinkers. Foot passengers, jostling one another's umbrellas, in a general infection of ill-temper, and losing their foothold at street-corners, where tens of thousands of other foot passen-gers have been slipping and sliding since the day broke (if this day ever broke), adding new deposits to the crust upon crust of mud, sticking at those points tenaciously to the pavement, and accumulating at compound interest.

Fog everywhere. Fog up the river, where it flows among green aits and meadows; fog down the river, where it rolls defiled among the tiers of shipping, and the waterside pollutions of a great (and dirty) city. Fog on the Essex marshes, fog on the Kentish heights. Fog creeping into the cabooses of collier-brigs; fog lying out on the yards, and hovering in the rigging of great ships; fog drooping on the gunwales of barges and small boats. Fog in the eyes and throats of ancient Greenwich pensioners, wheezing by the firesides of their wards, fog in the stem and bowl of the afternoon pipe of the wrathful skipper, down in his close cabin; fog cruelly pinching the toes and fingers of his shivering little 'prentice boy on deck. Chance people on the bridges peeping over the parapets into a nether sky of fog, with fog all round them, as if they were up in a balloon, and hanging in the misty clouds.

Gas looming through the fog in divers places in the streets, much as the sun may, from the spongy fields, be seen to loom by husbandman and ploughboy. Most of the shops lighted two hours before their time – as the gas seems to know, for it has a haggard and unwilling look.

The raw afternoon is rawest, and the dense fog is densest, and the muddy streets are muddiest, near the leaden-headed old obstruction, appropriate ornament for the threshold of a leaden-headed old corporation: Temple Bar. And hard by Temple Bar, in Lincoln's Inn Hall, at the very heart of the fog, sits the Lord High Chancellor in his High Court of Chancery.

Never can there come fog too thick, never can there come mud and mire too deep, to assort with the groping and floundering condition which this High Court of Chancery, most pestilent of hoary sinners, holds, this day, in the sight of heaven and earth. On such an afternoon, if ever, the Lord High Chancellor ought to be sitting here – as here he is – with a foggy glory round his head, softly fenced in with crimson cloth and curtains, addressed by a large advocate with great whiskers, a little voice, and an interminable brief, and outwardly directing his contemplation to the lantern in the roof, where he can see nothing but fog.

The Great Stink, Summer 1858

Charles Dickens and George Godwin

The water of London was as polluted as its air. The Thames had become, in the words of Disraeli, a 'Stygian pool'. Aside from industrial waste, the advent of the flushing water-closet meant that effluent gushed straight into the river instead of into a cesspit. The pollution in the Thames did not deter water companies from pumping it back out to service their customers. 'He who drinks a tumbler of London Water', Sydney Smith observed, 'has literally in his stomach more animated beings than there are Men, Women and Children on the face of the Globe.' (The 'animated beings' of course included the cholera bacillus.) Not that all sewers debouched into the Thames or the Fleet or the Wallbrook; some open sewers were so overfull that they had more than a decade of effluent blocked up in them. London's lack of sanitation hardly befitted a modern capital city.

Even so, it took the 'Great Stink' of 1858, a combination of a warm summer and a hyper-polluted Thames, to finally push legislators into action.

JULY 7, 1858:– You will have read in the papers that the Thames in London is most horrible. I have to cross Waterloo or London Bridge to get to the railroad when I come down here, and I can certify that the offensive smells, even in that short whiff, have been of a most head-and-stomach-distending nature. Nobody knows what is to be done; at least everybody knows a plan, and everybody else knows it won't do; in the meantime cartloads of chloride of lime are shot into the filthy stream, and do something I hope.

So great was the stench from the Thames that Parliament was abandoned. Little wonder – on close investigation of the Thames, George Godwin, the social scientist, found it to be thick with human excrement:

WHILST EXAMINING IN the summer the north shore of the Thames from the Houses of Parliament to London-bridge (a most unpleasant task), we made a rough measurement at about the time of low water, and are disposed to think that there is an average breadth of 100 feet of the most putrid soil skirting this edge of our great city for some hours during each day. We were told by several persons who are employed in this neighbourhood, that in parts the deposit is more than six feet deep: the whole of this is thickly impregnated with impure matter, and at the opening of such sewers as have not been passed into the river beyond low-water mark, the condition is too bad for description. Many of our readers may have noticed the black, offensive, and dangerous matter which is taken from choked drains in the neighbourhood of cesspools. There are many thousands of tons of equally poisonous stuff on the shore of the Thames. A considerable quantity of such matter is kept in solution by the action of the tide and the steam-vessels, which adds materially to the bad state of the water. While wandering along this putrid shore, which is both a shame and a wonder in the nineteenth century, thoughts arise, in spite of some overpowering feelings, of other days, of processions of stately barges, full of the influential citizens in whose hands the protection of Father Thames was placed.

Such was London's shame that a bill was rushed through Parliament charging the Metropolitan Board of Works with the creation of a capital-wide system of underground sewers. Under the direction of the Board's chief engineer, Sir Joseph Bazalgette, 1,300 miles of sewers were built in what was one of the great engineering triumphs of the Victorian era. The system still runs to this day.

Nine a.m.: Clerks on their Way to Work, 1858

George Augustus Sala

*I*F THE MORNING be fine, the pavement of the Strand
and Fleet Street looks quite radiant with the spruce
clerks walking down to their offices, governmental,
financial, and commercial. Marvellous young bucks some of
them are. These are the customers, you see at a glance, whom
the resplendent wares in the hosiers' shops attract, and in
whom those wary industrials find avid customers. These are
the dashing young parties who purchase the pea-green, the
orange, and the rose-pink gloves; the crimson braces, the kalei-
doscopic shirt-studs, the shirts embroidered with dahlias,
deaths' heads, race-horses, sun-flowers, and ballet-girls; the
horseshoe, fox-head, pewter-pot-and-crossed pipes, willow-
pattern-plate, and knife-and-fork pins. These are the glasses of
city fashion, and the mould of city form, for whom the legions
of fourteen, of fifteen, of sixteen, and of seventeen shilling
trousers, all unrivalled, patented, and warranted, are made; for
these ingenious youths coats with strange names are devised,
scarves and shawls of wondrous pattern and texture despatched
from distant Manchester and Paisley. For them the shiniest of
hats, the knobbiest of sticks, gleam through shop-windows;
for them the geniuses of 'all-round collars' invent every week
fresh yokes of starched linen, pleasant instruments of torture,
reminding us equally of the English pillory, the Chinese
cangue, the Spanish garotte, the French lucarne to the guillo-
tine (that window from which the criminal looks out into
eternity), and the homely and cosmopolitan dog-collar! There
are some of these gay clerks who go down to their offices with
roses at their button-holes, and with cigars in their mouths;

there are some who wear peg-top trousers, chin-tufts, eye-glasses, and varnished boots. These mostly turn off in the Strand, and are in the Admiralty or Somerset House. As for the government clerks of the extreme West-end – the patricians of the Home and Foreign Offices – the bureaucrats of the Circumlocution Office, in a word – *they* ride down to Whitehall or Downing Street in broughams or on park hacks. Catch them in omnibuses, or walking on the vulgar pavement, for sooth! The flags of Regent Street they might indeed tread gingerly, at three o'clock in the afternoon; but the Strand, and at nine o'clock in the morning! Forbid it, gentility! I observe – to return to the clerks who are bending citywards – that the most luxuriant whiskers belong to the Bank of England. I believe that there are even whisker clubs in that great national institution, where prizes are given for the best pair of *favoris* grown without macassar. You may, as a general rule, distinguish government from commercial clerks by the stern repudiation of the razor, as applied to the beard and moustaches, by the former; and again I may remark, that the prize for the thinnest and most dandy-looking umbrellas must be awarded, as of right, to the clerks in the East India House – mostly themselves slim, natty gentlemen, of jaunty appearance, who are all supposed to have had tender affairs with the widows of East India colonels. You may know the cashiers in the private banking houses by their white hats and buff waistcoats; you may know the stock-brokers by theit careering up Ludgate Hill in dog-carts, and occasionally tandems, and by the pervading sporting appearance of their costume; you may know the Jewish commission agents by their flashy broughams, with lapdogs and ladies in crinoline beside them; you may know the sugar-bakers and the soap-boilers by the comfortable double-bodied carriages with fat horses in which they roll along; you may know the Manchester warehousemen by their wearing gaiters, always carrying their hands in their pockets, and frequently slipping into recondite city taverns up darksome alleys, on their way to Cheapside, to make a quiet bet or so on the Chester Cup or the Liverpool Steeplechase; you may know, finally, the men with a million of money, or thereabouts, by their being ordinarily very shabby, and by their wearing shocking bad hats, which have seemingly never been brushed, on the backs of their heads.

'Every road,' says the proverb, 'leads to Rome;' every commercial ways [sic] leads to the Bank of England. And there, in the midst of that heterogeneous architectural jumble between the Bank of England itself, the Royal Exchange, the Poultry, Cornhill, and the Globe Insurance Office, the vast train of omnibuses, that have come from the West and that have come from the East – that have been rumbling along the Macadam while I was prosing on the pedestrians – with another great army of clerk martyrs outside and inside, their knees drawn up to their chins, and their chins resting on their umbrella handles, set down their loads of cash-book and ledger fillers. What an incalculable mass of figures must there be collected in those commercial heads! What legions of £. *s. d.*! What a chaos of cash debtor, contra creditor, bil [sic] payable, and bills receivable; waste-books, day-books, cash-books, and journals; insurance policies, brokerage, agio, tare and tret, dock warrants, and general commercial bedevilment! They file off to their several avocations, to spin money for others, often, poor fellows, while they themselves are blest with but meagre stipends. They plod away to their gloomy wharves and hard-hearted counting-houses, where the chains from great cranes wind round their bodies, and they dance hornpipes in bill-file and cash-box fetters, and the mahogany of the desks enters into their souls. Upon my word, I think if I were doomed to clerkdom, that I should run away and enlist; but that would avail me little, for I am equally certain that, were I a grenadier, and my commanding officer made me mount guard, that I should pop my musket into the sentry-box and run away too.

So the omnibuses meet at the Bank and disgorge the clerks by hundreds; repeating this operation scores of times between nine and ten o'clock. But you are not to delude yourself, that either by wheeled vehicle or by the humbler conveyances known as 'Shanks's mare,' and the 'Marrowbone stage' – in more refined language, walking – have all those who have business in the city reached their destination. No; the Silent highway has been their travelling route. On the broad – would that I could add the silvery and sparkling – bosom of Father Thames, they have been borne in swift, grimy little steamboats, crowded with living freights from Chelsea, and Pimlico, and Vauxhall piers, from Hungerford, Waterloo, Temple, Blackfriars, and Southwark – straight by the hay-boats, with their lateen sails discoloured in a manner that would delight a painter, straight by Thames police hulks, by four and six-oared cutters, by coal-barges, and great lighters laden with bricks and ashes and toiling towards Putney and Richmond; by oozy wharves and grim-chimneyed factories; by little, wheezy, tumbledown waterside public-houses; by breweries, and many-windowed warehouses; by the stately gardens of the Temple, and the sharp-pointed spires of city churches, and the great dome of Paul's looming blue in the morning, to the Old Shades Pier, hard by London Bridge. There is landing and scuffling and pushing; the quivering old barges, moored in the mud, are swaying and groaning beneath trampling feet. Then, for an instant, Thames Street, Upper and Lower, is invaded by an ant-hill swarm of spruce clerks, who mingle strangely with the fish-women and the dock-porters. But the insatiable counting-houses soon swallow them up; as though London's commercial maw were an hungered too, for breakfast, at nine o'clock in the morning.

White Slavery: Maids and Match Girls, 1860–83

Hannah Cullwick and James Greenwood

A Maid's Life, Hannah Cullwick

In the Victorian period, there were more domestic servants than at any other time in British history, and most of them were women. The 1851 Census reveals that 575,162 females and 74,323 males were in service. Only the working classes did not employ servants.

Hannah Cullwick, a maid-of-all-work for a Kilburn upholsterer, kept a diary. Here is the entry for 14 July 1860, a typical working day:

O PENED THE SHUTTERS and lighted the kitchen fire – shook my sooty things in the dusthole and emptied the soot there, swept and dusted the rooms and the hall, laid the cloth and got breakfast up – cleaned two pairs of boots – made the beds and emptied the slops, cleared and washed the breakfast things up – cleaned the plate – cleaned the knives and got dinner up – cleared away, cleaned the kitchen up – unpacked a hamper – took two chickens to Mrs Brewer's and brought a message back – made a tart and picked and gutted two ducks and roasted them – cleaned the steps and flags on my knees, blackleaded the scraper in the front of the house – cleaned the street flags too on my knees – had tea

– cleared away – washed up in the scullery – cleaned the pantry on my knees and scoured the tables – scrubbed the flags round the house and cleaned the window sills – got tea at 9 for the master and Mrs Warwick in my dirt but Anne (a fellow-servant) carried it up – cleaned the privy and passage and scullery floor on my knees – washed the door and cleaned the sink down- put the supper ready for Anne to take up, for I was too dirty and tired to go upstairs.

Cullwick's typical working day had lasted from 6.30 a.m. to 11 p.m.

Match Girls, James Greenwood

... IT IS not amongst the factories and warehouses of the City proper that one should seek for the seamiest side of girl labour. To discover that it will be necessary to go a little further afield. Not very far. A twopenny ride by tram from Aldgate will carry you to a likely preserve of the sort. At Stratford and near Stratford Bridge, in an awfully evil-smelling place called Marsh Gate Lane, there are several lucifer-match manufactories, at which the hands employed appear to be chiefly females. I chanced to arrive there just as the clanging bells all round about were announcing dinnertime, and presently there came swarming out into Stratford High Street a troop of petticoated toilers, such as an Englishman, and especially a Londoner, could not contemplate without feelings of shame and humiliation. From one lucifer-match factory gate alone I saw at least a hundred young girls emerge, sharp set, as the briskness of their steps betrayed, for the mid-day meal, but with lamentably small means to satisfy that not unnatural craving. They were not a nice-looking lot of girls. Indeed, I think I may go so far as saying that a more draggletail, poverty-stricked crowd of poor little wretches I never set eyes upon. Their coarse, heavy aprons charitably concealed the greater part of their tattered and flimsy skirts, but there certainly was not one in six who could boast of a mud-proof pair of boots.

As a rule, although the day was intensely cold, they wore neither shawl nor bonnet, but, in almost every instance, the most elaborate pains had been taken with the hair. Bedaubed and plastered with grease or oil, it was arranged according to the latest mode as pictured in the lady's penny book of fashions. 'Fringe on the forehead' was the all-prevailing style; and it may be very well where the brow is of average intellectual dimensions, and the contour of the face, if not perfection, is passable, but its effect on the appearance of a young lady whose birth and abiding place is one of London's 'back settlements,' must be seen to be believed. Take a coarse, broad face, with small deep-set eyes and prominent cheekbones, a stubby nose, with a mouth that in the glove trade would be called an 'out size,' and clap a frizzle of fringe between where the hair's 'parting' should be and the eyebrows, and if a human face can be made to look more tigerish I should be very sorry to behold it.

That the majority of these girls of the lucifer-match factory did not reside in the immediate neighbourhood was evident from the fact that they nearly all of them hurried to the local cookshops to spend their few halfpence. In many instances it was only one penny a girl expended. Experience, no doubt, has taught them what is the best value for such a coin obtainable in that region, and the popular voice is unmistakably in favour of a thick slice of bread and a piece of fried fish – not a large one, no bigger, perhaps, than the palm of one's hand – but possessed of potent 'relishing powers,' if a judgment may be formed on the extraordinary long way off that the fried fish shop appeals to one's sense of smell: and capable of bestowing an appetising flavour to the last bite of the thickest slice that might be cut from a loaf.

A door or two from the fish shop there was a hot soup establishment, where a substantial preparation of the pea was to be obtained for the marvellously low sums of a halfpenny and a penny a basin; and the shop was so full of customers within ten minutes of the factory dinner bells ceasing their din, that three young females were glad to have their 'pen'orths' handed over the heads of the earlier arrivals, and to eat it as they stood in the street. It was a painful spectacle – so poor and pitiful and poverty-stricken. It would have been bad enough had they been boys, but with all their coarseness and untidiness, one could not forget their sex, and that in a few years they would be women and wives – mothers probably. I spoke to one girl, about sixteen years old, and she told me that she lived in Shadwell (about two miles distant), and that working twelve hours a day she could earn seven shillings a week, out of which she gave her mother half-a-crown a week for her lodging and washing, and 'kep' herself' in food and clothes with the remaining four-and-sixpence. That was about the average earnings in that trade, she informed me, for girls of her age and experience – she had been a year and a half at the business.

Lucifer-match making, accordingly to this young lady's statement, 'was a much better game one time. But I'm a speaking now,' she continued, 'of when my mother was a gal. She worked at it, and so did my Aunt Loo. She died in the London Hospital of it.'

'Of what?'

'Of the matches. There wasn't no new-fangled ways of making matches in them times, at least so I've heard my mother say, on'y brimstone and fosterous [yellow phosphorus], and the fosterous used to get into your bones and eat zem away in your face and jaws mostly; that's what my Aunt Loo died of. But see what she used to earn, and my mother too! Eighteen shillings or a pound a week!'

'And with the prospect of a dreadful death by phosphorus poisoning?' I suggested.

'That's 'cordin' to your luck,' responded the reckless young matchmaker, 'it's like being in a raffle. Some wins and some loses.'

'And would you risk it if you had an opportunity?'

'Rather,' she replied, with an emphatic wag of her head, that left no doubt as to her earnestness, 'wouldn't you if you was me?'

In 1888 1,400 match girls of the Bryant & May factory, led by the Fabian journalist Annie Besant, won a three-week strike for better conditions.

A Day at the Races: The Derby, Epsom, 28 May 1861

Hippolyte Taine

A Frenchman's view:

RACES AT EPSOM: it is the Derby Day, a day of jollification; Parliament does not sit; for three days all the talk has been about horses and their trainers.

We start from Waterloo station. The sky is cloudless, free from mist; my English neighbours remark that they have never seen such a day in London. All around may be witnessed green husbandry, meadows encompassed with hedges, and the hedgerow is often interspersed with trees. The splendour of this green, the mass and the vigour of lustrous golden, bursting flowers, are extraordinary. Velvets constellated with diamonds, watered silks, the most magnificent embroideries do not match this deep hue; the colour is excessive, beyond the reach of painting; but never have the blooming and blossoming of plants, the luxury and the joy of the adorned earth, dazzled me with such bright pomp.

Epsom course is a large, green plain, slightly undulating; on one side are reared three public stands and several other smaller ones. In front, tents, hundreds of shops, temporary stables under canvas, and an incredible confusion of carriages, of horses, of horsemen, of private omnibuses; there are perhaps 200,000 human heads here. Nothing beautiful or even elegant; the carriages are ordinary vehicles, and toilettes are rare; one does not come here to exhibit them but to witness a spectacle: the spectacle is interesting only on account of its size. From the top of the Stand the enormous ant-heap swarms, and its din ascends. But beyond, on the right, a row of large trees, behind them the faint bluish undulations of the verdant country, make a magnificent frame to a mediocre picture. Some clouds as white as swans float in the sky, and their shadow sweeps over the grass; a light mist, charged with sunshine, flits in the distance, and the illuminated air, like a glory, envelops the plain, the heights, the vast area, and all the disorder of the human carnival.

It is a carnival, in fact; they have come to amuse themselves in a noisy fashion. Everywhere are gypsies, comic singers and dancers disguised as negroes, shooting galleries where bows and arrows or guns are used, charlatans who by dint of eloquence palm off watch chains, games of skittles and sticks, musicians of all sorts, and the most astonishing row of cabs, barouches, droskies, four-in-hands, with pies, cold meats, melons, fruits, wines, especially champagne. They unpack; they proceed to drink and eat; that restores the creature and excites him; coarse joy and open laughter are the result of a full stomach. In presence of this ready-made feast the aspect of the poor is pitiable to behold; they endeavour to sell you penny dolls, remembrances of the Derby; to induce you to play at Aunt Sally, to black your boots. Nearly all of them resemble wretched, hungry, beaten, mangy dogs, waiting for a bone, without hope of finding much on it. They arrived on foot during the night, and count upon dining off crumbs from the great feast. Many are lying on the ground, among the feet of the passers-by, and sleep open-mouthed, face upwards. Their countenances have an expression of stupidity and of painful hardness. The majority of them have bare feet, all are terribly dirty, and most absurd-looking; the reason is that they wear gentlemen's old clothes, worn-out fashionable dresses, small bonnets, formerly worn by young ladies. The sight of these cast-off things, which have covered several bodies, becoming more shabby in passing from one to the other, always makes me uncomfortable. To wear these old clothes is degrading; in doing so the human being shows or avows that he is the off-scouring of society. Among us [the French] a peasant, a workman, a labourer, is a different man, not an inferior person; his blouse belongs to him, as my coat belongs to me – it has clothed no one but him. The employment of ragged clothes is more than a peculiarity; the poor resign themselves here to be the footstool of others.

One of these women, with an old shawl that appeared to have been dragged in the gutter, with battered head-gear, which had been a bonnet, made limp by the rain, with a poor, dirty, pale baby in her arms, came and prowled round our omnibus, picked up a castaway bottle, and drained the dregs. Her second girl, who could walk, also picked up and munched a rind of melon. We gave them a shilling and cakes. The humble smile of thankfulness they returned, it is impossible to describe. They had the look of saying, like Sterne's poor donkey, 'Do not beat me, I beseech you – yet you may beat me if you wish.' Their countenances were burned, tanned by the sun; the mother had a scar on her right cheek, as if she had been struck by a boot; both of them, the child in particular, were grown wild and stunted. The great social mill crushes and grinds here, beneath its steel gearing, the lowest human stratum.

However, a bell rings, and the race is about to begin. The three or four hundred policemen clear the course; the stands are filled, arid the meadow in front of them is but a large black patch. We ascend to our places; nothing seems at all imposing. At this distance the crowd is an ant-heap; the horsemen and carriages which move forward and cross each other resemble beetles, May-bugs, large sombre drones on a green cloth. The jockeys in red, in blue, in yellow, in mauve, form a small group apart, like a swarm of butterflies which has alighted. Probably I am wanting in enthusiasm, but I seem to be looking at a game of insects. Thirty-four run; after three false starts they are off; fifteen or twenty keep together, the others are in small groups, and one sees them moving down the far side of the circuit. To the eye the speed is not very great; it is that of a railway train seen at a distance of half a league – when the carriages look like toy coaches which a child pulls along on a string. For several minutes the brown patch, dotted with red and bright spots, moves steadily over the distant green. It turns; one perceives the first group approach. 'Hats off!' and all heads are uncovered, and everyone rises; a repressed 'hurrah' runs through the stands. The frigid faces are on fire; brief, nervous gestures suddenly stir the phlegmatic bodies; below, in the betting ring, the agitation is extraordinary – like a general St Vitus's dance; picture a mass of puppets receiving an electric shock, and gesticulating with all their members like mad semaphores. But the most curious spectacle is the human tide which instantly pours forth and rolls over the course behind the runners, like a wave of ink; the black, motionless crowd has suddenly become molten; in a moment it spreads itself over a vast area. The policemen make a barrier in two or three ranks, using force when necessary to guard the square to which the jockeys and horses are led. Measures are taken to weigh and see that all is right ...

We descend; there is a hustling and crushing in the staircases, at the refreshment counters; but most of the carriages are provisioned for the day, and the people feast in the open air in small knots ... Over the whole downs jaws are at work, bottles are emptied, and towards evening the carnival is in full swing. Twenty-four gentlemen triumphantly range on their omnibus seventy-five bottles which they have emptied. Groups pelt each other with chicken bones, lobster shells, pieces of turf. Two parties of gentlemen have descended from their omnibuses and engaged in a fight, ten against ten; one of them gets two teeth broken . . .

On our return, the road is hidden by dust; the fields, near the roadside, are reddened by feet; everybody returns frightfully dirty, and powdered with white; there are drunken people along the whole road; up to eight o'clock in the evening they might be seen staggering and sick on Hyde Park Corner; their comrades support them, laughing, and the spectators' faces do not betoken disgust. Today everything is allowable, it is an outlet for a year of repression.

The 1861 Derby was won by Kettledrum at 16 to 1.

Tothill Fields, 1861

Henry Mayhew and John Binny

In 1616 Tothill Fields became the site for a 'bridewell' – a house
of correction which punished able-bodied prisoners by setting
them to work. Later Tothill Fields Bridewell was rebuilt and
given over solely to the incarceration of women and convicted
boys under the age of 17.

AT A LATER part of the day we accompanied the
warder to the airing-yard, to see the boys exercising.
This was done much after the fashion of other
prisons, the lads circling round and round, and each walking
some six or seven feet apart from those next him. There were
about forty boys altogether in the yard. 'They exercise', said
the warder, 'in detachments, for about an hour each; we keep
them walking briskly, and in cold mornings we make them
move along in double quick time.'

As the little troop paced over the flag-stones, their heavy
prison boots sounded very differently from what their naked
feet are wont to do when outside the prison gates; and we
could tell, by their shuffling noise and limping gait, how little
used many of them had been to such a luxury as shoe leather.
Then each boy had a small red cotton pocket-handkerchief
tied to the button-hole of his jacket (for no pockets are
allowed in the prison garb), and we could not help wondering
how many of the forty young 'offenders' there had ever before
known the use of such an article.

While the lads kept on filing past us, the chief warder, at
our request, called over the number of times that those who
had been recommitted had been previously in prison. This he

did merely by quoting to us the red figures stitched to the arms of the 'known' delinquents.

The following cyphers indicate the number of recommittals among the band:– 4, 3, 2, 4, 2, 10, 3, 3, 10, 7, 6, 3, 4, 3, 4, 4, 2, 4, 6, 4, 3, 9, 2, 4, 2. Thus we see that out of the 40 exercising in the yard, there were no less than 25 who had paid many previous visits to the prisons.

After this, one of the lads, who had been ten times recommitted, was called from out of the ranks, and questioned as to his age and antecedents.

'How old are you, boy?'

'Thirteen years, please, sir.'

'What are you in for?'

'Coat and umbereller, sir. This makes seven times here and three times at Coldbath Fields, please, sir.'

'How long have you got now?'

'Three calendar months. This makes four times, please, sir, that I've had three calendar months, and I've had two two-monthses as well – one of the two monthses here, and one at Coldbath Fields; and I've done one six weeks, and one two days besides, sir. It's mostly been for prigging,' added the young urchin.

'What did you take?'

'I took a watch and chain once, sir, and a pair of goold bracelets another time. I did a till twice, and this time it's for the coat and umbereller as I told you on afore. The two days I had was for a bottle of pickles, but that there was three or four years ago.'

'Oh, father's in a consumptive hospital down in the country,' he went on, in answer to our queries. 'Mother's at home, and she lives in S— Street, in the Gray's Inn Road.'

'Why, I began thieving about four years ago, please, sir,' he said, in answer to us. 'I went out with a butcher-boy. He's got four year penal servitude now.'

'Did I ever go out to work? Oh yes, sir. I was at work at a brush-maker's for about five months, and I've worked at Mr. Cubitt's in the Gray's Inn Road. I go out with one boy when I go prigging. I went into the shop with a bit of a old seal to sell, when I took the watch; and I tried on the same dodge when I took the pair of goold bracelets. Mother mends china and glass, please, sir. I don't mean to go out prigging no more. Not if I can get any work, I won't.'

This boy was a sharp-featured cunning-looking young vagabond, with a pucker at the corner of his mouth, that showed (though his eyes were cast down in affected penitence) that he was ready to break into laughter at the least breach of gravity. Indeed, he needed but the man's body-coat with the tails dragging on the ground, and the trousers tied up with string instead of braces, and bare muddy feet, to mark him as one of the confirmed young London thieves . . .

Here is the case of another of the boys, whose red mark on the sleeve of his jacket showed that he, too, had been ten times in prison before.

'Sixteen years of age, please, sir,' said the lad, 'and in for stealing a coat. I've been at prigging about four year. I had one calendar month here for a pair of boots. Then I stole a box of silver pencil-cases from a jeweller's shop. I bought an old aypenny ring, and broke it up, and while the gennelman was looking at it to see whether it was goold or not, I slipped the pencil-cases under my coat. I got four calendar months for that there, sir. Then I was took for two bundles of cigars, and had one month here. After that I was took for some meerschaum pipes, and had another month. I was took for a coat besides, and got three calendar months in Coldbath Fields. I guv my age seventeen that time, so as to get sent there. I guv it seventeen this time, too, but they was fly to it.'

'Why would you rather go to Coldbath Fields?' we inquired.

'Oh, I'd choose anything for a change, sir,' was the characteristic and candid reply.

'Then I was sent to Holloway for tossing,' went on the boy, 'and had fourteen days of it there. I don't know what I was took for the other time. Father's a hingineer, and I aint got no mother, please, sir. I've been to work with father when I've come out from my 'prisonments, but I've soon cut it and gone thieving again. I've been in a national school and a philanthropic over by Bedlam – it's called the House of Occupation.'

We next inquired as to what he intended to do when he regained his liberty once more.

'Do?' he answered, without the least fear, though the warder stood at his side, 'why, when I gets out here I shall go thieving again.'

The prison was closed in 1877. Westminster Cathedral now stands on the site.

Prostitutes on the Haymarket, 1862
Fyodor Dostoevsky

At the time of Dostoevsky's perambulation, there were estimated
to be 80,000 prostitutes in London.

ANYONE WHO HAS ever visited London must have
been at least once in the Haymarket at night. It is a
district in certain streets of which prostitutes swarm
by night in their thousands. Streets are lit by jets of gas –
something completely unknown in our own country. At every
step you come across magnificent public houses, all mirrors
and gilt. They serve as meeting places as well as shelters. It is a
terrifying experience to find oneself in that crowd. And, what
an odd amalgam it is. You will find old women there and
beautiful women at the sight of whom you stop in amazement.
There are no women in the world as beautiful as the English.

The streets can hardly accommodate the dense, seething
crowd. The mob has not enough room on the pavements and
swamps the whole street. All this mass of humanity craves
for booty and hurls itself at the first comer with shameless
cynicism. Glistening, expensive clothes and semi-rags and
sharp differences in age – they are all there. A drunken tramp
shuffling along in this terrible crowd is jostled by the rich and
titled. You hear curses, quarrels, solicitations and the quiet,
whispered invitation of some still bashful beauty. And how
beautiful they sometimes are with their keepsake faces! I
remember once I went into a 'casino'. The music was blaring,
people were dancing, a huge crowd was milling round. The
place was magnificently decorated. But gloom never forsakes
the English even in the midst of gaiety; even when they dance

they look serious, not to say sullen, making hardly any steps and then only as if in execution of some duty. Upstairs, in the gallery I saw a girl and stopped in amazement. She was sitting at a little table together with an apparently rich and respectable young man who, by all the signs, was an unaccustomed visitor to the casino. Perhaps he had been looking for her and they had at last found each other and arranged to meet there. He spoke to her little and only in short, jerky phrases as if he was not talking about what really interested him. Their conversation was punctuated by long and frequent silences. She, too, looked sad. Her face was delicate and fine, and there was something deep-hidden and sad, something thoughtful and melancholy in the proud expression of her eyes. I should say she had consumption. Mentally and morally she was, she could not fail to be, above the whole crowd of those wretched women; otherwise, what meaning would there be in a human face? All the same, however, she was then and there drinking gin, paid for by the young man. At last he got up, shook hands with her and went away. He left the casino, while she, her pale cheeks now flushed deep with drink, was soon lost in the crowd of women trading in their bodies.

In the Haymarket I noticed mothers who brought their little daughters to make them ply that same trade. Little girls, aged about twelve, seize you by the arm and beg you to come with them. I remember once amidst the crowd of people in the street I saw a little girl, not older than six, all in rags, dirty, bare-foot and hollow-cheeked; she had been severely beaten, and her body, which showed through the rags, was covered with bruises. She was walking along, as if oblivious of everybody and everything, in no hurry to get anywhere, and Heaven knows why loafing about in that crowd; perhaps she was hungry. Nobody was paying any attention to her. But what struck me most was the look of such distress, such hopeless despair on her face that to see that tiny bit of humanity already bearing the imprint of all that evil and despair was somehow unnatural and terribly painful. She kept on shaking her tousled head as if arguing about something, gesticulated and spread her little hands and then suddenly clasped them together and pressed them to her little bare breast. I went back and gave her sixpence. She took the small silver coin, gave me a wild look full of frightened surprise, and suddenly ran off as fast as her legs could carry her, as if afraid that I should take the money away from her. Jolly scenes, altogether ...

Into Hades:
The Metropolitan Underground Railway
Commences Service, 9 January 1863
The Times

Like Bazalgette's sewers, the Underground Railway was another triumph of Victorian engineering and took a similarly long gestation; local solicitor Charles Pearson campaigned for 20 years before the Metropolitan Railway from Paddington to Farringdon opened on 9 January 1863. The Prime Minister, Palmerston, refused to attend the ceremony on the basis that he 'wished to remain above ground as long as possible'. The first trains were pulled by steam engines, and to avoid passengers and crews suffocating from smoke and steam in the tunnels these waste products were ducted into a tank behind the engine, then released when the engine was above ground. Or so the theory went.

*Y*ESTERDAY THE METROPOLITAN (underground) Railway was opened to the public, and many thousands were enabled to indulge their curiosity in reference to this mode of travelling under the streets of the metropolis. The trains commenced running as early as six o'clock in the morning from the Paddington (Bishop's-road) station, and the Farringdon-street terminus, in order to accommodate workmen, and there was a goodly muster of that class of the public, who availed themselves of the advantages of the line in reaching their respective places of employment. At eight o'clock the desire to travel underground in the direction of the City began to manifest itself at the various stations along the line; and by nine it became equally evident to the authorities that neither the locomotive power nor the rolling stock at their disposal was at all in proportion to the requirements of the opening day. From this time, and throughout the morning, every station became crowded with anxious travellers who were admitted in sections; but poor were the chances of a place to those who ventured to take their tickets at any point below Baker-street, the occupants being, with but very rare exceptions, 'long distance,' or terminus, passengers. This circumstance tended to increase the numbers at every station every minute, until there became sufficient to fill any train of empties which might be sent to overflow; and we believe we are correct in stating that ultimately a number of the Great Western narrow gauge carriages as well as engines, were brought into requisition, and by this means the temporary wants of the public were accommodated. Possibly the greatest point of attraction, if the collection of numbers may be taken as any criterion, was King's cross, which is certainly the finest station on the line throwing even the termini into the shade. At this point, during the morning, the crowds were immense, and the constant cry, as the trains arrived, of 'No room', appeared to have a very depressing effect upon those assembled. Between eleven and twelve, at this station, and continuously for the space of an hour and a half, the money takers refused to take money for passengers between King's-cross and Farringdon-street, but they issued tickets between that station and Paddington, and many, whose destination was City-wise, determined to ride on the railway on its first day of opening, took tickets for the opposite direction, in order to secure places for the return journey. At twelve o'clock the clerks informed the public, who were certainly then assembled to the number of some 500 or 600 at King's-cross, that there were enough people at Paddington to fill four trains in succession; and that, therefore, their instructions were to issue no Farringdon-street tickets for an hour. This announcement had the effect of getting rid of very large numbers. Whilst, however, all the tendency of the traffic was towards the Farringdon-street terminus during the morning, the public were enabled to proceed westward with but little inconvenience. Towards afternoon, however, the tide set in the other way, and the approaches to the trains at Victoria-street can be compared to no other than the crush at the doors of a theatre on the first night of a pantomime. Between one and two o'clock thousands of anxious travellers by the new route were collected outside the Victoria-street terminus, and when the outer doors were opened, which was only at intervals, the rush was tremendous, and on reaching the ticket office the difficulty of exchanging cash for a ticket was an equally difficult task. The platform gained, the next grand struggle was for a seat in the incoming and presently outgoing train. Classification was altogether ignored, the holders of No.1 being obliged to be compelled to go in No.3 or not at all, and vice versa. Hundreds on each occasion, however, had to be left behind, to take their chance of the next train in rotation. Once in motion, all appeared to be right, the riding very easy, and a train which left Farringdon-street at 2:15 reached King's-cross station at 2:18 (a little over a mile), bringing up at the platform in three minutes. Gower-street was reached at 2:25, Portland-road at 2:30, Baker-street at 2:36, Edgware-road at 2:42, and the terminus at Paddington at 2:48; thus performing the journey in 33 minutes, including stoppages at the various stations. There were other journeys performed which were longer, reaching over 40 minutes, but the time above specified may be taken as about the average time of the running of the trains throughout the day. With regard to this point, however, the time occupied yesterday in the running of the trains from terminus to terminus can scarcely be taken as a fair criterion of what may be the actual time when the excitement of an opening day is over, and the line shall have sobered down to its ordinary traffic. The excitement of the public to get places, and the running about of officials at every station to each carriage to see if there was a seat for one here and for two there, no doubt took up more than half the time which will be occupied by the stoppage of a train at each station on ordinary occasions.

Of the general comfort in travelling on the line there can be no doubt, and the novel introduction of gas into the carriages is calculated to dispel any unpleasant feelings which passengers, especially ladies, might entertain against riding for so long a distance through a tunnel. Yesterday, throughout every journey, the gas burnt brightly, and in some instances was turned on so strong in the first-class carriages, in each of which there were two burners, that when the carriages were stationary, newspapers might be read with facility; but, in motion, the draft through the apertures of the lamps, created so much flickering as to render such a feat exceedingly difficult. The second-class carriages are very nicely fitted with leathered seats, and are very commodious, and the compartments and arms in the first-class render overcrowding impossible.

There is one point to which attention was attracted as

being adverse to the general expectation, and that was that it was understood that there was to be no steam or smoke from the engines used in working this tunnel railway. All we can say is, that on one of the journeys between Portland-road and Baker-street, not only were the passengers enveloped in steam, but it is extremely doubtful if they were not subjected to the unpleasantness of smoke also. This may have arisen from the circumstance before alluded to, that in consequence of the extreme pressure upon their resources, the workers of the metropolitan line were compelled to avail themselves of locomotive as well as rolling stock of the Great Western, and that it is only a temporary inconvenience. Up to six o'clock the computation was that somewhere about 25,000 persons had been carried over the line, and it is gratifying to remark that, notwithstanding the eagerness of the public to get into the carriages, even when the trains were in motion, no single accident, of any kind, was reported.

To the relief of suffocating Londoners the Underground was electrified from 1890. At around the same time, improved tunnel technology allowed the Underground to burrow safely and economically through central and West End London. Accordingly, the Central Line opened in 1900, Piccadilly in 1906, Baker Street & Waterloo ('Bakerloo') in 1906 and Northern in 1907. The extension of the Underground to the suburbs during the twentieth century speeded up the depopulation of the city begun by the railways.

Murder on the North London Railway, July 1864

Illustrated London News

16 JULY 1864

A MURDER WAS COMMITTED last Saturday in a carriage on the North London Railway. Mr. Thomas Briggs, chief clerk in the bank of Messrs. Robarts, Curtis, and Co., Lombard-street, left the Fenchurch-street station, by the 9.45 p.m. for Hackney, where he resided. On the arrival of the train at Hackney, the compartment in which he had travelled – the centre one of a first-class carriage – was found to be covered with blood, which in some places lay in pools. There were in it a walking-stick and a leather bag, both belonging to Mr. Briggs; and a hat, bearing the maker's name, which the murderer or one of the murderers had left behind. Shortly afterwards the insensible and almost lifeless body of Mr. Briggs was found lying between the lines by the driver and the stoker of an engine which was returning from the Hackney-wick station to Bow, and it was removed to an adjacent tavern. The head seemed to have been battered in by some sharp instrument; the clothes were covered in blood; and the broken link or hook of a watch-chain hung to a buttonhole of the waistcoat, the rest of the chain and the watch being missing. The wounded gentleman was quite insensible. On the left side of the head, just over the ear, which was torn away, was found a deep wound; the skull was fractured and the bone driven in. On the base of the skull there were four or five lacerated wounds; there were more wounds on other parts of the head. Stimulants were applied with a view of restoring consciousness but to no purpose, and Mr. Briggs, having been removed to his home, died on Sunday night. The money which Mr. Briggs had in his pocket had not been taken, but his watch was missing. It appears that the crime was committed between Bow and Hackney-wick. The distance between these places is traversed in about five minutes, so that in that brief space the deceased was attacked, robbed, and thrown out of the carriage. The next compartment was occupied by some ladies, but they did not hear any cries, although on the arrival of the train at Hackney they called the notice of the guard to the circumstance that some blood had been spurted through the carriage window on to their dresses as the train came from Bow. The chain belonging to Mr. Briggs was on Monday exchanged at a silversmith's in the City for another, by a man who is thus described:- 'Age thirty; height, 5 ft. 6 or 7 in.; complexion sallow; thin features; a foreigner – supposed German; speaks good English; dress, black frock coat and vest, dark trousers, and black hat.' This person took in exchange for Mr. Briggs' chain, a square oval secret-link gold Albert chain, with knot-pattern twisted key, swivel seal, and a plain gold finger-ring, white cornelian stone, oblong shape, engraved head. A reward of £300 has been offered for the apprehension of the murderer or murderers.

23 JULY 1864

The murder of Mr. Briggs in a carriage on the North London Railway, on Saturday week, was, there seems little doubt, committed by Franz Müller, a German tailor. The manner in which the crime was traced to him is curious. He was in the habit of calling at the house of a cabman named Matthews. Two days after the murder he visited this house, and produced a box containing a gold chain, which he said he had just purchased. He fastened the chain to his watch and gave the box to Matthew's little daughter. Matthews, happening some time afterwards to look at the box, saw inside it the name and address of Mr. Death, the jeweller, at whose shop he was aware Mr. Briggs's chain had been exchanged. The box was taken to Mr. Death, who identified it, and, a photograph of Müller having been produced, he at once recognised the man's features. The cabman was shown the hat left in the railway-carriage, and he declared it to be the one which he had himself bought for Müller some months ago. Müller left the Thames for New York in a sailing-vessel on Thursday week. This fact was ascertained by means of a letter which he wrote from on board that ship and sent ashore by the pilot, who landed at Worthing. Last Wednesday Inspector Tanner, of the metropolitan force; Mr. Death, the jeweller; and the cabman, left Liverpool in the Inman steamer City of Manchester in pursuit of Müller. Mr. Tanner is armed with the necessary warrants for the apprehension of the culprit, and bears despatches from Mr. Adams, the American minister in London, so that any proceedings in America will be facilitated to the utmost. The City of Manchester will in all probability arrive out sooner than the Victoria, and every precaution will be taken to secure Müller's arrest. If the New York Associated Press boat is seen off Cape Race telegrams for the Canadian stations will be at once forwarded, and then chances in favour of Müller escaping will be few indeed.

The Founding of the International Working Men's Association, Covent Garden, 28 September 1864

Karl Marx

The International Working Men's Association was formed in St Martin's Hall by French and British trade union workers, who asked Karl Marx to be their general secretary. So it was that London became the crucible of Communism, just as it was capital of capitalism. Marx writes to Engels in Manchester:

DEAR FREDERICK:
Sometime ago London workers sent an address about Poland to Paris workers and summoned them to common action in this matter.

The Parisians on their part sent over a deputations headed by a worker called Tolain, the real workers' candidate at the last election in Paris, a very nice fellow. (His companions too were quite nice lads.) A public meeting in St. Martin's Hall was summoned for September 28, 1864, by Odger (shoemaker, president of the Council here of all London trade unions and also especially of the Trade Unions Suffrage Agitation Society, which is connected with Bright), and Cremer, mason and secretary of the Masons' Union. (These two organized the big meeting of the trade unions in St. James's Hall for North America, under Bright, ditto the Garibaldi demonstrations.) A certain Le Lubez was sent to ask me if I would take part on behalf of the German workers, and especially if I would supply a German worker to speak at the meeting, etc. I provided them with Eccarius, who came off splendidly, and ditto was present myself as a mute figure on the platform. I knew that this time real 'powers' were involved on both the London and Paris sides and therefore decided to waive my usual standing rule to decline any such invitations.

(Le Lubez is a young Frenchman, i.e., in his thirties, who has however grown up in Jersey and London, speaks English excellently, and is a very good intermediary between the French and English workers.) (Music teacher and French lessons.)

At the meeting, which was packed to *suffocation* (for there is now evidently a revival of the working classes taking place), Major Wolff (Thurn-Taxis, Garibaldi's adjutant) represented the London Italian Working Men's Society. It was decided to found a 'Working Men's International Association', the General Council of which should be in London and should act as an 'intermediary' between the workers' societies in Germany, Italy, France, and England. Ditto that a General Working Men's Congress should be summoned in Belgium in 1865. A provisional committee was appointed at the meeting: Odger, Cremer, and many others, some of them old Chartists, old Owenites, etc., for England; Major Wolff, Fontana, and other Italians for Italy; Le Lubez, etc., for France; Eaccrius and I for Germany. The committee was empowered to co-opt as many members as it chose.

So far so good. I attended the first meeting of the committee. A sub committee (including myself) was appointed to draft a declaration of principles and provisional statutes. Being unwell, I was prevented from attending the meeting of the subcommittee and the meeting of the whole committee which followed.

In these two meetings which I had missed – that of the subcommittee and the subsequent one of the whole committee – the following had taken place:

Major Wolff had handed in the reglement [statutes]

of the Italian Workers' Societies (which possess a central organization but, as later transpired, are really associated benefit societies) to be used for the new association. I saw the stuff later. It was evidently a compilation of Mazzini's, so you alredy know the spirit and phraseology in which the real question, the workers' question, was dealt with. Also how nationalities were shoved in.

In addition an old Owenite, Weston – now a manufacturer himself, a very amiable and worthy man – had drawn up a program of indescribable breadth and full of the most extreme confusion.

The subsequent general committee meeting instructed the subcommittee to remodel Weston's program, ditto Wolff's regulations. Wolff himself left in order to attend the Congress of Italian Working Men's Associations in Naples and get them to decide on joining the London Central Association.

Another meeting of the subcommittee – which I again failed to attend, because I was informed of the rendezvous too late. At this a 'declaration of principles' and a new version of Wolff's statutes were put forward by Le Lubez and accepted by the committee for submission to the general committee.

The general committee met on October 18.

As Eccarius had written me that delay would be dangerous, I appeared and was really frightened when I heard the worthy Le Lubez read out an appallingly wordy, badly written, and utterly undigested preamble, pretending to be a declaration of principles, in which Mazzini could be detected everywhere, the whole thing crusted over with the vaguest tags of French socialism. Added to this, the Italian statutes were taken over in the main, and these, apart from all their other faults, aim at something which is in fact utterly impossible, a sort of central government of the *European* working classes (with Mazzini in the background, of course). I put up a mild opposition and after a lot of talking backwards and forwards Eccarius proposed that the subcommittee should submit the thing to further 'editing'. On the other hand the 'sentiments' contained in Lubez' declaration were voted for.

Two days later, on October 20, Cremer (for the English), Fontana (Italy), and Le Lubez assembled at my house. (Weston was prevented.) Hitherto I had never had the documents (those of Wolff and Le Lubez) in my hand so could not prepare anything, but was firmly determined that if possible not one single line of the stuff should be allowed to stand. In order to gain time I proposed that before we 'edited' the preamble we should 'discuss' the rules. This took place. It was an hour after midnight by the time the first of forty rules was agreed to. Cremer said (and this was what I had aimed at): We have nothing to put before the committee, which meets on October 25. We must postpone the meeting til November 1. But the subcommittee can get together on October 27 and attempt to reach a definite conclusion. This was agreed to and the 'papers' 'left behind' for my opinion.

I saw that it was impossible to make anything out of the stuff. In order to justify the extremely strange way in which I intended to present the 'sentiment' already 'voted for', I wrote an Address to the Working Classes (which was not in the original plan: a sort of review of the adventures of the working classes since 1845); on the pretext that everything material was included in the address and that we ought not to repeat the same things three times over, I altered the whole preamble, threw out the declaration of principles, and finally replaced the 40 rules with 10. Insofar as international politics come into the address, I speak of countries, not of nationalities, and denounce Russia, not the lesser nations. My proposals were all accepted by the subcommittee. Only I was obliged to insert two phrases about 'duty' and 'right' into the preamble to the statutes, ditto 'truth, morality, and justice', but these are placed in such a way that they can do no harm.

At the meeting of the general committee my address, etc., was agreed to with great enthusiasm (unanimously). The discussion on the method of printing, etc., takes place next Tuesday. Le Lubez has a copy of the address to translate into French and Fontana one to translate into Italian. (For a state there is a weekly paper called the *Bee-Hive*, edited by Potter the trade unionist, a sort of *Moniteur*.) I myself am to translate the stuff into German.

It was very difficult to frame the thing so that our view [Engels and Marx] should appear in a form acceptable from the present standpoint of the workers' movement. In a few weeks the same people will be holding meetings for the franchise with Bright and Cobden. It will take time before the re-awakened movement allows the old boldness of speech. It will be necessary to be *fortiter in re, suaviter in modo* [*bold in matter, mild in manner*]. As soon as the stuff is printed you will get it ...

                    Yours,
                    K.M.

Marx died in 1883 and was buried in Highgate Cemetery.

William Morris at Home, 10 March 1869
Henry James

William Morris was a Romantic anomaly in London. The 'improving' zeal of his fellow Victorians razed whole tracts of old London – including 17 of Wren's churches – to make way for new developments. Its ancient pedigree aside, London was the most modern city in the world. (By 1900 two-thirds of London was less than 50 years old). In reaction to modernity and its frequently shoddy, mass-produced goods, Morris founded in 1861 the firm of Morris, Marshall, Faulkner and Company, purveyors of craftsman-made furniture and artefacts.

MORRIS LIVES ON the same premises as his shop, in Queen's Square, Bloomsbury, an antiquated ex-fashionable region, smelling strong of the last century, with a hoary effigy of Queen Anne in the middle. Morris's poetry, you see, is only his sub-trade. To begin with, he is a manufacturer of stained glass windows, tiles, ecclesiastical and mediaeval tapestry, altar-cloths, and in fine everything quaint, archaic, pre-Raphaelite – and I may add, exquisite. Of course his business is small and may be carried on in his house: the things he makes are so handsome, rich and expensive (besides being articles of the very last luxury) that his *fabrique* can't be on a very large scale. But everything he has and does is superb and beautiful. But more curious than anything is himself. He designs with his own head and hands all the figures and patterns used in his glass and tapestry, and furthermore works the latter, stitch by stitch, with his own fingers – aided by those of his wife and little girls. Oh, ma chère, such a wife! *Je n'en reviens pas* – she haunts me still. A figure cut out of a missal – out of one of Rossetti's or Hunt's pictures – to say this gives but a faint idea of her, because when such an image puts on flesh and blood, it is an apparition of fearful and wonderful intensity. It's hard to say whether she's a grand synthesis of all the pre-Raphaelite pictures ever made – or they a 'keen analysis' of her – whether she's an original or a copy. In either case she is a wonder. Imagine a tall lean woman in a long dress of some dead purple stuff, guiltless of hoops (or of anything else, I should say,) with a mass of crisp black hair heaped into great wavy projections on each of her temples, a thin pale face, a pair of strange sad, deep, dark Swinburnian eyes, with great thick black oblique brows, joined in the middle and tucking themselves away under her hair, a mouth like the 'Oriana' in our illustrated Tennyson, a long neck, without any collar, and in lieu thereof some dozen strings of outlandish beads – in fine complete. On the wall was a large nearly full-length portrait of her by Rossetti, so strange and unreal that if you hadn't seen her you'd pronounce it a distempered vision, but in fact an extremely good likeness. After dinner (we stayed to dinner, Miss Grace, Miss S. S. and I,) Morris read us one of his unpublished poems, from the second series of his un-'Earthly Paradise', and his wife, having a bad toothache, lay on the sofa, with her handkerchief to her face. There was something very quaint and remote from our actual life, it seemed to me, in the whole scene: Morris reading . . . and in the corner this dark silent mediaeval woman with her mediaeval toothache. Morris himself is extremely pleasant and quite different from his wife. He impressed me most agreeably. He is short, burly, corpulent, very careless and unfinished in his dress, and looks a little like B. G. Hosmer, if you can imagine B. G. infinitely magnified and fortified. He has a very loud voice and a nervous restless manner and a perfectly unaffected and business-like address. His talk indeed is wonderfully to the point and remarkable for clear good sense. He said no one thing that I remember, but I was struck with the very good judgment shown in everything he uttered. He's an extraordinary example, in short, of a delicate sensitive genius and taste, saved by a perfectly healthy body and temper. All his designs are quite as good (or rather nearly so) as his poetry: altogether it was a long rich sort of visit, with a strong peculiar flavour of its own.

As well as being a craftsman and poet, Morris had a quite distinct reputation as a socialist thinker. He was an early and influential member of the Marxist-inclined Social Democratic Federation, led by Henry Hyndman, which livened up the London political scene in the late nineteenth century.

A Socialist March Through the West End, Autumn 1886
H.M. Hyndman

*T*HERE HAD GROWN up in the east end of London during 1885 and 1886 a more or less subsidized agitation, arising out of the collapse of the sugar refineries and the consequent throwing of a large number of men out of work, which led to an organization called 'The Fair Trade League'. I am willing to admit that there was a good deal to be said for their contentions in themselves, but brought up as they were in direct opposition to Socialist palliatives and Socialism as a cure for unemployment, the whole movement was used by the Capitalists against us.

These people, headed by two shrewd persons, Peters and Kelly, called a meeting in Trafalgar Square in favour of Fair Trade in the autumn of 1886. The Social-Democratic Federation at once summoned a counter demonstration against it. The two bodies met, many of the Fair Traders, as is now well known, being people who had been brought up at so much a head, ready for any little diversion. There was a good deal of friction in the Square itself between the two factions, and the whole thing seemed likely to degenerate into a free fight, when the police came to me and suggested that our folk should go off to Hyde Park, and thus avoid a serious breach of the peace ... So Burns took a red flag to lead the way, and we called upon the people to follow. Many of the other side came too, and a wholly unorganized mob went rushing down Pall Mall and up St. James's Street where, as speedily appeared, there were no police at all.

The trouble began at the Reform Club. There, owing to a member wishing to get into either that Club or the Carlton, a halt occurred: some of our supporters helping him to get through without being crushed or assaulted. Champion and I who were in Pall Mall among the crowd, on the opposite side of the pavement, saw some of the servants of the Reform Club throw down missiles at the crowd in the shape of old nail-brushes, shoes, etc. Thereupon stones were thrown at the windows, and a great hubbub ensued. Happily the people did not raid the Club, but hurried along. As we passed up St. James's Street, however, we noted that much heavier stone-throwing had begun – the roadway was then macadamized, and there was more than one big heap of metal ready broken for laying down – and that many of the Club windows were smashed all to pieces, including the windows of the New

University Club, from which I had not long before been expelled for making a speech on the Embankment in favour of the unemployed ...

As we left St. James's Street, however, and went along Piccadilly, things got worse and worse. Nearly all the shops, especially the tailors' and hosiers', had their windows broken and were looted. It was a funny enough scene to observe these people from the East End of London, brought up from their poor quarters at five shillings a head by the funds of the Fair Trade League, freely helping themselves to new garments and then putting them on ... in the Green Park. Later we learnt that the whole of South Audley Street had been pretty thoroughly looted, and that several ladies in carriages and on foot had thought themselves lucky to get off with the loss of their jewellery and purses. But of that we saw nothing, as we made our way to the Achilles statue, where we held our renewed meeing ...

We, *nous autres pauvres apôtres*, numbering at the time a few score thorough-going Socialists in the world of the metropolis at the outside, read with delighted laughter the placards, 'London in Danger from Socialist Plots', '75,000 Socialists marching on the West End from Dept-ford', 'Arrangements perfected to protect private property'.

(above) The Quadrant at the Piccadilly end of Regent Street, designed by John Nash, May 1852.

Triumphal Arches. H. Handels Statue &c. in the South Walk of VAUXHALL GARDENS. Les Arcs de Triomphe avecla Statue de celebre musicien. Handel &c. le jardin de Vauxhall.

(above) Vauxhall Gardens, a leading public entertainment venue in Georgian London.

(above) A chromo-
lithograph of the Great
Exhibition of 1851,
housed in a 'crystal
palace' designed by the
Duke of Devonshire's
gardener, Joseph Paxton.

(right) In 1888 the match
girls at Bryant & May's
factory by the River Lea
won a three-week strike
for better conditions.

above) The upper pool of the Thames, with Tower Bridge in the background, 1930. The Empire ensured London's position as the globe's chief port until the 960s.

(above) The residents of a slum street in East London, early twentieth century.

(above) A crowd of Londoners crossing London Bridge, 1909.

London can take it: St Paul's Cathedral survives Hitler's Blitz, 1940.

(above) A bus is guided by its fog lamps aong the Embankment during a 'pea souper' at midday on 6 December 1952.

(right) The Kray brothers (from left to right, Reginald, Charles, Ronald) were East End gangsters who mixed with West End socialites during the swinging Sixties.

above) An East End street celebrating the 1977 Queen's Silver Jubilee; one of the last appearances of the old Cockney London of street life; knees-ups in pubs and hop-picking in Kent in the summer.

The bombed bus at Tavistock Square on '7/7' 2005.

Madame Blavatsky in Norwood, c. 1887

W.B. Yeats

A Russian émigré, Helena Petrovna Blavatsky was the co-founder of the Theosophical Society. Annie Besant, the London socialist and birth control proponent, was one of her disciples.

I FOUND MADAME BLAVATSKY in a little house at Norwood, with but, as she said, three followers left – the Society of Psychical Research had just reported on her Indian phenomena – and as one of the three followers sat in an outer room to keep out undesirable visitors, I was kept a long time kicking my heels. Presently I was admitted and found an old woman in a plain loose dark dress: a sort of old Irish peasant woman with an air of humour and audacious power. I was still kept waiting, for she was deep in conversation with a woman visitor. I strayed through folding doors into the next room and stood, in sheer idleness of mind, looking at a cuckoo clock. It was certainly stopped, for the weights were off and lying upon the ground, and yet, as I stood there the cuckoo came out and cuckooed at me. I interrupted Madame Blavatsky to say, 'Your clock has hooted me.' 'It often hoots at a stranger,' she replied. 'Is there a spirit in it?' I said. 'I do not know,' she said, 'I should have to be alone to know what is in it.' I went back to the clock and began examining it and heard her say: 'Do not break my clock.' I wondered if there was some hidden mechanism and I should have been put out, I suppose, had I found any, though Henley had said to me, 'Of course she gets up fraudulent miracles, but a person of genius has to do something: Sarah Bernhardt sleeps in her coffin.' Presently the visitor went away and Madame Blavatsky explained that she was a propagandist for women's rights who had called to find out 'why men were so bad.' 'What explanation did you give her?' I said. 'That men were born bad, but women made themselves so,' and then she explained that I had been kept waiting because she had mistaken me for some man, whose name resembled mine and who wanted to persuade her of the flatness of the earth.

When I next saw her she had moved into a house at Holland Park, and some time must have passed – probably I had been in Sligo where I returned constantly for long visits – for she was surrounded by followers. She sat nightly before a little table covered with green baize and on this green baize she scribbled constantly with a piece of white chalk. She would scribble symbols, sometimes humorously explainable, and sometimes unintelligible figures, but the chalk was intended to mark down her score when she played patience. One saw in the next room a large table where every night her followers and guests, often a great number, sat down to their vegetable meal, while she encouraged or mocked through the folding doors. A great passionate nature, a sort of female Dr. Johnson, impressive I think to every man or woman who had themselves any richness, she seemed impatient of the formalism and the shrill abstract idealism of those about her, and this impatience broke out in railing and many nicknames: 'Oh you are a flap-doodle, but then you are a theosophist and a brother.' The most devout and learned of all her followers said to me, 'H.P.B. has just told me that there is another globe stuck on to this at the north pole, so that the earth has really a shape something like a dumb-bell.'

The Whitechapel Murders,
6 August–9 November 1888

Dr Thomas Bond and 'Jack the Ripper'

Over the course of autumn in 1888 the corpses of six murdered and mutilated prostitutes were found in rooms and alleys near Whitechapel High Street in the East End. Something of the sadistic cruelty inflicted on the victims was attested to by the post-mortem on Mary Jane Kelly carried out by Dr Thomas Bond:

T HE FACE WAS gashed in all directions the nose cheeks, eyebrows and ears being partly removed. The lips were blanched & cut by several incisions running obliquely down to the chin. There were also numerous cuts extending irregularly across all the features.

The neck was cut through the skin & other tissues right down to the vertebrae the 5th & 6th being deeply notched. The skin cuts in the front of the neck showed distinct ecchymosis.

The air passage was cut at the lower part of the larynx through the cricoid cartilage. Both breasts were removed by more or less circular incisions, the muscles down to the ribs being attached to the breasts. The intercostals between the 4th, 5th & 6th ribs were cut through & the contents of the thorax visible through the openings.

The skin & tissues of the abdomen from the costal arch to the pubes were removed in three large flaps. The right thigh was denuded in front to the bone, the flap of skin, including the external organs of generation & part of the right buttock.

The left thigh was stripped of skin, fascia & muscles as far as the knee.

The left calf showed a long gash through skin & tissues to the deep muscles & reaching from the knee to 5 ins above the ankle.

Both arms & forearms had extensive & jagged wounds.

The right thumb showed a small superficial incision about 1 in long, with extravasation of blood in the skin & there were several abrasions on the back of the hand moreover showing the same condition.

On opening the thorax it was found that the right lung was minimally adherent by old firm adhesions. The lower part of the lung was broken & torn away.

The left lung was intact: it was adherent at the apex & there were a few adhesions over the side. In the substaces of the lung were several nodules of consolidation.

The Pericardium was open below & the Heart absent.

In the abdominal cavity was some partially digested food of fish & potatoes & similar food was found in the remains of the stomach attached to the intestines.

The perverted nature of the Whitechapel killings and the elusiveness of their perpetrator caused terror to sweep the capital. Even in the west of the city, people became afraid to go out after dark. On 27 September the Central News Agency received the following letter, initially thought to be a hoax but then considered to be written by the Whitechapel murderer himself. It was the first time that the sobriquet Jack the Ripper was used.

DEAR BOSS,

I keep on hearing the police have caught me, but they won't fix me just yet. I have laughed when they look so clever and talk about being on the right track. The joke about Leather Apron gave me real fits.

I am down on whores and I shan't quit ripping them till I do get buckled. Grand work, the last job was. I gave the lady no time to squeal. How can they catch me now? I love my work and want to start again. You will soon hear of me and my funny little games.

I saved some of the proper red stuff in a ginger beer bottle over the last job, to write with, but it went thick like glue and I can't use it. Red ink is fit enough, I hope. Ha! Ha!

The next job I do I shall clip the lady's ears off and send them to the police, just for jolly, wouldn't you? Keep this letter back until I do a bit more work, then give it out straight. My knife's so nice and sharp, I want to get to work right away if I get a chance. Good luck,

Yours truly,

JACK THE RIPPER

Don't mind me giving the trade name. Wasn't good enough to post this before I got all the red ink off my hands; curse it. No luck yet. They say I am a doctor now. Ha! Ha!

On 1 October the Central News Agency received a postcard, bearing a bloody thumbprint and the following message:

I WAS NOT codding, dear old Boss, when I gave you the tip. You'll hear about Saucy Jack's work tomorrow. Double event this time. Number One squealed a bit. Couldn't finish straight off. Had no time to get ears for police. Thanks for keeping last letter back till I got to work again. – JACK THE RIPPER

The identity of 'Jack' has never been established. The Cable Street hairdresser George Chapman (born Severin Klosowski in Poland) is a favourite contender; if Jack was Chapman he was hanged for an unrelated homicide in 1903. If Jack was the demented barrister Montague Druitt he escaped the noose by drowning himself in the Thames in December 1888.

⚘ ⚘ ⚘

The Dock Strike, August–September 1889
Beatrice Webb

London's dockworkers suffered a 'casual' system of employment that saw thousands of men scrambling for work every morning outside the dock gates. Henry Mayhew, the social investigator, vividly described 'the Call':

THEN BEGINS THE scuffling and scrambling forth of countless hands high in the air, to catch the eye of him whose voice may give them work . . . All are shouting. Some cry aloud his surname, some his christian name, others call out their own names, to remind him that they are there . . . To look in the faces of that hungry crowd is to see a sight that must ever be remembered . . . For weeks they may have gone there, and gone through the same struggle – the same cries; and have gone away, after all, without the work they had screamed for.

On a busy day the London docks might employ over 20,000 men; on a slack day perhaps 10,000. The work – when it came – was notoriously poorly paid. In the summer of 1889, inspired by the successful match girls' strike of 1888, the dockworkers went on strike. Their demand was for four hours' continuous work at a time and a minimum rate of a 'tanner' (sixpence) an hour. The Fabian social reformer Beatrice Webb, who had investigated dockers' lives, recorded in her diary:

DIARY, 29 AUGUST 1889

The dock strike becoming more and more exciting – even watched at a distance. Originally 500 casuals marched out of the West and East India Docks – in another day the strike spread to the neighbouring docks – in a week half East London was out. For the first time a general strike of labour, not on account of the vast majority of strikers, but to enforce the claims to a decent livelihood of some 3,000 men. The hero of the scene, John Burns the socialist, who seems for the time to have the East London working men at his feet, with Ben Tillett as his lieutenant and ostensible representative of the dockers.

The strike is intensely interesting to me personally, as proving or disproving, in any case modifying, my generalization on 'Dock Life'. Certainly the solidarity of labour at the East end is a new thought to me – the dock labourers have not yet proved themselves capable of permanent organization but they have shown the capacity for common action. And what is more important, an extraordinary manifestation of practical sympathy, of effectual help, has been evoked among all classes in East London, skilled artisans making common cause with casuals, publicans, pawnbrokers and tradesmen supporting them.

DIARY, 22 SEPTEMBER 1889

The dock strike has ended in a brilliant victory to the men; all their demands (with the exception of fixed times for taking on) conceded – the concessions come into force in November. Burns' parting words 'Be good to your wives and your children and remember what a man who drinks water can do'. Fifty thousand pounds subscribed (£24,000 from Australia), pressure from all other capitalist interests, and public opinion of all classes have carried the dockers through to victory.

After the successful strike, the dockers formed a new General Labourers' Union. Ben Tillett was elected general secretary. In London alone, 20,000 men joined this new union. The year 1889 was a turning point in London politics: London finally secured a properly elected local authority – the London County Council (LCC).

One other event dominated late Victorian London, capital of the world's greatest ever empire: Victoria's Diamond Jubilee in 1897. The Queen recorded in her diary on 22 June: 'A never-to-be-forgotten day. No one ever, I believe, has met with such an ovation as was given to me, passing through those six miles of streets, including Constitution Hill.'

Only three years later, the crowds would again take to the streets of London – this time unscripted, as a release from anxiety.

Mafeking Night, 18 May 1900
Daily Mail

The Boer War, which began in 1899, saw the British garrison at Mafeking surrounded on 12 October. Week after week passed, with no British force able to break the siege. Public anxiety settled over Britain, in a barely conscious understanding that the country's standing as the globe's superpower was slipping away. On 17 May 1900 Mafeking was finally relieved. When the news was transmitted back to Britain the land – especially the 'imperial city' – went mad with a patriotic delirium that needed a neologism to express it: 'mafficking'.

*M*AFEKING IS FREE! ... At 9.30 last night the announcement came that the Boers had abandoned the siege ... London simply went wild with delight.

Fleet Street, which, on ordinary nights, contains only its usual number of pedestrians, was, as if by magic, transformed into a thoroughfare crowded and jammed with an excited throng of cheering, shouting, gesticulating, happy people. Whisdes were blown, even the innocent shovel that is used to stoke the May-Day fireplace was utilised for demonstrative purposes. Hawkers were on the scene with that rapidity which is only equalled by the vulture when it scents its prey. They were bereft of their 'B-P' buttons, their Union Jacks and their paper hats, sometimes receiving pay for them and as often not. In front of the newspaper offices the crowds became thick and impassable. The police were there, but that is all, for they were as atoms in a mighty sea.

At 9.30 the Mansion House presented its usual evening appearance of respectable desertion. The few passers-by did not even heed the empty bulletin board which so many had anxiously scanned during the day. The omnibus went by west and east as usual, and only the two huge footmen, so familiar to London pageantry, stood by, waiting and anxious to display the Baden-Powell picture that had been prepared for the great moment.

Five minutes later the Lord Mayor received the news, and the two footmen, in their wild desire to display 'BP' to the empty streets, nearly dropped it on the head of an unsuspecting passer-by. One of them shouted excitedly: 'Mafeking is relieved.'

Instantly the cry was taken up on the omnibuses and the people came clambering down in hot haste to hear the news repeated over and over again. Most of them stopped still as if it were too good to be true. Others rushed off into the byways, carrying the tidings further and further away, and all the time the streets became thicker with people cheering, shouting and singing.

Within five minutes of the announcement so unconventionally made by the Mansion House footman to the policeman below, the historic home of the Lord Mayor was surrounded by a crowd of no fewer than 20,000 madmen, all yelling: 'Mafeking is relieved!' or singing 'God Save the Queen' in all the notes possible to music.

Women absolutely wept for joy and men threw their arms about each others necks – strangers' necks for the most part; but that made no difference, for Mafeking was relieved ...

The death of Queen Victoria on 22 January 1901 confirmed the end of a glorious era. London was still the mightiest city in the world, both in extent (around 16 miles across) and in population (6.5 million), but it was definitely on the slide. Within 20 years, it would be outsized by New York.

Of course, some things remained the same. Street crime, for instance.

❧ ❧ ❧

Underworld: Whizzers, Knife-fights and Garrottings, 1904–19
Arthur Harding

I WAS DISCHARGED FROM Borstal in September 1904 and went back to Bethnal Green. I had no 'prospects' but I had supreme confidence in my ability to survive. Borstal had made me fitter, stronger, taller. I was no longer a kid, and when I went back to my old associates I found that I was something of a hero. I had had a good education at Dr Barnardo's. I was more intelligent than the other boys. I had a reputation for being tough. And I was the only one in the younger age group to have done time. They began to look up to me as a sort of leader.

There was a crowd of us went together, and what I told them to do they would do because they trusted me and perhaps because they were now a wee bit afraid of me. We youngsters began to mix more with the older thieves. There were about a dozen of them who used to hang out at Clark's. They were six or seven years older than us. But we used the same coffee shop and so we became known to them. The young lads looked up to the 'heads', as they called the older thieves, and some of them helped to carry stolen goods. You could say the older ones were the first eleven team, and me and my pals were the second.

I learnt pickpocketing from a chap I'd met at Wormwood Scrubs. His name was Edward Spencer. He was four years older than me and a real criminal. He thieved all his life. He was a real bloody villain, a complete criminal. He'd turn his hand to anything. His father worked for the Port of London Authority and his mother was respectable – they lived in Canrobert Street, Bethnal Green. He went thieving all over the place – him and a crowd of others. In the early years he used to go what they call 'shoot-flying' – stealing watch chains by getting hold of them and tugging. They would go into a street with a lot of turnings and when they made their catch they would shoot down the turnings – that's why they called it 'shoot-flying'. They also called it 'blagging'. About four of them used to do it, regular of a morning, just like going to business. They worked where the City toffs were – Broad Street, Finsbury Square.

I learnt about pickpocketing just like the Artful Dodger in Dickens. The other fellows were much older and took a real pride in their work. Spencer wouldn't let me go with him, but he told me how it was done and helped me to practise. Women were the easiest to take from. They didn't have handbags then, but used to have pockets at the back of their skirts. It was easy to cut them away – they didn't even notice what had happened. Whoever invented these pockets must have been a whizzer. Wallets were more difficult because they were kept in breast pockets, and shoot-flying you had to be ready to run. Pickpocketing men and women were two completely different lines. The Jewish boys, down in Whitechapel, were very good whizzers, but only went in for women. Spencer's lot only went in for men, and One-Eyed Charlie's gang were the same – though mostly he was a van-dragger – he wasn't a clever thief at all.

Soon I had my own little team. Mostly we went pickpocketing about Whitechapel and Petticoat Lane, where the crowds were, for the market. Sometimes we would take a little ride out, say to Peckham. And we used to go to market places like Whitecross Street in Finsbury and Leather Lane, Holborn. You went to market places because that's where people were in crowds. I was the gaffer. I looked after the others, always got them to do the pickpocketing. When they got it they would give it to me and I would do the selling and sharing out of the proceeds. People trusted us. Holiday times – holiday Mondays – we would go to New Cross or to Deptford where there was a big fair on. We never used to go to Hampstead Heath. That was because it was in Middlesex and the judge at Middlesex Sessions – Sir Ralph Littler – was the hottest judge in England. My friend Spencer got six years from him for attempting to steal a watch at White City. He said he would make Middlesex so safe that a man could hang his watch and chain on a lamp post and nobody would take it.

Brick Lane was a hotbed of villainy. Women paraded up and down the streets, took the men to their 'doubles' and sold themselves for a few pence. Thieves hung about on the corner of the street, waiting, like Mr Micawber, for something to turn up. In the back alleys there was garotting – some of the brides would lumber a seaman while he was drunk and then he would be dropped – 'stringing someone up' was the slang phrase for it. There were some wild characters about. One of them was 'China Bob'. I believe he was of Jewish extraction. He always carried a small chopper or hatchet in a poacher's pocket of his coat or jacket. He once fought a duel in Dorset Street with a man named 'Scabby'. Coats and shirts off, both had small knives. Both had small wounds when taken to London Hospital and had their cuts attended to. An enterprising reporter of the *Star* newspaper took some photos of their bodies. May I say that both of these two men were more like animals – and wild animals at that – than human beings. They inflicted terrible injuries on each other. China Bob had many scars and half-healed cuts upon his body, he smelt of decaying flesh. He was found one morning in the gutter in Commercial Street, which he had terrorized for so long. He was dead; no one was sorry, no one cared, least of all the police. This was after the First World War.

The man they called 'Scabby' was the same type of character. He would pick his victims from people who showed fear, and make them give him money for protection. One night in a doss-house in Dorset Street Scabby came in with a parcel of fish and chips. He offered the chips round, which was the custom then and still is. But one drunken fool took his piece of fish instead of just the chips and started eating it. Scabby had a knife in his hand, because he was about to cut a loaf of bread. When he realized what had happened he stabbed the man fatally. He was put on trial for murder, pleaded provocation and was acquitted. Later after drinking in the Frying Pan, a pub at the corner of Thrawl Street and Brick Lane, he crossed the road, walked into Mother Wolff's, picked up a penny cake and walked out of the shop without paying, after using some threats. He was charged with stealing a penny cake and sentenced to 12 months' jail. Such is justice.

Another character who haunted Brick Lane at that time was Biddy the Chiver. She and China Bob were natural enemies – he inflicted injuries upon her with his little hatchet what he carried about in his inside pocket. Biddy would have a go at anything, 'lumbering' a man and all the rest of it – i.e. luring him into some dark alley and then stripping him. There were a lot of people like that. They wouldn't thieve but they would terrorize people. Biddy was an attractive woman, while she was young. She had everything that men admire in a woman except the power to control her evil nature. She easily lost control. I first met her when I went to a party in a friend's house. Our eyes met across a crowded room. I liked the look of her. We talked and I wanted to know more about her. Someone warned me of her reputation for violence, so I left her alone. Biddy lived by making other women pay up to her, know what I mean? She'd terrorize all them people who got a living from lumbering sailors and that kind of thing. Men as well as women were afraid of her. With her, you couldn't be sure you would get away with superficial wounds. Sometimes a knife goes just too deep – or too near a vital spot – they are dangerous things to play with, and Biddy always worked with a knife. Her evil nature made her notorious. They called her 'Biddy the Chiver' and she lived up to her name. She slashed a woman's face with broken glass, inflicting nasty injuries. She was acquitted at her trial at the Old Bailey because the witness swore it was an accident.

Years slipped by. She looked what she was. Just like every other woman did at the other end of Brick Lane. She was dark-haired and slim – no superfluous flesh on her – but she wasn't attractive in any shape or form. She had a couple of nasty scars on her face and her reputation was very, very bad. Not many people would associate with her, not even men. She wasn't a desirable sort of person. She lived in Flower and Dean Street and carried on in the same old way, with small convictions for fighting, but nothing to put her away. Old Smithy owned the rooms and I think he was a wee bit wary of turning her out when she didn't pay the rent. Then she met and married a man who treated her very badly; she was frequently seen with bruises on her face. One day it happened. She went to look for him, found him with another woman and stabbed him to death. She was sentenced to three years for manslaughter, diminished responsibility. She died in Holloway prison.

Suffragettes Stone the Windows of 10 Downing Street, 1 March 1910

Emmeline Pankhurst

Founded in 1903 by Emmeline Pankhurst, the Women's Social and Political Union (WSPU) agitated for votes for women, initially peacefully, then militantly. They secured the right of women to sit on borough and county councils (they could already vote in local elections and sit on parish and district councils), yet Parliament steadfastly refused the extension of the national franchise. Pankhurst's response was to launch a campaign of window-breaking, declaring, 'The argument of the broken pane is the most valuable in politics.'

LATE IN THE afternoon of Friday, March 1st, I drove in a taxicab, accompanied by the Hon. Secretary of the Union, Mrs. Tuke and another of our members, to No. 10 Downing Street, the official residence of the Prime Minister. It was exactly half-past five when we alighted from the cab and threw our stones, four of them, through the window panes. As we expected we were promptly arrested and taken to Cannon Row police station. The hour that followed will long be remembered in London. At intervals of fifteen minutes relays of women who had volunteered for the demonstration did their work. The first smashing of glass occurred in the Haymarket and Piccadilly, and greatly startled and alarmed both pedestrians and police. A large number of the women were arrested, and everybody thought that this ended the affair. But before the excited populace and the frustrated shop owners' first exclamation had died down, before the police had reached the station with their prisoners, the ominous crashing and splintering of plate glass began again, this time along both sides of Regent Street and the Strand. A furious rush of police and people towards the second scene of action ensued. While their attention was being taken up with occurrences in this quarter, the third relay of women began breaking the windows in Oxford Circus an Bond Street. The demonstration ended for the day at half-past six with the breaking of many windows in the Strand. *Daily Mail* gave this graphic account of the demonstration:

From every part of the crowded and brilliantly lighted streets came the crash of splintered glass. People started as window shattered at their side; suddenly there was another crash in front of them; on the other side of the street; behind – everywhere. Scared shop assistants came running out to the pavements; traffic stopped; policemen sprang this way and that; five minutes later the streets were a procession of excited groups, each surrounding a woman wrecker being led in custody to the nearest police station. Meanwhile the shopping quarter of London had plunged itself into a sudden twilight. Shutters were hurriedly fitted, the rattle of iron curtains being drawn came from every side. Guards of commissionaires and shopmen were quickly mounted, and any unaccompanied lady in sight, especially, if she carried a hand bag, became an obejct of menacing suspicion.

At the hour when this demonstration was being made a conference was being held at Scotland Yard to determine what should be done to prevent the smashing of windows on the coming Monday night. But we had not announced the hour of our March 4th protest. I had in my speech simply invited women to assemble in Parliament Square on the evening of March 4th, and they accepted the invitation . . .

The demonstration had taken place in the morning, when a hundred or more women walked quietly into Knightsbridge and walking singly along the streets demolished nearly every pane of glass they passed. Taken by surprise the police arrested as many as they could reach, but most of the women escaped.

For that two days' work something like two hundred suffragettes were taken to the various police stations, and for days the long procession of women streamed through the courts.

Soon even breaking windows was not enough. An extremist wing of the WSPU, led by Pankhurst's daughter Christabel, organized bombings and arson. Public support for the Pankhursts leaked away. The upcoming First World War made a stronger case for suffrage – by doing the work of men in factories, so as to free them to fight on the Front, women earned the same rights as men. In 1928 the vote was extended to women over 21.

The Siege of Sidney Street, 3 January 1911
Philip Gibbs

In December 1910 a group of Russian-speaking anarchists led by 'Peter the Painter' were disturbed as they burgled a jewellery shop in Hatton Garden. Three policemen were shot as the gang got away. Eventually the police and the army trapped the suspects at 100 Sidney Street in the East End.

FOR SOME REASON, which I have forgotten, I went very early that morning to the *Chronicle* office, and was greeted by the news editor with the statement that a hell of a battle was raging in Sidney Street. He advised me to go and look at it.

I took a taxi, and drove to the corner of that street, where I found a dense crowd observing the affair as far as they dared peer round the angle of the walls from adjoining streets. Heedless at the moment of danger, which seemed to me ridiculous, I stood boldly opposite Sidney Street and looked down its length of houses. Immediately in front of me four soldiers of one of the Guards' regiments lay on their stomachs, protected from the dirt of the road by newspaper 'sandwich' boards, firing their rifles at a house halfway down the street. Another young Guardsman, leaning against a wall, took random shots at intervals while he smoked a Woodbine. As I stood near him, he winked and said, 'What a game!'

It was something more than a game. Bullets were flicking off the wall like peas, plugging holes into the dirty yellow brick, and ricocheting fantastically. One of them took a neat chip out of a policeman's helmet, and he said, 'Well, I'll be blowed!' and laughed in a foolish way. It was before the war, when we learned to know more about the meaning of bullets. Another struck a stick on which a journalistic friend of mine was leaning in an easy, graceful way. His support and his dignity suddenly departed from him.

'That's funny!' he said seriously, as he saw his stick neatly cut in half at his feet.

A cinematograph operator, standing well inside Sidney Street, was winding his handle vigorously, quite oblivious of the whiz of bullets, which were being fired at a slanting angle from the house, which seemed to be the target of the prostrate Guardsmen.

A large police inspector, of high authority, shouted a command to his men.

'What's all that nonsense? Clear the people back! Clear 'em right back! We don't want a lot of silly corpses lying round.'

A cordon of police pushed back the dense crowd, treading on the toes of those who would not move fast enough.

I found myself in a group of journalists.

'Get back there!' shouted the police.

But we were determined to see the drama out. It was more sensational than any 'movie' show. Immediately opposite was a tall gin palace – 'The Rising Sun'. Some strategist said, 'That's the place for us!' We raced across before the police could outflank us.

A Jew publican stood in the doorway, sullenly.

'Whatcher want?' he asked.

'Your roof,' said one of the journalists.

'A quid each, and worth it,' said the Jew.

At that time, before the era of paper money, some of us carried golden sovereigns in our pockets, one to a 'quid'. Most of the others did, but, as usual, I had not more than eighteenpence. A friend lent me the necessary coin, which the Jew slipped into his pocket as he let me pass. Twenty of us, at least, gained access to the roof of 'The Rising Sun'.

It was a good vantage point, or O.P., as we should have called it later in history. It looked right across to the house in Sidney Street in which Peter the Painter and his friends were defending themselves to the death – a tall, thin house of three storeys, with dirty window blinds. In the house immediately opposite were some more Guardsmen, with pillows and mattresses stuffed into the windows in the nature of sandbags as used in trench warfare. We could not see the soldiers, but we could see the effect of their intermittent fire, which had smashed every pane of glass and kept chipping off bits of brick in the anarchists' abode.

The street had been cleared of all onlookers, but a group of detectives slunk along the walls on the anarchists' side of the street at such an angle that they were safe from the slanting fire of the enemy. They had to keep very close to the wall, because Peter and his pals were dead shots and maintained something like a barrage fire with their automatics. Any detective or policeman who showed himself would have been sniped in a second, and these men were out to kill.

The thing became a bore as I watched it for an hour or more, during which time Mr Winston Churchill, who was then Home Secretary, came to take command of active operations, thereby causing an immense amount of ridicule in next day's papers. With a bowler hat pushed firmly down on his bulging brow, and one hand in his breast pocket, like Napoleon on the field of battle, he peered round the corner of the street, and afterwards, as we learned, ordered up some field guns to blow the house to bits.

That never happened for a reason which we on 'The Rising Sun' were quick to see.

In the top-floor room of the anarchists' house we observed a gas jet burning, and presently some of us noticed the white ash of burnt paper fluttering out of a chimney pot.

'They're burning documents,' said one of my friends.

They were burning more than that. They were setting fire to the house, upstairs and downstairs. The window curtains were first to catch alight, then volumes of black smoke, through which little tongues of flame licked up, poured through the empty window frames. They must have used paraffin to help the progress of the fire, for the whole house was burning with amazing rapidity.

'Did you ever see such a game in London!' exclaimed the man next to me on the roof of the public house.

For a moment I thought I saw one of the murderers standing on the window sill. But it was a blackened curtain which suddenly blew outside the window frame and dangled on the sill.

A moment later I had one quick glimpse of a man's arm with a pistol in his hand. He fired and there was a quick flash. At the same moment a volley of shots rang out from the Guardsmen opposite. It is certain that they killed the man who had shown himself, for afterwards they found his body (or a bit of it) with a bullet through the skull. It was not long afterwards that the roof fell in with an upward rush of flame and sparks. The inside of the house from top to bottom was a furnace.

The detectives, with revolvers ready, now advanced in Indian file. One of them ran forward and kicked at the front door. It fell in, and a sheet of flame leaped out. No other shot was fired from within. Peter the Painter and his fellow bandits were charred cinders in the bonfire they had made.

The Sidney Street siege caused an outcry against Jews and leftist refugees in the East End. There were mob attacks on the Anarchist Club in Jubilee Street and Russian Jewish shops were stoned. Like all political panics, this one was soon superceded by another, and the East End continued as the foundry of

Communism and Anarchism – both ideologies originated in London.

Children in Lambeth Walk, c. 1912

Maud Pember Reade

*T*HERE IS ONE little picture which must be described, though the child and its mother were unknown. The visitor in Lambeth Walk met a thin, decent woman carrying a pot of mignonette. By her side, a boy about seven years old was hopping along with a crutch under one arm. His other arm encircled a pot in which was a lovely blooming fuchsia, whose flowers swung to his movements. The woman was looking straight ahead with grave, preoccupied eyes, not heeding the child. His whole expression was one of such glorified beatitude that the onlooker, arrested by it, could only feel a pang of sharpest envy. They went on their way with their flowers, and round the next corner the visitor had to struggle through a deeply interested crowd, who were watching a man being taken to prison.

Questions are often asked as to how these children amuse themselves. They are popularly supposed to spend their time at picture palaces. As far as close observation could discover, they seemed to spend their playtime – the boys shrilly shouting and running in the streets, and the girls minding the baby and looking on. They played a kind of hop-scotch marked out in chalk, which reminded the visitor of a game much beloved by her in extreme youth. Boys whose parents were able to afford the luxury seemed to spend hours on one roller skate, and seemed to do positive marvels when the nature of the roadway and the nature of the skate are considered. Girls sometimes pooled their babies and did a little skipping, shouting severe orders as they did so to the unhappy infants. One party of soldiers, whose uniform was a piece of white tape round the arm and a piece of stick held over the shoulder as a weapon, marched up and down a narrow street for hours on the first day of the August holidays, making such a noise of battle and sudden death that the long-suffering mothers inside the houses occasionally left their work to scream to them to be quiet. The pathways were full of hatless girls and babies, who looked on with interest and envy. Needless to state, no notice was taken of the mothers' remonstrance. The best game of all is an ambulance, but that needs properties, which take some finding. A box on wheels, primarily intended for a baby's perambulator, and with the baby inside, makes a wonderful sort of toboggan along the paved path. The boy sits on one corner and holds with both hands on to the edges, the baby occupies the centre, and off they go, propelled by vigorous kicks.

In holiday-time elder brothers or sisters sometimes organise a party to Kennington Park or one of the open spaces near by, and the grass becomes a shrieking mass of children, from twelve or thirteen years of age downwards. The weary mother gives them bread and margarine in a piece of newspaper, and there is always a fountain from which they can drink. When they come home in the evening, something more solid is added to their usual tea. On Bank Holiday these children are taken by their parents to the nearest park. The father strolls off, the mother and children sit on the grass. Nobody talks. There is scolding and crying and laughing and shouting, and there is dreary staring silence – never conversation.

Indoors there are no amusements. There are no books and no games, nor any place to play the games should they exist. Wet holidays mean quarrelling and mischief, and a distracted mother. Every woman sighs when holidays begin. Boys and girls who earn money probably spend some of it on picture palaces; but the dependent children of parents in steady work at a low wage are not able to visit these fascinating places – much as they would like to. Two instances of 'picktur show, 2d.' appeared in the budgets. One was that of a young, newly married couple. The visitor smilingly hoped that they had enjoyed themselves. "E treated me,' said the young wife proudly. 'Then why does it come in your budget?' asked the visitor. The girl stared. 'Oh, I paid,' she explained; 'he let me take 'im.' The other case was that of two middle-aged people, of about thirty, where there were four children. A sister-in-law minded the children, they took the baby with them, and earnestly enjoyed the representation of a motor-car touring through the stars, and of the chase and capture of a murderer by a most intelligent boy, 'not bigger than Alfie.' Here again the wife paid.

The outstanding fact about the children was not their stupidity nor their lack of beauty – they were neither stupid nor ugly – it was their puny size and damaged health. On the whole, the health of those who lived upstairs was less bad than that of those who lived on the ground-floor, and decidedly less bad than that of those who lived in basements. Overcrowding in a first-floor room did not seem as deadly as overcrowding on the floor below. It is difficult to separate causes. Whether the superior health enjoyed by a first baby is due to more food, or to less overcrowding, or to less exposure to infection, is impossible to determine; perhaps it would be safe to say that it is due to all three, but whatever the exact causes are which produce in each case the sickly children so common in these households, the all-embracing one is poverty. The proportion of the infantile death-rate of Hampstead to that of Hoxton – something like 18 to 140 – proves this to be a fact. The 42 families already investigated in this inquiry have had altogether 201 children, but 18 of these were either born dead or died within a few hours. Of the remaining 183 children of all ages, ranging from a week up to sixteen or seventeen years, 39 had died, or over one-fifth. Out of the 144 survivors 5 were actually deficient, while many were slow in intellect or unduly excitable. Those among them who were born during the investigation were, with one exception, normal, cosy, healthy babies, with good appetites, who slept and fed in the usual way. They did not, however, in spite of special efforts made on their behalf, fulfil their first promise. At one year of age their environment had put its mark upon them. Though superior to babies of their class, who had not had special nourishment and care, they were vastly inferior to children of a better class who, though no finer or healthier at birth, had enjoyed proper conditions, and could therefore develop on sound and hygienic lines.

Office Boy, c. 1916
V.S. Pritchett

Pritchett, born in 1900, worked as an office boy in the leather trade on leaving Dulwich College.

W E WORKED UNTIL seven in the evening. On Saturdays we left between two and four, this depending on the mail. In the evenings I went home from London Bridge Station. In *The Waste Land* T. S. Eliot wrote of the strange morning and evening sight of those thousands of men, all wearing bowlers and carrying umbrellas, crossing London Bridge in long, dull regiments and pouring into that ugly, but to me most affecting, railway station which for years I used. I was captivated by it as I suppose every office worker is by the station in the great city that rules his life. Penn Station in New York, St Lazare in Paris, Waterloo, Paddington and Liverpool Street, are printed on the pages of a lifetime's grind at the office desk. Each is a quotidian frontier, splitting a life, a temple of the inexorable. The distinction of London Bridge Station, on the Chatham side, is that it is not a terminus but a junction where lives begin to fade and then blossom again as they swap trains in the rush hours and make for all the regions of South London and the towns of Kent. The trains come in and go out over those miles of rolling brick arches that run across South London like a massive Roman wall. There were no indicators on the platforms in my day and the confusion had to be sorted out by stentorian porters who called out the long litanies of stations in a hoarse London bawl and with a style of their own. They stood on the crowded platform edge, detected the identifying lights on the incoming engine and then sang out. To myself, at that age, all places I did not know seemed romantic and the lists of names were, if not Miltonic, at any rate as evocative as those names with which the Georgian poets filled up their lines. I would stare admiringly, even enviously, at the porter who would have to chant the long line to Bexley Heath; or the man who, beginning with the blunt and challenging football names of Charlton and Woolwich would go on to comic Plumstead and then flow forward over his long list till his voice fell to the finality of Greenhythe, Northfleet and Gravesend; or the softer tones of St Johns, Lewisham, and Blackheath. And to stir us up were the powerful trains – travelling to distances that seemed as remote as Istanbul to me – expresses that went to Margate, Herne Bay, Rochester and Chatham. I saw nothing dingy in this. The pleasure of my life as an office boy lay in being one of the London crowd and I actually enjoyed standing in a compartment packed with fifteen people on my way to Bromley North. How pleasant it was, in the war years, to stop dead outside Tower Bridge and to see a maroon go off in an air-raid warning and, even better, for a sentimentalist, to be stuck in one of those curry powder fogs that came up from the river and squashed London flat in its windless marsh. One listened to the fog signals and saw the fires of the watchmen; there was a sinister quiet as the train srood outside the Surrey Docks. And when, very late, the train got to Bromley North and one groped one's way home, seeing the conductors with flares in their hands walking ahead of the buses, or cars lost and askew on the wrong side of the road, and heard footsteps but saw no person until he was upon you and asking where he was, one swanked to oneself that at last one had had a load of the traditional muck on one's chest.

The thing I liked best was being sent on errands in Bermondsey. They became explorations, and I made every excuse to lengthen them. I pushed down south to the Dun Cow in the Old Kent Road, eastward by side streets and alleyways to Tower Bridge. I had a special pleasure in the rank places like those tunnels and vaults under the railway: the smells above all made me feel importantly a part of this working London. Names like Wilde's Rents, Cherry Garden Street, Jamaica Road, Dockhead and Pickle Herring Street excited and my journeys were not simply street journeys to me: they were like crossing the desert, finding the source of the Niger. London was not a city; it was a foreign country as strange as India and even though I knew the Thames is a small river compared with the great ones of the world, I would patriotically make it wider and wider in my mind. I liked the Hide Market where groups of old women and children hung about the hide men who would occasionally flick off a bit of flesh from the hides: the children like little vultures snatched at these bits and put them in their mothers' bags. We thought the children were going to eat these scraps, but in fact it is more likely – money being urgent to all Londoners – they were going to sell them to the glue merchants. The glue trade haunted many busy Cockney minds. Owing to the loop of the river, Bermondsey has remained the most clannish and isolated part of London; people there were deeply native for generations. Their manner was unemotional but behind the dryness, there was the suggestion of the Cockney sob.

'What'll y'ave? Lovin' mem'ry or deepest sympathy?' the woman in the shop asked when I went to buy a mourning card for one of our office cleaners.

I would pass the Tanners Arms and wonder at the peculiar fact that the owner had a piece of tanned human skin 'jes like pigskin'. The evenings came on and a procession of women and children would be wheeling their mattresses up to the railway tunnels or the deep tube station to be safe from the occasional raids. I would see other office boys wearing their bowler hats as I wore mine: we were a self-important, cracked-voice little race, sheepish, yet cocky, regarding our firms with childish awe.

But my work was dull. The terrible thing was that it was simple and mechanical; far, far less difficult than work at school. This was a humiliation and, even now, the simplicity of most of the work in offices, factories and warehouses depresses me. It is also all trite child's play and repetition and the correcting of an infinitude of silly mistakes, compared with intellectual or professional labour. Most people seemed to me, then, and even now, chained to a dulling routine of systematized and tolerated carelessness and error. Whatever was going to happen to me, I knew I must escape from this easy, unthinking world and I understood my father's dogged efforts to be on his own, and his own master. In difficulty lay the only escape, from what for me seemed to be deterioration of faculty.

The dullness, the long hours, the bad food, the low pay, the paring away of pleasure to a few hours late on Saturday afternoon, the tedious Sundays brightened only by that brief hour at the Sunday School – all these soon stunned and stunted me in my real life however much they moved me to live in my imagination. I accepted, with the native London masochism, that these were hard times and that this was to be my life. London has always preferred experience to satisfaction. I saw myself a junior clerk turning into a senior clerk comfortable in my train, enjoying the characters of my fellow travellers, talking sententiously of the state of affairs in France, Hong Kong and Singapore and, with profound judiciousness, of the government. Over the years one would know these season ticket holders – perhaps not speaking to them – as well as the characters in a novel. Sometimes there was an oddity – the man who read Virgil as he travelled up and down. And there was always, for diversity, the girls who knitted for the soldiers and read novels. There was also the pride I felt in being enslaved in a city so world-famous, in being submerged in its brick, in being smoked and kippered by it. There was the curious satisfaction, in these months, of a settled fate and the feeling that here was good sense and, under the reserve, humour and decency.

The Great War:
The Shooting Down of Zeppelin L31,
1 October 1916

On 31 May 1915 the front line of war came to London for the first time in three centuries. On that day Captain Linnartz flew Zeppelin airship LZ38 over the docks and East End and dropped 120 high-explosive bombs, killing seven people. Zeppelin raids continued throughout 1915 and 1916. Not until the autumn of 1916 did the city's air defences live up to their name, when they downed Zeppelin L31:

I SAW LAST NIGHT what is probably the most appalling spectacle associated with the war which London is likely to provide – the bringing down in flames of a raiding Zeppelin.

I was late at the office, and leaving it just before midnight was crossing to Blackfriars Bridge to get a tramcar home, when my attention was attracted by frenzied cries of 'Oh! Oh! She's hit!' from some wayfarers who were standing in the middle of the road gazing at the sky in a northern direction. Looking up the clear run of New Bridge Street and Farringdon Road I saw high in the sky a concentrated blaze of searchlights, and in its centre a ruddy glow which rapidly spread into the outline of a blazing airship. Then the searchlights were turned off and the Zeppelin drifted perpendicularly in the darkened sky, a gigantic pyramid of flames, red and orange, like a ruined star falling slowly to earth. Its glare lit up the streets and gave a ruddy tint even to the waters of the Thames.

The spectacle lasted two or three minutes. It was so horribly fascinating that I felt spellbound – almost suffocated with emotion, ready hysterically to laugh or cry. When at last the doomed airship vanished from sight there arose a shout the like of which I never heard in London before – a hoarse shout of mingled execration, triumph and joy; a swelling shout that appeared to be rising from all parts of the metropolis, ever increasing in force and intensity. It was London's *Te Deum* for another crowning deliverance. Four Zeppelins destroyed in a month! . . .

On getting to the office this morning I was ordered off to Potter's Bar, Middlesex, where the Zeppelin had been brought down, about thirteen miles from London. These days trains are infrequent and travel slowly as a war economy. The journey from King's Cross was particularly tedious. The train I caught was packed. My compartment had its twenty seats occupied and ten more passengers found standing room in it. The weather, too, was abominable. Rain fell persistently. We had to walk the two miles to the place where the Zeppelin fell, and over the miry roads and sodden fields hung a thick, clammy mist . . .

I got from a member of the Potter's Bar anti-aircraft

battery an account of the bringing down of the Zeppelin. He said the airship was caught in the beams of three searchlights from stations miles apart, and was being fired at by three batteries also from distances widely separated. She turned and twisted, rose and fell, in vain attempts to escape to the shelter of the outer darkness. None of the shells reached her. Then an aeroplane appeared and dropped three flares – the signal to the ground batteries to cease firing as he was about to attack. The airman, flying about the Zeppelin, let go rounds of machine-gun fire at her without effect, until one round fired into her from beneath set her on fire, and down she came a blazing mass, roaring like a furnace, breaking as she fell into two parts which were held together by internal cables until they reached the ground.

The framework of the Zeppelin lay in the field in two enormous heaps, separated from each other by about a hundred yards. Most of the forepart hung suspended from a tree . . .

The crew numbered nineteen. One body was found in the field some distance from the wreckage. He must have jumped from the doomed airship from a considerable height. So great was the force with which he struck the ground that I saw the imprint of his body clearly defined in the stubbly grass. There was a round hole for the head, then deep impressions of the trunk, with outstretched arms, and finally the widely separated legs. Life was in him when he was picked up, but the spark soon went out. He was, in fact, the Commander, who had been in one of the gondolas hanging from the airship . . .

With another journalist I went to the barn where the bodies lay. As we approached we heard a woman say to the sergeant of the party of soldiers in charge, 'May I go in? I would like to see a dead German.' 'No, madam, we cannot admit ladies,' was the reply. Introducing myself as a newspaper reporter, I made the same request. The sergeant said to me, 'If you particularly wish to go in you may. I would, however, advise you not to do so. If you do you will regret your curiosity.' I persisted in my request ...

Explaining to the sergeant that I particularly wanted to see the body of the Commander, I was allowed to go in. The sergeant removed the covering from one of the bodies which lay apart from the others. The only disfigurement was a slight distortion of the face. It was that of a young man, clean-shaven. He was heavily clad in a dark uniform and overcoat, with a thick muffler round his neck.

I knew who he was. At the office we had had official information of the identity of the Commander and the airship (though publication of both particulars was prohibited), and it was this knowledge that had determined me to see the body. The dead man was Heinrich Mathy, the most renowned of the German airship commanders, and the perished airship was his redoubtable L31. Yes, there he lay in death at my feet, the bugaboo of the Zeppelin raids, the first and most ruthless of these Pirates of the Air bent on our destruction.

With the downing of L31 the German High Command switched to airplane raids on the city; ordnance dropped by 14 Gotha bombers on 13 June 1917 killed 160 people – the most deadly air raid of the war.

War from the air caused worsening morale. Diarist Beatrice Webb noted on 5 October 1917: 'Six successive air raids have wrecked the nerves of Londoners, with the result of a good deal of panic even among the well-to-do and the educated.' Eventually Webb found that 'an additional cigarette' enabled her to recover her self-possession during raids. In the East End, citizens overcame their fright and started coping with the situation when they found ideal air-raid shelters on their doorsteps: the underground platforms of the Tube system.

670 Londoners died in bomb raids during the First World War

℀ ℀ ℀

Scenes from the Ghetto: Jewish Life in the East End, c. 1920–30

Bill Belmont (Solomon Belernof)

Belernof's Lithuanian family settled in Langdale Street in 1903, joining some 42,000 East European Jews who had settled in Stepney over the previous 30 years. Most had fled pogroms.

EVERY OTHER SATURDAY, Dad took us to Schewzik's (Benjamin Schewzik, 86 Brick Lane). These were the original Russian Vapour Baths, used by everybody in the East End throughout the week. Wednesdays were reserved for women, and Mum also went there with my sisters once a fortnight. When we got there, Dad paid his few coppers (half price for me) and was given a key to one of the clothes lockers. Dad tied a towel round his body, for decency's sake, and put the string with the key round his neck. I stayed naked. First we went into a communal washroom, where we collected a basin each and filled it with hot water. We had brought a piece of soap, and scrubbed ourselves and rinsed ourselves clean, in the company of scores of people doing the same, and chatting away to each other at the same time.

When we were thoroughly clean and dried off, we went into the hot room. This was pleasantly warm (about 80 degrees Fahrenheit, I suppose) and we sat on long stone steps, going higher if we wanted more heat, and lower if we became too hot. We only stayed here a little while, to get acclimatized to the heat, and then moved into the second hot room. This was much hotter (over 100 degrees Fahrenheit), and I remember having to sit on my hands because the steps were too hot for my thin-skinned behind. Dad now began promoting my circulation with his besom, a small birch broom which he had brought with him. He would beat me all over with this, and my flesh would tingle and feel almost alive. When he thought I'd had enough, I took the besom and pummelled him with it. I felt parboiled and wanted to go out, at least to the first hot room. But there was still another hot room (temperature 130 degrees Fahrenheit) which Dad wanted to visit. I poked my nose into it and could hardly see a thing for the steam. A couple of minutes was enough for me, but Dad stayed there for about ten minutes, beating his arms and legs with the besom. I waited in the second hot room until he came out, and we then went back through room one to the shower room. Here we stood under an ice-cold shower until I felt as if I was frozen; then we started the whole rigmarole again by going back into the hot rooms.

IN FEBRUARY 1921 practically the whole class was sent into the Great Hall one Monday afternoon, where we were surprised to see what looked like hundreds of boys and girls sitting at individual desks. We were told that they were doing 'The Scholarship'. I had no idea what this meant, and certainly didn't realize that it was to prove a passport to a grammar school. To me, it was just a page of sums to do, and a 'composition' to write on one of four subjects. I have no memory of the arithmetic, except that I couldn't do all the sums, but I do remember the title I chose for my composition. It was 'Bells', and I am quite sure that my use of one word was instrumental in my gaining the scholarship. The word was 'tin-tinnabulation', which I had picked up somewhere or other, and which I used in my description of bells ringing.

At the end of the afternoon, we were freed and burst out of school in our normal disorderly rout. I forgot all about it immediately, and did not even mention it at home. About two months later, my teacher, Sammy Rich, gave me an envelope in the classroom. Everybody looked at me as I opened it; I hadn't the faintest idea what it could be about. It was a letter from County Hall informing me that I had been provisionally awarded a London County Council scholarship, with a returnable slip for my parents to sign, if they agreed to my acceptance of the scholarship. This was necessary in those days, since not all parents, by any means, were desirous of their children carrying on education beyond the age of fourteen, since they felt it more important for their kids to get out to work as soon as possible to augment the family budget.

As I entered our street on my way home, I heard a large cheering from above. I looked up and saw my mother leaning out of our second floor window shouting 'Hooray, hooray.' The grapevine had been in action, and the other kids in the street had shouted the news up to my mother – 'Solly's won a scholarship.' I'm sure she had no idea what it was all about, but she knew I'd won something, and that was enough.

At home I read the form to my parents and encountered a difficulty that I was to contend with many times later. My father couldn't sign the acceptance form because he couldn't write. I asked around and found that this wasn't exceptional. All he had to do was to make a cross and I would write beside it 'Israel Belanoff – his mark'.

'THE STREET' WAS the focus of our lives and an absolute extension of the house one lived in. It was the unit, and all who lived in it owed a loyalty to every other street-dweller. When we first moved to Grey Eagle Street this was a bit difficult, because it was at the very edge of the ghetto, bordering on to the business and commercial side of London. We were, in fact, Jews who were encroaching on to Christian territory – and we were made very aware of this. Grey Eagle Street was not very long – about 150 yards – with a pub at one corner and a small grocery shop at the other. It was roughly divided by race – the southern half being mainly Jewish and the northern half almost entirely Christian. This led to almost daily fights between north and south – fist-fights usually, but, occasionally, more seriously pursued with lengths of wood and iron bars. It normally started with the cry, 'Who killed Christ?' – answered by some brave soul with, 'I did, and I'll bloody well kill you if I catch you.'

Every fight was led on our side by the members of the largest and most famous of the street families – the Frescos. Their house was roughly in the centre of the street, and whenever a scrap started someone would shout, 'Call the Frescos' and out they would swarm with their fists flying. They were a large family – about twelve of them – who had lived in England for generations and were, in fact, by looks and dress indistinguishable from the 'natives'. One particular characteristic was that the Fresco children never wore boots (shoes were unknown to us), and this matched with all the goyim (or 'yoks') in the neighbourhood. Jewish kids, on the other hand, always wore boots – as a sign of respectability, I presume – and these were very useful in fights, particularly as they were often studded.

On the corner of Old Montague Street, where I was born, was the original Blooms'. This was, at first, just a little shop, specializing in selling salt-beef sandwiches for ten pence each (4p). It was only one of six or seven little 'bookties' (tiny shops) which specialized in the same delicacy. But Blooms' always had the best beef (or perhaps the trick lay in the pickling brine) and certainly had the most enormous

fillings. Business prospered, and in the early 30s the shop
was demolished and a brand new restaurant was built in
its place. It now provided all sorts of meat and delicacies
– pickled herring, chopped liver, laktas, etc. – as well as the
basic beef sandwich, with dill cucumbers and mouthwatering
cheesecake to follow. This became the eating centre for
anybody with money, and was crowded every Saturday night.
I myself seldom patronized it – too dear! – and together
with most of the young East Enders was a customer of a
nearby café called 'Snelwars' after the owner's name. Alec
Snelwar, a stout easy-going old gent, ran a very relaxed joint,
where we could go in for a coffee or an ice cream soda and
sit there chatting all evening. The main occupation, apart
from just talking, was draughts. Alec provided draughts sets
to anybody requiring them, and he, his two sons, and his
daughter Sadie were always willing to sit down and play
with the customers. God knows how he made any profit
– certainly not from us. Draughts players from all over the
East End congregated here, including the then champion of
England. He was a tailor named Sammy Cohen and he used
to come in and play a dozen games simultaneously – and
win them all.

The post-war slump hit the East End – dependent as it was on
the docks for its livelihood – harder than most of the capital. In
1921 the Labour Mayor of Poplar, George Lansbury, refused to
set the local rates in full, since many households were unable to
pay. The action was unlawful and 36 councillors and the town
clerk were ordered to appear at the High Court.

The Poplar councillors, accompanied by 2,000 supporters,
walked the five miles to the High Court under a banner that
read:

POPLAR
BOROUGH COUNCIL
Marching to the
HIGH COURT
And possibly to
PRISON
To secure
EQUALISATION OF RATES
For
POOR BOROUGHS

Thirty councillors were imprisoned. The rates revolt received huge support across London, to the embarrassment of the Home Office, which brokered a deal whereby a rates equalization conference was established. Effectively the Poplar councillors had won: subsidy for poor relief was to be shared more equally between London's boroughs, which meant that Poplar's own rates were cut by 5s 6d in the pound. After six weeks in prison the councillors were released to triumphal scenes in Poplar.

'Poplarism' – meaning direct action by councils on behalf of the disadvantaged – cast a long red shadow. Poplarism inspired left-wing socialists for decades to come (the Greater London Council's 'Fares Fair' transport policy in the 1980s was only one imitation), just as it put many middle-class voters off voting for 'law-breaking' Labour.

The First Wembley, 29 April 1923
News of the World

T HE BATTLE OF Wembley is over. If future generations ask sometimes who won it, they will be told a policeman on an old grey mare. It was intended as everybody knows to be the greatest final in the history of the Football Association Cup. By the most unimaginable good fortune, it just missed being the greatest catastrophe. Two hundred thousand people will agree that this statement is no exaggeration.

Wembley was an experiment it is true, but at what a cost when the casualties numbered a thousand or more! Long before Bolton Wanderers and West Ham came on the field to battle for the cup, seasoned campaigners who had watched every final for thirty years, prophesied that there would be no match. One had to be there to realize and understand why. It was the biggest football tragedy in history and in some respects a reflection on the common sense of sporting London and sporting Lancashire. For weeks and weeks it had been taken for granted that a record crowd would invade the magnificent stadium for the first final at Wembley. Most elaborate and – so they thought – adequate arrangements had been made to deal with an attendance of a hundred and thirty thousand. That is where the scheme of things went wrong.

Two hundred thousand people wanted to see the game and it was impossible to crowd them all in. What actually happened is a trifle obscure. Whether an elaborate organization broke down or whether the walls and gates of Wembley failed ito withstand the crush of the multitude no one seems to know. But here roughly are the facts. About two o'clock – just an hour before the game was due to commence

– pandemonium and riot entered into possession of the great arena of Wembley and the most amazing and bewildering hour in English football followed.

Long before that time, covered stands and concrete terraces, the spacious cheap banks and every enclosure were filled as comfortably as the F.A. treasurer would wish to see them. Bank upon bank of humanity filled the eye at every turn; it was one vast sea of white faces with a guardsman's red tunic showing up sharply here and there. The smoke from thousands of comforting tobacco pipes hung like a haze in the warm spring sunshine. We – the hundred odd thousand of us – were gathered round the most wonderful football field in England; the arena itself a verdant virgin green, with the white chalk boundaries, the terrible 'penalty spot' and the centre ring standing out in bold relief. In a quarter of an hour the King would be there. Suddenly a roar from the eastern stand, another from the west, a mad stampede, a rushing torrent of humanity at both ends, and the shame of Wembley had begun. One hundred thousand people locked outside the gates got into the ground without payment. They smashed one set of entrance doors, clambered over the turnstiles, swarmed up the steel girders that gave them entrance to the reserved stands and let pandemonium loose. Those spectators who had already taken up their positions and stood perhaps for hours to hold them were bundled unceremoniously across the running track and into the field of play by the exulting multitude pressing on behind.

Three thousand police it is said were there but the three thousand were impotent and helpless. They were swallowed up in the armies advancing from both ends of the field. Two hundred thousand people were then on a ground the full capacity of which is estimated at one hundred and thirty thousand. Gone was the verdant virgin sward trampled and crushed under the feet of the throng who wandered aimlessly from end to end and side to side. They congregated in two gigantic rings round the bands of the Guards and seemingly the football final was forgotten. Stretcher bearers and ambulance men were worked to distraction. Men and women fainted and fell from the crush and excitement, and lots were badly injured in that mad stampede. Twenty cases lay on the field at one time – just when the King was due as a matter of fact – and the total casualties were well over a thousand. Each moment the crowd on the field was reinforced by deserters from the legitimate view-points. Squads of police rushed up by motor car to assist their harassed comrades but were swallowed up in the multitude and became units of the crowd. So menacing was the position that pistols in holsters were handed to the constables before they joined the scene of action. Looking down from the magnificent Press Stand on to that turbulent mob it was plain to see that only a miracle could save the Cup-tie. And the miracle happened in the form of a dashing masterful policeman riding a lively grey mare. There were ten mounted policemen altogether, but the one on the grey was the tactician. He rode at the crowd, he charged, he wheeled, he shouted and gesticulated, and, wonder of wonders, the crowd fell back. Only a foot at a time, it is true – and that sullenly and grudgingly – but they went back all the same. The grey mare and her relentless rider were everywhere, and each yard of conquest was mightily cheered. Then the King came – the signal for a deafening roar from London and Lancashire together and after His Majesty the teams. On to the playing field they filed, and tried peaceful persuasion with the reluctant crowd. It was not so successful, however, as the more vigorous methods of the mounted men, and that astute grey mare still rounding up the stragglers in the centre and barging into the knots of obstinate men who would have wrecked the cup final as cheerfully as they would have kicked the ball. But the policeman on the grey mare was

a Wellington yesterday afternoon, and all the honours of that
football Waterloo were his. Back, back, back, went the surging
crowd, and at long last the field was clear to the touchlines
and the corner flags. Further they would not go, but planted
themselves down on the green turf and prepared for the play.
In front of them, and all the way round the ground, policemen – rank and file – sat shoulder to shoulder in front of
the spectators, determined that Bolton and West Ham should
fight the battle the world and his wife had come to see. To
another mighty roar the respective captains trotted up for the
spin of the coin. Bolton won it, the teams took up positions,
the whistle blew and the game was on forty minutes late.
Only once thereafter was there any stoppage from encroach-
ment of the field of play. It threatened to develop into another
disastrous invasion, but the policeman on the old grey mare
came to the rescue again. For ninety minutes the men in the
white jerseys and those in the claret and blue, ran and kicked
themselves to a standstill in the battle for the English cup and
to the accompaniment of a ceaseless roar from the excited
multitude. The whites – Bolton, of course – won it, as they
deserved to do on the run of the play. After the great game it
was possible to take stock of the incidents of the afternoon.
The casualties were abnormally heavy and some very severe.
At least sixty of the thousand odd patients had to be taken
to hospital, including one man who fell through a stand roof
on to which he had clambered for a better view. Another
badly-injured man courted disaster in the same way as scores
of others. He climbed up the back of a terrace, dropped over
the top, and rolled on the heads of the tightly-packed people
on the running track below. No one else attempted the trick
thereafter. Perhaps the most seriously-injured individual of
all was a policeman at one of the turnstiles. The keeper of
the gate was knocked out by the clamouring crowd, and the
constable dashed up to check the rush. He got his foot to

the lever of the turnstile, but was overwhelmed, and the gate flying back, he was so badly crushed that practically every rib was flattened. It was not a brilliant beginning for Wembley. There were scenes that those who witnessed them will want to forget and never experience again. But there was one that a few will like to remember. Behind the cheap stand, as the multitude streamed away, stood a young policeman with a double row of ribbons across the left breast. A quiet smile played on his lips and he patted the neck of an old grey mare.

There were other developments in north-west London, aside from housing, which caught the collective imagination.

All around London, the Tube was sending out tentacles into the green belt, but it was in Middlesex that the exemplar of the leafy suburb, away from 'The Smoke', was achieved. In 1925 the Metropolitan Line reached Uxbridge and then, in 1932, Stanmore – a vast new tract of metropolitan commuterdom cleverly dubbed 'Metro-Land'. T.R. Fyvel was a child of Metro-Land:

I DISTINCTLY REMEMBER that when I was a schoolboy in North-West London, there were still batches of fields around Wembley. It grew between the wars, the creation of the speculative builder; street upon street of box-like, semi-detached houses sprung into full existence, indistinguishable from those of other London suburbs. There they all are; 'Chatsworth' beside 'Knole', 'Blenheim' next to 'Balmoral'; the tiny front gates, the back gardens with patches of lawn and scarlet runners and pink Alexandra roses; brick and mortar of English suburb-life – a life where the youthful hero of the local tennis club or amateur dramatic group seems far too early changed to the captured young family man showing snapshots of his offspring in the 8.42 to London, and, almost before he knows, to 'Dad', middle-aged, working in the garden and worrying over insurance installments and school bills.

A good life, a mild civilised life, whose superficiality still masks native English strength (remember the Blitz!) but not a life likely to produce English poets, adventurers, empire builders – or Olympic champions.

✗ ✗ ✗

Chinatown, 28 April 1925
Arnold Bennett

The Chinese settled in Limehouse before 1850, arriving as seamen and launderers.

*A*PR. 28, 1925:– I went to Chinatown last night with Beaverbrook and Ashfield. Pennyfields is the name of the chief street, Limehouse. We went to the Limehouse Police Station first. It took us exactly fifteen minutes to drive there from Ciro's. Great change in a short time. We saw some 'curios' (as the Chief Inspector called them) first. Explanation of 'Fantan' and 'Pluck Pigeons'. The first seems a purely childish game in which the bank pays 2 to 1 winnings on a 4 to 1 chance.

Then out with the Inspector to Pennyfields. No gambling after 8 o'clock, he said, usually not later than 7. We entered two Chinese restaurants (11 p.m.) where lots of people were drinking tea. Humble people. All very clean and tidy indeed, and the people looked decent. A few nice-looking prostitutes – chiefly Jewesses. Nearly all houses closed. Some windows, said the Chief Inspector, were always shuttered. 'They don't like the light.' Glimpses of curtained bedrooms higher up. We went into a Chinese Music Club, where four men were playing Mah Jong and one strumming a sort of Chinese guitar, with very large string-pegs. Their singing nights were Wednesday and Saturday. A suggestion that they should sing was not well received. They were very polite but did not want us. We were to have seen the Chinese Chapel, where the religion of Confucius is practised; but it was locked up.

Then we went into a pub (closed) and found one or two old topers (friends of the proprietor's) drinking stout after hours. We were taken up stairs and there saw a wonderful collection of Chinese carving of all sorts – chiefly picked up from sailors. Lastly, return to police station. No prisoners. Cells marvellously clean and sanitary. Steam heating. Temp. must be 63 at least. Plank bed, white as a yacht's forecastle, but a pretty comfortable pillow: one rug. On the whole a rather flat night. Still we saw the facts. We saw no vice whatever. Inspector gave the Chinese an exceedingly good character.

The General Strike, 4–12 May 1926
Philip Gibbs

The General Strike was called by the Trades Union Congress
(TUC) in support of the mineworkers, who were 'locked out'
by their employers as a means of enforcing wage cuts. In the
first days of the strike London came to an almost complete
standstill, with public transport suspended and about half of the
city's 61 power stations shut down. Such paralysis of the nation's
capital was not to be endured by the Conservative government,
particularly its bellicose Chancellor of the Exchequer, Winston
Churchill. On 8 May Churchill organized a supply convoy
from the docks to Hyde Park with the Grenadier Guards
and armoured cars as escort. On the following day Churchill
ordered pockets of troops to be stationed around London.
There were running battles between strikers and police in New
Cross, Deptford and Poplar but the TUC had little stomach
for constitutional or armed conflict with the government. Even
more detrimental to the effectiveness of the strike was the vast
army of volunteer strike-breakers (as many as 114,000 in London
alone) who had come forward to staff essential services.

MY SYMPATHIES HAVE always been on the side of
the underdogs and the underpaid, but they were
not in favour of this general strike, which was an
attempt by the T.U.C. to coerce the Government of the
country and take over its power. It was an attack on our
Parliamentary system and tradition, and, if successful, would
have been the tyranny of a minority over the commonweal.

The Government called for volunteers to carry on the
essential services of the country and to maintain order. It was
answered by the 'plus-four boys' as they were called – young

gentlemen from the Universities and the public schools, the sons of the Middle Class, who at week-ends wore the baggy breeches and tasselled stockings which gave them their nickname. It all looked very serious. Foreign correspondents came to England anticipating riots and bloodshed in a social revolution. But they were astonished by the good nature of both sides. The police played football matches with the strikers in Wales. The 'plus-four boys' did their jobs on the buses and tramcars with a great sense of humour.

'This bus goes anywhere you like,' was chalked up on one of them ... 'No fares and kind treatment.' ... 'Joy rides to the East End.'

One young gentleman, diverting his bus from its normal route, stopped outside his house in Eaton Square to call for his morning letters.

Boy and girl drivers handled great lorries full of milk churns, and drove them all through the night to bring milk to London where there was a dump in Hyde Park. Elderly ladies established canteens for the volunteers who had long hours and little food.

I had a look at all this, and one morning went down to the docks which were supposed to be hot spots and very dangerous because of the temper of the men. At the approach to the East India Docks I enquired my way to the dock gates.

'Better not go there!' said a man. 'You might not get as far as that.'

'Why not?' I asked.

The man spat on the pavement

'I'm just telling you,' he said, with an ugly look.

I went on further and saw a group of dockers lounging about, and went up to them.

'How do I get into the Docks?' I asked.

One man answered me.

'You don't! They're in the hands of the military. Nobody's allowed in.'

'I bet you I'll get in,' I told him.

There was a general laugh.

'Not you! Sentries with loaded rifles at the gates.'

They came as far as the gate with me to see what happened, and we had a talk on the way. I found them very decent fellows, with no desire to declare war on the nation or any class of it. What they wanted was a bit more pay and regular work, instead of being turned off for long spells because trade was bad and few ships were coming in.

'We've a right to live, haven't we?' said one of them.

I agreed with him.

At the dock gates I was questioned by a tall policeman who looked suspicious.

'No one allowed in here,' he said grimly. 'What do you want? What's your name?'

When I told him my name he stared at me and then laughed and grabbed my hand.

'Good God!' he exclaimed. 'I knew you in Flanders, and on the Somme. Come in. I'll get a chit for you from the O.C.'

The group of dockers outside the gate were impressed. They thought I must be a hell of a fellow – the Home Secretary or something big.

The docks were deserted. Nothing moved. Only here and there a Guardsman marched up and down on sentry-go.

From one great shed came the sound of merry music. It was playing 'Dear Little Buttercup'. It seemed to me very odd, and I went into the shed and found a Guards' band playing a selection from Gilbert and Sullivan, without an audience.

'Doing their bit,' said the officer who led me round.

Only in England I think could such a thing have happened. Truly we are a very amusing people.

By 12 May – the day the TUC called off the General Strike
– volunteers were running 100 Underground trains, 500 buses
and 100 trams.

✖ ✖ ✖

Down and Out:
George Orwell in a Doss-house, c. 1931

George Orwell

Donning tramp's clothes, George Orwell set off to explore
down-and-out London:

AT ABOUT ELEVEN I began looking for a bed. I had
read about doss-houses (they are never called doss-
houses, by the way), and I supposed that one could
get a bed for fourpence or thereabouts. Seeing a man, a navvy
or something of the kind, standing on the kerb in the Waterloo
Road, I stopped and questioned him. I said that I was stony
broke and wanted the cheapest bed I could get.

'Oh,' said he, 'you go to that 'ouse across the street there,
with the sign "Good Beds for Single Men". That's a good kip
(sleeping-place), that is. I bin there myself on and off. You'll
find it cheap *and* clean.'

It was a tall, battered-looking house, with dim lights in
all the windows, some of which were patched with brown
paper. I entered a stone passage-way, and a little etiolated

boy with sleepy eyes appeared from a door leading to a cellar. Murmurous sounds came from the cellar, and a wave of hot air and cheese. The boy yawned and held out his hand.

'Want a kip? That'll be a 'og, guv'nor.'

I paid the shilling, and the boy led me up a rickety unlighted staircase to a bedroom. It had a sweetish reek of paregoric and foul linen; the windows seemed to be tight shut, and the air was almost suffocating at first. There was a candle burning, and I saw that the room measured fifteen feet square by eight high, and had eight beds in it. Already six lodgers were in bed, queer lumpy shapes with all their own clothes, even their boots, piled on top of them. Someone was coughing in a loathsome manner in one corner.

When I got into the bed I found that it was as hard as a board, and as for the pillow, it was a mere bard cylinder like a block of wood. It was rather worse than sleeping on a table, because the bed was not six feet long, and very narrow, and the mattress was convex, so that one had to hold on to avoid falling out. The sheets stank so horribly of sweat that I could not bear them near my nose. Also, the bedclothes only consisted of the sheets and a cotton counterpane, so that though stuffy it was none too warm. Several noises recurred throughout the night. About once in an hour the man on my left – a sailor, I think – woke up, swore vilely, and lighted a cigarette. Another man, victim of bladder disease, got up and noisily used his chamber-pot half a dozen times during the night. The man in the corner had a coughing fit once every twenty minutes, so regularly that one came to listen for it as one listens for the next yap when a dog is baying the moon. It was an unspeakably repellent sound; a foul bubbling and retching, as though the man's bowels were being churned up within him. Once when he struck a match I saw that he was a very old man, with a grey, sunken face like that of a corpse, and he was wearing his trousers wrapped round his head as a nightcap, a thing which for some reason disgusted me very much. Every time he coughed or the other man swore, a sleepy voice from one of the other beds cried out:

'Shut up! Oh, for Christ's —— *sake* shut up!'

I had about an hour's sleep in all. In the morning I was woken by a dim impression of some large brown thing coming towards me. I opened my eyes and saw that it was one of the sailor's feet, sticking out of bed close to my face. It was dark brown, quite dark brown like an Indian's, with dirt. The walls were leprous, and the sheets, three weeks from the wash, were almost raw umber colour. I got up, dressed and went downstairs. In the cellar were a row of basins and two slippery roller towels. I had a piece of soap in my pocket, and I was going to wash, when I noticed that every basin was streaked with grime – solid, sticky filth as black as boot-blacking. I went out unwashed. Altogether, the lodging-house had not come up to its description as cheap *and* clean. It was however, as I found later, a fairly representative lodging-house.

The poor had always been part of London but the Great Depression spawned more of them. As the hungry 1930s wore on, protests against poverty became louder and more violent.

The Hunger Marchers in Hyde Park, 27 October 1932

Wal Hannington

The hunger marchers were led to London by the National Unemployed Workers' Movement. Their aim was to present a petition against the means test to the House of Commons.

*N*EXT MORNING, 27TH October, the general public of London, emerging into the streets, found that special constables had taken over all the normal duties of the policemen on patrol and on traffic duty. This was a clear indication of the elaborate preparations for struggle which the police had made. By mid-day approximately 100,000 London workers were moving towards Hyde Park from all parts of London, to give the greatest welcome to the hunger marchers that had ever been seen in Hyde Park. By two o'clock Hyde Park and the streets around Marble Arch were black with the multitude of workers who had arrived and were now awaiting the arrival of the hunger marchers. It is estimated that 5000 police and special constables were gathered round the park, with many thousands more mobilized in the neighbourhood in readiness for action.

The press had announced that morning that all leave had been stopped for the Coldstream Guards in Wellington barracks, and that they were being held in readiness in case of trouble. As the various contingents of marchers began to enter the park at 2.30 there were signs of tremendous enthusiasm. London's warmest welcome, shouted from 100,000 throats in Hyde Park, was the working-class reply to the impudent campaign of lies by the capitalist press against the marchers.

As the last contingent of marchers entered the park gates, trouble broke out with the police. It started with the special constables; not being used to their task, they lost their heads, and, as the crowds swept forward on to the space where the meetings were to be held, the specials drew their truncheons in an effort to control the sea of surging humanity. This incensed the workers; they felt particularly bitter towards the specials, whom they had dubbed 'blackleg cops'. The workers turned on the special constables and put them to flight, but the fighting which they had been responsible for starting continued throughout the whole afternoon, whilst speakers from the marchers were addressing huge gatherings on the green.

The workers kept the police back from the meetings; several times mounted police charged forward, only to be repulsed by thousands of workers who tore up railings and used them as weapons and barricades for the protection of their meetings. Many mounted men were dragged from their horses. From the streets the fighting extended into the park and back again into the streets, where repeated mounted police charges at full speed failed to dislodge the workers. The foot police were on several occasions surrounded by strong forces of workers, and terrific fights ensued. Many workers and police were injured. Inside the park one could hear the roar of the crowd as they fought tenaciously around the Marble Arch and along Oxford Street. At one juncture a plain-clothes detective stepped forward to speak to a chief inspector; as he did so a zealous special constable struck him down with a terrific blow on the head with a staff. He was about to kick him as he lay on the ground, but was prevented from doing so by the officer in uniform, who stepped forward to reprimand him for the foolish mistake which he had made.

Some of the edge was taken off London's hardship by the job-creating building programme of the London County Council (LCC) under Labour's Herbert Morrison ('Up with the Houses! Down with the Slums!'), but only partially. And where there was poverty there was discontent. The impoverished East End, it seemed, would be a likely recruiting ground for Sir Oswald Mosley's blackshirted, jackbooted British Union of Fascists.

The Battle of Cable Street, 4 October 1936
East London Advertiser

Organized anti-Semitism in the East End, which was the main area of Jewish settlement in Britain, began in 1901 when the British Brothers League held meetings that resounded to the call to 'Wipe Them [the Jews] Out!' In 1936 Sir Oswald Mosley took his turn at whipping up anti-Semitism in the East End, announcing that his British Union of Fascists (BUF) would march through Shoreditch, Limehouse, Bow and Bethnal Green on 4 October.

The BUF's progress was opposed by the Labour Party, the Independent Labour Party, the Jewish People's Council against Fascism and Anti-Semitism, and the Communist Party:

The Fascists Gather

*A*T TWO O'CLOCK in the afternoon the Fascists began to gather at Tower Hill. The first part of Mosley's bodyguard arrived in special vans with barred windows. As they jumped from these vehicles, the crowds gathered on the historic hill surged forward. The mounted police were compelled to draw their batons and charge the crowd, driving them into side streets. Two Fascists were beaten up at Mansell street on their way to the meeting. 'The Red Flag' could be heard. Wireless vans passing through the streets reported the movements of the crowd. Sir Phillip Game had his headquarters in a street off Tower Hill. Overhead a police aeroplane flew, keeping observation.

A large number of men who had met at Aldgate to take part in the I.L.P. demonstration against the Fascist march, collided with a contingent of Fascists coming from Mark Lane station. Anti-Fascists attempted to occupy the Minories and a car bearing the slogan, 'Mosley shall not pass,' swept into Royal Mint street. Crowds surged round that and the police had to clear the road with a baton charge. Barriers were thrown across the road. By half-past three a hundred casualties, women amongst them, had been treated at Leman street police station.

About this time Sir Oswald Mosley arrived in a long black sports car. He was wearing a new uniform in place of the severely plain back shirt and trousers he has affected formerly. Now he was wearing a black military cut jacket, grey riding breeches and jack boots. He had a black peaked military cap and a red arm band. As his car moved along the ranks of some 5,000 Fascists escorted by a guard of Fascists on motor cycles, the Blackshirts shouted out letter by letter. 'M. O. S. L. E. Y. We want Mosley!' Sir Oswald then reviewed his troops. He had a long talk with Staff Officer Moran, who had been struck during one of the earlier scuffles with a stick wound with barbed wire. He had been taken to hospital and returned to the parade. Sir Oswald was asked to see Sir Phillip Game, who informed him that in view of the large crowds and previous clashes, and the risk of further ones the procession would have to be diverted to the Embankment

Sir Oswald then led his army on a 'West End' march escorted by hundreds of constables.

At the Temple the police formed a cordon, allowing only Fascists to pass and on the Embankment the parade was dismissed.

Seventy Arrests Made

Altogether some seventy arrests were made. They were made in between a score of baton charges in various places on the route. On Tower Hill during the early part of the afternoon, Fascists and their opponents of the I.L.P. and Communist sections, both had their own dressing stations where casualties were treated. After it was over, iron bars, chair-legs wrapped with barbed wire, and broken bottles were picked up from the gutters.

Cable Street Barricaded

There was tremendous excitement at Cable street, down whose narrow width it was expected that Sir Oswald and his blackshirts would pass. There large numbers of people joined in the erection of a great barricade. A builder's lorry was dragged from a neighbouring yard and overturned in the street. This was the foundation of a barricade which was added to with barrels, corrugated iron, lengths of timber, and piles of bricks. The police tried to stop the men, but were met with a shower of bricks.

As they retreated paving stones were torn out of the pavement and piled against the barricade to strengthen it. The police later returned with reinforcements, a baton charge was made, and when the street was clear again they had the task of taking down a formidable structure. Several hours later, piles of timber, bricks and barrels and iron roofing beside the road, and pavements with gaping spaces where there should have been stones, looked like the aftermath of a battle in Spain. Before the barricade, those who had erected it had scattered broken glass in front, to check the police horses.

The people living in Cable street were highly jubilant at the abandonment of the march and claimed that the news of their barricade had as much to do with it as the fighting at Tower Hill.

Shop Windows Broken at Aldgate

No Fascists reached Gardiner's Corner but there were clashes there with the police also. There a great surging crowd awaited the coming of the Fascists. Someone tied a red flag to a lamp-post and someone else let off a firework.

The police found it difficult to control the crowd and a baton charge was ordered. The people were hemmed together on the pavement and in the panic there was a surge against the windows of Messers Kirtz the clothiers on the south side of the road, and their window was broken, as was also a big plate glass window in a shop on the opposite side or the road. Several people were injured here.

The Scene at Lime House

It had been announced by the Fascists that the first meeting to be addressed by Sir Oswald Mosley would be opposite the Memorial Hostel Limehouse. A Blackshirt meeting was in fact started here and addressed by Blackshirt speakers for two hours. Every point of vantage was taken and a cordon of police was thrown across the narrow entrance to Salmons Lane. The meeting was in most of its manifestations a good-natured one, the crowd heckling the speakers whose speech it was impossible for almost any of the crowd except those in the narrow front circle to hear. The speakers were surrounded by a ring of policemen.

As the hands of the clock on Limehouse Church neared five o'clock the crowd grew more thick, and there were shouts or 'Get him off that perch,' referring to the speaker. The crowd pushed forward towards him, and were sent surging back by the police. A little later there was another rush forward by the crowd, and it was seen that the police ring was sagging under the strain. Mounted police who had been standing quietly on the outskirts of the crowd, then pushed their way in among the people up to the speaker, and he was removed under police protection, leaving his stand behind him. The mounted police then rode among the crowd calling out 'All over. There will be no march. You can go home.' This was a big surprise to the people there who had not heard of the events of Tower Hill.

Quiet Gathering at Bow

Sir Oswald Mosley had also announced that there would be a meeting at Stafford Road, Bow, at its junction with Roman Road. About 200 people gathered here to await the coming of the Fascists. Everything was very quiet, the crowd at this meeting place being considerably less than at the junction of Mile End Road and Barrett Road, where a huge throng stood waiting for a long time. 'I'm going to get my place now,' said an onlooker, taking up his stand opposite the La Boheme at two o'clock, and she was one of the many who waited three hours for a procession that never arrived.

As many as 100,000 anti-Fascist demonstrators had gathered for the 'Battle of Cable Street'. If Cable Street was a victory over Fascism in the East End, it was only a brief victory. Within days, BUF youths were out smashing windows of Jewish shops on Mile End Road; in 1937 the BUF contested the LCC elections, winning 23 per cent of the vote in Bethnal Green. Only with the outbreak of war in 1939 did the BUF's campaign in the East End truly falter, when its far-right politics aligned it ineluctably with Britain's enemies, Germany and Italy.

The Abdication, 11 December 1936

Duff Cooper

The monarchy presided over London's tribulations during the 1930s – once seen as the capital's 'rival', now it was the one thing that bound it together. Even the abdication of Edward VIII did not tarnish the city's affection for royalty.

There were various religious, legal and political reasons why Edward VIII could not remain king and marry twice-divorced Wallis Simpson. Edward chose 'the woman I love' over the crown.

*I*N THIS WINTER [1936] occurred the abdication of King Edward VIII. I had known His Majesty for some years and he had always shown me the greatest kindness ... I was aware of his affection for his present wife [the Duchess of Windsor] but had not guessed that he was contemplating matrimony. I learnt this from the Prime Minister [Baldwin], whom I happened to meet one afternoon in one of the corridors of the House of Commons. 'Just the person I was looking for,' he exclaimed. 'Come to my room for a minute.' When he reached it he told me that the King meant to abdicate and marry, and had asked him, for the King behaved with punctilious constitutional rectitude throughout the crisis, whether he might see one or two Cabinet Ministers with whom he was on friendly terms. I was one of them and I had an audience on the following day.

I began by asking the King whether it was any use my trying to dissuade him from his intention or whether I should merely be wasting my time and his. He said that it would be quite useless, and I believed him. I then suggested postponement, which seemed to me the only alternative to abdication. It was a solution that I had known to work in the affairs of humbler folk and I had accepted it in my own case. I thought that if they would agree not to meet for a year, during which he would be crowned and perhaps attend a Durbar, of which there was some possibility at that time, he would at the end of that period have grown more accustomed to his position and loth to leave it. I also secretly thought that he might in the interval meet somebody whom he would love more. He never has. He refused to consider the suggestion for a reason which did him credit. He felt it would be wrong to go through so solemn a religious ceremony as the Coronation without letting his subjects know what it was his intention to do. I could not argue against such scruples, but could only respect them. When we parted he said that we would have further conversations on the subject, but I did not see him again for many years, for soon afterwards the matter was given full publicity and there followed the rapid events that led to the abdication.

I was sad at his going. No such event had ever happened in English history. I felt that we were losing a personality of value to the State and I feared lest the prestige of the monarchy should suffer, a fear which happily proved groundless. He had many qualities that fitted him for his great position – charm of manner, sympathy with suffering, courage and sincerity, keen interest in politics and in the services.

Children Evacuated, 1 September 1939

Anonymous Schoolgirl

The Second World War started at 4.45 a.m. on 1 September 1939, when German tanks rolled into Poland. Britain was not yet at war, but prudence dictated that London's children were evacuated in case of bombing.

The writer was a pupil at the North London Collegiate School:

AUGUST 21ST–28TH [1939] was a week of suspense. The Soviet-German pact was announced and people suddenly realised that a European upheaval was imminent. The six o'clock news became an event of national importance. We were most of us on our holidays, but returned hastily to London, waiting for the order: 'All children in danger areas to stand by for evacuation.'

On Monday the 28th of August we turned up, laden with changes of underclothes, and barley sugar, at a strangely unfamiliar Sandall Road. The one thing that really brought home to us the seriousness of the situation was the sight of everyone carrying what have now become so commonplace, gasmasks. We went up to our form rooms, heartily greeting our friends again, just as on the first day of term, but with what a difference. Everyone gave her solemn opinion (including first-hand information) on the outcome of the crisis, and even holidays had to take second place. By now carefully labelled, we went down to prayers. Only a little more than a third of the school was present. We sat in the half empty hall and were told by Miss Drummond that the order to evacuate might come through at any moment and we must always be ready.

So, all that week, we came to school in the morning after fond farewells and the hurried making of sandwiches, and all that week, until the fateful Friday, we returned home in the evening and ate our sandwiches for supper. But we had by no means a dull time at school. We had meetings for poetry and play-reading, scrapbook making, the study of astronomy, and rummy in room 5. We were briskly organised into squads, and played energetic if somewhat unusual games of rounders at the Home Field, watched with amusement (and funny remarks) by the men in charge of the local barrage-balloon, which reposed gracefully on the lower pitch. The ball had frequently to be retrieved from the precincts of the balloon and the upper netball court where the men were usually to be seen, dressed in singlets and shorts and an occasional Air-Force cap, eating lunch off trestle-tables. Back at school, education was supplied in the form of travel-talks by one member of staff, talks on 'how to recognise our feathered friends' by another, lectures on the history of Poland, and communal and somewhat hectic washing-up.

On Thursday the uncertainty was ended – Friday was to be the day. The barley-sugar was hastily replenished and we said good-bye in earnest. Friday morning was much the same as any of the others, and passed quickly, and after a substantial lunch and a last re-checking we set off on our journey.

We marched in twos to Kentish Town Station, feeling intensely like a Sunday children's outing, or a caravan of camels. We were heartily cheered on our way by the inhabitants of Camden Town who stood at their front gates gazing sympathetically upon us and murmuring 'Cheer up, ducky'.

We reached the High Road, and there were the placards: 'Germans invade Poland'.

We stood on the station platform for about twenty minutes feeling rather subdued and wishing that our rucksacks were not quite so heavy. At last the train came and we bundled in. Only the engine driver knew our destination. However, we kept our spirits up, for it was rather an adventure and we were all in it together. We did crossword puzzles, munched sweets, sang, and a member of staff even produced a wireless. The train stopped at St. Albans and our hearts sank, for after all, we wanted to go somewhere new and interesting, and St. Albans was too near home. But to our relief the train started off again, and finally stopped at Luton, which to most of us was an unknown quantity. Somebody yelled to us to get out, and out we came. It began to drizzle as we walked down to Dunstable Road School, and the adventure began rather to pall.

※ ※ ※

The House of Commons Discusses War and Peace, 2 September 1939

Ralph Glyn, MP

SEPTEMBER 3. LAST night in London was one of the great times in modern history. The half-hour in the Commons – 7.30 to 8 – was perhaps the most decisive half-hour that we have known.

All through the day the House had been in a schoolboyish, almost hysterical mood; they were laughing and shuffling. There was a feeling that something fishy was happening in

Downing Street. The Cabinet was still sitting. Ministers were telephoning Paris – and the Germans were bombing Poland. *Why* were we not at war?

At half-past seven we met again, this time subdued and tense. Chamberlain we knew would declare war. The Ambassadors were looking down; Count Edward Raczijnsky pale and worn. Chamberlain came in looking grey – a kind of whitish-grey – and glum, dour. Captain Margesson, the Secretary to the Treasury, came behind him, purple with anxiety. Chamberlain's statement! . . . In the House we thought he was only half-way through when – he sat down. There was a gasp, first of horror, then anger. His own backbenchers leant forward to cry, 'Munich, Munich!' The House seemed to rise to its feet with Mr. Arthur Greenwood, the Labour leader.

Mr. L.S. Amery [Conservative MP for Sparkbrook, Birmingham], sitting very small near Anthony Eden, jumped up to shout at Greenwood – 'speak for England.' Others took up the cry. Chamberlain white and hunched. Margesson with sweat pouring down his face, Sir John Simon, [and] the Foreign Secretary [Lord Halifax], punctiliously looking holy.

Greenwood spoke slowly and very simply. He spoke for England and what is more he saved Chamberlain by most skilfully suggesting that it was the French who were delaying. Then one or two backbenchers, Chamberlain's own supporters, got up. It was not a joint Anglo-French pledge to Poland, they said, it was a *British* pledge – why were we not fulfilling it? The House swung against Chamberlain again. Winston Churchill, I saw, was getting whiter and grimmer. He turned round to look at Eden, who nodded as if to say, 'You speak, I'll follow.' I know that Churchill was about to move a vote of censure on the Government – which would have fallen. But Chamberlain looked across at Churchill: 'I'm playing straight,' his glance seemed to say, 'there really *are* reasons for delay.' Churchill sat back, relaxed, uneasy.

Then James Maxton [Independent Labour MP for Bridgeton, Glasgow], the pacifist, rose, gaunt, a Horseman from the Apocalypse, doom written across his face: 'Don't let's talk of national honour: what do such phrases mean? The plain fact is that war means the slaughter of millions. If the Prime Minister can still maintain the peace he will have saved those lives, he mustn't be rushed.' Again the House swung and was poised. We all thought in the curious hush: What if the gaunt figure of doom were right after all? Slaughter – misery – ruin – was he right? But the alternative: Hitler trading on our fears, Germany treading on freedom, Europe under terror. The whole House was swayed in unison with the drama which itself was living.

Another backbencher spoke: 'We must keep our pledge – Hitler must be stopped.' Once again we were swinging against Chamberlain, when Margesson, damp and shapeless, rose to move the adjournment. In a kind of daze it was carried.

We broke up, some feeling sick from the reaction – two members *were* sick – all were uneasy and ashamed. I went home, lay awake all night, slept a bit towards morning, and was awakened by the air-raid warning. Had the Germans read the feelings of the country? Were they attacking first?

From my window I could look over London – it is the clearest and sunniest and freshest day we have had this year. St. Paul's dome shone blue, and to the east I could see the smoke and masts of the ships at the wharves all peaceful under a blue sky. Later – at 11.15 – I heard Chamberlain's announcement. We had gone out to meet Hitler, we were at war.

The Blitz, September 1940
Len Jones, Virginia Woolf and Edward R. Murrow

Frustrated in his desire to win the Battle of Britain by bombing RAF airfields, Hitler switched the battle's 'Schwerpunkt' (focal point) to a terror attack by the Luftwaffe on Britain's capital.

It was Hitler's belief that war from the air would terrorize London into defeat. He was wrong. The city's inhabitants, on the contrary, took a perverse and particular pleasure from being the front line of the war. 'We can take it' became the catchphrase of the Blitz.

Day One came on 7 September 1940 when 375 aircraft unloaded their bombs on London:

Len Jones, 7 September 1940

Len Jones was an 18-year-old living in Poplar, which was targeted like the rest of the East End because of its gasworks, warehouses and docks.

THAT AFTERNOON, AROUND five o'clock, I went outside the house. I'd heard the aircraft, and it was very exciting, because the first formations were coming over without any bombs dropping, but very, very majestic; terrific. And I had no thought that they were actually bombers. Then from that point on I was well aware, because bombs began to fall, and shrapnel was going along King Street, dancing off the cobbles. Then the real impetus came, in so far as the suction and the compression from the high explosive blasts just pulled you and pushed you, and the whole of this atmosphere was turbulating so hard that, after an explosion of a nearby bomb, you could actually feel your eyeballs being sucked out. I was holding my eyes to try and stop them going. And the suction was so vast, it ripped my shirt away, and ripped my trousers. Then I couldn't get my breath, the smoke was like acid and everything round me was black and yellow. And these bombers just kept on and on, the whole road was moving, rising and falling.

The lucky and the prepared took refuge in Nissen or Anderson shelters. Everyone else hid under the bed, under the stairs, under the kitchen table or just sat it out. Tube stations, which had been used in the First World War, were the obvious sanctuaries from Hitler's ordnance but only 4 per cent of Londoners used them – the Tube's overcrowded, unsanitary conditions deterred nearly all. Henry Moore, the sculptor, was reminded of 'the holds of slave ships'. Neither were Tube stations impregnable. In January 1941 a bomb bounced down the escalator at Bank and exploded on the platform, killing 117 people.

Virginia Woolf, 10 September 1940

The docks and East End took the brunt of the Luftwaffe's bombs, but everywhere in the city 'copped it'. The novelist Virginia Woolf recorded bomb damage in literary Bloomsbury:

TUESDAY, 10 SEPTEMBER

Back from half a day in London – perhaps our strangest visit. When we got to Gower St a barrier with Diversion on it. No sign of damage. But, coming to Doughty St a crowd. Then Miss Perkins at the window. Meek S. roped off. Wardens there, not allowed in. The house about 30 yards from ours struck at one this morning by a bomb. Completely ruined. Another bomb in the square still unexploded. We walked round the back. Stood by Jane Harrison's house. The house was still smouldering. That is a great pile of bricks. Underneath all the people who had gone down to their shelter. Scraps of cloth hanging to the bare walls at the side still standing. A looking glass I think swinging. Like a tooth knocked out – a clean cut. Our house undamaged. No windows yet broken – perhaps the bomb has now broken them. We saw Sage Bernal with an arm band jumping on top of the bricks – who lived there? I suppose the casual young men & women I used to see, from my window; the flat dwellers who used to have flower pots & sit on the balcony. All now blown to bits – The garage man at the back – blear eyed & jerky told us he had been blown out of his bed by the explosion; made to take shelter in a church – a hard cold seat, he said, & a small boy lying in my arms. 'I cheered when the all clear sounded. I'm aching all over.' He said the Jerrys had been over for 3 nights trying to bomb Kings X. They had destroyed half Argyll Street, also shops in Grays Inn Road. Then Mr Pritchard ambled up. Took the news as calm as a grig. 'They actually have the impertinence to say this will make us accept peace – !' he said: he watches raids from his flat roof & sleeps like a hog. So, after talking to Miss Perkins & Mrs Jackson (a bloodless sand hopper), but both serene – Miss P. had slept on a camp bed in her shelter – we went on to Grays Inn. Left the car & saw Holborn. A vast gap at the top of Chancery Lane. Smoking still. Some great shop entirely destroyed: the hotel opposite like a shell. In a wine shop there were no windows left. People standing at the tables – I think drink being served. Heaps of blue green glass in the road at Chancery Lane. Men breaking off fragments left in the frames. Glass falling. Then into Lincolns Inn. To the N.S. office: windows broken, but house untouched. We went over it. Deserted. Wet passages. Glass on stairs. Doors locked. So back to the car. A great block of traffic. The Cinema behind Mme Tussaud's torn open: the stage visible; some decoration swinging. All the R[egent's]. Park houses with broken windows, but undamaged. And then miles & miles of orderly ordinary streets – all Bayswater, & Sussex Sqre as usual. Streets empty. Faces set & eyes bleared. In Chancery Lane I saw a man with a barrow of music books. My typists office destroyed. Then at Wimbledon a Siren – people began running. We drove, through almost empty streets, as fast as possible. Horses taken out of the shafts. Cars pulled up. Then the all clear. The people I think of now are the very grimy lodging house keepers, say in Heathcote Street; with another night to face: old wretched women standing at their doors; dirty, miserable. Well – as Nessa said on the phone, its coming very near. I had thought myself a coward for suggesting that we shd. not sleep 2 nights at 37. I was greatly relieved when Miss P. telephoned advising us not to stay, & L. agreed.

Edward R. Murrow, 13 September 1940

Murrow was war correspondent for America's CBS.

THIS IS LONDON at 3:30 in the morning. This has been what might be called a 'routine night' – air-raid alarm at about 9 o'clock and intermittent bombing ever since. I had the impression that more high explosives and few incendiaries have been used tonight. Only two small fires can be seen on the horizon. Again the Germans have been sending their bombers in singly or in pairs. The anti-aircraft barrage has been fierce but sometimes there have been periods of twenty minutes when London has been silent. Then the big red busses would start up and move on till the guns started working again. That silence is almost harder to bear. One becomes accustomed to rattling windows and the distant sound of bombs and then there comes a silence that can be felt. You know the sound will return – you wait, and then it starts again. That waiting is bad. It gives you a chance to imagine things. I have been walking tonight – there is a full moon, and the dirty-gray buildings appear white. The stars, the empty windows, are hidden. It's a beautiful and lonesome city where men and women and children are trying to snatch a few hours' sleep underground.

In the fashionable residential districts I could read the TO LET signs on the front of big houses in the light of the bright moon. Those houses have big basements underneath – good shelters, but they're not being used. Many people think they should be.

The scale of this air war is so great that the reporting is not easy. Often we spend hours traveling about this sprawling city, viewing damage, talking with people, and occasionally listening to the bombs coming down, and then more hours wondering what you'd like to hear about these people who are citizens of no mean city. We've told you about the bombs, the fires, the smashed houses . . .

On Friday and Saturday morning the sky grew darker and darker as the oily smoke rose and spread in heavy, immobile columns, shutting out the sun.

At the barracks, drill quickly became monotonous. We had work to do, and we weren't the target. But we couldn't keep our eyes off those sickening, solid columns climbing up like the convolutions of a lazy snake into a torpid sky.

I suppose our masters felt that, although the Battle of Britain had begun, the worst might already be over – I don't know; but they decided to put us recruits in the hat and draw out three for week-end leave. My name came out of the hat first, and I sent a wire to my parents in Sevenoaks to say that I was coming home. My pass was from midday on Saturday, and I got down to the centre of London by Underground. Bombers were coming over at monotonously regular intervals. I walked down to Charing Cross. There was a lot of noise still, and a lot of smoke. As I entered the station the loudspeakers were ordering everyone out because planes were overhead and they were frightened of casualties if the place were hit. I strolled out to the top of that long flight of stone steps down into Villiers Street and sat on the balustrade watching.

Up in the lonely sky there was still one bomber, gleaming silver, and then he dropped a stick just across the Thames from us. Back in the station the loudspeaker announced that the main line was gone and that there wouldn't be any more trains out for hours. Hundreds of people stood around like a flock of sheep which is frightened and can't make up its mind which way to turn. You could see the dead mask of indecision on their faces as they looked about, hoping someone would tell them what to do. I walked out of the station and decided to hitch-hike home. I was lucky; somewhere on the south bank of the river I met a man on a motor-cycle who was going through Blackheath, and he took me on his pillion.

Now we were nearer to the docks. The columns of smoke merged and became a monstrous curtain which blocked the sky; only the billows within it and the sudden shafts of flame which shot up hundreds of feet made one realize that it was a living thing and not just the backdrop of some nightmare opera. There were fire-hoses along the side of the road, climbing over one another like a helping of macaroni, with those sad little fountains spraying out from the leaks, as they always seem to do from all fire-hoses. Every two or three minutes we would pull into the gutter as a fire-bell broke out stridently behind us and an engine in unfamiliar livery tore past at lull tilt, chocolate or green or blue, with gold lettering – City of Birmingham Fire Brigade, or Sheffield, or Bournemouth. The feeling was something you had never experienced before – the excitement and dash of fire-engines arriving to help from so far away, and the oily, evil smell of fire and destruction, with its lazy insolent rhythm.

It looked terrible and hopeless, but there was a kind of *Gotterdämmerung* grandeur about it.

The culmination of the Blitz came on the night of 29 December 1940, when the bull's eye was the City of London. It was as if the Great Fire had been rekindled: flames reached from Aldersgate to Cannon Street. Nineteen churches and 31 guild halls were destroyed. The roll of dead Londoners now reached over 9,000.

However, although no one yet knew it, the worst of the Blitz was over. London had taken it.

For four years after the Blitz Hitler left London in comparative peace. But he had not quite finished with the capital. On 12 June 1944 a V1 flying bomb, launched from a site near Dunkirk, landed on Bethnall Green, where its one-ton warhead killed six people. The 'V' in V1 stood for *Vergeltungswaffe*, meaning 'Vengeance weapon'. Soon after, V1s were crossing the English Channel at the rate of over 100 a day.

Never ones for following Nazi nomenclature, Londoners called the V1s – on account of the spluttering noise they made – the slang name for cheap cars: 'doodlebugs'.

Doodlebugs, June–July 1944
Vere Hodgson

SUNDAY, 18TH. THESE last three days have been one long Air Raid Alert, and we have had little sleep. Must get some tonight if I am to work in the day. So I have decided to come and bed down on the Sanctuary sofa. It is on the ground floor. I do not mind the guns, but the shrapnel danger through my skylight in the flat makes me hop out of bed to the door.

These Robot Planes go on after daybreak, which the old raids never did. I could hear the wretched thing travelling overhead at 6 a.m. They did not fall on us – but they fell on someone. Our guns barked out and spat and fussed until they had gone. They travel quickly and on Thursday night were low over Kensington. In fact everyone of us was perfectly convinced the thing was exactly three inches above the roof.

Nothing is said on the wireless or in the papers except . . . Southern England! That is us – and we are all fed-up.

Monday was our fire-watch. Mrs Hoare light-heartedly remarked: 'I don't think there will be any more air-raids.' And in my heart I agreed with her. But not a bit of it! Hitler has still got a sting in his Nasty Tail. At 4 a.m. we were amazed to be roused by a Warning. We all got up. In 20 minutes All Clear. Just as I had bedded down another went. I sat on the steps. It was just getting light. Mr Bendall reported to the Street Leader.

In the morning much discussion, for no one knew about Robot Planes. Cannot remember all the events of Thursday night. We had little sleep. I was in my flat – something trundled across the sky. In the morning nothing on the wireless, and we felt injured – as we needed the sympathy of our friends! On and off all day we had Warnings and gunfire. One Robot fell in Tooley St in the City. One of the women from our Printing Works rang up to say at Eltham they had had a terrible night – all her windows and doors blown out.

JULY 1944

Sunday, 2nd. The week before I went away I slept at the Sanctuary, and managed to get about five hours sleep every night. One can keep going on this. One night I was wakened by a light on my face, and thought it was the tail of the wretched thing overhead. But it was caught in the searchlights, and they travelled with it across the sky. To my fevered imagination, however, it seemed as if the thing was creeping up the front of the house, across the roof, and that it burst in the back garden. But in reality it was a mile away.

Monday, just as I had had lunch in the flat and was going to shop – a bumble sounded near. We all gathered in the front hall. Terrific explosion shook the house. We knew it was near – smoke and debris were rising. Obviously Church St. Feeling shaken I went out, saw police cars, ambulances and fire brigades tearing up Campden Hill Rd. All Notting Hill came out, and we thanked God we had escaped. It was on the bend of the Carmelite Church. Many killed and injured – any one of us might have been there. I go frequently.

A little cripple came to ask if we could send her away. A man had pushed her inside a public house as the bomb fell. She was only shaken but was unnerved. The authorities are on the spot so quickly, and the injured are attended to with amazing speed, everything cleared away, that one does not see the horrors. You only imagine it.

Went on like this all the week. We lost count of Warnings. However, we are so busy that we have little time to think about them. The papers call it the baby blitz. It is annoying to have it all the time. You just dodge out for a few minutes to shop. People are amazingly unconcerned – except the old. All the men think about is to get into the open and see one! But all London has slept dressed night after night . . .

Monday, 3rd. Life is one long air-raid Alert, and things that go bump in the night. Not a whit better, really worse. Fetched my air-raid mattress – all the household is on the ground floor as in the Big Blitz. With the shutters closed we are as safe as it is possible to be, short of a direct hit. One listens fascinated to the Doodle Bugs passing over, holding one's breath, praying they will travel on, but feeling a wretched cad, because you know that means they will explode on someone else.

Our London Shelter in China Walk has had a bomb. The old place shook itself, and settled down again. But Mrs Johnson is not sleeping there.

Friday, 7th. Today I really saw one. Walked to the flat as the Alert went. Half-way up heard a Thrum Thrum. A Platinum Blonde, the other side of the road lifted her head from reading a letter, and called out: 'Can you see it?' I replied 'no.' 'Come over here,' she shouted. And there, between the clouds, sure enough right over our heads, was a horrible black thing. It gave me a turn. The Platinum Blonde pursued her way, unmoved, still reading her letter. I regret to say I hastened my pace – though there is little likelihood, if it is directly above you, that it will fall on you. But it might have been rose petals for all the Platinum Blonde seemed to care!

Saturday, 8th. A disturbed night. Turned in just before midnight. Dozing off when I heard two explosions. One Robot had dithered over this house for some time. I put my head beneath the nearest desk – and waited. It came. Terrific

– as if in the back garden. House shook to its foundations – windows rattled in their sockets, but held. Got up, undid the shutters, found the yellow kitten asleep – but all intact. Slept little all night.

During July 1944 20,000 houses a day were destroyed by V1s. The worst incident, however, concerned a church – when the Guards Chapel near St James' Park was hit, 119 died.

By the end of August 1944 the Allied invasion of Europe had seized the main V1 launch sites and doodlebug raids waned.

Something more terrible than the V1, however, was to descend from the sky onto London: the V2. Travelling at 3,600 mph, the V2 carried its one-ton warhead for 220 miles. There was no defence. There was no warning. As Vere Hodgson remarked: 'They seem to be rockets which drop from the stratosphere. You may be out peaceably walking and one drops. Nice prospect!'

Between September 1944 and March 1945 some 500 V2s fell on London.

And then, after five long years, the Battle of London was over. A total of 29,890 Londoners had been killed and 50,000 seriously injured. London had lost 116,000 houses (with 2 million damaged) and some of her greatest landmarks, including 14 churches designed by Wren.

But London had taken it. There was cause for celebration, which came on 8 May 1945, with the announcement of the end of the war in Europe.

VE Day, 8 May 1945
James Lees-Milne

TUESDAY, 8TH MAY

*T*HIS IS V-DAY at last. I got home at 9.30, had a bath and changed. At midday went to Bridget's flat, and with her and Anne to lunch with John Sutro at Driver's. We were joined by Oliver Messel and a quiet, mystery man of about 50. We ate oysters and lobsters and drank sweet champagne. Then returned to hear Churchill's speech at 3 o'clock. It was merely a short announcement that peace had been declared. We were all rather disappointed, and wondered what the necessity was for telling us what we already knew.

I went to John Sutro's house and found Bridget there. Had it not been for the mystery man arriving uninvited at 8 o'clock, the evening would have been unalloyed fun. The three of us being such old friends were perfectly contented by our own company. Bridget was more beautiful and alluring than ever I remember her. We drank muscat wine, and listened to the King's speech at 9. It was perfect, well-phrased, well-delivered in his rich, resonant voice, expressed with true feeling and tinged with an appropriate emotion for the occasion. Bridget and I cooked the dinner, she scrambling eggs, I frying the bacon in great quantity. This was all we had, but it was delicious. We drank a bottle of excellent white wine and some very old brandy, sitting till 11.45 at the table. All the while the sad mystery man sat speechless. John played Chopin on the piano. At midnight I insisted on our joining the revels. It was a very warm night. Thousands of searchlights swept the sky. Otherwise there were no illuminations and no street lights at all. Claridge's and the Ritz were lit up. We walked down

Bond Street passing small groups singing, not boisterously. Piccadilly was however full of swarming people and littered with paper.

We walked arm in arm into the middle of Piccadilly Circus which was brilliantly illuminated with arc lamps. Here the crowds were yelling, singing and laughing. They were orderly and good-humoured. All the English virtues were on the surface. We watched individuals climb the lamp posts, and plant flags on the top amidst tumultuous applause from bystanders. We walked down Piccadilly towards the Ritz. In the Green Park there was a huge bonfire under the trees, and too near one poor tree which caught fire. Bridget made us push through the crowd collected on the pavement to a ring of people round the bonfire. Six or seven people were struggling under barricades of wood including whole doorways from air raid shelters which they dragged on to the fire. The fire's reflection upon thousands of faces, packed on the pavement, squatting on the grass and cramming the windows of the Piccadilly houses reminded me for some reason of a Harrison Ainsworth illustration of the crowds witnessing Charles I's execution. One extraordinary figure, a bearded, naval titan, organised an absurd nonsense game, by calling out the Navy and making them tear round the bonfire carrying the Union Jack; then the RAF; then the Army; then the Land Army, represented by three girls only; then the Americans; then the civilians. If we had been a little drunker we would have joined in. As it was Bridget took a flying leap over the pyre in sheer exuberance of spirits. The scene was more Elizabethan than neo-Georgian, a spontaneous peasant game, a dance round the maypole, almost Breughelian, infinitely bucolic. No one was bullied into joining who didn't want to, and the spectators enjoyed it as much as the participants. I thought, if we could have a V-night once a month, and invite the Poles, Germans, even

Russians to do what we were doing now, there might never be another war.

We left Bridget at Mount Street. John and I went to his house where I slept the night. This was about 3 a.m.

Like the rest of the country, London voted overwhelmingly for Labour in the General Election of 1945; like the remainder of the country, London soon became desperate for glamour and excitement in the post-war era of continued rationing and National Service. American culture held a particular lure for many

❧ ❧ ❧

Hep-cats:
Jive at the Paramount Ballroom, 1947
William Sansom

THREE OF THE main dance halls in London that cater for jive – on every night some of the time, on some nights all of the time – are the Paramount Ballroom in Tottenham Court Road, the Hammersmith Palais-de-danse and the Lyceum Theatre in Drury Lane. Many others radiate outwards through the suburbs. Mecca Dancing alone runs some dozen and a half halls. Not only jive is danced at these halls – waltzes, foxtrots and tangos and rumbas and sambas and beguines and much else seduce the fantastic, bobby-soxed toe; but although each dance has its own enthusiasts, jive has become in all the most popular. When the band starts to swing, a distinct emanation can be sensed through the hall, an eagerness is lit, the walls and pillars seem to echo a zest that is cheerful and vicious, gay and anaesthetic, by different standards beautiful and hideous.

But to the particular – and the Paramount Dance Hall in Tottenham Court Road. This is part of the Mecca chain. It serves its session of dancing twice daily on all days of the week – from 3 to 5.15 p.m. and from 7.30 to 11 p.m. On Sundays it becomes a club, with a small yearly membership fee. On an ordinary evening (and there are many extraordinary evenings, jive nights, competition nights, extension nights) you pay two shillings and receive a ticket which includes your cloakroom fee (an extra 3d. refunded if you don't use it). Down the carpeted stairway, and you are in the hall. It lies underground, the ceiling is low and warmly lit; chocolate and crimson pillars are topped with heavy gilt Corinthian capitals; fans like aeroplane propellors hang motionless from the ceiling. One wall of the immense room is ornate with heavy rose damask, with mirrors, with curling gold baroquish plaster work. The opposite wall encloses within similar gilt flamboyances several large tapestried panels involving such heterogeny as nymphs round a fountain and an ancient barque in full sail. Opposite, across the shining pale wood floor a raised and draped dais provides a platform for one of the two bands. From the glitter of metal instruments there now rises and falls, in the slow drawl of a hesitation waltz, the melody of *Heilige Nacht*.

It seems at first that the hundred or more couples on the floor are just waltzing, at the dream-drugged pace of any modern ballroom waltz. But then you notice one couple, and then another and another, who perform a curious rhythmic throw-away of each other, so that half the time they are apart and spinning round by themselves, while when they meet again they raise a finger or join hands in a jerked stylized motion that seems to represent some symbolic ritual understanding between them, as though repeatedly they are exchanging masonic signs. Their feet move to a short-stepped, decided, paused routine that has nothing to do with the waltz. They are in fact jivers who cannot stop jiving. To any music they will continue, though in a dejected and adulterated measure, the motions of their obsession. And as *Heilige Nacht* draws to a close you might observe two of these eccentrics more closely and notice that the young man wears a jacket reaching almost to his knees, narrow trousers short enough to show his socks, and a watch-chain hanging from his waistcoat to his ankles; the girl wears a particularly short skirt, much pleated so that when she spins it will rise up to the tops of her thighs, which in their turn are covered by a tight, short, determinedly modest pair of pants. These are jive clothes – a *zoot* suit and a *swing* skirt – and only when you have had time to digest their detail can you begin to realize the full involution of the culture dispersing itself around the jive idea.

But now *Heilige Nacht* has ended, the last notes like toothpaste have been squeezed from the tubular saxophone, the muted trumpet. A short pause and then all the brass of the orchestra crashes open the first tidal chord of a fast swing tune. An epithet much used in the idiom of swing is 'solid'. A 'solid' driving beat is produced that 'sends' the dancers. It seems almost as if an invisible material force is at work, as though the instruments emit successive walls of sound that force the dancers on their way. And now these walls have already galvanized the floor with a strange excitement. The force of sudden movement, the unison enthusiasm, is palpable. The hep-cats are at it, the jive is on, they're in a groove. Swing skirts are circling, zoot-tails flying; smiles are set solid on their lips, eyes glazed in a tremendously concentrated inward scrutiny of the body's motion. They throw each other away, then, magnetized, come together. Within this simple mathematical framework the improvization thrives: legs are kicked in special ways, arms extended, the whole body bent in calculated distortion, the torso shivered in a movement half intendedly lunatic. Sometimes either partner succeeds in a particularly inspired acrobatic and then the glaze is lifted, the face comes to the surface with delight, laughs its triumph. Once one of the men throws his girl right over his shoulder – a sublime feat, but one not favoured by a cautious management.

However, not all wear zoot suits and swing skirts. Those who do are the *élite*, the most regular regulars who come every day of the week, twice a day at week-ends; the absolutely possessed. Otherwise the clientele prove surprising varied. A tall most English-looking man in grey flannels and a sports coat contrasts with a smoother Latin gentleman in a rich brown suit and a red carnation; a spiv with padded shoulders and a flash hair-cut bumps into an elderly gentleman in a quiet grey suit who might be a tea-taster or a dentist. A soberly-dressed woman wearing pince-nez spins next to a seventeen-year-old working girl with a wan, excited face; a tweedy lady with a fresh-air face and a well-filled figure whirls past a slinky silken snake painted and dressed for manslaughter. There is a strong colony of coloured men, mostly in uniform, particularly here in the Paramount. Of all these mixed types, however, the most prevalent is the working girl of adolescence or early twenties and her male counterpart. Dressed in no particular mood, except that it be free and easy, these attend in their hundreds, forming by far the majority and proving, with their adulation of all things American, the backbone of the movement . . .

The Lyceum theatre presents an amazing spectacle to-day. It is a theatre more gilded than most, and the tiers of boxes and circles still flash their ornate gold over the immense new

dance floor covering auditorium and stage. Huge faceted chandeliers hang above and on these are directed coloured beams of light – astringent violet, sharp blazing green, murderous rose. Around the sides of this vast oval, under the dizzying dome of the roof, there remain remnants of the old theatre decoration – tiled walls, iron brackets, shaded lamps. The floor itself descends and ascends to form a gentle valley dipping where the orchestra pit must have been; and now every night in these hallowed precincts of pantomime the new mime of old Africa proceeds apace, at a fast bewildering pace, with almost authentic intensity. In the circle above tables are set, a long bar for soft drinks ranges the back of the pit, girl attendants in strange military uniforms parade the corridors, a large orchestra delivers from underneath the flies a steaming brand of music that seems to make the whole immense edifice and the thousand dancers shake in one ecstatic unison. But despite the disturbing mixture of old things and new, despite a sensation of panic at the impact of such large-scale obsession, an atmosphere of gaiety, cheerfulness and liveliness prevails, and so much delighted movement seems in itself a virtue. By four o'clock on Saturday mornings the band has played its

last notes. The dancers make their way to the street and stand in doorways or sit on the kerb waiting for the all-night bus home – waiting for a 'workman's bus' to take them home.

Lastly, on a fortissimo note, there is the night of a special jive competition. Back again at the Paramount; under the low lighted ceiling, by the red damask walls, under the sinister fans, to see the hall crowded as never before. The huge band plays only jive, and almost without a pause. There is little general dancing, the floor is split into huddled circles of enthusiasts pressing forward to see virtuoso exhibitions by experts. News cameras are there, flash bulbs ignite, people sit on the bandstand, or stand on chairs cheering; the scene has some of the dazzled, hysterical atmosphere of an election night press, a boxing gala, a Victory Night. The experts themselves dance now with unexampled fury, at great speed, contriving the most immaculate precisions of movement, arabesques of jive. One may pick them at random; the little five-foot girl in a white swing suit and a blue sailor hat, a six-foot soldier in a battle-dress, a negro with a curious low movement that keeps his zoot-tails nearly brushing the floor, two girls in woollen jumpers who dance arm in arm like skipping horses, a dancer from the Ballet Nègre exaggerating the movements with his technical knowledge, and other less distinct but equally energetic enthusiasts jiving the night out to cheers and clapping and cries of 'Harry!' and 'Go it, Bert!' till the selections are made and the winners announced. And then it is only the semi-final.

In fact, the whole movement looks now to be semi-final. It may be just a craze that will die – a diabolo, a Charleston, a pogo-stick. But so far it has lasted longer than usual. It sometimes happens that presumed novelties persist and become an habitual part of the national behaviour – the foxtrot did. Much lies in the American lead, for if the Americans get tired and move on to something else, that something is likely to find favour among film-bred youth here; and along with bumble-puppy, miniature golf, and the Black Bottom, will go the epideictic zoot boy and his swell swing skirt.

Some pre-war entertainments carried into the new world of late 1940s London. Attendance at football matches soared, with Arsenal regularly pulling in crowds of 60,000. 'Going to the dogs' (greyhound racing) became a working-class London obsession; on some nights more than 100,000 spectators turned up at White City. Jive, football, the dogs, cinema – nothing, however, quite banished the greyness of austerity London, not even the 1948 Olympic games.

There was, at least, work to be had. Among those called to Britain to take up employment were colonial subjects from the West Indies.

The Empire Windrush *Arrives at Tilbury,* 21 June 1948
Daily Express

Blacks had lived in London for centuries (there may well have been blacks in the Roman army that established Londinium), but the 450 West Indians who arrived aboard the *Windrush* were the first of the large-scale African and Asian immigrations.

FOUR HUNDRED AND fifty Jamaicans crowded the rails of the *Empire Windrush* as she anchored in the Thames last night. They sailed as refugees from their island's unemployment problem, and have provided a new problem to the Colonial Office and the Ministry of Labour here. Loudspeakers called the 450 work-seekers to a pep talk by Mr Ivor Cummings, a principal officer of the Colonial Office, who welcomed them. They were told: Things will not be too easy.

Some of the men were resentful. But when they learned that the Colonial Office had only heard of their coming 12 days ago, they switched the blame to the Jamaican Government. An ex-RAF man returning to seek a welder's job said: 'Now we know how much our government cares for us.'

The Jamaicans – and others with them – have been sorted into two groups: Group One: 82, who are volunteering for the Forces, will go to a Wimpole Street hostel (cost to them £1 1s a week). Group Two: 104 who have friends in England. Group Three: the rest with no contacts, who will go by motor coach to deep shelters on Clapham Common (cost 2/6d a week).

The ship will not berth until 7 a.m. and all non-official

communications with her have been barred by Transport Ministry officials and military police. Reporters were refused permission to go on board from a launch.

Footnote: Three men reported as stowaways as the anchor was dropped near Tilbury. They had eluded several searches. This brings the stowaway total to six, including one woman.

As Mr Cummings had warned, things were not too easy for the *Windrush*'s passengers. Vince Reid, who accompanied his father, recalled:

I DON'T KNOW how, we stayed one night in a hotel in Victoria, but my father knew some people who were quite willing to put us up. And it was over in Valetta Road. And then we eventually got a room over in King's Cross, in Argyle Square. And that's where, that's where we lived, all three of us in one room: two adults and a young boy in one room, that was it. You couldn't get any place to rent. I mean, you had usually notices, about 'No Irish' and not even 'No Blacks', but 'No Niggers'. I mean, this is 1948, you know, and already you had those things in shop windows.

So we were forced to live in one room, all three of us. You can imagine the tension, two adults and a thirteen-year-old boy in one room. It was horrendous. But that's how it was. I had no sort of personal impression of how I'm going to be received, because, as I say, I was a boy. And I wasn't expecting anything. But how I was received was when I went to school, first of all, I was a subject of curiosity, which is quite surprising when you think that you had black soldiers in England. And, you know, people would come up and rub your skin and see if it would rub off the black, and rub your hair and, you know, it's really insulting. And, of course, there was always the latent violence, you know, people want to fight you. Fortunately, I was quite big and could handle myself, so that didn't persist very long, because they couldn't deal with me on that basis. But, even at that time, one was very aware of hostility, quite serious hostility, you know, being beaten up, even at that time.

I was the only black child in the school. And, funnily enough, one of the other things about the school was they didn't even give me a test to see – it was a secondary modern school – they didn't even give me a test to see which grade I should be put in, you know, they just put me in the lowest grade. Then they had a sort of end of year examination and I moved up into the top class. But I remember a teacher, teaching Shakespeare and the soliloquy from *Julius Caesar*. And this teacher said, 'Who can explain what this soliloquy means?' So I put my hand up, you know. And, of course the way I spoke then is not like I speak now, I had this funny Jamaican accent. And this teacher just rolled around. I felt so ashamed, that he was basically mocking me, you know, and I felt so ashamed. And I stopped, I really basically stopped going to school, because I felt so angry and ashamed. It still hurts to this day, you know, because it was bloody upsetting. And that was what it was like. You weren't expected to know anything and they just took the mickey. And that was then, 1949, '49, and it still hurts.

It was fairly demoralising. I mean, you go to a secondary modern school, you come out with no kind of certificates whatsoever. I remember when, at fifteen, I left school, and I actually wanted to be a tailor. And I went along to the youth services thing, and this bloke just laughed. Want to be a tailor? You know, no way. So I ended up in the Post Office as a junior postman. And I didn't want to be a postman, so, eventually, at the age of about sixteen, you could become a boy entrant to join the Royal Air Force. And given the kind of conditions in which I was living, I thought, well, it's a way out. So that's what I did, I went and joined the Air Force, signed on for twelve years, in fact. Bought myself out after three years, 256 days, for £250, which was a lot of money in those days.

I mean, I would have to go in anyway, because you had National Service at that time, so I thought, rather than wait, I could go in and perhaps learn a trade, which I did. I was trained as a radio mechanic. And in fact, my entry, I was the first one to be trained as what they call a ground wireless fitter. And I was the first one in my entry to be made an NCO. I was a corporal when I was about nineteen. So, although the whole thing had been humiliating to some extent, I wasn't exactly demoralised, 'cos I always had this belief in my own ability and nobody was ever going to eradicate that. So, of course, going in the Air Force and becoming one of the first to be made an NCO reinforced that opinion of myself.

The Festival of Britain, 1951
John Betjeman

Only in 1951, when the Labour government unveiled 'A Tonic to the Nation' – the Festival of Britain – did the post-war drabness begin to lift.

Staged on 27 acres of wasteland to the side of County Hall, the Festival of Britain was visited by more than 8.5 million people in the five months it was open. Among its main attractions was the 'Dome of Discovery' (which, like the 1851 'Crystal Palace', exhibited the best of British goods), the 'Skylon' (a 296-foot pencil-thin obelisk) and the Royal Festival Hall.

SUN SHONE ON the South Bank site. Over their teas and their strip cartoons and sports pages the busy workers were resting in threes and fours, as they had been before when I visited the site with the illustrator of these pages. As before, some of their mates were hard at it. All honour to these mates. They have built the gayest and best of exhibitions. Modern artists and sculptors have been given a chance, so have modern architects. Hugh Casson has collected a team of talent and guided it with genius. The South Bank is treated with imagination and happiness: for the first time Londoners will realise the river in their midst. For the first time for a long time they will see things done for the fun of the thing. The Festival lacks the ponderousness of Wembley, the elaboration of White City, and it is a bigger affair altogether than Earl's Court. Though the site is small and thundered through by the Southern electric it would take days to see all the exhibits.

These were the highlights of what I saw.

The Regatta Restaurant by Messrs Black & Gibson. It seems built of crystal and planks. It surveys the lovely outline of the Royal Palace of Westminster, Shaw's Scotland Yard and the domes and turrets of Colonel Edis' Whitehall Court across the sliding water. The details of the restaurant are thoughtful and simple, not fussily modern as they are in the Thames-Side Cafeteria. I like the door handles which are brass hands with fingers open to clutch on the pull side. On the push side is the brass back of a hand.

The seaside section with its model town by Reginald Brill and nets and buckets and kiosks, arranged round it by the Simpson's window-dresser.

Eric Brown's seaside promenade with masts.

The 1851 Centenary Pavilion designed by Hugh Casson. It is made of cast iron from moulds still in stock at Macfarlane's. It is far the prettiest building in the exhibitions.

The wall of coloured balls on the Waterloo side, through which the chimney pots of dead old London look like a backcloth in pantomime.

The skylon, though it is best at night. In the day I am for ever wanting to pull it by its end on elastic and see if it shoots to the moon.

The landscape gardening by Mr G. Sheppard as seen from the Lion and Unicorn pavilion.

The roof of that pavilion and flight of doves from a wicker cage. Much of the other decoration there makes me think of Heath.

In the more solemn, permanent style of the thirties is Wells Coates' Telecinema.

THE ONE CERTAINLY permanent feature of the exhibition, the Festival Hall, is forbidding outside. The outline of the roof is very ugly, the side elevations are decorated to look like the Tote. Because they had to be permanent the architects, Messrs Matthew & Martin, seem to have lost their nerve and missed the gaiety of the merry exhibitionists outside in the sun. But the interior of the Hall is amazing. Again, its decoration is rather self-consciously severe or modishly modernistic, but the scale, size and complete efficiency of the building make one realise that here one is standing in what must be the finest Concert Hall in the world. Sitting in the front row and looking through the *open* doors, I saw a Southern train pass outside not a hundred yards away, but I could hear no sound of it.

The Dome of Discovery by Ralph Tubbs is another partial success. Outside it looks well from across the river. Inside it is a disappointment and this is no fault of the architect, I am sure. The structure of the dome would have been unusual and impressive if left alone, but the numerous exhibits and decorations put it out of scale. I felt I might just as well have been in Olympia or any other large covered area. The interior is the most prominent example of the chief failing of the exhibition. Science seems to have obsessed the decorators. There are patterns in coloured tubes of nuclear whatever they are. There are bits of ships and engines and aeroplanes and patterns of them and patterns of plans and plans of patterns. In many parts of the exhibition I was not sure whether an objective science made it look like art or vice versa and that convinced me, that neither was either.

There are few really ugly objects so far as buildings are concerned. The most notable are the kiosks illustrated here and the hideous walls on the Homes and Gardens' pavilion, which are snail-pointed like a scraped Victorian church. If they are meant to illustrate methods of stonewalling they are warnings of how not to do it. All the walls are wrongly pointed and painfully insensitive.

I went to the Festival Buildings expecting to find gambolling functionalists trying to be funny. I returned over that endless Bailey bridge exhausted but enchanted.

As well as administering a pick-me-up to the people, the Festival birthed the South Bank as a centre for culture.

The Last Tram, 6 July 1952
George Gale

THE JOURNEY FROM Woolwich to New Cross of the last tram in London was incomparable. No triumphal car this, yet it had more glory in its dying than ever it had in its living. Its passage through Greenwich and Deptford was neither that of king nor of clown, yet majesty was affronted and levity confounded. The ridiculous cortege prompted cheers, and tears and jeers were alike dispelled. It was Saturday night in South-East London, and the last tram had become a pretext for a Cockney bacchanalia.

Imagine a crowd along a prescribed route to see a king or queen pass by. Let it keep its squealing children about its knees and hoist up its infants with flags in their hands. Give it torn paper hats, flamboyant holiday-camp hats and ribbons, football rattles, tin trumpets, dustbin drums and scrubbing-board drums, real and tin-tray cymbals, piano-accordions, and a welter of whistles. Let it line up not in daylight but late at night, after all the public-houses from the Old Kent Road to the free ferry at Woolwich and beyond to Abbey Wood have sent away their tens of thousands of customers filled with beer, their arms and pockets filled with bottles, and their throats in full voice. Take away most of the policemen a stately procession would command and then, at midnight, with the moon almost full and the night air hot, send out, to run this crazy gauntlet, a tram.

This tram had no name – only a number, 1951. Queueing up behind other trams at Woolwich free ferry, it looked like all the rest, dingy, mechanical, uncomfortable, certainly soulless. Woolwich at a quarter to eleven seemed normal enough, until you realized that the soldiers and their giggling girls, moving into the dark alleys, had left a noisy crowd behind in the full light, jostling in the pies-and-peas, fish-and-chips, and jellied-eels stalls, that the stragglers outside the doss-house were waiting on the kerb before claiming their beds, that flags hung from a few windows and men in their vests and wives in their nightdresses from others, and that women were dancing reels of sorts on the pavements.

As soon as the tram moved off – to go to Abbey Wood and back before it began its last journey – you realized that it was no longer an ordinary tram but had been made by the crowd at Woolwich into more than an object of affectionate derision or a scrap-album relic. It had become a festival queen, and as the festival was rowdy, beery, middle-aged, and merry, so was its queen. The last tram was a fattish woman of fifty, her tubes a little wheezy, her joints choked with arthritis, with a little bright lipstick and dry powder, her hair dyed and thinning, her resolution and her vanity indomitable. The huge crowd from Abbey Wood through Woolwich to New Cross were celebrating themselves when they celebrated the tram.

Off it moved, filled with a noisy babble of passengers, and

escorted by policemen on motor-cycles, hundreds of cyclists, scores of motor-cyclists, and dozens of cars. There was a great cheer, flares were lit, horns and whistles blown. A woman leaped on to the rear of the tram and clung there, her frock, underclothes, and blasphemies streaming out behind her. She fell off soon, but others clambered on the sides. By the end of the journey there were twenty youths sitting on the roof and dozens strung along the sides. There was singing all the way, and the tunes came easily to mind. 'Maybe It's Because I'm a Londoner', 'Any Old Iron', and so on to 'Auld Lang Syne'.

There were people dressed as monkeys, people dressed as gipsies, people sporting huge theatre bills, people wanting to pat the tram or break a bottle against it or have a penny squashed by it. There were people who stood in front of it waving wildly. The tram could hardly move at times, and the whole road was filled with this exuberant crowd. Patients at a hospital threw out bandages as it passed. Someone flung out a bundle of torn newspapers. The last tram was an hour late getting to New Cross, and it was exhausted.

Outside the depot the crowd was vast. The moment of triumph was at hand. There were only a few yards to go into the sheds. First the boys on the roof had to be got off, and that took half a dozen policemen. Then the last paying passengers had to be cleared off. This was easier since they all scuttled off quickly so that no one would notice the mementoes they had torn off, unscrewed, and broken away from the tram. Then the people climbing up the sides had to be pulled down, and firemen had to be brought in to clear the tracks.

A great cheer went up. Another. And another. But the last tram did not move. She clung to life, so it seemed, but in truth she was deader than ever. A break had occurred in her electrical system. The glory was too much for her. And so another tram came out of the shed and was tied to the last tram. It gave a jerk, the last tram shook and moved up to the sheds. Newsreel cameras whirred, cameras flashed. The last tram had gone inside so that the officials could receive it with official publicity.

It will come out again, unheralded, to make its last journey to the scrap-yard. On its road of glory it had passed that scrap-yard at Charlton and the rows of trams awaiting destruction. It did not shudder, although there were plenty of wits to remind it of its fate. But then the last tram, even if it had become more than a machine, was all the way supremely unsentimental.

For all of the bright new world conjured up by the Festival of Britain and the dispensing of the tram system, old problems lingered on. The 'Great Smog' of December 1952 caused as many as 500 deaths from pneumonia, bronchitis and other diseases. A 'pea souper' in 1957 contributed towards the Lewisham railway disaster in which 90 people died. Successive Clean Air Acts, together with the demise of heavy industry, finally killed the 'eternal smoke' of London.

Then there was the perennial local difficulty of xenophobia.

Notting Hill Race Riots, 1 September 1958
Colin Eales

Throughout the summer of 1958 there were isolated attacks on individual black men in West London. Conspicuous among the assailants were 'Teddy Boys' – déclassé white youths dressed like extravagant Edwardians (hence 'Teddy') with a love of the new rock'n'roll sound from America – and hanging around in the background was the definite shadow of resurgent fascism. The Union for British Freedom operated from Westbourne Grove. On 24 August the attacks stepped up a gear when white youths armed with razors and bottles went 'nigger hunting' in a car. A week later the racial hostility spilled over into outright rioting in Notting Hill. The worst incidents came on Monday 1 September. Colin Eales was a reporter with the *Kensington News and West London Times*:

AS I TURNED into Bramley Road I saw a mob of over 700 men, women and children stretching 200 yards along the road. Young children of ten were treating the whole affair as a great joke and shouting, 'Come on, let's get the blacks and the coppers. Let's get on with it.' In the middle of the screaming, jeering youths and adults, a speaker from the Union Movement was urging his excited audience to 'get rid of them' (the coloured people). Groups of policemen stood at strategic points carefully watching the 'meeting', while police cars and Black Marias waited round the corner. Suddenly, hundreds of leaflets were thrown over the crowd, a fierce cry rent the air and the mob rushed off in the direction of Latimer Road, shouting, 'Kill the niggers!' Women grabbed their small children and chased after their menfolk. Dogs ran in among the crowds barking. Everywhere there was riotous confusion. Police cars and vans wheeled out to cut off the mob. Meanwhile other police cars and vans in the area stood by to deal with the impending wave of violence.

Within half an hour the mob which had by now swelled to uncontrollable numbers had broken scores of windows and set upon two negroes who were lucky to escape with cuts and bruises. Women from the top floor windows laughed as they called down to the thousand strong crowd, 'Go on boys, get yourself some blacks.' As the crowd swung into Blenheim Crescent milk bottles rained down from tenement roofs where coloured men were sheltering. Accompanied by a dozen bottles, down came a petrol-bomb in the middle of the mob. One eighteen-year-old youth was led away with blood streaming from a head wound. Unable to get at their attackers, the inflamed rioters moved off to vent their wrath on other coloured men. Whilst the mob was active in another street, a young boy of five was dragged off his bicycle in Westbourne Park Road, and beaten up by coloured men. The news spread like wildfire through the streets until it reached the ears of the rioters. Screaming for revenge they broke off from their window smashing. The mob was now moving towards Ladbroke Grove. Cars and lorries were halted as the inflamed rioters poured across the main road into Westbourne Park Road. One youth at the head of the mob ran straight into a passing car in his enthusiasm for window smashing and blood. He was taken to hospital with a suspected broken leg. Once in Westbourne Park Road the rioters, hundreds strong, swore and shouted at a house where West Indians lived. Scores of milk bottles were hurled through the air, smashing the windows where coloured men had appeared. Broken glass and bricks were strewn across the road. The rioters left to continue their rampage through the streets.

Apart from the mob itself, smaller groups of fifteen to twenty were moving around the district independently. All through the evening, gangs of hooligans from all over London came to join in. They came on foot, by train, bus, motorbike, car and lorry, shouting, 'Alright boys, we're here.' Those on motorbikes and in cars toured the district looking for coloured people. When they found them they went back to tell their friends. In this way I saw many coloured people suddenly pounced on . . . Stopping in Talbot Grove I talked to a group of cheerful housewives and their husbands. I was told that they were expecting a gang of negroes, led by a female brothel-keeper, to come down and set on them. As we chatted amicably on the doorstep, a woman shouted, 'Here comes Madame.' Men and women alike pulled out railings and iron bars. Some grabbed milk bottles. A solitary coloured man ran down the street being pelted with bottles. When the excitement had subsided, one woman breathed a sigh of relief and said, 'Wrong ones.'

The riots petered out on 5 September. Race hatred in London did not.

Suburban Life:
Mr and Mrs Matthews in Woodford, October 1959
Peter Willmott and Michael Young

From Willmott and Young's *Family and Class in a London Suburb*:

*H*OME AND WORK place are certainly separated by distance. Of the 572 people in the general sample who were in paid work, 76 per cent worked outside the borough. Taking London as a whole the average time taken from door to door in the journey to work was 42 minutes, in Woodford many people have much longer to go than that.

'I have to walk to the station first of all. It takes me altogether an hour and a half to get to work and more to get home at night. They push them into the trains like sardines. I can't even read my evening paper till Leytonstone, there's such a crush.'

What the wife does in Essex and the husband in London are quite different. Here are some extracts taken every three-quarters of an hour or so from the diaries written by a teacher and his wife for a particular Thursday morning in October 1959.

MR MATTHEWS

7.15 a.m.

Got up reluctantly when the alarm rang. Went downstairs, put the dog out and made a pot of tea, taking a cup to Doris. Took my own cup of tea into the bathroom, while I washed and shaved. Finished dressing and then downstairs to breakfast.

MRS MATTHEWS

Frank brought me my usual cup of tea in bed. Got up and went down in my dressing-gown to get his breakfast. Said good morning to our little Sealyham, Dennis – he rolls on his back and waits for me to tickle him.

8 a.m.

Left the house. A brisk walk to the station as usual – otherwise I would miss the train that goes through Snaresbrook at about 8.10. Bought my *Times* at the station bookstall, where I have one ordered. Read *The Times* on the train and was irritated by being turned out at Leytonstone to wait for another.

Frank left for work and Dennis and I walked to the gate to see him off. Waited until Frank had disappeared round the bend in the road, then went indoors and called the children and prepared their breakfast.

8.45 a.m.

Arrived at school. Collected the classroom key and went to unlock door. Eastwood and Good, who are monitors, were waiting outside the

Got Susan ready for school and took her round there. Then went on to the shops. On the way back saw Mrs. Rayburn, who has been ill door as usual. Took my coat to the staff room, and when I got back found that most of the other boys had arrived. Took the register and went up to Assembly with the class. The Head announced the times of the Record and Chess clubs, but as usual no one could hear him.

with flu – I stopped to ask her how she was feeling.

9.15 a.m.

Returned to classroom for first period. Awaited arrival of 4C, which takes ten minutes longer than anyone else. We made a start on the trial scene from *The Merchant of Venice*; they seemed to get the general feeling of it well, but will they understand most of the detail when we come to examine it more carefully next week?

Arrived home. Combed Dennis, then did the bed-making, then started on the dishes. I like to see the bright cheerful colours of the plates emerge from the soapy water. 'House-wives' Choice' on the radio also cheers me up.

10 a.m.

Second Period. I took the Second-year 6th A-level group. Harrington announced that he did not intend to go on to do S-level after all, because his

My friend Joyce called. She wanted to know if I would go over to her house for tea that afternoon, instead of the next day, as previously arranged. I agreed. We parents couldn't afford any more years at school. I tried to dissuade him and the period developed into quite a discussion.

started a discussion about washing machines.

10.45 a.m.

Morning break. I went to the staff room for tea. Talked with Anderson about two boys in my class. He says he caught them fighting quite violently yesterday. This might not matter so much if they were younger, but they are 16. Anderson and I discussed tactics – which made a change from the interminable political discussions we've had lately in the staff room.

Joyce having gone, I took Dennis out for his morning walk in the Forest. We have made a lot of friends on these walks – dog-owners seem to find it very easy to get talking to each other. Saw my friend Shirly out with her Dachshund, Oscar. We stopped for a chat about the party we both were at last Saturday.

Obviously it is not easy for Mr. and Mrs. Matthews to share their interests in the way they would if they ran a farm together. Mrs. Matthews likes to hear about the people her husband works with; she is not thrilled to hear about S-level candidates, and even if she were once, the excitement would not last long.

Mr and Mrs Matthews had never had it so good. The late 1950s and early 1960s were London's age of affluence. Building boomed, partly because 100,000 families had been deprived of their homes by Hitler and partly because of 'slum clearances', where utopian planners replaced traditional housing with concrete tower blocks (384 of which were built between 1964 and 1974). Manufacturing boomed too. Only six miles or so from Woodford, Ford's car plant at Dagenham was turning out 250,000 cars a year. Mr Matthews preferred to catch the train to work, but a Ford Zodiac or a Cortina was a feasible purchase for the working as well as the middle classes. London lived in a virtuous economic circle: Londoners spent their wages on consumer goods often made in London itself.

❧ ❧ ❧

Speakers' Corner, c. 1963
Heathcote Williams

THE FIRST SPEAKER arrives: Robert Mathews of the Coloured Workers Welfare Association. He buys a cup of tea, and then wanders back across the tarmac to fetch his platform, with his cracked bowler hat on one side of his head and his briefcase, tied onto his waistband, hanging round his knees.

The West Indian known as Jahweh arrives in his white coat, dabbling with the calico strings of his wooden harp. He stands by the gate, opens his hebrew bible and begins to chant from it. His mouth begins to lather, his ringleted hair shakes in the wind. He gathers a crowd.

Van Dyn comes in the East Gate dragging his tea chest. He sits down on it, sorts out his newspaper cuttings, and wanders across to the catering stall to buy a cup of tea with no milk and five lumps of sugar. He looks about for the police and tries to sell some handbills with his photograph on them. They advertise a selection of tattoo artists, none of whom ever tattooed Van Dyn. He walks back to the tea chest, stomping the discarded paper cups with his heels. He screeches, kicks an oil drum across the tarmac and starts his meeting.

The man with the silent message hooks a milk crate from under the refreshment stall with his umbrella, brings it into the open, mounts it and reads his newspaper.

Mathews returns, drinks his tea with both hands for he has no fingers, erects his platform, climbs up on it and knocks the board at the top of it with his stumps shouting: OPPOSITION! COME ON ... OPPOSITION! COME ON POOR WHITE BASTARD, POOR WHITE TRASH, COME ON ... OPPOSITION ... He gathers a crowd.

The park fills.

Platforms, notices and banners slowly rise above the heads of the listeners: THE END IS NIGH in slab letters on flapping sail cloth; THE COMMUNIST PARTY OF GREAT BRITAIN; THE PROTESTANT TRUTH SOCIETY; THE SALVATION ARMY; THE MOVEMENT FOR FREEDOM IN KASHMIR; THE CATHOLIC EVIDENCE GUILD; THE MOVEMENT OF PAN-AFRICAN EXPONENTS AND OF PEOPLES OF AFRICAN DESCENT, and beneath it: GIVE US THE LIBERTY TO KNOW, UTTER AND TO ARGUE FREELY ACCORDING TO CONSCIENCE ABOVE ALL LIBERTY; THE NATIONAL SECULAR SOCIETY; THE EX-SERVICE MOVEMENT FOR PEACE; THE NATURAL LAW RELIGION; POBLACHT OIBRITHE IN EIREAN AR GCUSPOIR: THE CAUSE OF LABOUR IS THE CAUSE OF IRELAND, written awkwardly on a board, the outside layer of wood corrugated with the rain; THE SOCIETY FOR EVANGELIZING LONDON; HOW THE WAR OFFICE ROBS INVENTORS; Stanley Broder's INDIVIDUALISM; and then the faint syllogism of the Church Army: GOD loves you. GOD wants you. YOU need God.

Winston Churchill Lies in State,
January 1965
John Stewart Collis

IT WAS THE last week of January 1965. Churchill's funeral took place on Saturday 30 January. The Lying in State lasted throughout the previous fortnight. The queue, starting from the gates of the House of Commons, curled round over Westminster Bridge, then along Lambeth Palace Road, thence over Lambeth Bridge to Millbank leading to Westminster Hall in which the catafalque was placed. I understood that it meant about four hours in the queue before reaching the Hall. It flowed on throughout every day and every night.

It occurred to me that this was one of those historic occasions in which it would be good to participate. I was living in Ewell in Surrey at the time, and I thought that if I drove up on the Tuesday of the second week in the middle of the night, arriving at about 3 a.m., the queue would surely be short, and I wouldn't have to join it for more than an hour before reaching the catafalque. So I went up and parked my car in the vicinity of Parliament Square – for no policeman was making the slightest objection as to where one put a car on this occasion.

I hastened to walk across the Square and was pleased to find no queue in sight. Then in high spirits I walked quickly over Westminster Bridge, and turned to the right into Lambeth Palace Road – to be confronted almost at once by an enormously wide queue, a long distance from the bridge. My heart sank. It is an eccentricity of mine to do things on impulse without taking simple precautions. It was a cold night, and I was wearing only a light overcoat and thin socks, and absolutely the wrong kind of shoes. By the time I had reached Lambeth Bridge, I had become alarmed by my predicament, but hoped that I would make it.

I looked round at this great queue of people, so long and wide. Many were young and must have been children during the war, perhaps not yet born at its outset. Many others were middle-aged – they had heard that voice coming to them over the wireless, whether to groups or into lonely rooms. Twenty years had passed since the final triumph of this man. But neither the young nor the middle-aged were thinking of those last years, but of what he had been, of what he was in their imagination. He was the man who had overcome Hitler. He had promised nothing. He did not rant. He never smiled. There was melancholy in his cadence, and there was understanding of simple people when he spoke of 'that bad man over there'. Now his body was soon to disappear from the surface of the earth.

I spoke to nobody, and I heard no memorable remark. It had become very cold. I welcomed this. It was far more appropriate for the sombre scene than a warm summer night would have been. But on account of my faulty clothing I became anxious. Something must be done. After we had at last crossed Lambeth Bridge, the queue took an enormous loop around a Green before joining Millbank. In the middle of this Green a marquee had been erected to serve the purposes of a lavatory. I had a hat on and it occurred to me that if I stepped out of my place in the queue, entered the tent, and then emerged hatless from it, I could join the far end of the loop without attracting any notice. And indeed I did accomplish this quite easily.

This reprehensible tactic cut out at least an hour of my queue-crawling, yet it was not until 6.30 a.m. that I was able to mount the steps of Westminster Hall and go inside. What a change! I came into wonderful warm air and a cathedral peace. A long staircase led down to the floor of the great hall in which the catafalque stood. Our queue, the river of people come to pay homage to Churchill, flowed slowly down this long staircase. We were not chivvied by any policemen, there was no 'keep moving, please', all was discreet courtesy. In fact I paused on my way down and stood still to watch something. There were four sentinels stationed at the catafalque, one at each corner. They were relieved at regular intervals by fresh guards. It was my good fortune while descending the stairs to see a relief party in action.

From a door on the left side of the catafalque, and higher up, four sentinels appeared. The other four standing by the coffin had their rifles in the 'at ease' position, their legs apart, their heads bowed. They were motionless as any statue. Gradually the four men from above, in obedience to no verbal command, with incomparable grace of movement, each soundlessly approached the separate sentinels, and stood behind them. Then quietly the statues came to life; their limbs assumed slow motion; their bowed heads were raised: silently they came to attention and sloped arms, and each with the same rhythm left the catafalque by the way the others had come – who now slowly ordered arms, stood at ease, bowed their heads, until their figures too were frozen.

After passing the catafalque I stopped before the exit to look back at the steady stream of people descending the stairs. That stream had flowed during all the previous week, night and day, and would continue day and night until the ending of this second week.

As I left the Hall I stumbled and fell to the ground. Two policemen quietly restored me to the perpendicular. This indignity did not bother me at all. I had seen something I would not forget. After seventeen years I put it in words now as if, for me, it had been yesterday. There was a message too, could I but read it, as to the meaning of Homage and of Leadership.

Like Victoria's death six decades before, Churchill's passing marked the end of an era. Austerity London was out, Swinging London was in.

ℋ ℋ ℋ

The Sixties: Swinging London, April 1965
John Crosby

In spring 1966 *Time*'s front cover read 'London – The Swinging City'. Inside, Piri Halasz breathlessly announced that, 'In a decade dominated by youth, London has burst into bloom. It swings, it is the scene.'

Halasz' phrase 'Swinging London' stuck in the world's mind but London's cultural revolution had already been identified and pinned to the specimen board a year before by John Crosby in the *Weekend Telegraph* (somewhat ironically, since the *Telegraph* was the epitome of the staid, bowler-hatted, snobbish London the revolution was meant to be *against*). A mini-boom had put money in teenage pockets and years of grey rationing had put a desire for colour in teenage hearts. The city's fashion garment industry was ideally placed to provide for the new 'Mod' image, while the perversity of Liverpool as the beacon of the new 'pop' music was soon overcome: the Beatles relocated to London as quickly as they decently could, some boys from Deptford formed the Rolling Stones, while the Small Faces and the Who showed themselves to be the rock poets of the 'My Generation'. So, the capital got the music too. Sex and drugs were easily arranged. The 'pill' facilitated sex without procreation, while other pills (supposedly) enhanced recreation.

Some observers had seen it all coming; looking at the skiffle, jazz and beat clubs of Soho in 1958, the London writer Colin McInnes had noted: 'Contemporary England ... has produced ... the dullest society in western Europe: a society blighted by blankets of negative respectability, and of dogmatic domesticity. The teenagers don't seem to care for this, and have organized their underground of joy.'

In 1965 the underground went overground. The revolution was classless. For the first time since the Blitz, the two cities of London – the rich and the poor – shared the same space.

Fly me to the moon and let me play among the stars
Let me know what spring is like on Jupiter and Mars

A N AMERICAN GIRL from Natchez, Mississippi, singing at the new Cool Elephant. Blue walls. Cigarette smoke. The gleam of a trombone through the nightclub blackness.

At Annabel's in Berkeley Square are the elegant crowd – the Duchess of Northumberland, Frank Sinatra when he's in town, King Constantine dancing with his young queen, Anne-Marie, Aristotle Onassis, a sprinkling of Saudi Arabians, perhaps Princess Margaret. In Soho, at the Ad Lib, the hottest and swingingest spot in town the noise is deafening, the beat group is pounding out *I Just Don't Know What to Do with*

Myself, on the floor, under the red and green and blue lights, a frenzy of the prettiest legs in the whole world belonging to models, au pair girls or just ordinary English girls, a gleam of pure joy on their pretty faces, dancing with the young bloods, the scruffy very hotshot photographers like David Bailey or Terry Donovan, or a new pop singer – all vibrating with youth. At the corner table more or less permanently reserved for the Beatles (you'll always find at least one of them there when they're in town) Ringo proposes to Maureen (that's where he did it).

These are for the rich and famous. But London's throbbing nightlife has room for everyone. At the Marquee, a jazz club, non-alcoholic, on Wardour Street, you'll find the young kids from the offices. The Scene on Great Windmill Street brings in the Mods. Ronnie Scotts in Soho is a classless place – the sons of dukes and working men rubbing elbows in mutual appreciation of jazz; the Flamingo, a beat spot, caters to the West Indians.

Diana Vreeland, who as editor of *Vogue* is almost supreme arbiter of taste in America, has said simply, 'London is the most swinging city in the world at the moment' – putting into words what a lot of us Americans living here have long felt. The young bloods from Madrid and Rome – for reasons they only dimly understand – suddenly converge on London. London is where the action is, as New York and then Paris were right after the war, as Rome was in the mid-Fifties. Now it's London – the gayest, most uninhibited, and – in a wholly new, very modern sense -most wholly elegant city in the world. It seems to me that the last people to find it out are the Londoners themselves, under whose nose these changes in mood and tone have taken place, almost imperceptibly over the past four or five years.

> *Fill my heart with song, let me sing for ever more*
> *You are all I long for, all I worship and adore*

There's a quality of eager innocence in that old song and that's exactly the tone of London's nightlife. In an English girl's eyes is a starry innocence only possible in an island that has not been invaded for 1,000 years. Behind the dark-eyed invitation in a French girl, a Spanish girl, an Italian girl, there always lies a hint of wariness, a tiny veil of distrust, the ancient memory of ancient rapes, forgotten pillage.

I asked Leslie Linder, proprietor of those Elephants, The White Elephant (restaurant), and the Crazy and Cool Elephants, both night-clubs, what made London a swinging town. He answered simply and immediately. 'It's the girls. Italian and Spanish men are kinky for English girls. When I opened The White Elephant we had the prettiest girls I ever saw.'

Mark Birley, the immensely tall and coolly elegant owner of the coolly elegant Annabel's says the same thing. 'The girls are prettier here than anywhere else – much more so than in Rome or Paris.'

They're more than pretty; they're young, appreciative, sharp-tongued, glowingly alive. Even the sex orgies among the sex-and-pot set in Chelsea and Kensington have youth and eagerness and, in a strange way, a quality of innocence about them. In Rome and Paris, the sex orgies are for the old, the jaded, the disgusting and disgusted. Young English girls take to sex as if it's candy and it's delicious.

England, in fact, is getting something of a corner on all the pretty girls who are flying in from all the other capitals of Europe. 'The au pair girls started all that,' says Leslie Linder. 'All these pretty young chicks from Sweden and Denmark. London is getting very Continental. We've got all these French chicks. Spanish chicks, German chicks. Of course,

Rome has a lot of foreign chicks, too, but it seems to me the girls are nicer here and more natural: In Rome, all the chicks are grabbing – they want to be film stars or they want to marry a millionaire. Here, they're just students or au pair girls. They don't want anything except to be girls. It's a healthier atmosphere than either Rome or Paris.'

The deluge of pretty girls is on all levels. Betty Kenward, who writes the social column under the name of Jennifer for *Queen* magazine, points out, 'The young King and Queen of Greece may fly in for a ball and that brings in all those young princesses from Holland or Denmark. Then there are so many international marriages. Tina Onassis, a Greek, married to the Marquess of Blandford. Lord Bessborough is married to a chic American girl. So is Kenneth Keith. Young David Montagu has a charming young French wife. We have charming young Italian wives, charming Spanish wives – and they all bring in their friends from their countries of birth.'

The nightlife is just a symptom, the outer and visible froth, of an inner, far deeper turbulence that boiled up in Britain around – if we must date it – 1958, though some are astounded at what is happening. Why – they say – is this happening here and not in America, and they go right home and start young men's shops in their own stores.

There's a revolution in men's clothes here that is very much part of the London swinging scene, partly because it's adding so much dash and colour and glamour to the London street scene, but also as a sign of deeper social turmoil that is transforming England, especially among the young. English men's clothes were once almost uniform: staid, sober and, above all, correct, advertising your precise rung on the social ladder and even your bank account. Today the working-class boys – many of them fresh out of the Army or Navy and in full revolt against conformity of dress – their pockets full of money, are splurging on suede jackets, skin-like tweed trousers, double-breasted pin-striped suits (the very latest mode) with two buttons – or perhaps six. The impact of Carnaby Street is becoming worldwide. Tony Curtis wears Carnaby Street clothes. So do Peter Sellers and the Beatles.

The same thing on a different social and income level can be seen at Blades in Dover Street where the custom-made suits cost £52. At Blades the clothes have an elegance and a sort of look-at-me dash not seen since Edwardian times. On the racks I found, just as an example of what goes on there, a jet black velvet dinner jacket – trousers the same material – with a mandarin collar and buttons that I would never have the courage to wear.

A typical customer of Blades is Hercules Bellville, not long out of Oxford, who swathes himself in brown corduroy of velvety texture, long skirted, with waspish pants, which he tops with a short fur-collared coat. Fully assembled, with his flowing blond hair and almost classical good English looks, Hercules looks like something straight out of Max Beerbohm.

The proprietor of Blades is Rupert Lycett-Green, and both he and Bellville typify the revolt of the upper-class young. Bellville toiled in advertising a while, a socially acceptable occupation, then threw the whole thing up to get into movie-making. He's an assistant-assistant director now, frequently out of work, but he's doing what he wants.

Lycett-Green worked for a bit in the family engineering firm in the north of France. Two years ago, he quit and started Blades with his own money. After a shaky start it is doing quite well.

'Twenty-five years ago,' says Lycett-Green, 'young people would be almost afraid to speak out and do something like this with their money. They'd have followed their fathers into the City, or estate management. Now the young people want to see what they can do on their own. Some of my friends have started their own insurance companies, their own restaurants or their own nightclubs. They're all doing what they want to do, not what's expected of them.'

Another case is Noel Picarda, another Oxonian, who comes from a long line of lawyers. His father and brothers are barristers and they wanted Noel in the law firm, too. But he's in love with show business and he's performing at the Establishment, writing and appearing in sketches at the Poor Millionaire and has started a talent agency.

Richard de la Mare, grandson of Walter de la Mare, declined a nice safe job in the publishing house of Faber & Faber, where his father is chairman, to undertake the extremely precarious and not at all lucrative task of making *avant garde* films like *Carousella* about the life of strip-teasers.

The caste system, in short, is breaking down at both ends. The working-class young are busting out of the lower depths and invading fields where they can make more money and the upper-class is breaking down walls to get into the lower levels where they can have more fun. Caroline Charles says: 'Here they're so much more democratic than America – everybody mixes!' It's the bounce and vitality of these youngsters, both upper and lower class, that contributes most of the fizz to London.

De La Mare observed also, 'My mother told me that, after she and my father were married for about five years, they settled down. But she says that my wife and I have been married five years and haven't settled down. By settling down, they mean moving to the country, playing golf and raising roses and children. The young marrieds don't settle down like that any more. They keep right on swinging right here in London.'

This has changed the nature of their entertaining much for the better, according to *Queen*'s Mrs Kenward. English upper-class dinner parties used to be renowned for the quantities of servants and the tastelessness of the food. Now, the servants have disappeared and the food is much better. Mrs Kenward credits the late Constance Spry who taught many of the young brides how to cook. 'Cooking is much better than it was,' she said, 'Young married couples know how to entertain much better – without staff or with temporary staff.'

Much of the stuffiness, in fact, has been knocked out of the Royal entertaining. The Queen's party for Princess Alexandra and Angus Ogilvy was a really swinging affair that went on to the wee hours, my American friends who attended it told me. Those used to be dreary affairs. Not long ago, Prince Charles and Princess Anne gave a twist and shake party for their young friends at Windsor Castle. Princess Margaret is usually found with actors, writers or painters rather than Guards officers.

London, says Leslie Linder – and everyone else – has lost its reputation as a bad food city. Largely, I suspect, because the English are travelling abroad more, they are demanding and getting better food in the restaurants. The young swingers prefer the little restaurants – places like Trattoria Terrazza in Soho, Pavilion or Au Pere de Nico in Chelsea, or Chanterelle on Old Brompton Road – rather than the stuffier big places like the Savoy Grill which used to get the play. The White Tower on Percy Street has magnificent food and superb wines for the well-heeled. Tiberio's Italian food is marvellous. Even the penniless young ones eat better – at Buzzy's Bistro under the footpath on King's Road, Chelsea, or at Hades in Exhibition Road, South Kensington, where the girls are beautiful, the prices rock bottom and the food not at all bad.

The most astonishing change of all to me is the muscular virility of England's writers and dramatists and actors and artists – this from an island we'd mostly thought of in terms of Noel Coward and drawing-room comedy. English plays used to be jaded, fey, rococo – and so were the actors. Now, it's all anger, sweat and the working classes, and expresses the vitality and energy and virility among the young people I meet.

Vitality was the keynote of *Tom Jones* which made a fortune (for the Americans because the British film companies didn't have the sense to invest in it) and was also one of the principal ingredients of the James Bond film *Goldfinger* which has already earned £7,800,000 and of *Lawrence of Arabia* and the Beatles film – all British-written, directed and acted. (And all of them American-owned. Why haven't you British any faith in your own writers and directors and actors?)

Talent is getting to be Britain's greatest export commodity. Not long ago, the New York film critics made their nominations for the year's best acting and every last actor was English (and two of the actresses were English, too.) In Paris, at New Jimmy's or at Kastel's, they dance now to the records of the Beatles or Cilla Black or the Rolling Stones where only a year ago the music came from Frank Sinatra, Tony Bennett and Dean Martin – all Americans.

The new National Theatre has presented almost casually one masterpiece after another, from *Uncle Vanya*, which was described as the supreme achievement of the English stage, to *Othello*, a somewhat more controversial masterpiece. To a theatregoer, the variety to pick from is sumptuous. And in that great pile of red plush and crystal chandeliered elegance, Covent Garden, Kenneth Macmillan has unveiled a wholly new, very renaissance, very masculine version of Prokofiev's *Romeo and Juliet*. The theatres themselves with their 19th-century opulence and curves and charm are a perennial lure to visitors.

This explosion of creative vitality, a sort of English renaissance, has occurred on the very highest levels, as well as the more frivolous ones. On the topmost sphere of pure thought. Fred Hoyle, the Cambridge astronomer, has just advanced a theory about the physical nature of the universe as sweeping in its implications as those of Copernicus, Newton or Einstein.

Several theories have been suggested as to why all this is happening, where all this explosion of creative energy came from. It has been suggested that England, shorn of its world-wide responsibilities for keeping the peace, has turned its energies, previously dissipated in running the colonies, inward toward personal self-expression.

I think this is quite true but there's another factor. The English, I think, had a long Dark Age which started in the depression of the Thirties, continued through the long and terrible war and culminated in a long period of austerity, much longer than anyone else's. Longer even than Germany's, that didn't end really until about 1958. After any prolonged darkness, the Middle Ages, or the Napoleonic Wars, there's a renaissance, a flowering, a release of pent-up energy – and London is right in the middle of it.

Or perhaps just at the beginning. Most of these kids, who are starting dress shops or writing songs or making films, are in their twenties or early thirties. The best years, several decades of them, might well lie ahead when these talents mature.

Swinging London was meritocratic: a dustman might dance with a deb. The East End could go to the West End. Among those taking advantage of the new social mobility were some London villains called the Krays.

Gangland: The Shooting of George Cornell at the Blind Beggar, 9 March 1966

Ronald Kray

The Kray twins, Ronnie and Reggie, ran a Mafia-type gang ('the Firm') in the East End in the 1950s and 1960s. During a brief move into nightclub ownership in the West End they socialized with celebrities such as Diana Dors and Frank Sinatra. David Bailey photographed them.

George Cornell was a member of the Richardson gang from south of the river, and had been implicated in the shooting of the Krays' associate, Richard Hart. The Blind Beggar public house is situated in Whitechapel Road.

RICHARD HART HAD to be avenged. No one could kill a member of the Kray gang and expect to get away with it. The problem was, both of the Richardsons and Mad Frankie Fraser were in custody and likely to remain so. That left Cornell. He would have to be the one to pay the price. And, let's face it, who better? All I had to do was find him. The next night, 9 March, I got the answer. He was drinking in the Blind Beggar.

Typical of the yobbo mentality of the man. Less than twenty-four hours after the Catford killing and here he was, drinking in a pub that was officially on our patch. It was as though he wanted to be killed.

I unpacked my 9mm Mauser automatic. I also got out a shoulder holster. I called Scotch Jack Dickson and told him to bring the car round to my flat and to contact Ian Barrie, the big Scot, and to collect him on the way. As we drove towards the Blind Beggar, I checked that Barrie was carrying a weapon, just in case.

At eight-thirty p.m. precisely we arrived at the pub and quickly looked around to make sure that this was not an ambush. I told Dickson to wait in the car with the engine running, then Ian Barrie and I walked into the Blind Beggar. I could not have felt calmer, and having Ian Barrie alongside me was great. No general ever had a better right-hand man.

It was very quiet and gloomy inside the pub. There was an old bloke sitting by himself in the public bar and three people in the saloon bar: two blokes at a table and George Cornell sitting alone on a stool at the far end of the bar. As we walked in the barmaid was putting on a record. It was the Walker Brothers and it was called 'The Sun Ain't Gonna Shine Any More'. For George Cornell that was certainly true.

As we walked towards him he turned round and a sort of sneer came over his face. 'Well, look who's here,' he said.

I never said anything. I just felt hatred for this sneering man. I took out my gun and held it towards his face. Nothing was said, but his eyes told me that he thought the whole thing was a bluff. I shot him in the forehead. He fell forward on to the bar. There was some blood on the counter. That's all that happened. Nothing more. Despite any other account you may have read of this incident, that was what happened.

It was over very quickly. There was silence. Everyone had disappeared – the barmaid, the old man in the public and the blokes in the saloon bar. It was like a ghost pub. Ian Barrie stood next to me. He had said nothing.

I felt fucking marvellous. I have never felt so good, so bloody alive, before or since. Twenty years on and I can recall every second of the killing of George Cornell. I have replayed it in my mind millions of times.

After a couple of minutes we walked out, got into the car and set off for a pub in the East End run by a friend called

Madge. On the way there we could hear the screaming of the police car sirens. When we got to the pub I told a few of my friends what had happened. I also told Reg, who seemed a bit alarmed.

Then we went to a pub at Stoke Newington called the Coach and Horses. There I gave my gun to a trusted friend we used to call the Cat and told him to get rid of it. I suddenly noticed my hands were covered in gunpowder burns, so I scrubbed them in the washroom. I showered and put on fresh clothing – underwear, a suit, a shirt and tie. (We had spare sets of 'emergency' clothes at several places.) All my old clothing was taken away to be burned. Upstairs in a private room I had a few drinks with some of the top members of the firm – Reg, Dickson, Barrie, Ronnie Hart and others. We listened to the radio and heard that a man had been shot dead in the East End. As the news was announced I could feel everyone in the room, including Reg, looking at me with new respect. I had killed a man. I had got my button, as the Yanks say. I was a man to be feared. I was now the Colonel.

A year later Reggie Kray knifed to death Jack 'The Hat' McVitie, a minor member of his own gang, for failing to fulfil a contract 'hit'. The twins were tried for murder at the Old Bailey in 1969, where they were found guilty and sentenced to life imprisonment. Ronnie Kray died in 1995. Reggie Kray died of cancer in 2000.

Grosvenor Square, 17 March 1968
Dick Pountain and Mick Farren

Along with sit-ins at the London School of Economics and Hornsey College of Arts and Crafts, the demonstrations against the Vietnam War held in Grosvenor Square – site of the US Embassy – were the height of student protest in London.

DICK POUNTAIN: THE first one [Grosvenor Square demonstration], in March, turned into a real free-for-all afterwards – running down Park Lane, trashing cars and bank windows, very very heavy. We, the Situationists, actually had a presence on the march and made this huge banner that said 'Storm the Reality Studio and Retake the Universe'. Yellow letters on blue . . . it was very professionally done. We joined the march amidst all these Trots, all chanting 'Ho, Ho, Ho Chi Minh!' and we were chanting 'Hot chocolate, drinking chocolate!' and getting lots and lots of aggravation from all the Trots around us. And as we went past Hyde Park Corner this figure clad in black leather from head to foot came out of the crowd and joined us and it was Micky Farren and it was the first time I ever spoke to him.

MICK FARREN: Saturday night, we'd been playing somewhere like Mother's Club in Birmingham and we were coming back down the M1 and ran into these humungous police roadblocks and they pulled out all our equipment. We said, 'What the fuck do you want?' and they said, 'We're looking for weapons.' And we get back to London and me and Sandy plan to go to the riot the next day. So we got up about lunch-time, two o'clock as was our wont, and got our shit together. Nobody else could be bothered to go because they were still asleep. We went downstairs and there were maybe 50 motorcycle cops at the top of Endell Street and buses full of these geezers who look like they feed on vodka and raw meat and don't get let out except on riots. I thought, 'Mother-fucker! what's goin on here?' There weren't exactly tanks on the boulevards but … shit, it was like Chile or something. So we went marching up to Centrepoint where we ran into Miles and we hooked up with the march somewhere by Tottenham Court Road and Oxford Street.

We were marching along and there were reports that Mick Jagger had been seen and this was happening and that was happening and it was all very sort of aggressive. There were all sorts of Germans who were a real nuisance because they kept linking arms and getting into that run that the Japanese had invented. We didn't really want to go that fast – we'd just got up and we didn't feel too good and we didn't need a lot of mad Krauts doing the Japanese run, very disruptive, like Zulu impis getting wound up, and they kept doing these flurries of running on the spot which got people very excited to the point that somebody tried to nose his car out of somewhere like Berwick Street through the crowd and Miles kicked in his headlamps! I thought, 'Jesus!' Me and Sandy were coming down off speed and we weren't as rambunctious as a lot of people around us. We had just meandered along.

So we got to South Audley Street and started streaming down there and everything halts and nobody knows what's going on and there's all these rumours that they're tear-gassing people here and there (in fact they weren't). We hadn't seen the US Embassy yet, although there was another rumour that there were armed marines who'd kill you if you actually got inside. Then everything started to move and we went charging down Audley Street and it seemed like the police had given way, that's what everybody assumed. We arrived on the grass in Grosvenor Square, where, although I didn't know it at the time, we had immediately been surrounded. So there we have these thousands of people boxed in on the grass, though it's not that crowded, there's room to stroll around, except down the end by the Embassy where it's so crowded you can't see anything. And we just started wandering about and I remarked to Sandy, 'It's like a fucking love-in.' Then there was a thunder of hooves and there we were in the middle of the charge of the Light Brigade, which was fucking scary. What little I knew, basically from Napoleonic history, was get under a tree, because it's very hard to swing one of those truncheons when you're on a horse and the other guy is under a tree. So the first charge goes through and they're sort of whacking people and one geezer on a white horse, who became quite notorious, whacked this girl on the head – at which point everybody became exceedingly annoyed and dragged him off his horse and kicked him. He got away a couple of times but then he was surrounded and when everyone closed ranks he was just left there. And then people were hurling bits of turf and rocks and stuff and then they'd retreat and charge again and retreat and charge and people were getting hit and hurt and injured and then we went home. Just like that. And watched it on TV.

In 1968 Paris was shaken to its foundations by student protest. London could only manage some half-hearted 'demos', proving once again that London did not do political insurrection.

In truth, it did not do cultural revolution either. By the end of the 1960s it was apparent that 'Swinging London' was no such thing. It had been a trick of the light. As soon as the rain clouds of recession gathered over the economy Swinging London disappeared. Somehow the self-conscious, meretricious, would-be-daring nude revue staged by Ken Tynan only proved the point.

Oh! Calcutta!, *18 August 1970*
Frances Partridge

GEORGIA [TENNANT] TOOK me to Ken Tynan's pornographic revue *Oh! Calcutta!* at the Round House. I got there early and stood watching the mixed crowds coming in – self-conscious, demure, hearty and 'beat'. The show presented no surprise except perhaps that beautiful naked bodies are more beautiful when fully displayed and the bush is an adornment. There were some lovely girls, particularly a negress; two muscular Michael-Angelesque young men and two others that were flabby and unattractive. There was something inevitably phoney in the assumed lustfulness of their movement and dancing, when no male had the ghost of an erection. And the little sketches were despicably feeble, their prep-school humour sprinkled with defiantly uttered four-letter words. Could anything have been made of such a performance? Yes, if it had been (a) really funny and (b) really pornographic.

I got a fearful tickle in my throat and nearly expired of trying to stop coughing. Georgia thought I was upset by the performance, and said she was, and 'had no idea it would be all about SEX'. I'm not sure if I managed to convince her that

I was not in the faintest degree embarrassed, but I've had a brute of a summer cold for a fortnight and can't get rid of it.

1970s Britain became the 'Sick Man of Europe', with London at its head. The capital suffered an economic downturn greater than any other part of the nation. Manufacturing in London went into freefall. So did trade in and out of the Port of London. At their 1950s peak the docks employed 30,000; by the end of the 1970s they employed barely 2,000 men.

The tune of the times became cynicism. London heard it first.

❧ ❧ ❧

The Sex Pistols Play their First Gig, St Martin's Art College, 6 November 1975

Various

Punk rock was made in London. Specifically at SEX, the sado-masochist-influenced boutique on the King's Road, Chelsea, run by Malcolm McLaren and Vivienne Westwood. There McLaren introduced a band called The Strand (Steve Jones, Paul Cook, Glen Matlock) to a customer wearing an 'I Hate Pink Floyd' T-shirt, called John Lydon. After singing along to an Alice Cooper song on the jukebox Lydon got the job as vocalist.

John Lydon changed his name to Johnny Rotten. The enterprising McLaren changed the name of the band to the Sex Pistols.

GLEN MATLOCK *(Sex Pistols bassist. Now touring with Glen Matlock and The Philistines)*

*J*SET THE GIG up. I was at St Martins doing a foundation course. In the second year, I was going to be the social sec but over the summer holidays I decided to take the band seriously after John had joined that August, so I gave my place to someone else and, as I left, I blagged the gig with Bazooka Joe.

PAUL MADDEN *(photographer)*

I was at London College doing a printing course; a friend in the year below me said he was going to see Bazooka Joe at St Martins. We went down early at half seven. It was on the fifth floor in an open common room with no stage. There were no lifts and it was stairs all the way up. It was empty 'no tables or anything' pretty dark. There were no more than 40 people there. They were selling cheap white wine at 20p a cup. It was real throw-down-your-neck typical student ruin, really vile.

NICK WELLS *(St Martins student)*

The Sex Pistols were very loud and grubby. They were extremely unpleasant but you couldn't ignore them. It was a tiny little venue with students milling round the bar, no more than 100 at most. It was also very loud, as loud as Can who had been the loudest gig I'd ever been to before then.

PAUL COOK *(Sex Pistols drummer)*

We rehearsed across the road and wheeled all the equipment down Charing Cross Road at about six in the evening.

GLEN MATLOCK

So we had to push our gear through the rush-hour crowd. There was a frosty atmosphere and after four numbers someone pulled the plug on us because we were a horrible din and a bit of a fracas started.

PAUL MADDEN

Before they came on I thought, 'Who's that weird bloke with weird trousers on?' He was wearing peg-leg trousers and it was Malcolm McLaren. The trousers were baggy at the waist and going to nothing at the ankles. Very strange. He stood out a mile. He kept running back and forth. I thought, what's he so angry about? He was trying to start trouble. They had an attitude that was basically 'Fuck off, we're the Sex Pistols'. They were all going in the same direction at maximum speed.

PAUL COOK

We set up and played for 20 minutes. Total chaos. None of us knew what we were doing. We were very nervous and all over the place. We played 'No Lip', 'Satellite', 'Substitute', 'Seventeen', and 'What'cha Gonna Do About It'.

ADAM ANT *(aka Stuart Goddard, Bazooka Joe bass player)*

For their first gig, the Sex Pistols were support group to the band I was in, Bazooka Joe. I'll never forget it. They came in as a gang; they looked like they couldn't give a fuck about anybody. Jonesy was tiny, he looked like a young Pete Townshend. Matlock had paint-spattered trousers and a woman's pink leather top. I watched them play; Malcolm was at the front, orchestrating them, telling them where to stand. Viv[ienne Westwood] was there. They had a confidence in what they were doing, a cheeky-chappie confidence.

STEVE JONES *(Sex Pistols guitarist)*

It was fucking wild. I was so nervous I took a Mandrax. When we started playing, the Mandrax was hitting me and I cranked the amp up. It was a 100-watt amp in a little room with no stage and it was great. Everyone was looking at us. It seemed like millions of people at the time.

ADAM ANT

There weren't many there, maybe a dozen or so people, Jordan, Michael Collins, Andy Czezowski. They did 'Substitute,' and 'What'cha Gonna Do About It' with the lyrics changed, 'I want you to know that I hate you baby.' Then John lost interest. He'd eat sweets, pull them out and suck them and just spit them out. He just looked at the audience, glazed.

PAUL COOK

It must have been a terrible racket, because someone pulled the plug on us. There was a big fight. People yelled at us to get off because they wanted Bazooka Joe. We nearly had a fight with them. They thought we were an oddity because of our attitudes. We weren't being nice. That was the main difference between us and them.

NICK WELLS

Jeremy Diggle, who was the president of the students' union, switched them off, they had done their 20 minutes. It didn't seem that significant at the time.

JOHN LYDON

There was not one single hand clap. The college audience had never seen anything like it. They couldn't connect with where we were coming from because our stance was so anti-pop, so anti- everything that had gone before.

Soon Matlock would be replaced in the Sex Pistols line-up by another SEX customer, Sid Vicious.

London's role as the manufactory of punk was almost total. The short-lived London SS (the SS supposedly stood for Social Security in reference to the band's white proletarian background) produced both The Damned and The Clash, the latter providing late-1970s inner London with its signature soundtracks – 'White Riot', '(White Man) In Hammersmith Palais' and 'London Calling'.

But ultimately the sound and the fury of punk signified nothing. City commercialism co-opted it. Its resting place was the tourist postcard.

In fragmented, nihilistic 1970s London there were two cohesives – sport and royalty. They came together in the Queen's Silver Jubilee year in one potent patriotic moment.

Wade Wins Wimbledon, 1 July 1977
Frank Keating

VIRGINIA WADE IS the Wimbledon champion at last – and it didn't matter one jot that it was one of the worst finals in memory. The day will be long recalled for the ecstatic scenes at the very end when the Queen gave her the trophy and even starchy All England men and matrons relaxed upper lips and thunderously let go with 'For she's a jolly good fellow'. Whether the anthem was addressed to the Queen or Miss Wade they cared not a fig. And nor did England.

But, by jove, Miss Wade made the nation sweat as ever. She has been trying to win the thing for 16 years now and it was not until well into the afternoon that nails stopped being bitten. She beat the mountainous Dutch girl, Betty Stove, 4–6, 6–3, 6–1.

Miss Wade's first year at Wimbledon was in 1962 and coincided with the Queen's first visit. Afterwards Virginia said it had been so joyously noisy that she had not heard all the Queen had said to her at the end. 'It didn't matter, it was just great to see her lips moving.'

Rampant patriotism apart, it must be said that it was an awfully dank, dull match full of terrible unforced bloomers by both girls. The Queen's long-known aversion to lawn tennis cannot have been changed. Indeed she had pulled on her white gloves, was straightening her skirt, glancing at the clock and looking to get away to the tea-time racing results mid-way through the third set.

From the start both players were as nervous as field mice at harvesting, the Dutch girl seemingly the less so, for she won the first set – at the end of which you could probably hear the silence a mile away. It looked as if we were in for the biggest anti-climax since the *Titanic* similarly came across something large and unexpected all those years ago.

It was 3–3 in the second set before the despairing, muttered prayers of 14,000 people got through to their girl in the cathedral. It worked! Virginia reeled off seven games on the trot to take the second set and squat, unassailable, on a 4-0 lead in the last.

The power of prayer! Miss Wade's father, a retired archdeacon, also did his stuff. 'Yes,' he admitted before the match, 'I did pray for Virginia this morning.' Though he added after some meditative thought: 'But then I always pray for everyone each morning.'

꧁ ꧂

Enter Mrs Thatcher, 4 May 1979
Margaret Thatcher

Margaret Hilda Thatcher was elected leader of the Conservative Party in 1975.

W E KNEW WE had won by the early hours of Friday 4 May, but it was not until the afternoon that we gained the clear majority of seats we needed – 44 as it eventually turned out. The Conservative Party would form the next government.

There were many friends with me as we waited for the results to come in during those long hours in Conservative Central Office. But I can remember an odd sense of loneliness as well as anticipation when I received the telephone call which summoned me to the Palace. I was anxious about getting the details of procedure and protocol right; it is extraordinary how on really important occasions one's mind often focuses on what in the cold light of day seem to be mere trivia. But I was haunted by tales of embarrassing episodes as one prime minister left and his successor entered office: Ted Heath's departure from No. 10 was a case in point. I now could not help feeling sorry for James Callaghan, who just a little earlier had conceded victory in a short speech, both dignified and generous. Whatever our past and indeed future disagreements, I believed him to be a patriot with the interests of Britain at heart, whose worst tribulations had been inflicted by his own party.

At about 2.45 p.m. the call came. I walked out of Central Office through a crowd of supporters and into the waiting car, which drove Denis and me to the Palace on my last journey as Leader of the Opposition.

The Audience at which one receives the Queen's authority to form a government comes to most prime ministers only once in a lifetime. The authority is unbroken when a sitting prime minister wins an election, and so it never had to be renewed throughout the years I was in office. All audiences with the Queen take place in strict confidence – a confidentiality which is vital to the working of both government and constitution. I was to have such audiences with Her Majesty once a week, usually on a Tuesday, when she was in London and sometimes elsewhere when the royal family were at Windsor or Balmoral.

Perhaps it is permissible to make just two points about these meetings. Anyone who imagines that they are a mere formality or confined to social niceties is quite wrong; they are quietly businesslike and Her Majesty brings to bear a formidable grasp of current issues and breadth of experience. And, although the press could not resist the temptation to suggest disputes between the Palace and Downing Street, especially on Commonwealth affairs, I always found the Queen's attitude towards the work of the government absolutely correct.

Of course, under the circumstances, stories of clashes between 'two powerful women' were just too good not to make up. In general, more nonsense was written about the so-called 'feminine factor' during my time in office than about almost anything else. I was always asked how it felt to be a woman prime minister. I would reply: 'I don't know: I've never experienced the alternative.'

After the audience, Sir Philip Moore, the Queen's Secretary, took me to his office down what are called the 'the Prime Minister's stairs'. I found my new principal private secretary, Ken Stowe, waiting there, ready to accompany me to Downing Street. Ken had come to the Palace with the outgoing prime minister, James Callaghan, barely an hour before. The civil service already knew a good deal about our policies because they carefully scrutinize an Opposition's manifesto with a view to the hasty preparation of a new administration's legislative programme. Of course, as I quickly learnt, some senior civil servants would need more than a conscientious reading of our manifesto and a few speeches truly to grasp the changes we firmly intended to make. Also, it takes time to build up relationships with staff which reach beyond the formal level of respect to trust and confidence. But the sheer professionalism of the British civil service, which allows governments to come and go with a minimum of dislocation and a maximum of efficiency, is something other countries with different systems have every cause to envy.

Denis and I left Buckingham Palace in the prime ministerial car: my previous car had already gone to Mr Callaghan. As we drove out through the Palace gates, Denis noticed that this time the Guards saluted me. In those innocent days before security had to become so much tighter for fear of terrorism, crowds of well-wishers, sightseers, press and camera crews were waiting for us in Downing Street itself. The crowds extended all the way up Downing Street and out into Whitehall. Denis and I got out of the car and walked towards them. This gave me the opportunity to run through in my mind what I would say outside No. 10.

When we turned to the cameras and reporters, the cheers were so deafening that no one in the street could hear what I was saying. Fortunately, the microphones thrust in front of me picked it up and carried it over the radio and television.

I quoted a famous prayer attributed to St Francis of Assisi, beginning, 'where there is discord, may we bring harmony.' Afterwards a good deal of sarcasm was expended on this choice, but the rest of the quotation is often forgotten. St Francis prayed for more than peace; the prayer goes on: 'Where there is error, may we bring truth. Where there is doubt, may we bring faith. And where there is despair, may we bring hope'. The forces of error, doubt and despair were so firmly entrenched in British society, as the 'winter of discontent' had just powerfully illustrated, that overcoming them would not be possible without some measure of discord.

The election of a Conservative government under Margaret Thatcher had profound implications for London. The Greater London Council (GLC, the successor to the LCC) was headed by Ken Livingstone, a populist Labour politician bent on pursuing affirmative-action programmes for 'minorities' and a subsidized 'Fares Fair' transport policy that slashed Tube and bus fares. Mr Livingstone also had the pronounced habit of using the GLC as a platform to criticize the Conservative government's policies on nuclear armament and Northern Ireland.

All of the above were anathema to Margaret Thatcher, doyenne of traditional values and free enterprise. Soon Thatcher would deal with Livingstone, but first there were other enemies within London.

The SAS Storm the Iranian Embassy, Prince's Gate, 5 May 1980

Anonymous SAS Trooper

The Iranian Embassy was seized by terrorists demanding the liberation of Khuzestan on 30 April 1980. Five days later the terrorists started shooting their hostages; at this point a counter-terrorist team from 22 Special Air Service Regiment was ordered by the Conservative Home Secretary, William Whitelaw, to raise the siege.

W E TOOK UP a position behind a low wall as the demolition call sign ran forward and placed the explosive charge on the Embassy french windows. It was then that we saw the abseiler swinging in the flames on the first floor. It was all noise, confusion, bursts of submachine-gun fire. I could hear women screaming. Christ! It's all going wrong, I thought. There's no way we can blow that charge without injuring the abseiler. Instant change of plans. The sledge-man ran forward and lifted the sledge-hammer. One blow, just above the lock, was sufficient to open the door. They say luck shines on the brave. We were certainly lucky. If that door had been bolted or barricaded, we would have had big problems.

'Go. Go. Go, Get in at the rear.' The voice was screaming in my ear. The eight call signs rose to their feet as one and then we were sweeping in through the splintered door. All feelings of doubt and fear had now disappeared. I was blasted. The adrenalin was bursting through my bloodstream. Fearsome! I got a fearsome rush, the best one of my life. I had the heavy body armour on, with high-velocity plates front and back. During training it weighs a ton. Now it felt like a T-shirt. Search and destroy! We were in the library. There were thousands of books. As I adjusted my eyes to the half-light – made worse by the condensation on my respirator eyepieces – the thought occurred to me that if we had blown that explosive charge we might have set fire to the books. Then we would really have had big problems: the whole Embassy would have been ablaze in seconds.

The adrenalin was making me feel confident, elated. My mind was crystal clear as we swept on through the library and headed for our first objective. I reached the head of the cellar stairs first, and was quickly joined by Sek and two of the call signs. The entry to the stairs was blocked by two sets of step-ladders. I searched desperately with my eyes for any signs of booby-traps. There wasn't time for a thorough check. We had to risk it. We braced ourselves and wrenched the ladders out of the way.

Mercifully there was no explosion. The stairs were now cleared and we disappeared into the gloom of the basement. I fished a stun grenade out of my waistcoat and pulled the pin. Audio Armageddon, I thought as I tossed the grenade down into the darkness. We descended the stairs, squinting into the blinding flashes for any unexpected movement, any sign of the enemy, and then we were into the corridor at the bottom. We had no sledge, no Remington with us, so we had to drill the locks with 9-milly, booting the doors in, clearing the rooms methodically as we went along. Minutes turned into seconds; it was the fastest room clearance I'd ever done.

It was when I entered the last room that I saw the dark shape crouched in the corner. Christ! This is it, I thought. We've hit the jackpot. We've found a terrorist. I jabbed my MP5 into the fire position and let off a burst of twenty rounds. There was a clang as the crouched figure crumpled and rolled over. It was a dustbin!

Nothing, not a thing. The cellars were clear. I was now conscious of the sweat. It was stinging my eyes, and the rubber on the inside of the respirator was slimy. My mouth was dry and I could feel the blood pulsing through my temples. And then we were off again, no time to stop now, up the cellar stairs and into the Embassy reception area. As we advanced across the hallway, there was smoke, confusion, a tremendous clamour of noise coming from above us. The rest of the lads, having stormed over the balcony at the front and blasted their way into the first floor of the building with a well-placed explosive charge, were now systematically clearing the upper rooms, assisted by a winning combination of the stunning effect of the initial explosion, the choking fumes of CS gas, the chilling execution of well-practised manoeuvres and the sheer terror induced by their sinister, black-hooded appearance. We were intoxicated by the situation. Nothing could stop us now.

Through the gloom I could see the masked figures of the other team members forming into a line on the main staircase. My radio earpiece crackled into life. 'The hostages are coming. Feed them out through the back. I repeat, out through the back.'

I joined a line with Sek. We were six or seven steps up from the hallway. There were more explosions. The hysterical voices of the women swept over us. Then the first hostages were passed down the line. I had my MP5 on a sling around my neck. My pistol was in its holster. My hands were free to help the hostages, to steady them, to reassure them, to point them in the right direction. They looked shocked and disorientated. Their eyes were streaming with CS gas. They stumbled down the stairs looking frightened and dishevelled. One woman had her blouse ripped and her breasts exposed. I lost count at fifteen and still they were coming, stumbling, confused, heading towards the library and freedom.

'This one's a terrorist!' The high-pitched yell cut through

the atmosphere on the stairs like a screaming jet, adding to the confusion of the moment. A dark face ringed by an Afro-style haircut came into view; then the body, clothed in a green combat jacket, bent double, crouched in an unnatural pose, running the gauntlet of black-hooded figures. He was punched and kicked as he made his descent of the stairs. He was running afraid. He knew he was close to death.

He drew level with me. Then I saw it – a Russian fragmentation grenade. I could see the detonator cap protruding from his hand. I moved my hands to the MP5 and slipped the safety-catch to 'automatic'. Through the smoke and gloom I could see call signs at the bottom of the stairs in the hallway. Shit! I can't fire. They are in my line of sight, the bullets will go straight through the terrorist and into my mates. I've got to immobilize the bastard. I've got to do something. Instinctively, I raised the MP 5 above my head and in one swift, sharp movement brought the stock of the weapon down on the back of his neck. I hit him as hard as I could. His head snapped backwards and for one fleeting second I caught sight of his tortured, hate-filled face. He collapsed forward and rolled down the remaining few stairs, hitting the carpet in the hallway, a sagging, crumpled heap. The sound of two magazines being emptied into him was deafening. As he twitched and vomited his life away, his hand opened and the grenade rolled out. In that split second my mind was so crystal clear with adrenalin it zoomed straight in on the grenade pin and lever. I stared at the mechanism for what seemed like an eternity, and what I saw flooded the very core of me with relief and elation. The pin was still located in the lever. It was all over, everything was going to be okay.

But this was no time to rest, this was one of the most vulnerable periods of the operation, the closing stages. This is where inexperienced troops would drop their guard. The radio crackled into life. 'You must abandon the building.

The other floors are ablaze. Make your way out through the library entrance at the rear. The Embassy is clear. I repeat, the Embassy is clear.'

I joined Sek and we filed out through the library, through the smoke and the debris. We turned left and headed back for number 14, past the hostages, who were laid out and trussed up on the lawn ready for documentation, past the unexploded explosive charge, past the discarded sledgehammer and other pieces of assault equipment – all the trappings of battle in the middle of South Kensington. It was 8.07 p.m.

As we made our way through the french windows of number 14, the Gonze, ex-Para, a new boy in the regiment from one of the other call signs, removed his respirator and asked the Irish police sergeant on duty at the door what the Embassy World snooker score was. A look of total disbelief spread across the policeman's face and he just stood there shaking his head from side to side.

I crossed the room to my holdall and as I began pulling off my assault equipment I could feel the tiredness spreading through my limbs. It wasn't just the energy expended on the assault, it was the accumulation of six days of tension and high drama, of snatched sleep in a noisy room, of anxiety and worry over the outcome of the operation. I looked to my left. The Toad had just returned. He looked tired, his face was flushed and he was out of breath. He looked at me and shook his head. 'I'm getting too old for this sort of thing.'

'So am I,' I replied.

Within fifteen minutes most of the team members had stripped off their assault kit, packed it into their holdalls and parcelled their MP5s into plastic bags to be taken away for forensic examination. Before moving out through the front door of number 14 to the waiting Avis hire van, we had a dramatic visit from Home Secretary William Whitelaw, old Oyster Eyes himself. He stood before us, tears of joy unashamedly running down his cheeks, wringing his hands in relief. He thanked the assembled team members for what they had done for the country that day. 'This operation will show that we in Britain will not tolerate terrorists. The world must learn this.' It was a fine personal gesture and rounded the operation off perfectly.

⚜ ⚜ ⚜

The Brixton Riots, 10–12 April 1981
Martin Huckerby

Huckerby was a journalist on *The Times*.

AT 8 PM on Saturday night Brixton was burning. A pillar of smoke, hundreds of feet across, rose into the darkening sky; its base was tinged with red from the fires in Railton Road. Further north more smoke climbed from the blazing buildings in Brixton centre. Police in strength occupied the north end of Railton Road, and screened some of the side roads, but along much of the length of this street of sleazy shops, old terraced houses and derelict sites the mob ran wild. At the south end of Railton Road, at the junction with Shakespeare Road, there were no police. The only sign of authority was an abandoned fire engine astride the junction, its windows smashed and its wrecked, equipment strewn across the road. The view north up Railton Road was of an inferno, a tunnel of fire through the smothering smoke. Red hot debris dripped from a series of burning buildings along both sides of the road. Amid the roaring of the flames and crashing of collapsing buildings there were screams and shouts. Despite the furnace of heat, figures could be seen running through the smoke, hurling missiles at unseen police. At one point the splash of fire from an exploding petrol bomb pierced the swirling smoke. Three black men, one carrying a case of whisky, grabbed hold of me, wrenched my note-book away and hurled me away from the area, past a crowd of local residents, black and white together, standing watching the blaze in horror-struck silence.

At 8.15 pm, halfway along Railton Road, where Leeson Road links it to Mavall Road, the rioters ruled. At least five upturned cars, several burned out, stood in the short length of Leeson Road as running figures, mostly black but a few white, whirled back and forth. On the corner of Leeson Road and Mayall Road the three-storey Windsor Castle public house stood with smashed windows and broken down doors. The street outside was littered with broken bottles and an emptied cash register. From the top storey smoke began to trickle from a smashed window.

Some of the side streets leading into Railton Road from the west were the province of the rioters. I was chased out of Barnwell Road by a gang of shouting black youths; in the next street, Effra Parade, a police cordon barred the exit from Railton Road.

At 8.35 pm, the George public house, at the junction of Effra Parade and Railton Road, was being consumed with flames, a gutted fruit machine lying outside. Across the junction a car spares shop and a newsagents blazed in unison. In between stood a gutted fire engine, and around surged rioters and police, the latter trying to protect firemen as they sought to stem the flames.

At 8.40 two black men, both by no means youths, had been dragged out of the fighting and were loaded into a police van; one was screaming 'They are kicking me' when all the police were doing was marching him to the van. By 9.00 several police moved down Effra Road towards the centre of the riot, many lacking riot shields and equipped only with plastic milk crates or wooden boxes to protect themselves. Within minutes there was a line of police officers sitting with bandaged heads on the kerb beside a police first aid van. A woman emerged from a house nearby to offer drinks.

At 9.22 the Brixton shopping centre appeared almost calm by comparison to Railton Road. Rubbish was strewn across the main A23 Brixton Road; burglar alarms rang vainly from looted shops and knots of youths, black and white, drifted along in the almost complete absence of the police. Down the shopping street of Coldharbour Lane, linking the main road with Railton Road, fires burnt on both sides. In the main road, youths, boys and girls, black and white, climbed into the shattered windows of Dolcis shoe shop, calmly selecting particular shoes, before loading them into Dolcis carrier bags. Along Electric Avenue, the centre of the open air market, looters climbed in and out of shops, completely untroubled by the police.

By 9.30 one or two police stood nervously in Brixton Road. One uniformed constable said to a white teenager clutching four packets of cigarettes 'I don't want to know. I can't do anything about anything tonight.'

At 9.40 several dozen police with riot shields moved into Brixton Road from the south pushing through the mainly black crowds milling around. In the distance youths and older men could still be seen humping goods out of wrecked shops. As the police began clearing the entrance to Coldharbour Lane, two milk bottles came flying out of the retreating groups. A police constable was carried away unconscious by four of his colleagues. At 9.53 more police charged across Brixton Road, pursuing a group of youths into Brighton Terrace to the west. Private cars were still travelling along the main road, crashing over rubble and jinking to avoid running police. From Effra Road to the south a shower of rocks and bottles suddenly came flying in at the crowd and police alike. Waving truncheons, dozens of police rushed wildly in pursuit. More police, hastily brought in as could be seen from the white shoes of one constable, were gradually taking over the shopping centre but violence kept re-occurring. At 10.30 a freelance photographer, Mr Neil Martinson, of Hackney, was attacked by police with truncheons after he had taken pictures of them arresting a black man. His motor cycle jacket and helmet saved him from serious injury. By about 11 pm the violence and the looting began to die away. Police were posted outside the many looted jewellers, outside Woolworths where the aisles were covered with scattered sweets and cartons, outside Currys, where empty cartons for radios, calculators and food mixers filled the gutters. In Electric Avenue the street was awash with broken glass, smashed display cases, discarded jeans and sweaters, and empty Easter egg cartons. As least half the shops in the market area bore evidence of looting, or just pure destruction, as in the case of the Consumer Advice Centre. Away from that area of concentrated looting, the damage was less but many of the stores on Brixton Road had gaping windows and tumbled display cases. No jewellery shop appeared to have escaped unscathed.

By 11.15 Railton Road appeared quiet, littered with upturned burnt-out cars and at the north end covered with thousands of rocks and pieces of brick which had been taken from the adjoining derelict sites and hurled at police. Further south firemen continued to fight the fires, slowly bringing them under control. The Windsor Castle public house had virtually disappeared: just a pile of rubble lay where it had been, two broken gas mains flaring amid the debris. Eventually the firemen succeeded but too late to save most of the gutted buildings. At midnight they were still playing hoses on the smouldering wreckage In the centre of Brixton the streets were full of glaziers' vans, with the sound of men hammering boards over shattered windows almost drowning the still-ringing alarm bells. Along the gutters in the centre of Brixton there were fragments of glass and empty cartons smeared with blood, indicating that at least some of the looters paid a price for their spoils.

Who was to blame for the riots? The Archbishop of Canterbury, Dr Robert Runcie, despite being a conservative, irritated the Prime Minister by suggesting that the riots were not racial in cause but were manifestations of the hopelessness that existed amongst poor Londoners, caused by her monetarist policies. Neither did Runcie's *Faith in the City* report spare the 1960s architects whose concrete tower blocks dominated working-class estates: 'poor design, defects in construction ... no "defensible space" ... one or two shuttered shops, and main shopping areas a 20 minute expensive bus journey away.'

The Church proved to be a long-standing thorn in the side of Thatcherism. Another critic was more easily silenced. On 31 March 1986 the government abolished 'Red Ken' Livingstone's GLC. Norman Tebbit, Thatcher's most loyal lieutenant, who always had the merit of plain speaking, explained that the GLC was terminated because it 'was Labour-dominated, high-spending and at odds with the government's view of the world'. The GLC, in truth, had made itself an easy target, being a by-word for profligacy and 'loony Leftism' – the nadir being reached when the head of an infant school in Hackney banned her pupils from watching *Romeo and Juliet* because it was 'blatantly heterosexual'.

Whatever the reason, London was now the only capital in the West to not have its own government.

The GLC went out with a bang, holding a massive firework party outside County Hall. Across in the City, there was a 'Big Bang' of a different sort. On 27 October the City was deregulated. No longer was the City the site of small gentlemanly firms operating eons-old price-fixing cartels, it was an international casino where the game was stocks and shares. To prepare and run the deregulated system banks and brokerage firms paid bright young things handsome wages. So was born the 'Yuppie', the Young Urban Professional.

A favourite haunt of the Yuppie was the East End, then being redeveloped by the London Docklands Development Corporation into chichi housing and spangly glass office blocks. Or, at least, part of the East End was redeveloped – much of it remained untouched and hopeless.

Docklands: Days in the Life of a Bethnal Green GP, c. 1986–90

David Widgery

ANTENATAL CLINIC IN Hackney; only 'white' mother of the afternoon a nineteen-year-old Irish lass who is thin as a rake, marigold-haired and has a face like a crucifix. The others are a cheerfully polyglot mixture of Jamaican, Egyptian, Turkish, Sikh. Anarchist punk comes late dressed like a disintegrating tea cosy. Doesn't want to be examined. The woman consultant, strict and kindly, is distressed by the fact that so few of her patients are either married or Christian. The Turkish lady is lost in fear, pain and apprehension; her more experienced friend announces to me knowingly, 'She don't know what's coming.' The punk is enormously constipated. Boots holed and voluminous clothes smell of corporate squatting. Clinic walls have pictures of vegetables and eggs, useful ingredients of diet. 'Are you on a good diet?' the consultant asks. 'No, I don't want to lose weight.'

'I LIVE IN a block with fifty houses. There's only three men who don't wear a turban. Myself and an Irishman and an Egyptian,' says Edward Farthing. This is not true. But he has said it many times.

OUT-OF-DATE TATTOOS AND cracked knuckles. Heroin ... which means lost fathers, painful migrations, blocked veins and a succession of changes of address. Wants a letter for the court. Again.

CHRISTMAS HOME VISITS. Alka Seltzer and warm loathing. Pass print union picket line at Wapping; the union fulltimers are putting out the fires (literally). Baby cheered up by new arrival, bored by his circumstances. Exit strewn with litter and four or five supermarket trolleys buggering each other. Lift's surfaces tattoed with misspelt swearwords. Christmas wrapping and food packs blow up and down the corridors of concrete gloom. One flat made derelict full of broken machinery and rubble. In the corner broken mirrors and smashed reproduction portraits of big-eyed children that East Enders like. On way out, a cheerful pair stagger in: their fumes ignitable. A mess with people left to fight and love and laugh it out.

A BOY WITH stomach pain at 1 in the morning. Eventually decide he had eaten too much and proved right by prodigious vomiting over my trousers. Enter Teviot, ghoulish, low-rise corridors, past a smashed mountain bike, newish, as if masticated by giant jaws. Big graffiti: 'Beware. You Are Entering The Teviot Estate' which no-one has bothered to paint out. This one's probably only gastric flu but in view of the empty one-litre vodka bottle in the inbuilt bar may be dehydrated for other reasons. Then called about a baby which had been crying for four hours. It has 'just settled' by the time I arrived.

MR WALLER, EX-DOCKER. 'Downloader', went into hold with hook and ropes. Fruit, refrigerated meat, veg., nuts from Beirut, Damascus and Limassol. Via barge or bogies into the sheds and bays until the Covent Garden lorries picked them up. In turn reloaded boats with old axles, scrap metal, machinery. Registered here since 1916, born in the surgery road. Moved to Stepney, then Bow, then back to Rhodeswell Road according to ascent up housing ladder. Now has pernicious anaemia, skin with a citrus gleam.

Also woman obsessed by her desire for sexual events: a female Casanova. Another woman, acute anxiety, mothering son and husband. Then cross they can't stand up for themselves. Thin girl who turns out to have been a prostitute in Rugby of all places. 'Open the door less,' I say. 'Try shielding yourself from men.' Flotsam and jetsam: the female foot-soldiers of mental illness. Nothing grand, just everyday sadness.

THEN TO LADY of ninety-six who has just died. Already stiffening as family slowly assemble round the bed, formally like a wedding photo in a developing tank. Devout: the incense, nicotine. The older sister devastated; her mortality ablaze. Considerate district nurse, her blue uniform makes formal the loss. Me respectful of a body I never knew but will see again in a galvanised box in the undertaker's. After I sign the cremation form, a shifty man gives me £18 cash in a dirty brown envelope. I see him later chainsmoking in the cafe and obsessively playing the fruit machine. Save us from dodgy undertakers.

IN PEKING RESTAURANT LDDC executives are parcelling up the docklands' visual vistas for advertising clients. Arguing about percentages. 'We'll supply everything: film, catering, birds.' Getting drunker and noisier. 'Let's get bottom line on this. If you were me, what would you be thinking?' 'The world's your oyster here in Docklands. We run things. When we got your letter, our first reaction was, send in the heavy mob. Kick 'em. Then the more liberal among us said, let's talk to them, we can screw 'em afterwards.' Gangsters in pinstripes.

Outcast London in the time of Thatcher and Major did not end at the City and the greenbelt. By 1992 over 10 per cent of London's population subsisted on income support. Homelessness was endemic.

To the bewilderment of many Londoners, London ceased – at some indefinable point – to be an English city. It became a cosmopolis, with a babel of languages. Of London's population of 6.6 million two out of every six were born outside the UK.

And at some other impossible-to-pin-down point London had ceased to be a city with a street life, beyond shopping 'up West'. Fear of traffic (up by 20 per cent over the course of the 1980s) and fear of crime (reported incidents rose from 584,000 in 1979 to 834,000 in 1990) kept people inside, with their doors locked.

It was small wonder that many fled from the inner city to *beyond* the suburbs.

There were, however, some things that still brought London to the street.

✗ ✗ ✗

The Funeral Procession of Diana, Princess of Wales, 6 September 1997
Deborah Bull

THE MORNING OF Diana's funeral, and my friend David and I joined several thousand people in Hyde Park to watch her cortege pass by. It has been the most extraordinary occasion, the most comprehensive and controlled display of public grief I am ever likely to witness. It was a bright and sparkling day, and the simplicity of the horse-drawn gun carriage contrasted sharply with the glamour of Diana's life. But I am sensing a mood here in the country which I find unsettling, a mood which verges on anarchy. I hope 'the people' have thought about where this will take them; the funeral demonstrated the need for formality and tradition to hold us together in times of tragedy, and yet I'm strongly aware of a potentially destructive element in the emotions on display. Charles, Earl Spencer, Diana's brother, brought the house down at Westminster Abbey with his bold and emotional condemnation of the gross intrusions which plagued his sister's life, in particular her difficult relationship with the media and the Royal Family. As much as I admire him for saying so eloquently what he did, I cannot help feeling that this is not a time for division, unless his intention was revenge and the downfall of the monarchy. If those were his aims, he did very well indeed. If not, then he only achieved personal catharsis and a familial defence of Diana and her sons. There was something ancestral, almost Shakespearean about it. The 'people' applauded as one, and I know what the headlines will be in the morning. The broadsheets will ask serious questions about the future of the monarchy. The tabloids will probably herald the arrival on the scene of the people's choice of a new King Charles – except this one will be a Spencer, not a Windsor.

Diana may have been mortal, but the monarchy – despite the reservations of Bull and countless others – survived into another century. So too did one of London's other great institutions, despite the attempts of the IRA to bomb it to bits and of other countries to steal its business: the City.

The City had achieved its international status in the seventeenth century because of the expansion of the British economy and the nation's rise to imperial mastery. During the twentieth century the City's fortunes sank in line with the contraction of British trade. However, courtesy of the Big Bang of 1987 the City was able to establish highly-competitive, multi-purpose financial conglomerates that used electronic dealing technology instead of the old scrummage on the Stock Market trading floor. By the late 1990s the City was processing over $300 billion of exchange per day. The City had become the globe's capital for processing capital.

Like the City burghers of old, the City players of the twenty-first century celebrated their wealth and power in buildings.

Arisen from the Wreckage:
30 St Mary Axe, December 2003

Jonathan Glancy

THE DAY I visited 30 St Mary Axe, the City of London was smothered in a Dickensian mist. Norman Foster's 180m tour de force was all but invisible. Its spectacular top-floor bar offered panoramic views not of a great carpet of buildings patched with parks and threaded with rivers, but of nothing at all. Nothing, that is, save the eerie sight of spidermen absailing the outside of the great steel-and-glass sheath, fixing its 7,500 windows permanently into place ...

The poor weather was useful in that it concentrated my mind on the building itself rather than any mesmerising views. This seemed right. For this is an extraordinary building, one that every Londoner, every visitor to the capital, should want to get to know.

The curious have watched the skywards odyssey of this radical skyscraper since construction began in 2001 and have known about it for at least five years. It rises from the site of the former Baltic Exchange building bombed by the IRA in 1992. Last December, the skeletal structure was decorated like a Christmas tree. It was visible night and day from the least likely corners of the capital, above rooftops, scrapyards, marshes and motorways. Like the dome of St Paul's Cathedral, Canary Wharf and the future London Bridge Tower, designed by Renzo Piano, 30 St Mary Axe will define the London skyline for generations to come. It already has a nickname. A dumb one: the Gherkin. I am not sure where this name originated, but it is hopelessly inappropriate, even if, like the 'wobbly bridge', it is likely to stick. Gherkins do not look like this. Nor is 30 St Mary Axe, in any accepted understanding of the word, 'organic'. If it resembles anything, it is one of the great dirigibles of the 1930s, or one of Wernher von Braun's early space rockets. Tethered firmly to the ground, this sleek and sensational machine for making money, this 'towering innuendo' commissioned and owned by financial services group Swiss Re, will be home to up to 4,000 workers . . . In a Britain of largely cynical, fast-buck, skin-deep, government-approved new architecture, this is one new building – not a gherkin – that deserves to be relished.

✷ ✷ ✷

The London Bombings, 7 July 2005
Various

It was the best of times, it was the worst of times. On 6 July 2005 the capital celebrated the news that it had been chosen to host the 2012 Olympics. On the next day, at 8.50 a.m., during the commuter rush hour, three bombs exploded on the Underground (at King's Cross, Edgware Road and Liverpool Street/Aldgate) and a fourth bomb detonated at 9.47 a.m. on the Number 30 double-decker bus as it entered Tavistock Square. Altogether 56 people died in what was the deadliest terrorist attack on British soil since the 1988 bombing of Pan Am flight 103. To no one's great surprise, Al-Qaeda claimed responsibility for '7/7'.

Alice O'Keefe, 25, a freelance journalist, was caught in the tube blast near King's Cross.

WHEN THE TRAIN slammed to a halt and the carriage flooded with thick black smoke, I thought, 'That's it, this is how I'm going to die.' The train's on fire and we're all going to asphyxiate slowly. I heard screams from the carriage in front. Beside me, a woman was moaning, 'Jesus, Jesus', which seemed appropriate, although I'm not a believer. I wanted to pray too but couldn't quite let myself.

I'm claustrophobic, and if anyone had asked me to describe hell, this would have been it. I felt myself shutting down. I curled up against the glass partition and wrapped my coat around my face, trying to keep my breathing under control.

The first five minutes were the worst. After that, it became clear that the smoke wasn't getting any thicker and some air was still circulating. Somewhere, a woman was still screaming hysterically, much to the annoyance of everyone around me. There was a feeling that if anyone lost their nerve, the situation would become impossible. I didn't let myself imagine the screamer was in a carriage full of corpses, as I now realize she probably was.

It was thirty interminable minutes until we were evacuated. As we straggled towards the bright lights of King's Cross I saw the injured for the first time: one young man staggering and soaked in blood, whose staring eyes are still imprinted on my brain; a middle-aged woman with her eye a sticky mess. I realized that I had been one of the lucky ones. I was crazed with shock when I got out of the station. I got through to my mum on the phone. She told me that there had been several incidents across London, but neither of us knew that my train had been bombed. I decided to try and get to her office in Old Street. I was still so confused that I walked in the wrong direction and found myself lost in the scrum of commuters.

Nobody seemed to notice that my face and hair were black with soot. After wandering in circles for a while, I found a black cab.

My mum didn't recognize me, as I was blackened and my eyes were still goggling with shock when I arrived at her office. I then watched events unfold on television. Now it all seems like a bad dream.

Bernie Scranney 33, from Shepherd's Bush, west London. At Edgware Road blast.
I GOT ON a Circle line tube at Notting Hill and was heading towards the *Guardian*, where I work in the advertising department. The train was full and I stood immediately behind the driver's cab in the first carriage. We set off and another tube began to pass in the opposite direction.

Almost immediately there was a huge bang and flash. I knew it was a bomb. Our train came to a halt and there were clouds of black smoke. A second later and the explosion would have punched a hole in our carriage. The emergency lighting came on and we heard screaming from under the other train. We could hear a guy shouting 'Help me, help me.' Some people tried to get out but the doors wouldn't open.

We didn't know if our driver was OK and I started banging on the cab door. At first there was no answer. Eventually he opened it. He was quite dazed, perhaps concussed. His windows had shattered but not blown in. He opened the outer door and looked at the track ahead. There were huge pieces of metal which had been ripped out of their rivets lying about. The driver warned it would not be safe to get out if the track was live. The guy under the train was still screaming.

The driver must have taken the brunt of the blast but he got it together very quickly and made an announcement that there had been an accident. No one was hurt on our train and after a while he walked down the track and met transport officials who had come down from Edgware station. We were down there for about 20 minutes. Eventually they led us out along the rails. The guy under the train had stopped screaming. I think he'd died.

There were passengers coming out of the other trains with cuts and lacerations to their faces. I had smoke black all over my face and hands. I went out and had a cup of tea in a cafe. My hands were shaking.

George Psarabakis, 41, driver of the No 30 bus blown apart in Tavistock Place.

I AM JUST relieved to be here and to be able to see my wife and children. Many other people have not been so fortunate. I feel for the people who have perished and for their families. Myself and the other drivers in London have an important job and we are going to continue to do that as best we can. We are going to continue our normal lives. We are not going to be intimidated.

So spoke an authentic Londoner. The Romano-Londoners who refused to budge because Boudicca was on the way would have understood. So too all those Londoners who showed they could take it during the Blitz.

Sources and Acknowledgements

The editor has made every effort to secure permission to reproduce copyrighted material. Any errors or omissions should be addressed to the editor c/o the publishers.

Anglo-Saxon Chronicle, 'Viking Raids', from *The Anglo-Saxon Chronicle*, trans. G.N. Garmonsway, 1953. Copyright (1953) JM Dent

Anglo-Saxon Poet, 'Abandoned British City', from *The Earliest English Poems*, Michael Alexander, 1992. Copyright © 1992 Michael Alexander. Reproduced by permission of Penguin UK

Anonymous, 'The Ordinances of the Spurriers', quoted in *Readings in English History*, ed. Arvel B. Erickson and Martin J. Havran, 1967

Anonymous, 'London Lickpenny', quoted in *The Oxford Book of London*, ed. Paul Bailey, 1996

Anonymous, 'Henry V's Victory March After Agincourt', quoted in *English Historical Documents*, vol. IV, 1329–1485, ed. A.R. Myers, 1969

Anonymous, 'The Dignity of the Mayor of London', quoted in *English Historical Documents*, vol. IV, *1329–1485*, ed. A.R. Myers, 1969

Anonymous, 'Elizabethan London: The Oath of Every Freeman' quoted in *London in the Age of Shakespeare: An Anthology*, ed. Lawrence Manley, 1986

Anonymous, 'The Restoration: The Arrival of Charles II in London', from 'England's Joy', *Harleian Miscellany*, vol. vii, 1810

Anonymous SAS Trooper, 'The SAS Storm the Iranian Embassy', from *Soldier 'I' SAS*, Michael Paul Kennedy, 1989. Copyright © 1989 Michael Paul Kennedy

Anonymous Schoolgirl, 'Children Evacuated', from *North London Collegiate School Magazine*, December 1939

Jane Austen , 'The Season: Jane Austen's Party', from *Voices from the World of Jane Austen*, Malcolm Day, 2006

Bede, 'Londoners Rejects Christianity', from *Bede's Ecclesiastical History of England*, trans. J.A. Giles, rev. A.M. Sellar, 1907

Bill Belmont, 'Scenes from the Ghetto: Jewish Life in the East End', from *Echoes of the East End*, Venetia Murray, 1989. Copyright © 1989 Bill Belmont

Arnold Bennett, 'Chinatown', from *Journals*, vol. III, ed. Norman Flower, 1932

John Betjeman, 'The Festival of Britain', from *Coming Home: An Anthology of Prose 1920–1977*, selected Candida Lycett Green, 1998. Copyright © The Estate of John Betjeman. Reprinted by permission of Aitken Alexander Associates

William Blake, 'London: A Georgian Poet's View', from *Songs of Experience*, 1794

Dr Thomas Bond, 'The Whitechapel Murders', from *The Ultimate Jack the Ripper Source Book*, Stewart P. Evans and Keith Skinner, 2002

James Boswell, 'Man About Town: A Rake's Progress', from *Bowell's London Journal*, ed. Frederick A. Pottle, London, 1992

Charlotte Brontë, 'A Visit to the Great Exhibition', quoted in *The Brontes' Life and Letters*, ed. Clement Shorter, 1908

Deborah Bull, 'The Funeral Procession of Diana, Princess of Wales', from *Dancing Away*, 1998. Copyright © 1998 Deborah Bull

Calendar of the Coroners' Rolls, 'Misadventures in Childhood', '"Then Kicked Him as He Lay"', 'A Home Owner Attacks Drunken Roisterers', 'A Hit and Run Cart Driver', quoted in *Chaucer's World*, compiled Edith Rickert, 1948. Copyright © 1948 Columbia University Press

Calendar of Plea and Memoranda Rolls, 'An Inventory of the Goods in a Fishmonger's City House', quoted in *English Historical Documents*, vol. IV, *1329–1485*, ed. A.R. Myers, 1969

Charles II, 'Notices for a Lost Dog', quoted in *Source Book of English History*, ed. E.K. Kendall, 1908

Chronicle of the Grey Friars, 'Evil May Day', from *Camden Society*, old series, vol. 53, 1852

Chronicle of the Grey Friars, 'Protestant Revolution: Edward VI Suppresses Popery in London', from *Chronicle of the Gray Friars of London*, ed. J.G. Nichols, 1857

City of London Letter-Book, 'Traders Riot', 'False Beggars', 'Trick of the Trade: A Fraudulent Beggar', 'Expulsion of a Leper', 'Richard Whittington is Elected Mayor for the Third

Time', quoted in *Memorials of London and London Life AD 1276–1419*, ed. H.T. Riley, 1868

Duff Cooper, 'The Abdication', from *Old Men Forget*, 1954. © 1954 The Estate of Duff Copper (Lord Norwich). Reprinted by permission of the Random House Group Ltd

John Crosby, 'The Sixties: Swinging London' (originally 'London, The Most Exciting City in the World', *Weekend Telegraph*, 16 April 1965. Copyright © 1965 John Crosby. Reprinted by permission of Telegraph Media Group Ltd

Hannah Cullwick, 'White Slavery', from *The Diaries of Hannah Cullwick*, 1984

Daily Courant, 'Handel's Water Music', quoted in *The London Anthology*, ed. Hugh and Pauline Massingham, n.d.

Daily Express, 'The *Empire Windrush* Arrives at Tilbury', *Daily Express* 22 June 1948

Daily Mail, 'Mafeking Night', *Daily Mail* 19 May 1900

Daniel Defoe, 'London Arisen from the Ashes: Wren Rebuild's St Paul's Cathedral', from *A Tour thro' the Whole Island of Great Britain Divided into Circuits or Journies by Daniel Defoe, Gent., 1724–1726*, 1727

Charles Dickens, 'Fog', from *Bleak House*, 1852–3

Charles Dickens, 'The Great Stink', quoted in *The London Anthology*, ed. Hugh and Pauline Massingham, n.d.

Fyodor Dostoevsky, 'Prostitutes on the Haymarket', from *Winter Notes on Summer Impressions*, trans. K. Fitz Lyon, 1985

Colin Eales, 'Notting Hill Race Riots', quoted in *Windrush*, Mike Phillips and Trevor Phillips, 1998. Copyright © 1998 Mike Phillips and Trevor Phillips

East London Advertiser, 'The Battle of Cable Street', *East London Advertiser*, 10 October 1936. Reprinted by permission of Malcolm Starbrook, editor of the *East London Advertiser*

Maria Edgeworth, 'Mrs Fry at Newgate', from *Life and Letters of Maria Edgeworth*, ed. A.J.C. Hare, 1894

Friedrich Engels, 'The Condition of the Working Class in London', from *The Condition of the Working Class in England*, trans. and ed. W.O. Henderson and W.H. Chaloner, 1958. Copyright © Basil Blackwell. Reprinted by permission of Blackwell Publishers Ltd

John Evelyn, 'The Great Frost', 'A Whale in the Thames', 'The Great Fire', *The Diary of John Evelyn*, ed. W. Bray, 1907

John Evelyn, 'The Dutch in the Thames', from *Diary and Correspondence*, ed. W. Bray, 1827

Sir John Fielding, letter, from *Grenville Papers*, ed. W.J. Smith, 1852

William Fitz Stephen, 'A Description of the City of London', quoted in *English Historical Documents*, vol. II, 1042-1189, ed. David C. Douglas and George W. Greenaway, 1981

William Fleetwood, 'A School for Pick Pockets', from *Original Letters*, ed. Henry Ellis, 1824

William Fleetwood, 'Riots, Puritans and Shakespeare', in *Life in Shakespeare's England*, ed. John Dover Wilson, 1911

Sergeant Henry Foster, 'The Battle of Newbury', from 'A True and Exact Relation of the Marchings of the Two Regiments of the Trained Bands of the City of London, Being the Red and Blue Regiments ... who Marched to the Relief of Gloucester', Thomason tracts, British Library, n.d.

John Foxe, 'Mary Persecutes the Protestants: The Burning of Bradford and Leaf at Smithfield', from *Foxe's Book of Martyrs*, ed. Rev. T. Pratt, 1858

Andreas Franciscus, 'Tudor London: A Portrait', from *Two Italian Accounts of Tudor England*, trans. C.V. Malfatti, 1953

Sir John Froissart, 'The Peasants' Revolt Comes to London', from *Chronicles of England, France and Spain*, trans. Lord Berners, 1523–5

George Gale, 'The Last Tram', *Manchester Guardian*, 7 July 1952

The General Court of the Mayor of the City of London, 'Public Nuisances', quoted in *English Historical Documents*, vol. IV, 1329–1485, ed. A.R. Myers, 1969

Father John Gerard, 'The Torturing of a Jesuit Priest in the Tower of London', from *The Autobiography of an Elizabethan*, trans. Philip Caraman, 1951

Philip Gibbs, 'The Siege of Sidney Street', from *Adventures in Journalism*, 1923. Copyright © 1923 Philip Gibbs

Philip Gibbs, 'The General Strike', from *The Pageant of the Years*, 1946. Copyright © 1946 Philip Gibbs

Jonathan Glancy, 'Arisen from the Wreckage: 30 St Mary Axe', from 'Space Odyssey', *Guardian*, 8 December 2003. Copyright © 2003 Guardian News & Media Ltd. Reprinted by permission

George Godwin, 'The Great Stink', from *Town Swamps and Social Bridges*, 1859

James Greenwood, 'White Slavery', from *Toilers in London*, 'One of the Crowd' (pseud. James Greenwood), 1883

Charles Greville, 'William IV Rambles the Streets', from *The Greville Memoirs*, ed. Roger Fulford, 1963

Charles Greville, 'King Cholera', from *Leaves from the Greville Diary*, 1929

Edward Hall, 'The Joust Between Lord Scales and the Bastard of Burgoyne', 'The Sweating Sickness', quoted in *The London Anthology*, ed. Hugh and Pauline Massingham, n.d.

Wal Hannington, 'The Hunger Marchers in Hyde Park', from *Unemployed Struggles, 1919–1936*, 1977. Copyright © 1977 Wal Hannington/Lawrence & Wishart

Arthur Harding, 'Underworld', from *East End Underworld: Chapters on the Life of Arthus Harding*, Raphael Samuel, 1981. Copyright © 1981 Raphael Samuel

Henry I, 'The Charter of Henry I in Favour of the Citizens of London', quoted in *English Historical Documents*, vol. II, *1042–1189*, ed. David C. Douglas and George W. Greenaway, 1981

Philip Henry, 'The Execution of Charles I', quoted in *They Saw it Happen: An Anthology of Eye-witnesses' Accounts of Events in British History 1485–1688*, comp. C.R.N. Routh, 1956

Paul Hentzner, 'Queen Elizabeth at Greenwich', quoted in *Life in Shakespeare's England*, ed. John Dover Wilson, 1911

William Hickey, 'The Lord Mayor's Banquet', from *Memoirs*, ed. Peter Quennell, 1960

Sir Edward Hoby, 'The Gunpowder Plot', quoted in *They Saw it Happen: An Anthology of Eye-witnesses' Accounts of Events in British History 1485–1688*, comp. C.R.N. Routh, 1956

Vere Hodgson, 'Doodlebugs', from *Few Eggs and No Oranges: The Diaries of Vere Hodgson 1940–45*, 1999. Copyright © Kensington Public Library/Veronica Bowater

John Howard, 'London Hospitals', quoted in *English Historical Documents*, vol. XI, *1783–1832*, ed. A. Aspinall and Anthony Smith, 1959

Martin Huckerby, 'The Brixton Riots' (originally 'Looters Moved in as Flames Spread'), *The Times*, 13 April 1981.

Copyright © 1981 News International. Reprinted by permission

H.M. Hyndman, 'A Socialist March Through the West End', from _The Record of an Adventurous Life_, 1911

Illustrated London News, 'Murder on the North London Railway', _Illustrated London News_, July 1864

Jack the Ripper, 'The Whitechapel Murders', from _The Ultimate Jack the Ripper Source Book_, Stewart P. Evans and Keith Skinner, 2002

Henry James, 'William Morris at Home', _The Letters of Henry James_, vol. I, ed. Leon Edel, 1974

Len Jones, 'The Blitz', quoted in _The First Day of the Blitz_, Peter Stansky, 2007. Reprinted by permission of Yale University Press

Frank Keating, 'Wade Wins Wimbledon', _Guardian_, 2 July 1977. Copyright © 1977 Guardian News and Media Group Ltd

Ronald Kray, 'Gangland: The Shooting of George Cornell at the Blind Beggar', from _Our Story_, Ronald and Reginald Kray (with Fred Dineage), 1988. Copyright © Bejubob Ltd

James Lees-Milne, 'VE Day', from _Diaries, 1942–1954_, abridged by Michael Bloch, 2007. Reprinted by permission of John Murray

London Assizes, 'Building Regulations', quoted in _Every One A Witness: The Norman Age_, ed. A.F. Scott, 1976

Lord Mayor and Aldermen, 'Riots, Puritans and Shakespeare', quoted in _Life in Shakespeare's England_, ed. John Dover Wilson, 1911

Michael MacDonagh, 'The Great War: The Shooting Down of Zeppelin L31', from _In London During the Great War_, 1935

Henry Machyn, 'Queen Mary Seizes the Crown', *Camden Society*, vol. 42, 1848

John Macky, 'Coffee-houses', from A *Journey Through England*, 1714

Henry Mayhew, 'Victorian London: Street Life', from *Mayhew's London*, ed. Peter Quennell, 1969

Henry Mayhew and John Binny, 'Tothill Fields', from *The Criminal Prisons of London*, 1862

Karl Marx, 'Karl Marx at Home', from *The Marx-Engels Correspondence*, ed. Fritz Raddatz, trans. C. Ewald Osers, 1981

Karl Marx, 'The Founding of the Working Men's Association, Covent Garden', *Marx Engels Collected Works*, vol. 21, 1955

A Monk of St Bertin's Abbey, 'Edward the Confessor Builds Westminster Abbey', from *The Life of King Edward who Rests at Westminster*, trans. and ed. Frank Barlow, 1962

The Monk of Westminster, 'Richard II Quarrels with the City of London', quoted in *English Historical Documents* , vol. IV, 1329–1485, ed. A.R. Myers, 1969

Karl P. Moritz, 'Ranelagh Pleasure Gardens', from *Travels in England in 1782*, ed. P.E. Matheson, 1924

Edward R. Murrow, 'The Blitz', CBS broadcast 13 September 1940. Copyright © 1940 CBS

John O'London, 'The Opening of the London to Deptford Railway', quoted in *Voices from Dickens' London*, Michael Paterson, 2006

George Orwell, 'Down and Out: George Orwell in a Doss-house', from *Down and Out in Paris and London*, 1933. Copyright © 1933 The Trustees of the Estate of George Orwell. Reprinted by permission of A.M. Heath Ltd

News of the World, 'The First Wembley', *News of the World*, 29 April 1923

Emmeline Pankhurst, 'Suffragettes Stone the Windows of 10 Downing Street', from *My Own Story*, 1914

Matthew Paris, 'The Thames Floods', quoted in *English Historical Documents*, vol. II, *1042–1189*, ed. D.C. Douglas and George W. Greenway, 1953

Parliamentary Committee on Climbing Boys, 'Death of a Climbing Boy', from evidence given before the Parliamentary Committee on Climbing Boys, 1817

Frances Partridge, 'Oh! Calcutta!', from *Life Regained: Diaries 1970–72*, 1999. Copyright © 1999 Frances Partridge

Sir Robert Peel, '"Peelers"', from *English Letters of the XIX Century*, ed. James Aitken, 1946

Maude Pember Reade, 'Children in Lambeth Walk', from *Round About a Pound a Week*, 1913

Samuel Pepys, 'Journal of the Plague Year', from *The Diary of Samuel Pepys*, ed. Henry B. Wheatley, 1913

Samuel Pepys, 'A Visit to a Gaming House', from *The Diary of Samuel Pepys*, ed. Robert Latham and William Matthews, 1970–83

Thomas Platter, 'Bear-Baiting', 'A Fishmarket' 'Bear-Baiting', 'Riots, Puritans and Shakespeare', from *Travels in England*, trans. Clare Williams, 1937. Copyright © 1937 Random House Archive and Library

Dick Pountain and Mick Farren, 'Grosvenor Square', from *Days in the Life: Voices from the English Underground, 1961–1971*, Jonathon Green, 1988. Copyright © 1988 Jonathon Green

V.S. Pritchett, 'Office Boy', from *The Cab at the Door*, 1968. Copyright © 1968 V.S. Pritchett. Reprinted by permission of the Random House Group Ltd

Vince Reid, 'The *Empire Windrush* Arrives at Tilbury', from *Windrush*, Mike Phillips and Trevor Phillips, 1998. Copyright © 1998 Mike Phillips and Trevor Phillips

Samuel Richardson, 'A Hanging at Tyburn', from *Familiar Letters on Important Occasions*, 1973

Robert of Avesbury, 'City of the Dead: The Black Death', quoted in *Translations and Reprints from the Original Sources of European History*, vol. II, 1902

Robert of Avesbury, 'Flagellants', from *British Latin Selections AD 500-1400*, ed. R.A. Browne, 1954

Roger of Wendover, 'Tax Riot', from *Flowers of History*, trans. J.A. Giles, 1849

William Roper, 'The Beheading of Sir Thomas More', from *More's Utopia*, ed. J.R. Lumby, 1879

John Rushworth, 'The Attempted Arrest of the Five Members', from *Historical Collections*, 1691

Lord John Russell, 'Chartist Demonstration', from *The Letters of Queen Victoria*, A.C. Benson and Viscount Esher, 1908

George Augustus Sala, 'Nine a.m.: Clerks on their Way to Work', from *Twice Round the Clock*, 1858

Ignatius Sancho, 'The Gordon Riots', quoted in *Through African Eyes*, vol. I, ed. Paul Edwards, 1966

William Sansom, 'Hep-cats: Jive at the Paramount Ballroom' (originally 'The Public's Progress'), *Contact*, 1947

César de Saussure, 'Coffee-houses', from *A Foreign View of England in the Reigns of George I and George II*, ed. Mme Van Muyden, 1902

Max Schlesinger, 'Some London Wonders: Gaslights, Penny Gaffs and Omnibuses', from *Saunterings in and about London*, 1853

Johanna Schopenhauer, 'Mr Whitbread's Brewery', from *A Lady Travels: Journeys in England and Scotland from the Diaries of Johanna Schopenhauer*, ed. and trans. Ruth Michaelis-Jena and Willy Merson, 1988

Louis Simond, 'Shooting Under London Bridge in a Boat', from *Journal of a Tour and Residence in Great Britain During the Years 1810 and 1811 by a French Traveller*, 1817

John Stodeley, 'Wars of the Roses: The Beginning of Strife', from *Paston Letters*, ed. J. Gairdner, 1872

John Stow, 'Theft from the Queen', 'A Legacy for the Relief of the Poor', 'Sentenced for Libel', 'A Scaffold Collapses at a Sports Match', *The Annales, or a General Chronicle of England*, 1631

John Stow, 'The Brothels of Southwark', *A Survay of London*, 1603

Lady Strafford, 'The Mohock Club', *The Wentworth Papers 1705–1739*, ed. Thomas Wentworth, 1883

Snorri Sturluson, 'London Bridge is Pulled Down by King Olaf', from *Heimskringla or the Chronicles of the Kings of Norway, the Saga of Olaf Haraldson*, Part 1, Online Medieval and Classical Library, http://omacl/org/Heimskringla/haraldson1

Jonathan Swift, 'Making Hay in Chelsea', quoted in *The London Anthology*, ed. Hugh and Pauline Massingham, n.d.

Tacitus, 'Boudicca Sacks Londinium', from *The Annals of Imperial Rome*, 1956. Copyright © Michael Grant Publications Ltd, 1956, 1959, 1971, 1973, 1975, 1977, 1989, 1996. Reprinted by permission of Penguin UK

Hippolyte Taine, 'A Day at the Races: The Derby, Epsom', from *Notes on England*, trans. N.F. Rae, 1872

John Taylor, 'Ranters', quoted in *The London Anthology*, ed. Hugh and Pauline Massingham, n.d.

Anne Thackeray Ritchie, 'High Society: A Fancy-dress Ball at Buckingham Palace', from *The Letters of Anne Thackeray Ritchie*, 1924

Margaret Thatcher, 'Enter Mrs Thatcher', *The Downing Street Years*, 1993. Copyright © 1993 Margaret Thatcher

The Times, 'Into Hades', *The Times*, 10 January 1863

Zacharias von Uffenbach, 'Cockfighting', from *London in 1710*, ed. and trans. W.H. Quarrell and Margaret Mare, 1934. Copyright 1934 W.H. Quarrell and Margaret Mare

Various, 'The Romans in London'; graffiti 1, 2, 6 from *The Archaeology of Roman Britain*, R.G. Collingwood, 1930; graffiti 3, 7 from *The Romans in Britain: An Anthology of Inscriptions with Translations and a Running Commentary*, A.R. Burn, 1932; graffiti 4–5 from *Some Inscriptions from Roman Britain*, London Association of Classical Teachers, Original Records, No. 4, n.d.

Various, 'The Sex Pistols Play their First Gig, St Martin's Art College', from *Punk: An Oral History*, John Robb and Oliver Craske, 2006. Reprinted by permission of The Random House Group Ltd

Various, 'The London Bombings', *Observer*, 10 July 2005 (Alice O'Keefe); and *Guardian*, 9 July 2005 (Bernie Scranney)

Orderic Vitalis, 'The Coronation of William the Conqueror', from *The Ecclesiastical History of Orderic Vitalis*, trans. Majorie Chibnill, Oxford University Press, 1978

John Verney, 'Highway Robbery', *Memoirs of the Verney Family During the 17th Century*, ed. F.P. Verney, 1904

Queen Victoria, 'Queen Victoria at Her Coronation', from *Letters of Queen Victoria,* ed. A.C. Benson and Viscount Esher, 1908

Baron Waldstein, 'The Diary of a Tourist', from *The Diary of Baron Waldstein*, trans. G.W. Groos, 1981. Copyright © 1981 Thames and Hudson. Reprinted by permission of Thames and Hudson

Horace Walpole, 'Earthquake', 'Wilkes and the Mob', 'The Rage for Building', from *Letters,* ed. Paget Toynbee, 1903

Beatrice Webb, 'The Dock Strike', from *The Diary 1873–92,* 1986. Reprinted by permission of the Little, Brown Group and the London School of Economics and Political Science

Lupold von Wedel, 'Swans and Freaks', quoted in *London in the Age of Shakespeare: An Anthology*, ed. Lawrence Manley, 1986

John Wesley, 'John Wesley Stoned', from *John Wesley's Journal,* ed. P. Parker, 1903

David Widgery, 'Docklands: Days in the Life of a Bethnal Green GP', from *Some Lives!,* 1991. Copyright © 1991 David Widgery

Heathcote Williams, 'Speakers' Corner', *The Speakers,* 1964. Copyright © 1964 Heathcote Williams

P. Willmott and M. Young, 'Suburban Life: Mr and Mrs Matthews in Woodford', from *Family and Class in a London Suburb*, 1960. Copyright © 1960 P. Willmott and M. Young

Virginia Woolf, 'The Blitz', from *A Writer's Diary,* 1954. Copyright © 1954 Leonard Woolf. Copyright renewed 1982 by Quentin Bell and Angelica Garnett. Reprinted by permission of the Society of Authors

Frederick, Duke of Wurtemberg, 'Chauvinism and Clothes', quoted in *England as Seen by Foreigners in the Days of Elizabeth and James the First*, ed. W.B. Rye, 1865.

W.B. Yeats, 'Madame Blavatsky in Norwood', from *The Trembling of the Veil*, 1922

Personal Acknowledgements

All books are cooperative efforts, and this has been no exception. My thanks are due to the following: Penny Lewis-Stempel, Julian Alexander at Lucas Alexander Whitley, Leo Hollis and Jan Chamier at Constable, Kathryn Fox, Jessica Cuthbert-Smith and Steve Williamson.

Index